Review and Herald® titles may be purchased in bulk for educational, business, fund-raising, or sales promotional use. For information, e-mail SpecialMarkets@reviewandherald.com.

The Review and Herald® Publishing Association publishes biblically based materials for spiritual, physical, and mental growth and Christian discipleship.

Scripture quotations identified CEV are from the Contemporary English Version. Copyright © American Bible Society 1991, 1995. Used by permission.

Texts credited to Clear Word are from *The Clear Word,* copyright © 1994, 2000, 2003, 2004, 2006 by Review and Herald Publishing Association. All rights reserved.

Texts credited to Message are from *The Message.* Copyright ã 1993, 1994, 1995, 1996, 2000, 2001, 2002. Used by permission of NavPress Publishing Group.

Scripture quotations marked NASB are from the *New American Standard Bible,* copyright © 1960, 1962, 1963, 1968, 1971, 1972, 1973, 1975, 1977, 1995 by The Lockman Foundation. Used by permission.

Bible texts credited to NIrV are from the *Holy Bible, New International Reader's Version.* Copyright © 1985, 1996, 1998 by International Bible Society. Used by permission of Zondervan. All rights reserved.

Texts credited to NIV are from the *Holy Bible, New International Version.* Copyright © 1973, 1978, 1984, 2011 by Biblica, Inc. Used by permission. All rights reserved worldwide

Texts credited to NKJV are from the New King James Version. Copyright © 1979, 1980, 1982 by Thomas Nelson, Inc. Used by permission. All rights reserved.

Scripture quotations marked NLT are taken from the *Holy Bible,* New Living Translation, copyright © 1996, 2004, 2007 by Tyndale House Foundation. Used by permission of Tyndale House Publishers, Inc., Carol Stream, Illinois 60188. All rights reserved.

Bible texts credited to NLV are from the *Holy Bible: New Life Version.* Copyright © 1969 by Christian Literature International, P.O. Box 777, Canby, Oregon 97013 Used by permission.

This book was
Edited by JoAlyce Waugh
Copyedited by Megan Mason
Designed by Emily Ford / Review and Herald® Design Center
Cover illustrations of tree, bubbles, and shark by Emily Ford / Review and Herald® Design Center
Cover photos © Thinkstock.com
Typeset: Minion Pro 10.5 / 12.5

PRINTED IN U.S.A.

17 16 15 14 13   5 4 3 2 1

Library of Congress Cataloging-in-Publication Data
Walker, Celeste Perrino.
    iChoose life [2015 young adult devotional] / Celeste Walker.
       pages cm
    ISBN 978-0-8280-2748-9
1. Young adults--Prayers and devotions. 2. Seventh-Day Adventist youth--Prayers and devotions. 3. Devotional calendars--Seventh-Day Adventists. I. Title. II. Title: i Choose life [2015 young adult devotional].
    BV4529.2.W34 2014
    242--dc23
                                2013015353
    ISBN 978-0-8280-2748-9

———

Also by Céleste Perrino-Walker:
More Power to Ya
The Secret of Being Content

To order, **call 1-800-765-6955.**
Visit us at **www.reviewandherald.com**
for information on other Review and Herald® products.

Inside Out

Dress yourselves in Christ, and be up and about! **Romans 13:14, Message.**

Imagine answering a casting call to play Jesus in a movie. Every day you'd go to work and try to think and act like Jesus. You'd go around all day asking yourself "WWJD—what would Jesus do?" Doubtless Jim Caviezel, who portrayed Jesus in Mel Gibson's *The Passion of the Christ,* asked himself that question a lot during filming.

Caviezel was 33 years old when he played Jesus—the age Jesus was believed to be when he was crucified—and suffered hypothermia, was struck by lightning, and had to deal with the pain of a separated shoulder during filming. Caviezel, a professed believer, says that he felt at times like a great presence came within him during filming. "This prayer that came from me was 'I don't want people to see me. I just want them to see Jesus. And through that conversions will happen.' That's what I wanted more than anything, that people would have a visceral effect to finally make a decision whether to follow Him or not."

Actors pretend to be someone else, but as Christians we aren't called to *act* like Jesus, we're called to *be* like Jesus. Anybody can act. In fact, most people pretend to be something they're not. *Being* like Jesus means that everything we do, everything we think, everything we are first goes through the filter of Jesus. We don't *act* like Him; we *are* like Him.

This year, try something different, something bold. Choose to let Jesus live out His life in you. Make that your only resolution as you begin this brand-new year. Changing outward behavior won't cut it, though; Jesus transforms us from the inside out, not the outside in.

If there was just one thing you could do this year that would bring you closer to God and keep you there, what would it be? What would it take to make that your reality? It's worth the effort.

Small Town, Big-Time

Abstain from all appearance of evil. **I Thessalonians 5:22, KJV.**

Is there a difference between doing something wrong and just *appearing* to do something wrong?

Well, yeah, but the Bible tells us to avoid both. I learned the importance of this lesson from none other than Christian singer Steven Curtis Chapman. Back in the olden days when cell phones didn't exist, he had a concert in the tiny town of Richford, Vermont. Even though he was relatively unknown, had just three CDs out, and hadn't yet been awarded 56 Gospel Music Association Dove Awards or five Grammy Awards, his concert was a big deal in such a small place. Where to put all those people?

Answer: The gym at the high school, which is precisely where I found myself, along with my family and a couple young kids who were friends with my little sister Joy. We had a great time. I even got bold enough to climb up onto my chair and take pictures. As a result, I have a photo of Steven Curtis Chapman pointing right at me while probably thinking, *You there! Get off that chair before you fall and break your neck!*

After the concert we hung around outside while Steven signed autographs. Sarah, a young girl who had come with us and who was just slightly overexcited about our encounter with a celebrity, barreled her way to the front and threw her arms around Steven's neck. He immediately put his hands up in the air and backed away from her. How was he to know she was only a tall-for-her-age little kid? All he could see was a tall girl and a lot of blond hair.

Today that image comes to mind whenever I hear one of his songs on the radio—Steven with his hands up in surrender, backing away from something that could easily be misinterpreted. Obviously he was avoiding even the appearance of impropriety with his body language (in case someone captured the event on film), and in that moment I gained a huge respect for him not as a singer but as a man of God.

Avoiding the appearance of evil is necessary because we human beings are wired with wicked minds. We don't think the best of people; we think the worst of them. And avoiding even the appearance of evil gives us much-needed help in avoiding the actual evil itself.

Lost and Found

Suppose one of you has a hundred sheep and loses one of them.
Doesn't he leave the ninety-nine in the open country and
go after the lost sheep until he finds it? And when he finds it,
he joyfully puts it on his shoulders and goes home. Then he calls his friends
and neighbors together and says, "Rejoice with me; I have found my lost
sheep." I tell you that in the same way there will be more rejoicing
in heaven over one sinner who repents than over ninety-nine
righteous persons who do not need to repent. **Luke 15:4-7, NIV.**

It was 7:00 p.m. at night when David Lavau, 68, was driving home and the headlights of an oncoming car temporarily blinded him. He hit his brakes but couldn't get enough traction to keep his car from plummeting off the side of the road and down 200 feet into a ravine. His car, oddly enough, landed right next to another car that had made the same plunge 10 days earlier and contained the body of an elderly man who had not survived the crash.

Two men, one ravine, and no one knew where they were. Lavau's family and friends all thought he was with his other family or friends. Eventually they started checking with one another and realized he was missing. The police were able to locate where he'd been the day he'd gone missing, but they weren't able to find him. That's when his grown kids took matters into their own hands. They started driving up the road from his house to Ventura County, where he liked to take shopping trips. They stopped at every ravine and hill and hollered down until finally they heard their father's faint cry of "Help! Help!"

Six days after crashing into the ravine, Lavau was rescued because his children wouldn't give up hope that he could be found. He had suffered some serious injuries, and was airlifted to the hospital, where he underwent two surgeries. It took six weeks for him to recover fully.

No matter what it took, Lavau's kids were determined to find their dad. But what if, after Lavau had been found, he had refused to leave because he wanted to stay with his smashed car in the ravine? What if he had told his kids that he wasn't worth the time and effort it took to find him and that they should leave him there to die? What if he had said it was just too difficult to get back up that mountainside? What if he'd said he preferred being hungry, thirsty, and lost?

Absurd, you say? You're right. But do you make these same excuses about allowing Jesus to rescue you from the wreckage of this sinful world? He's looking for *you* because you're worth saving.

The Farmer's Apples

The Lord does not look at the things people look at. People look at the outward appearance, but the Lord looks at the heart. **1 Samuel 16:7, NIV.**

Now there was a certain farmer and she had lots of animals, including a horse, some sheep, a llama, an alpaca, and more rabbits than you could pull out of a hat in 10 minutes. On her farm was a whole bunch of apple trees. And those apple trees, every year without fail, were covered with a whole bunch of apples (nope, not the Mac kind). Every year she ignored those apples because they were ugly. When I say ugly, I mean so ugly that if you saw them in the supermarket next to the pretty apples, you'd cover your eyes and scream, "What *are* those things?"

So those apples just rotted into the ground every year, except for the ones that the deer ate. They mostly came out to eat at night, and in the dark they couldn't tell the difference. One day the farmer thought the horse might not be too picky. So for a couple years she brought apples to the horse, and he ate them in broad daylight and didn't seem to mind too much.

Then one year, when she was picking up apples for the horse, the farmer noticed that some of the apples were fairly large for wild apples. Some of them didn't even look terrible, just kind of awful. So she thought she might make some applesauce with them since pretty apples weren't necessary for the afore-mentioned sauce, because they were only going to get mashed up anyway.

So the farmer picked some of the apples and made them into a very tasty applesauce. Lo and behold, one day when she was picking up some apples to give to the sheep (who wanted to get in on all the new apple action), she decided to taste one herself. And do you know it was one of the most delicious, crispest apples I ever ate?

I didn't think those apples had any value because they were ugly. I tend to think the same way about ugly things in my life—trials, irritating people, uncomfortable situations. I whine about them and wish they would go away. However, God can use everything, not just good things, to help us become more like Him. And it's often during the ugly times of life that we grow closer to Him. What's ugly in your life today, and how might God use it for good?

The Little Boy and the Road

A prudent person sees trouble coming and ducks;
a simpleton walks in blindly and is clobbered. **Proverbs 22:3, Message.**

There is a house along my road that has a front yard about the size of a postage stamp. Next to the house is a dirt pull-off (you can't really call it a driveway, because it's not big enough). In that pull-off I often see a little boy playing in the dirt. Not drawing pictures with a stick, mind you, or hunting ants. No, he's got elaborate rows of cars or soldiers all lined up there. Today, when I went by, it looked like a miniature used-car lot. And he had a friend with him.

Whenever I see him playing there so close to the road, all I can think is that it would only take one distracted driver, someone texting or talking on the phone, or trying to dial up a song on their iPod, and it's all going to be over for that little boy. He's so close to the road, so close to danger, that I can't believe his parents let him play there. I want to stop my car, jump out, and run over to him shrieking, "Run! Quick! It's too dangerous here! Stay back there a safe distance. Or, better yet, go play inside your house."

I suppose angels have the same trouble. Every day when they make flybys they see us dawdling around next to terrible dangers. We're surfing too close to an off-limits Web site, or taking risks in a bad relationship, or saying things we shouldn't. All it would take is one little thing: the wrong word, the wrong choice, the wrong move, and wham! We're toast. They probably want to yell at us to move away, to get back in the house.

Maybe God even sends them to warn us. If He does, it's only because our built-in early warning systems have failed. Our consciences are kept sensitive by the Holy Spirit, but they can become dull if we don't maintain a constant relationship with God. When our consciences are working properly, they warn us of danger long before we are near it. If we are wise, we will listen to God's voice and steer clear because we know that no good ever comes of ignoring God.

Think About It: What kinds of places have you been hanging around lately? Are they barely on this side of danger? Have you been ignoring warning signs that God has been sending to keep you safe? Make a decision today to listen to the Holy Spirit and move back into the safety zone.

Power Surge

"Who touched me?" Jesus asked. When they all denied it,
Peter said, "Master, the people are crowding and pressing against you."
But Jesus said, "Someone touched me; I know that power
has gone out from me." **Luke 8:45, 46, NIV.**

Crowds can be dangerous. There are many well-documented cases of crowds gone bad: people being killed, trampled, crushed, asphyxiated. If you've ever been in a crowd so large that you were lifted up and carried along by the sheer press of bodies you'll know what I mean. Even in smaller crowds you can be pushed and shoved.

One woman in the Bible knew this all too well. She'd been trying to reach Jesus for days, but the crowds around Him were always so large that she couldn't get close. She had been sick for 12 years and had spent all her money on doctors, hoping to get better. If anything, she was worse off than before. She knew that if she could only touch Jesus' robe she would be healed. The trouble was that she couldn't get anywhere near Him.

Jesus knew it too, and He wanted her to get close enough to touch Him because He wanted to point out her faith to everyone in the crowd. But think about this: everyone near Jesus was touching Him but no one else was healed. Why? Why this one woman who didn't even get to bump into Him, yet was able to touch the hem of His robe?

Because she asked and believed. By her act of faith she claimed God's healing power and believed that she would be healed. *And she was.* "He could distinguish the touch of faith from the casual touch of the careless throng. Someone had touched Him with a deep purpose and had received answer" (Ellen G. White, *The Ministry of Healing*, p. 60).

How many times have you prayed for something as if you were bumping into Jesus in a crowd? "Dear Lord, please give me this or that. Dear Lord, please do this or that." How many times have you prayed in desperation and faith—the way the woman who touched Jesus' robe prayed—believing that God would answer your prayer?

Will God answer all our prayers the way we want? Probably not. But He *will* answer all of them. And if we ask with intention instead of just mouthing the words, not only will He answer our prayers but also He will change our lives because we are asking in faith. Hold on to Him, ask, and believe.

I Dare You to Find It

All Scripture is given by inspiration of God,
and is profitable for doctrine, for reproof, for correction,
for instruction in righteousness, that the man of God may be complete,
thoroughly equipped for every good work. **2 Timothy 3:16, 17, NKJV.**

How well do you know your Bible? Do you know, for instance, where to find the verse that says that whenever God closes a door, He opens a window? Go ahead: you have five minutes to find it.

Did you find it? No? It's actually not a verse in the Bible, although a lot of people think it is.

How about the expression "another one bites the dust"? Do you think that is from a verse in the Bible? (Hint: Try a King James Version. If thou dost not have that version lying about in thy dwelling, check out www.Biblegateway.com, where thou canst verily read many different translations, one at a time or side by side.)

Did you find it? I'll admit it's a bit of a sneaky one, because the actual verse reads "They that dwell in the wilderness shall bow before him; and his enemies shall lick the dust" (Psalm 72:9). The phrase "lick the dust" morphed into "bite the dust" and was used by cowboys to describe what happened to gunslingers when they lost a quick draw and "bit" the dust.

Knowing what the Bible says is important because then we also know what the Bible *doesn't* say, which is important. Bank tellers spend hours handling real money, so they're pretty good at spotting counterfeit bills. Similarly, if we spend time reading the Bible every day, we'll have a solid grasp on truth and will be able to recognize Satan's counterfeits. That's *every* day, not a couple of times each week. You wouldn't eat just once or twice a week, and the Bible is your spiritual food.

The other reason it's important to spend time reading the Bible daily is because it is God's *living* word. There is power in it that will change our lives. But if we read it just to say we read the Bible, we'll know a lot about the Bible but it won't change us. Change happens only when the Holy Spirit is a part of the process.

One more challenge: Is there a verse in the Bible that says the Sabbath is Sunday?

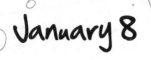

My Hope is in You

And we know that all things work together for good to those who love God, to those who are the called according to His purpose. **Romans 8:28, NKJV.**

It's easy to surf along during the good times and think that if you did a face-plant, or met up with a shark who wanted a piece of you, that you'd trust God and rely on Him every bit as much during the dark times as you are right at that beautiful, wonderful, happy moment. It's another thing entirely to actually be spitting out salt water, or trying to stop the bleeding from the stump of your arm or leg while you thrash around trying to get back to shore, and still be able to trust that God has a plan and that everything will work together in the end for His glory and for good. Not only for your good, but the good of others too.

That's exactly the situation in which Christian contemporary singer Aaron Shust and his wife, Sarah, found themselves when their second son, Nicky, was diagnosed with a rare disease called eosinophilic esophagitis (EE). Nicky couldn't eat or swallow food because his esophagus was severely inflamed. He had the worst case doctors had ever seen, and there was no known cure. But Aaron and Sarah had talked about the fact that if God chose to bless them with children they were only caretakers of those children. The children belonged to God and however long God chose to let them live was His perfect plan. So they clung to God and His plan even during the darkness of their son's suffering. That's when an amazing thing happened. Nicky was taken for further testing, and doctors couldn't find any trace of the disease.

A writer reporting on the story referred to their ordeal as a tragedy, but Aaron commented on the story himself, saying, "I have never called what God took us through a 'tragedy.' A tragedy implies, by definition, an unhappy ending, and while our boy still deals with aspects of EE, he is alive and happy and strong. And at age 2 he can quote John 1:1 and Matthew 5:16 verbatim. I'm a proud papa, more in love with my son and my Savior than I was a year ago."

What we must remember when we're fighting against the darkness and pain of hard times is that *all suffering is temporary*. God's own Son suffered and died. But He rose again. His suffering was temporary, and ours will be too. One day we'll be in heaven and there will be no more suffering or sadness. At all. Ever.

Regret and Redemption

God, make a fresh start in me, shape a Genesis week
from the chaos of my life. Don't throw me out with the trash,
or fail to breathe holiness in me. Bring me back from gray exile,
put a fresh wind in my sails! **Psalm 51:10-12, Message.**

Shackled hand and foot, Derek Seber was led into the courtroom. His prison suit looked disheveled. There was a small crowd hovering in the background: his parents and the parents of the girl who died in the car accident. But it was obvious that he didn't realize there was anyone else in the room at all. His face was ravaged with regret, twisted with remorse, and he was sobbing.

What brought this 22-year-old man to this courtroom when he should have been going to classes at Norwich University and having pizza with his friends?

One drink. One drink that led to another drink that led to another drink. You see, he'd been to a party with a lot of underage people who were drinking. When he left the party, seven other people crammed into the car he was driving—the same car he crashed while driving with a blood alcohol level nearly two and a half times the legal limit. The car looked like a building had fallen on it. One girl had died at the scene of the accident. Three other victims were in critical condition.

If he could go back in time, which of the events leading up to the crash do you think he'd change? Hopefully it wouldn't just be that he'd give the car keys to someone who hadn't been drinking, but that he would never have taken a drink at that party in the first place. Or, better yet, that he had not gone to a party at which so many other people were drinking.

Sadly, Derek will never be able to go back to the happy times before the accident. He will forever be responsible for causing someone's death. But there is hope for him still, as there is for anyone who will come to Jesus after a wrong turn in life.

Jesus can't eliminate our mistakes, but He can help us to move on from them. He can give us hearts committed to listening for His direction in our lives. Who knew that better than King David? He also was responsible for the death of an innocent person. When he asked God for a clean heart and a right spirit, he knew God was the only one who could bring something good from evil circumstances. Our God is a God of redemption, of second chances, of do-overs, of new starts. Make a commitment today to walk each step *in* His direction and *with* His direction.

January 10

Advertising Christ

Pray that I will proclaim this message
as clearly as I should. **Colossians 4:4, NLT.**

Native Americans were some of the most famous code talkers. They served in the United States Marine Corps in which they used their native languages as code for the military. Code talking was first used by the Choctaw during World War I, and later by other Native American tribes, including the Navajo, Lakota, Meskwaki, and Comanche. Native American languages were ideal for use in code talking because very few non-Native Americans could speak them and most of the languages had never been written down.

During the Battle of Iwo Jima, six Navajo code talkers worked around the clock. They sent and received more than 800 messages and didn't make a single mistake. Major Howard Connor, a 5th Marine Division signal officer, later said, "Were it not for the Navajos, the Marines would never have taken Iwo Jima."

The code was Navajo words in place of important military words. For example, the Navajo used their word for "buzzard" when they wanted to say "bomber." The word they used for "submarine" meant "iron fish" in Navajo.

Talking in code is great—when you don't want anyone to know what you're talking about. As Christians we often talk in our own code, "Christianese," if you will: washed in the blood, saved by grace, fellowshipping, dead to sin, backsliding. As Seventh-day Adventists we have even more code words: haystacks (a potluck dish), EGW (Ellen G. White), SOP (Spirit of Prophecy), the great controversy, sundown to sundown, unclean meat, and so on.

Yet the Bible calls us to make the gospel plain when we share it with others. When Paul talked about preaching the gospel, the word he used meant "to herald." A herald in those days was just a messenger. He wasn't to change the message, only proclaim it. We shouldn't make the gospel message indecipherable. Salvation is meant to be simple so *everyone* can understand it, not just those who know the code.

Think About It: How many more Christian code words can you think of? How could you make them plainer for non-Christians?

Limitless

I'm absolutely convinced that nothing—nothing living or dead,
angelic or demonic, today or tomorrow, high or low,
thinkable or unthinkable—absolutely *nothing* can get between us
and God's love because of the way that Jesus our Master
has embraced us. **Romans 8:38, 39, Message.**

D id you know that humans use only about 10 percent of their brains? You've probably heard that before and wondered why the other 90 percent of your brain was slacking off. The truth is more boring than fiction in this case—it's a myth that humans use so little of their brains. In fact, according to neurologist Barry Gordon at Johns Hopkins School of Medicine in Baltimore, the idea is ridiculous. "It turns out, though," he says, "that we use virtually every part of the brain, and that [most of] the brain is active almost all the time."

No one knows how or where the myth got started, but apparently people believe it because they know *they* are not particularly clever and can blame it on all those brain cells they aren't using. Based on that myth, someone made a movie about a pill that lets you access 100 percent of your brain power at once. The idea was that when you can use all of your brain all of the time, your potential is limitless. You can do, and be, and understand everything. Of course, the pill eventually wears off and needs to be taken again, and then the people who use it start getting headaches and dying. Typical Hollywood stuff.

But imagine if, instead of your brain, you could use 100 percent of your *heart*. Not just the little bit you use when you're feeling generous and having a great hair day, but all of it. On your own, though, you simply can't. We humans are too selfish—our "I" problem affects our hearts.

The only way is to let Jesus love *through* us. Then our love really can be limitless because then we don't rely on our own tiny heart with the little bit of love we give people when we're in a good mood and we happen to feel like it and they happen to be people we like anyway and want to be nice to. Instead, we have at our fingertips all the love of God, a love so big we can't even comprehend it. And all that love will flow effortlessly to everyone around us.

An Inside Job

These people make a big show of saying the right thing,
but their heart isn't in it. They act like they're worshiping me,
but they don't mean it. **Matthew 15:8, Message.**

*Order in the court! Order in the court! There will be order in this court,
or I'll hold you in contempt. Now, would you please take a seat? What's that?
You don't know why you're here? Didn't your lawyer tell you? Very well, you are
charged with being a Christian. How do you plead?*

*Guilty? We'll see about that. Now, it looks like you've been spending a lot of
time going to church and doing churchy things. I see here that you volunteer at
a soup kitchen once a month and that you do community service projects with a
group from your church. Is that correct? Yes, I see. And why do you go to church?
These are very serious charges, make no mistake about it.*

*Counselor, will you please hold up Exhibit A? The defendant will please
identify the object. It's your Bible, you say. Can you prove it's your Bible and
not just any Bible? There are markings? What kind of markings? So you've high-
lighted some of the texts, have you? Name some of them. OK, OK, that's enough.
Clearly this is your Bible, and you're very well acquainted with its contents.*

*Now, please tell the court the details of your relationship with someone called
Jesus . . .*

It's easy to identify yourself as a Christian; anyone can do it. It's easy to know
all about God and believe in Him but not actually *be* a Christian. Even the
demons believe in God—and tremble (see James 2:19). But what if someone pointed a finger at you, accusing you of being a Christian, and you were
dragged in front of a judge and jury? As the prosecuting attorney dug through
your life, exposing your innermost thoughts and beliefs, would there be
enough evidence to convict you of being a Christian?

Being a Christian is an inside job. The Holy Spirit begins by transform-
ing us inwardly and then works His way out. He'll change *you* first, and then
through you He'll change everything about your life and your world.

No, Thanks

Then the righteous will answer him, "Lord, when did we see you
hungry and feed you, or thirsty and give you something to drink?
When did we see you a stranger and invite you in, or needing clothes
and clothe you? When did we see you sick or in prison and go to visit you?"
The King will reply, "Truly I tell you, whatever you did for one of the least of
these brothers and sisters of mine, you did for me." **Matthew 25:37-40, NIV.**

Have you ever done something nice for someone and not even gotten a thank-you for your trouble? Social networking makes it easier than ever to help people out, which is probably why everyone automatically turns to it when they want advice before buying something or traveling away from home. They'll post a question to their friends and get pelted with answers and advice. Of course, there's the old-fashioned way of helping someone too: giving them a lift, pet-sitting, picking up their homework, saving them a seat. If we're walking the Christian walk, we do these things for people we know and like as well as for strangers and enemies.

The trouble comes when you invest time and energy to help someone and they don't even acknowledge your efforts. You think, *I went out of my way to help you and this is the thanks I get? Dude! Seriously?*

I get really annoyed when it happens to me because I'm compulsively helpful. It's almost a sickness. And when someone doesn't even give me a nod after all my help, I wonder why I bothered. But then I have to ask myself: Why am I helpful? Why do I take the time to do something for someone else, especially when it inconveniences me? Is it because I like people to thank me? Or is it because I want to be Christlike and help whether they are thankful or not?

Jesus had the same problem with being underappreciated. "He came to live in our behalf the life of the poorest and to walk and work among the needy and the suffering. Unrecognized and unhonored, He walked in and out among the people for whom He had done so much" (Ellen G. White, *The Ministry of Healing*, p. 19). Imagine what would have happened if He had decided to help humanity *only* if every one of us was appreciative of His sacrifice.

January 14

Pick Me! Pick Me!

But you are the ones chosen by God,
chosen for the high calling of priestly work,
chosen to be a holy people, God's instruments to do his work
and speak out for him, to tell others of the night-and-day
difference he made for you—from nothing to something,
from rejected to accepted. **I Peter 2:9, 10, Message.**

You know that sinking feeling you get when someone, usually a teacher, announces it's time to choose sides for a game, or to be on a team, or even to get into a small group? I hate that feeling. When I was in school, the teachers would select team captains and those two would get to pick who was on their team. The good players were chosen first and then the popular kids, even if they couldn't hit a baseball with a canoe. Then they'd pick the kids who had a little talent, then the kids who had broken legs. And then, to their great sorrow, one of the captains would get stuck with me.

Now, can I just say that I was a fair to middling baseball (or any team sport) player and I could run faster than most? I wasn't left until last because no one thought I could get the job done. It was just that I was different, usually new in school, and no one knew me. But always being the last one chosen affected my attitude about the game. I was afraid to try and fail, and I doubted myself and my ability. I *had* been picked last, after all. But I had to prove myself; I had to *show* them I could do it. I had to show whoever had gotten stuck with me that they really were *lucky* to have me.

That's why I'm so glad I'm on God's team. Not only did I make the team, but He picked me Himself. Not last, but first! I was chosen first. And so were you because God chose you before you were even born. He chooses each of us personally and He chooses each of us first. He wants us on His team.

We all will experience rejection in life but that is not what is important. What *is* important is that God has chosen us to be on His team and to do His important work. We need to get busy and do it, full of confidence because we are special, we are chosen, we are His.

Think About It: Ask yourself what would happen if you believed—and I mean *truly* believed—that God has chosen you, that you are special, and that He has important work for you. In what ways would this knowledge change your life?

Skunked

Don't be misled: No one makes a fool of God.
What a person plants, he will harvest. The person who plants selfishness,
ignoring the needs of others—ignoring God!—harvests a crop of weeds.
All he'll have to show for his life is weeds! But the one who plants
in response to God, letting God's Spirit do the growth work in him,
harvests a crop of real life, eternal life. **Galatians 6:7, 8, Message.**

My friend Bob made a new friend this spring—a smelly, black-and-white friend. Yes, a skunk. "They're so friendly," he told me. "Really, you'd think they wouldn't be, but they are." In fact, this skunk was so friendly that Bob made kind of a pet out of it. He fed it and let the skunk nose around his yard looking for whatever skunks look for.

But Bob has a dog. She's not a mean dog, but since she wouldn't appreciate a pet skunk, Bob decided he'd better stop feeding the skunk before there was trouble with his dog. Who knows how the skunk felt about being ignored suddenly, but I imagine it wasn't too happy.

One warm summer night, when Bob and his dog were on the couch watching television, the skunk sauntered in through the open French doors. The skunk looked at Bob (probably with reproach), Bob looked at the dog (probably with horror), the dog looked at the skunk (probably with disbelief), and then the dog launched itself across the room at the skunk. I don't need to tell you how the skunk reacted to that kind of welcome. Suffice it to say that Bob's house smelled so bad that he had to have it professionally cleaned. He probably wished the dog could be professionally cleaned too because it slept in his bed every night.

Why, you might well ask, would someone make friends with such a potentially nasty-smelling beast? For the same reason we sometimes play around with sin—it looks cute and cuddly on the outside and even seems harmless at first. Let's face it: sometimes the very fact that there's a little danger involved tempts us to flirt with sin. It isn't until you get burned (or sprayed) by it that you realize it's not innocent at all. It's mean and nasty, and the consequences are far worse than living in a stinky house for a while.

A Long Time Ago Yesterday

But in fact God has placed the parts in the body, every one of them, just as he wanted them to be. If they were all one part, where would the body be? As it is, there are many parts, but one body. **I Corinthians 12:18-20, NIV.**

A couple weeks ago I sang a song at church. It was by a group called Petra, a Christian rock band that was the first to be inducted into the Gospel Music Hall of Fame. The song I sang was "More Power to Ya," and it talks about how the Lord will give us strength and power to do His work if we will wait on Him. (Check it out on YouTube.)

The song went pretty well; it's in my range, which is a rarity because I'm a contralto. After the service a friend shook my hand and said, "I enjoyed your special music. You have such a beautiful voice." But do you know what I heard? I heard, "I enjoyed your special music. Shut up and let your sister sing."

Whoa, you may be thinking, *where did that come from?* I thought exactly the same thing, except that I know where it came from. When I was a kid, my sister and I were asked to sing at a wedding and we were practicing one day at our grandparent's house. My sister has a beautiful voice. I, on the other hand, hadn't yet discovered that my strength was in singing lower notes, so I was warbling along in a thin, high soprano. My grandmother looked at me and said, "Why don't you shut up and let your sister sing? You sound awful."

That was a long time ago, and I should have forgotten all about it. But I haven't. However, I choose to ignore it and sing anyway because God has put music in my life and given me some talent for it. In fact, I'm the music director at my church, and I lead out in the praise team because I choose to honor God and ignore my grandmother's condemnation.

Everyone lives with negative messages that demean and discourage. What cruel words have kept you from accepting God's full potential for your life? Let them go and step into the work that God has planned for you. We all have gifts, and God will bless us richly as we use them for His glory and in His worship.

Peekaboo, I See You—Forever

Don't you see what happens, you simpletons, you idiots? Carelessness kills;
complacency is murder. First pay attention to me, and then relax.
Now you can take it easy—you're in good hands. **Proverbs 1:32, 33, Message.**

When I was a teenager, I hiked Algonquin Peak (the second-highest mountain in New York) in the Adirondacks with my parents and some of their friends . . . during the winter. On the way up I became hypothermic, then when we got to the top it was snowing so hard we couldn't see anything, and then I almost fell off the mountain. I was wearing instep crampons on my boots (they're little metal teeth that give you traction on the icy trail) and climbing upward when I slipped off the metal grips and onto the smooth toes of my boots. That's when I started sliding off the side of the mountain.

Fortunately my mother was nearby. She reached out and I was able to grab her hand. She pulled me onto solid ground. If she hadn't, I would have tumbled right off the mountain and smashed onto the rocks below.

That feeling of free falling to certain doom should be a familiar feeling— and you don't even have to nearly fall off a mountain to get it. It's the same feeling you should have every time you send a text, an e-mail, a picture, or post something online. It's as if you take that information and dangle it over a big cliff and then—oops!—it slips out of your fingers and it's gone. You no longer have any control over it.

Many teens are discovering the hard way that what you say and pictures you send can come back to haunt you and really mess up your life. More and more teens face charges of possessing and distributing child pornography because they were sexting—sending sexually explicit pictures—to one another. The charges carry prison sentences, and some states require offenders to be registered in the sex offender registry for the rest of their lives. Imagine trying to get a job or live a normal life with that label hanging over you.

To protect yourself, never send a picture to anyone that you wouldn't want your parents to see (if you get caught, scarier people than your parents will see that photo). Hold yourself accountable to God; don't say anything digitally to someone that you wouldn't say to their face and that you wouldn't say if Jesus were standing next to them. And don't be afraid to blab. If anyone pressures you to send pictures that make you uncomfortable, tell someone.

The Man and the Rock

I can do all things through Christ who strengthens me. **Philippians 4:13, NKJV.**

There's a story I once heard about a man who was asked by God to push against an enormous rock. Every day the man pushed and pushed, but it was the size of a house and never budged a single inch. Satan, of course, decided to take advantage of the man's epic fail and he got in the habit of paying him a visit to rub it in.

"You're never going to be able to move that rock. Why don't you quit?" the devil taunted him.

Finally the man was so worn down that he asked God if he really should quit. God replied, "You think you've failed because you haven't moved the rock. But I never asked you to move it, I asked you to push it. You did that, and look at you! You've gotten really strong. Now step aside. I'm going to move the rock."

Have you ever been up against a situation you felt was hopeless? One that you were sure would become your own epic fail? We've all been there. But it doesn't matter whether you're up against something big, small, or microscopic. All situations have one thing in common: we need God's strength, wisdom, and power to get through all of it, whether big or small, important or trivial.

Ellen White says, "You may feel the deficiency of your character and the smallness of your ability in comparison with the greatness of the work. But if you had the greatest intellect ever given to man, it would not be sufficient for your work. 'Without Me ye can do nothing,' says our Lord and Savior. John 15:5. The result of all we do rests in the hands of God. Whatever may betide, lay hold upon Him with steady, persevering confidence" (*The Ministry of Healing*, p. 513).

What a relief! The outcome of everything—*everything*—is in God's hands. We could be as smart as a hundred Einsteins, as strong as a hundred Arnold Schwarzeneggers, as talented as all the winners of American Idol put together, and it still wouldn't matter. We can't be strong enough, fast enough, smart enough, or good enough to get God's work done. Unless God is working through us, on our side, we're going to fail, because it's God's work, and only God is great enough to do it. We just have to be willing to let Him use us and then stand aside and let *Him* move the rock.

Dark of Night

The night is far spent, the day is at hand. Therefore let us cast off the works of darkness, and let us put on the armor of light. **Romans 13:12, NKJV.**

I woke up and tried to remember what had awakened me. I thought I'd heard a screech of tires and the thud of impact. But I wasn't sure. Had it just been a dream? As I lay there in my bed, wondering if I should get up, get dressed, get in my car, and drive down the road to see if there had been an actual accident, I heard a shot and then an explosion! It hadn't been a dream after all. There really had been a car accident and the car had exploded, which meant that someone could be trapped inside burning alive.

My husband and I threw open the front door and strained to hear anything. We heard voices yelling, so he ran to his truck to locate the accident and see if he could help. I ran to the phone and made my first-ever 9-1-1 call. I prayed frantically for the poor people I was sure were trapped inside the car burning to a crisp.

When my husband came back, he said he'd seen a couple young guys wandering down the road looking a little confused. The police had stopped him and asked if he'd seen anyone, and he told them where the guys had gone.

The next day we found out the car had been stolen and the young men had actually been on a steal-and-crash spree for a couple of weeks. The police brought in dogs and tracked them down. They were arrested, and it'll be a while before they go joyriding again.

The difference in our *perception* of what had happened and what had *actually* happened was like the difference between night and day. By night we thought innocent people had accidentally crashed their car and were trapped in it while it burned. By day we discovered that the people who crashed the car weren't so innocent; they'd done it on purpose, and then ran away from the scene of the accident so they wouldn't be arrested.

In the same way, Satan tries to confuse and disorient us. He starts a little fire here, or a crash there, and while we're running around panicked, he pulls a little hat trick somewhere else. By the time we figure it out, we discover that we're miles away from God, wandering out in the wilderness somewhere lost and alone. We need to anchor ourselves in God so that Satan's distractions will appear to be just what they are, smoke and mirrors, and not worth our attention.

Worrywart

Therefore I say to you, do not worry about your life,
what you will eat or what you will drink; nor about your body,
what you will put on. Is not life more than food and the body
more than clothing? Look at the birds of the air, for they neither sow
nor reap nor gather into barns; yet your heavenly Father feeds them.
Are you not of more value than they? **Matthew 6:25, 26, NKJV.**

TheFreeDictionary.com defines "worrywart" as a noun referring to someone who worries too much, which applies to all of us because we all worry. However, Jesus Himself told us not to worry. Period. So if we worry at all, we're worrying too much.

Worried about that test you're taking this week? Don't. Worried about the fight you had with your best friend? Don't. Worried about whether or not you'll make it into the college you chose, onto the team you've been practicing for, or into the position at church that you are excited about? Don't. "Therefore I say to you, do not worry."

Worry is a perception problem. We *perceive* a problem, and we worry about it. But what we don't take into account is that as human beings we're stuck in this particular moment. We can't see past the end of this week, this day, even this minute. And anything at all beyond this very minute is really just our imagining, that which we suppose will happen based on the facts we have in hand. What we don't—in fact, can't—know is what other forces God has set in motion that will supply the very need we are fruitlessly worrying about.

George Müller was a man who became rather famous for his dependence on God's reality in place of his own. In the 1800s Müller built and ran orphanages in Ashley Downs, Bristol, England. He never asked for one penny from anyone except God. Many instances are recorded of needs that were met as they arose even though it would have been impossible to predict them. In one famous instance Müller and the children gave thanks for their breakfast (there was no food in the house). As they were sitting at the table prepared to eat, the baker and the milkman knocked on the door. The baker had enough bread to feed everyone in the house, and the milkman's cart broke down in front of the orphanage and he supplied the milk.

Worry is pointless. We serve a God who is in charge of everything. He has the solution to every problem and the resources to meet any need. Anchor yourself in God's reality today and let Him blow your mind with the possibilities.

Pawned

> Then from the top of the mountain God spoke to Moses and the people:
> "I am the Lord your God who brought you out of the land of Egypt,
> out of the house of bondage, and set you free. You are my people,
> and I want you to be holy, for I am holy." **Exodus 20:1, 2, Clear Word.**

Pawn shops are not just places for people with names like Chumlee and Big Hoss, two stars of the television series *Pawn Stars,* to hang out; they serve a legitimate need in society by providing quick cash. About 3,000 years ago in ancient China, peasants relied on pawn shops to lend them money. Through the years pawnbroking has continued to thrive. During the Great Depression pawn shops offered cash when banks failed. And Christopher Columbus owed his cruise to find a new world to a pawn shop; Queen Isabella of Spain pawned her jewelry to fund his trip.

If you're not familiar with pawnbroking, here's how it works. Let's say you need some money but you can't get a regular loan at a bank. You take the Mickey Mantle baseball card that your grandpa gave you (unless you, too, have crown jewels) to a pawn shop. The owner will tell you how much it's worth to him and offer you a loan. If you pay the loan back (with interest) you can have your card back. If not, the shop owner can sell it to someone else to make his money back.

You are more familiar with pawn brokers than you might realize because you, my friend, have been pawned. You are that Mickey Mantle baseball card in the grubby hands of Satan, sold into his pawnshop by your sins. There you sit on the shelf with a huge price tag around your neck. The most expensive items the stars of the television show *Pawn Stars* have sold were four one-kilo gold bars, which were worth $128,000. But you are far more expensive than that. In fact, only the sinless life of God's own Son can ransom you from Satan's pawn shop.

You could say that we belong to God twice: first because He created us, and second because He redeemed us. The question is, how long do you want to stay in that smoky old pawnshop? You are free to leave whenever you choose. All you have to do is accept God's payment for your sins and you can leave with Him. You'll never have to spend another minute listening to Satan gloat.

Infected

It only takes a spark, remember, to set off a forest fire.
A careless or wrongly placed word out of your mouth can do that.
By our speech we can ruin the world, turn harmony to chaos,
throw mud on a reputation, send the whole world up in smoke and
go up in smoke with it, smoke right from the pit of hell. **James 3:5, 6, Message.**

Are you a germaphobe, someone who has a deep and abiding fear of germs? Do you wipe down the handles of grocery carts, use a tissue to handle the pump at the gas station, and carry a utility-size bottle of hand sanitizer on your person at all times? I'm not talking about the very real condition of mysophobia, which is a pathological fear of germs and contamination. I'm talking about your average, garden-variety germ hating.

Let's face it, maybe you should be. Experts estimate that there are about 60,000 kinds of germs—and we come in contact with many of them on a daily basis. Fortunately for us, only 1 or 2 percent are significantly dangerous to healthy people. Still, researchers found that 70-80 percent of grocery carts tested in the United States had E. coli—a bacteria that can cause stomach cramps, vomiting, and diarrhea—on them. Your desk has 400 times more germs than a toilet. Scary, isn't it?

But germs aren't the only infectious little things that surround us every day. Words are every bit as plentiful and can be just as damaging as germs. They can be deceitful, too; sometimes you're not even aware of how bad they are until the damage is done. We're told in James 3:7, 8 that all kinds of animals can be tamed, but the tongue can't be tamed. When you consider some of the damage a tongue can do, a prowling tiger seems like a nice kitty.

James goes on to say that we praise God and curse with the same tongue! (See verse 9.) Can you imagine good water and sewage coming out of the same pipe? coming up out of the water fountain? Would you want to drink there? Me neither!

In order to keep our words pure, we need to ask the Holy Spirit to give them to us. That way we'll always be speaking God-approved words that will only be capable of infecting those around us with God's love and wisdom. Now, *that's* something I wouldn't mind catching!

Audience of One

Then He who sat on the throne said,
"Behold, I make all things new." And He said to me,
"Write, for these words are true and faithful." **Revelation 21:5, NKJV.**

What do Anne Frank, Samuel Pepys, Lewis Carroll, George Washington, Thomas Jefferson, Beatrix Potter, and Harry S. Truman have in common? They all kept diaries. Samuel Pepys and Beatrix Potter even wrote their diaries in codes they made up. Both of the codes were cracked after their deaths. Today we'd say their diaries were hacked; someone breached their firewalls. Since Pepys and Potter thought their words were safely hidden inside their codes they both wrote honestly about their lives. Shy, retiring Beatrix Potter—creator of Peter Rabbit and other stories—turned out to be a critic of the arts and politics of her day. Pepys chronicled the time period he lived in and unwittingly provided historians valuable insight into life in London during the 1660s.

Diaries, or journals, have been found in Japan that date back to the tenth century. Believe it or not, there is some evidence to suggest that all this writing might be good for your health. In addition to strengthening your immune system and helping with asthma, writing about how you feel, especially if you're going through a tough situation, can help you get a grip on the situation and reduce the negative impact on your life.

The Bible doesn't record any particular instances of journalkeeping. However, if paper had been more readily available, I think Paul would have been an avid journalkeeper, judging from the number of letters he wrote. A journal can be a great place to write down our thoughts about God and prayers to Him, and it can be a safe place to work through problems we have with other people, too.

Journaling often helps people begin to understand and process things that bother them. If you're honest when you write, you'll get to know yourself better and releasing your emotions on paper will help you let go of them. Try it yourself and see what you think.

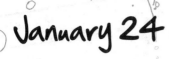

January 24

Stand Up and Be Counted

A word fitly spoken is like apples of gold in settings of silver. **Proverbs 25:11, NKJV.**

It's amazing the things you can't remember after time has passed. For instance, I can't remember the names of half of my high school teachers, or who was our class valedictorian, or any of the grades I got. But I remember Bruce Therrien, and I didn't even know him. I've never spoken to him—ever—but I'll never forget him.

He was older than I was; his brother was in my class. He was also "cool," something I definitely was not. The only thing we shared was that we liked to sit at the back of the bus. I don't know why he liked sitting there, but I sat there because I could stay out of the way, keep my head down, and avoid getting picked on too much. It was always like running the gauntlet as I made my way to the back because people would try to trip me or say something nasty, but once I made it, I always felt safe.

One day some kids began tormenting me as we were all filing off the bus, and to my surprise Bruce Therrien, who never said much at any time, told them to stop. And they did. Because he was popular? Because he was bigger? Because he said so? I don't know; but they stopped. Just like that. He never said one other thing to me, or about me that I know of, but I'll never forget him because of that one time he made the bullies stop picking on me.

You may think that you don't have a lot to offer as you go through your day, but the truth is, you have a great deal to offer. You have the great God of the universe living in *your* life. With God's love spilling out of you and onto other people you can effect major change for good in your life, your neighborhood, your family, your friends, and even your enemies. Never discount the value of a smile directed at someone who is down in the dumps, an act of kindness or a kind word for someone who is being bullied. Who knows, someone may remember *you* forever.

Take It to the Streets: No one is immune to bullying; it's not just for teenagers. If bullying is a problem in places where you hang out, whether physically or in cyberspace, recruit some friends who want to make a difference and spread your message of anti-bullying. Stand up for one another and let bullies know that you won't tolerate their abusive behavior in your circles. Don't be shy about getting adults involved either. The more people involved in stomping out bullying, the safer everyone will be.

Tebowing

Not only that—count yourselves blessed every time people
put you down or throw you out or speak lies about you to discredit me.
What it means is that the truth is too close for comfort and they
are uncomfortable. You can be glad when that happens—give a cheer,
even!—for though they don't like it, *I* do! And all heaven applauds.
And know that you are in good company. My prophets and witnesses have
always gotten into this kind of trouble. **Matthew 5:11, 12, Message.**

Football player Tim Tebow had an outstanding career as an amateur player that won him many awards before being recruited by the Denver Broncos. However, he went through the media wringer for . . . wait for it . . . praying. In fact, the act of dropping to one knee and bowing your head in a position of prayer has become known as "Tebowing."

Tebow started the movement himself, though not on purpose. Tebow's faith is strong and he publicly drops to one knee and rests his forehead on one hand as he prays. After a game a fan emulated him and then secured the Web site www.tebowing.com and began posting pictures of people in the Tebowing position. Soldiers, people in precarious positions, brides and grooms, even a kid during his chemo treatment, all Tebowing.

This isn't the first time Tebow has been caught in the spotlight for religious reasons. In 2010 the NCAA (National Collegiate Athletic Association) made a rule that players couldn't write messages in the black paint under their eyes. The media dubbed it "The Tebow Rule" because Tebow was known for writing scriptures in his black under-eye paint. After he once wrote "John 3:16" in the paint, 92 million people Googled the verse.

But the tide began to shift, and rather than emulating Tebow, his critics started to mock him and his "prayer position." Tebow shrugged off the incident, and graciously said he didn't consider them an attack on his religion, which is how the Bible tells us to respond when people mock our religion or our faith. It's easier said than done.

Let's face it, if you go public with your faith, chances are someone is going to mock you for it. Are you prepared? Are you fortified with spiritual strength to respond with grace when someone insults your beliefs? If you aren't, or you don't know, ask God to make you strong enough to endure insults for His sake. And remember, He was insulted first.

Angry Birds

*And everyone who competes for the prize
is temperate in all things. Now they do it to obtain a perishable crown,
but we for an imperishable crown.* **I Corinthians 9:25, NKJV.**

My sister Faith once posted as her status on Facebook: "Why aren't my angry birds talking to me?" To which I replied, "Why are your birds angry? Didn't you feed them?"

OK, so I didn't know Angry Birds was the name of a computer game. Stop laughing; I really didn't! The first time someone showed it to me I couldn't understand why anyone would want to launch cute little birds at pigs in the first place. (I didn't know the pigs stole the birds' eggs, which caused said birds to become angry.)

Not having an iPod, iPhone, or other iDevice on which to play Angry Birds, and not having enough time to play computer games anyway, I happily survived quite a long time before I found out that Google had a version I could play right there on my computer. And you know what else I found out? It's addictive! I tried using the game as a reward for completing writing tasks and I had to watch out that I didn't get caught up in the "if I try just one more time, I can beat this level" mentality that is so prevalent in gaming.

Internet addiction and gaming addiction, whether computer or game console, are very recent problems because digital gaming and the Internet are still pretty new. Five years after its launch, Angry Birds had been downloaded more than 1 *billion* times. It gets about 200 *million* minutes of play time *per day*. Along with many other licensed products are t-shirts, plush toys, books, soft drinks, and a board game—seriously, a board game of the digital game!—for sale, and a movie is in the works.

Gaming and Internet addictions are very real things; experts say these addictions have the characteristics of other psychological addictions such as gambling or impulse control disorder. In one extreme case, 3-month-old Kim Sa-rang died from malnutrition while her game-addicted parents raised a virtual child with magical powers. Addicted players withdraw from real-life activities and people, and into their own digital online world.

Because gaming and the Internet weren't around in Bible times, the Bible doesn't talk about them. However, the Bible does talk about principles we must use to guide our lives. Temperance, the practice of doing all good things in moderation and avoiding bad things entirely, is important for us to be well-rounded, healthy people. Letting any one thing control your life makes a god out of it (see Exodus 20:3). Put God in charge of your life in real time.

Rooted Deep

Then Christ will make his home in your hearts as you trust in him.
Your roots will grow down into God's love and keep you strong.
And may you have the power to understand, as all God's people should,
how wide, how long, how high, and how deep his love is.
May you experience the love of Christ, though it is too great
to understand fully. Then you will be made complete with all the fullness
of life and power that comes from God. **Ephesians 3:17-19, NLT.**

It was the only tree for miles around. It stood out like a sore thumb smack dab in the middle of the Sahara. Even if you were driving a vehicle the size of a building, you could have easily driven around it. But in 1973 a drunk Libyan trucker managed to plow right into it, and the tree died.

Called the Tree of Ténéré, the big acacia tree stood where trees hadn't lived since the Sahara was a lot wetter than it is now. This was the last acacia tree left from a group of trees that used to stand on that spot, marking a salt caravan route.

If you wonder where this tree was getting water from, the mystery was solved by some men when they dug a well in 1938. They discovered that the tree's roots went down all the way to the water table—around 110 feet below the ground. Can you imagine tree roots that long?

The tree meant so much to the people of Niger that after it was knocked down, they put it in the Niger National Museum and replaced it with a skeletal metal structure in its original spot.

Have you ever felt like a tree out in the middle of a desert? Or maybe like a tree alone despite being in the middle of a forest? Having other people around doesn't always protect us from loneliness and isolation. But no matter where God has planted you, He's given you the ability to plant your roots deep in His love so that He can nourish you in the middle of whatever circumstances you might find yourself.

No matter how lonely, discouraged, or shut out you may feel, you can never be lost to God's love if you sink your roots into it. Let God's love sustain you like the Tree of Ténéré.

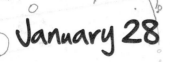

January 28

Murmuration of Christians

I have a serious concern to bring up with you,
my friends, using the authority of Jesus, our Master.
I'll put it as urgently as I can: You must *get along with each other.*
You must learn to be considerate of one another,
cultivating a life in common. **I Corinthians 1:10, Message.**

You've probably heard the expression "a flock of birds," used to describe a group of birds together. You may have even heard of a "gaggle of geese" or maybe even a "murder of crows." But have you ever heard of a "parliament of owls"? An "unkindness of ravens"? An "exaltation of larks"? A "pandemonium of parrots"? A "squabble of seagulls"? How about a "murmuration of starlings"?

These are all collective nouns used to fancifully describe a particular type of bird grouping. They aren't used often, which is why you might not be familiar with them, but as I write this, a "murmuration of starlings" is becoming very popular because of some video footage shot by Sophie Windsor Clive and Liberty Smith while on a canoe trip in the U.K. A quick search on YouTube should turn up some awesome footage if you want to check it out. Anyway, a murmuration of starlings is hundreds of thousands of these birds twisting and turning across the sky and forming shapes as they fly close together and then separate into different groups. Although terrific numbers of them are flying together swiftly, they don't collide. It's such an amazing and awe-inspiring phenomenon that scientists have been studying the starlings to try to figure out how they can communicate so quickly during flight.

Unity like this is God's plan for His church—us! We should be in tune with one another so much that we will go through life so harmoniously that the world can't help noticing and will figure it out only when they study what's behind this unity. God's ability to guide so many diverse individuals as a unified body of believers will astonish everyone who sees it and inspire them to want to know Him better. We will be a murmuration of Christians.

God can see the big picture, the image of His love that He wants to portray to the world through us. Even when we can't discern His plan, when all we can see is the individuals fluttering near us, we can trust that God has a purpose for everything He asks us to do.

Here and Now

*There's an opportune time to do things,
a right time for everything on the earth.* **Ecclesiastes 3:1, Message.**

There is no denying that texting has done some good in the world. In one particularly spectacular case, vascular surgeon David Nott was able to perform a difficult amputation on a teen while volunteering with Doctors Without Borders in the Congo because a colleague who knew how to do the surgery texted him directions. The teen made a full recovery. In less-flashy cases, texting can help pass along important information that's quick and easy to relay.

When used irresponsibly, texting results in car crashes, loss of life, suspension from school, regret, and various accidents. Alexia Longueira, 15, was texting and walking at the same time—don't try this at home—when she fell through an open manhole into a sewer.

Technology is here to stay, and there will be more, not less, gadgets to tinker with in the future. Maybe texting is already so last week that everyone is doing something completely new and different to keep in constant contact. There's nothing wrong with technology. But just like any other "good" thing, we can abuse it.

Deepak Sharma made the *Guinness Book of World Records* by sending 182,689 texts in a single month (that's about one text every 14 seconds). His goal is 300,000 texts in a month. Basically his whole life is texting. Think of all the things he's missing out on.

And that's kind of the point. You don't have to text every 14 seconds to miss out on a lot of life because of texting. Whenever you text you're missing out on the real life that's happening all around you. You become caught up in conversations with people who aren't physically present with you. Sure, there's a time for texting—there's a time for all technology. Texting can be useful and can enhance our lives. But when we use it too much, we cheat ourselves of actual experiences with real people, the ones in the room, in the house, in the car, or at the table with us.

If you are addicted to texting, try going on a texting fast. Don't text for a month (or a week, if you can't handle a month). Life will certainly be different, but you might discover that you've been missing out!

January 30

Gotcha!

*Keep a cool head. Stay alert. The Devil is poised to pounce,
and would like nothing better than to catch you napping.
Keep your guard up.* **1 Peter 5:8, Message.**

A friend of mine is all about birds. He loves them, owns them, raises them, writes about them, and watches them through his binoculars. His wife really likes them too, and one day she happened to look out the window and noticed some weird-looking geese near a little island up the river from where they lived. Because they both knew all about every kind of goose that lived in their area, they knew the geese were from somewhere else. They were excited! What kind of geese could these be? Unfortunately, the geese were far enough away that my friends couldn't see them well enough to identify them.

A couple weeks went by while they wondered about what sort of geese had landed on the island, and probably pored over their bird books trying to identify their visitors. The mystery was solved one day when they watched a man wearing hip waders slosh out to the geese and the geese didn't fly away.

They were plastic goose decoys.

Satan likes to play the same tricks on us. He shows us something interesting and different (it might even be a little familiar) just to catch our attention. But once he's got us hooked, it's always bad—for us, that is. Like my friends (and possibly some real geese) who were duped by the plastic decoys, we find out that things are not always as they seem—often they're worse. But by that time we're caught. Sometimes the only consequence is embarrassment or disappointment; sometimes the consequences are worse and we have to live with them forever.

God is familiar with all of Satan's decoys, and He also knows all our weaknesses. The principles contained within the Ten Commandments are there to help us avoid all the traps Satan lays for us. But in order for us to discern those pitfalls, we need to be immersed in God's Word and communicating with Him daily.

Satan doesn't work 40-hour weeks; he's on the prowl 24/7. He will try to catch us whenever he can. It's our job to listen for God's direction. The Bible says, "Whether you turn to the right or to the left, your ears will hear a voice behind you, saying, 'This is the way; walk in it'" (Isaiah 30:21, NIV).

January 31

Backwards Day

If you cling to your life, you will lose it;
but if you give up your life for me, you will find it. **Matthew 10:39, NLT.**

Today is National Backwards Day. You can eat supper for breakfast, walk backwards, wear your clothes backwards, write your name backwards, say the alphabet backwards, and no one will think you're strange. You won't get the day off, as it's not a federal holiday, but there are Web sites devoted to suggesting unique ways to celebrate the day.

Christians shouldn't have any trouble celebrating Backwards Day, because our very religion is full of beliefs the world thinks are backwards. Mathematician, inventor, and religious philosopher Blaise Pascal said, "Mahomet established a religion by putting his enemies to death; Jesus Christ by commanding his followers to lay down their lives."

To the Jews, Jesus' entire life seemed backwards. Instead of ruling as a king, He walked the earth in such poverty that He didn't even have a place of His own to lay His head at night. Instead of demanding that people serve Him, He served people. Instead of being worshipped and adored, He was crucified and killed. Jesus didn't look the way people expected, He didn't act the way they expected, and He didn't rule the way they expected.

They were accustomed to the "eye for an eye, tooth for a tooth" method of justice, yet here was Jesus telling them to turn the other cheek. At that time it was legal for Roman soldiers to force Jewish citizens to carry their loads for them, something the Jews hated. Yet Jesus urged them not only to walk the mile they were legally required to walk but to walk an *additional mile*. People who saw Jesus in action must have wondered, "Who is this guy?"

Everything Jesus teaches is the opposite of what we naturally want to do. If we want to keep our life, we must lose it; instead of holding on tight to what we want, we must let God take over. When we submit ourselves to His will, which makes us slaves or captives, Jesus sets us free to become the people we were really meant to be. By losing we gain, by dying we live; everything is backwards. There is only one way we can learn how to live like this: the Holy Spirit has to change us from the inside out, back to front. Start living backwards today!

February 1

Waiting

Then the Kingdom of Heaven will be like ten bridesmaids
who took their lamps and went to meet the bridegroom.
Five of them were foolish, and five were wise. The five who were foolish
didn't take enough olive oil for their lamps, but the other five were wise
enough to take along extra oil. When the bridegroom was delayed,
they all became drowsy and fell asleep. **Matthew 25:1-5, NLT.**

I live in a pretty small city, more a large town. So when I heard that the release of a certain video game drew more than 600 teens who stood in line for hours to get their hands on a copy, I could hardly believe it. Apparently, if you went to the store early in the day, you could get an armband with a number on it that would let you cut in line later so you wouldn't have to wait so long. Still, more than 600 kids waiting in line for hours to buy a game?

Is there anything you want so badly that you'd stand in line for hours on end? Evidently the bridesmaids in Jesus' parable wanted to be part of the wedding procession so badly that they waited for hours. In fact, they waited so long that they fell asleep, and they ran out of oil. Can you imagine the angst if some of those kids waiting in line at the store found out when they reached the counter that they didn't have enough money to pay for the game after they waited so long in line?

In parables everything represents something. In this case the oil and the money represent our spiritual condition—the Holy Spirit in our life. We are each responsible for our own spiritual condition, just as each bridesmaid and teen was responsible for bringing enough oil or money. We can't borrow someone else's if we find that we don't have any. You can't claim your parents', or your best friend's, or your sibling's spiritual life; you have only your own.

Today find a quiet place and have a heart-to-heart with God. Be honest about your spiritual life, and ask God to help you grow closer to Him. Is there anything you need to eliminate from your life that prevents you from becoming closer to God? Is there anything you should be doing that you aren't? Ask God to show you and to give you the strength to follow Him so that when He comes back, you will have plenty of oil in your lamp and will be ready to step in line with the bridal party and follow Jesus to the wedding feast.

You've Got Talent

Again, it will be like a man going on a journey,
who called his servants and entrusted his wealth to them.
To one he gave five bags of gold, to another two bags,
and to another one bag, each according to his ability.
Then he went on his journey. **Matthew 25:14, 15, NIV.**

America and Britain have had their differences in the past (there was that whole Revolutionary War squabble, for instance), but there is one thing they both agree on: their citizens have a lot of talent. Both countries have their own version of *Got Talent,* which showcases aspiring artists to demonstrate that talent. During the 2007 season of *Britain's Got Talent* 6-year-old Connie Talbot, a tiny, gap-toothed tot at the time, entered for fun and wowed the judges with an a cappella rendition of "Over the Rainbow." Seven years later—and with a full set of teeth—she has recorded four albums and is continuing her singing career around her primary school activities. She even received an offer for a movie role.

When you start talking to people about talent, they're either loaded with it, or they have a list of excuses as long as your arm for believing they have no talent. The truth is that God has given everyone talent of some kind. It may not get you a record deal but it is still talent. You don't get to choose your talent, and you may have to work hard to increase it so that you can use it to your full potential.

Some people really struggle to know what they are good at, while others seem to have been born with that knowledge. If you have trouble identifying your talent, ask people who know you well what talent they see in you—and don't forget to talk to God about it. Ask Him to make your talents clear to you.

It doesn't matter if your talent is encouraging others or performing intricate brain surgery, whatever talent God has given you is important and it should be used for Him. When He comes back, He's going to ask you what you did with the talent He gave you, and the six little words you'll want to hear are: "Well done, good and faithful servant" (Matthew 25:21, NKJV).

February 3

Something Smells Sheep-y

When he finally arrives, blazing in beauty and all his angels with him,
the Son of Man will take his place on his glorious throne.
Then all the nations will be arranged before him and he will sort
the people out, much as a shepherd sorts out sheep and goats,
putting sheep to his right and goats to his left. **Matthew 25:31-33, Message.**

If you've been paying attention (pop quiz!), you may have noticed that this is the third day we've spent in Matthew 25 and that this final day is the last of a trilogy of Jesus' parables. Just as a camera tripod needs all three legs to balance properly, these three stories should be considered together because they each talk about one part of how we should live as we wait for Jesus to return.

The final area Jesus describes is caring for others. The sheep represent the people in the parable who cared about others and helped when they saw suffering. The goats represent those who didn't care.

"Wait," you say, "I'd love to help, but I can't go on a mission trip to help needy people."

That's all right. Going on a mission trip isn't the only way to help people. Can you pray with someone who is hurting? Can you share your lunch with someone who forgot theirs? Can you smile at someone who seems stressed out? Can you help someone reach something that's up high on a grocery store shelf?

"God calls not only for your benevolence, but your cheerful countenance, your hopeful words, the grasp of your hand. Relieve some of God's afflicted ones. Some are sick, and hope has departed. Bring back the sunlight to them. There are souls who have lost their courage: speak to them. Pray for them. There are those who need the bread of life. Read to them from the word of God. There is a soul sickness no balm can reach, no medicine heal. Pray for these, and bring them to Jesus Christ. And in all your work, Christ will be present to make impressions upon human hearts" (Ellen G. White, *The Health Food Ministry*, p. 42).

Caring means sharing ourselves, and *everyone* has something they can share.

Check It Out: Go back to Matthew 25 and read the parables through from start to finish. Which one do you identify with most? least? Ask God to show you which areas you are weak in and to help you grow in those areas so you'll be ready to meet Him when He comes to separate the sheep from the goats.

Spy Games

*Watching for their opportunity, the leaders sent spies
pretending to be honest men. They tried to get Jesus
to say something that could be reported to the Roman governor
so he would arrest Jesus. **Luke 20:20, NLT.***

Most people love a good spy story, especially when there's a lot of action. One of the most interesting parts of all the cloak and dagger stuff is the gadgets: shoe phones, button cameras, eavesdropping ear buds, night vision goggles. Spying means intrigue and danger.

If you had to list biblical spy stories, you'd probably think of the spies Rahab hid, or the 12 spies Moses sent to check out Canaan, or even King David's spies. The Bible has lots of spy stories in it. I just never realized there was a spy story in the New Testament too, did you?

Ellen White tells us that "during His ministry He [Jesus] was continually pursued by crafty and hypocritical men who were seeking His life. Spies were on His track, watching His words, to find some occasion against Him. The keenest and most highly cultured minds of the nation sought to defeat Him in controversy. But never could they gain an advantage. They had to retire from the field, confounded and put to shame by the lowly Teacher from Galilee" (*The Ministry of Healing*, pp. 51, 52).

Jesus didn't need any fancy gadgets, because He had the greatest weapon of all against evil plots and plans; He had God on His side. We don't find Jesus skulking around in the shadows trying to stay out of sight so the spies wouldn't catch Him. We don't see Him holed up in a dark cellar sending out messages to be proclaimed while He stayed inside where it was safe. He was out in the open speaking the plain truth without fear. And that's what we should do.

Sooner or later you'll encounter people who will try to trap you, trip you up, and scoff at you. They'll say you're not a "real" Christian, as if real Christians aren't real humans but some kind of perfect beings who can't make mistakes. This kind of attack can be devastating, and you might wonder if you actually are a "real" Christian.

When this happens, anchor yourself in God and trust that He will support you. Harriet Tubman, who famously brought hundreds of slaves to freedom through the Underground Railroad, said, "Lord, I'm going to hold steady on to You, and You've got to see me through."

February 5

Mercy Me

*Because I love Zion, I will not keep still.
Because my heart yearns for Jerusalem, I cannot remain silent.
I will not stop praying for her until her righteousness shines like the dawn,
and her salvation blazes like a burning torch. The nations will see
your righteousness. World leaders will be blinded by your glory. And you
will be given a new name by the Lord's own mouth.* **Isaiah 62:1, 2, NLT.**

What do you think of your name? It identifies you. You answer to it. It represents you legally. But you didn't choose it. Someone else chose your name, probably your parents unless they gave the honor to a friend or relative. Maybe you were named after a favorite aunt or uncle, or maybe a grandparent or great-grandparent. Or you could have received a name that was popular when you were born; popular names tend to go through phases. But no one consulted you. They chose your name, and that was that.

Or is it? Some people legally change their names. Chris Garnett, 19, changed his name to KentuckyFriedCruelty.com to protest the way the fast-food chain treats its chickens at the processing plant. Steve Kreuscher, a bus driver and amateur artist, changed his name to In God We Trust. And in New Zealand a 9-year-old girl's name was changed from the outrageous Talula Does The Hula From Hawaii to something more sedate that wouldn't get her picked on in school.

I find it fascinating that God Himself has many names. A few of the names listed in the Bible are El Shaddai: "God Almighty"; El Elyon: "The Most High God"; El Olam: "The Everlasting God"; and Yahweh: "to exist, be." How many more can you find?

Sometimes God changed a person's name to reflect something they had learned or passed through, for instance giving Jacob the name "Israel" after they wrestled. A number of other people had more than one name: Abram/Abraham, Sarai/Sarah, Paul/Saul, Simon/Peter.

If God ever gave me a new name, I hope it would be "Mercy," because His mercy is important in my life and it would be a reminder to extend that mercy to everyone I dealt with each day. I pray He would make me a fountain of mercy. If God gave you a new name, one that reflected your personality or some special attribute that He gave you or that was important to you, what do you think it would be?

Sing a New Song

Let the whole earth sing to the Lord! Each day proclaim the good news that he saves. Publish his glorious deeds among the nations. Tell everyone about the amazing things he does. **I Chronicles 16:23, 24, NLT.**

Music is a touchy subject. The different generations have grown up with different types of music and sometimes have a hard time appreciating the music that others enjoy. Am I right? Then there is the whole debate about the merits of Christian rock versus hymns versus Christian rap versus Christian screamo that could go on and on without end, amen. And by the time that debate was exhausted and we got to the one about Christian music versus secular music, we'd all be gray-haired.

As a church music director, I know what it's like to try to please people with different tastes in music. I can't say I have all the answers, but at least I do know the question, which is something that most people overlook when they launch into an argument—I mean, discussion—about music. If you are not a Christian, then the only question you need to ask yourself about your choice of music is, "Do I like it?" Christians, though, have a different question to ask: "Does this music bring me closer to God?"

Ellen White says, "Music, when not abused, is a great blessing; but when put to a wrong use, it is a terrible curse. It excites, but does not impart that strength and courage which the Christian can find only at the throne of grace while humbly making known his wants and, with strong cries and tears, pleading for heavenly strength to be fortified against the powerful temptations of the evil one. Satan is leading the young captive. Oh, what can I say to lead them to break his power of infatuation! He is a skillful charmer luring them on to perdition" (*The Adventist Home,* p. 408).

But, you protest, *it's just music!* That's like saying, "It's just dynamite." Dynamite can do some awesome things. It can blow up mountains and level ground for roads to be built. It's used in construction, demolition, and quarrying. It's been a great benefit to mankind when used for noble reasons. But dynamite can also be deadly. Manufacturing accidents have killed workers in dynamite plants, and it has been used for terrorist activities.

And that brings us back to our original question: "Does this music bring me closer to God?" You, with God's help, are the only one who can answer that question.

February 7

Plan A

*But Moses pleaded with the Lord, "O Lord, I'm not very good with words. I never have been, and I'm not now, even though you have spoken to me. I get tongue-tied, and my words get tangled." **Exodus 4:10, NLT.***

I grew up in a small town not far from the city of St. Albans, Vermont, which you might remember from history class as the farthest place north that saw any action in the Civil War. St. Albans was raided by a group of Confederate soldiers who held up three banks and stole $208,000 before escaping to Canada. But there's something else this city is known for that you won't read about in history books. People who live here like to shorten their words—they slur them together. So if you ask a resident where they are from, it is likely to sound more like "Snobbins" than "St. Albans."

The trend migrated north and a lot of the kids in my school slurred their words even though they weren't from St. Albans. One of my teachers complained about this one day and the class laughed at him. To prove his point, he asked a girl who had just come into the room and missed the conversation, "Tina, jeep (did you eat)?" She replied, "Yeah, I had a burger and some fries."

Maybe Moses, too, had this problem; he said he had trouble speaking. Or maybe he had a stutter. Or maybe he had the same problem I have—his words were great if he had time to think them out and write them down, but they got all confused if he had to spit them out all unedited. In any case, God finally agreed to send Aaron along with Moses to be his spokesman.

Do you ever find yourself wondering what might have happened if Moses had said, "I will," instead of, "I can't"? If God had been able to use Plan A instead of Plan B, would Pharaoh have given in right away, before all the plagues? Would the people have trusted God sooner and avoided wandering around in the wilderness for 40 years? We don't know because the Bible doesn't say, "If only Moses had agreed to do what God asked, things would have been very different for the people of Israel."

One thing you can be sure of: God has a plan for your life. Whatever it is, ask Him to make you ready and willing to go where He sends you and do what He asks you. Expect Him to provide whatever you need to carry out His plan. That's part of any good Plan A.

The Friendly Skies

God doesn't come and go. God *lasts.* He's Creator of all you can see
or imagine. He doesn't get tired out, doesn't pause to catch his breath.
And he knows *everything,* inside and out. He energizes those who get
tired, gives fresh strength to dropouts. For even young people tire and drop
out, young folk in their prime stumble and fall. But those who wait upon
God get fresh strength. They spread their wings and soar like eagles, they run
and don't get tired, they walk and don't lag behind. **Isaiah 40:28-31, Message.**

I love to fly; it's just the thought of crashing that keeps me firmly on the ground most of the time. Don't get me wrong—planes are great. How else could you start watching a movie in New England and finish in jolly old England? In a matter of hours you could be in another state or country. Flying definitely has its advantages. The possibility of crashing just isn't one of them.

Oh, I know, crashes are relatively rare. There's a far greater chance I'll be run over by a rhinoceros in Times Square or abducted by mosquitoes than my plane will crash. I try to keep that in mind while I'm actually flying. I'm sure the other passengers appreciate it because all that concentrating keeps me relatively quiet during the flight. But I can never quite figure out how everyone else does it.

It was while flying, though, that I got to see something I could never have seen from the ground: every day the sun is shining and the sky is blue. We don't realize it because we can't see above the clouds, but it's true. On the other side of those gloomy gray clouds and that drizzling rain is a perpetually sunny day.

In that way, flying is like life. From down here with only our human view of things, we merely see the looming gray clouds in our lives. Our problems feel depressing and heavy, yet just above them God is waiting to pull us up to where it is always light.

Praise is the vehicle into His presence. From up there we can see that all our problems are only temporary; they won't last. God will give us new strength to face them. When we dwell on our problems first, God seems small, but when we start by praising Him for all the blessings we have in our lives, our problems seem small.

Challenge Yourself: Having a gray day and think you have nothing to praise God for? Make a list of things you're grateful for, starting with: I am alive.

Do-Over

Suddenly, Jesus' words flashed through Peter's mind:
"Before the rooster crows, you will deny three times that you
even know me." And he went away, weeping bitterly. **Matthew 26:75, NLT.**

If anybody in the history of the world wanted a do-over it had to be Peter. Just hours after declaring that even if everyone else deserted Jesus, he would never leave his Savior, and that he would never disown Him even if he had to die with Him, Peter denied that he knew Jesus.

Not just once. Not just twice. Three times he said that he had never laid eyes on Jesus before and that he was most definitely not one of His disciples. Ouch. The Message translation of the Bible says, "He went out and cried and cried and cried" (Matthew 26:75). Wouldn't you?

We've all made mistakes. Some of them are huge, whopping humdingers that can, and sometimes do, change life forever, while some are just embarrassing for a short time. Hopefully we learn from them so that we don't repeat the same mistakes twice.

Some people who have made huge mistakes think that they can't go on. First there is the embarrassment to get through, then there are the apologies and trying to make things right, and then you must go on with the weight of your mistake crushing the life out of you every day for the rest of your life.

It's easy to think that way, but it's not true. When you are trapped in remorse and guilt and feel like the stuff that makes the stuff under the refrigerator say, "Eww," it may be hard to imagine life getting any better any time soon. But the truth is that Jesus willingly became our sacrifice precisely *because* He knew we would make mistakes—all have sinned, after all—and He can forgive your mistakes because dying for us gave Him the right to do so.

After rising from the dead, Jesus didn't linger on earth very long, so you can be sure that whatever occupied His time during those days was very important to Him. Forgiving Peter was right up there on the list. Not only did He forgive Peter but He also gave him the important job of taking care of His flock when He returned to heaven. His message was clear: "Yes, you messed up. I forgive you; don't beat yourself up over the past. I have important work for you." That's the same message He gives each one of us when we mess up: "Dry your eyes; I have work for you."

Oops, Sorry

Then Jesus stood up again and said to the woman,
"Where are your accusers? Didn't even one of them condemn you?"
"No, Lord," she said. And Jesus said, "Neither do I.
Go and sin no more." **John 8:10, 11, NLT.**

It's one o'clock in the morning, and you're sleeping soundly in your bed. I, on the other hand, am driving down the road way too fast. Your cat dashes out in front of my car and—splat—I hit it. Oh, man! I can't believe I just hit your cat! Why was I driving that fast? I should have been driving slower. I should have known something like that would happen. I feel terrible!

I knock on your door and hand you your poor little kitty. "I'm so sorry. I was driving too fast, and I hit your cat."

You start crying, and now I feel even worse. "Poor little Fluffy!" you wail.

"Will you forgive me?" I beg.

You sniff and wipe your nose on your sleeve. "Yes," you say sadly because you can see that I really mean it.

The next night I'm driving fast again and I hit one of your other cats. I bring it to the door. "I'm so sorry. Will you forgive me?" You take Peaches from me and again say, "yes," through your tears.

Next night. Same story. You take Mittens and you probably forgive me, but it's beginning to dawn on both of us that I'm not really all that sorry since I keep repeating the same behavior again and again. *I'm not sorry enough to stop.*

I may be sorry for the consequences—the dead cats—and sorry for the grief I caused you but not sorry enough for it to change how I drive. Jesus told the woman caught in adultery to "go and sin no more." If I had been really sorry about killing your cats, I would have asked God to help me stop driving fast. I would have held myself accountable by obeying speed limit signs and asking people to drive me places if I couldn't trust myself not to go over the speed limit. I would go and speed no more.

If you're sorry for something you've done but you keep doing it, you might want to ask yourself if you're really sorry for what you're doing. If you aren't, ask God to help you get to that place—true repentance—and sin no more.

Telephone, Telegraph, Tell a Friend

Who may worship in your sanctuary, Lord? Who may enter your presence on your holy hill? Those who lead blameless lives and do what is right, speaking the truth from sincere hearts. Those who refuse to gossip or harm their neighbors or speak evil of their friends. **Psalm 15:1-3, NLT.**

Did you ever play a game called telephone? It's a popular party game. Everyone stands in a line and someone starts the game by whispering a phrase or story into the ear of the first person in line. That person whispers it into the ear of the next person, and on down the line it goes until the last person has to repeat it out loud. Usually it changes so much from the original that everyone gets a good laugh. In one game, for example, the original phrase was "Ally alligator ate eleven avocados at noon," and by the time it got to the end it had become "Hippos are purple."

There's even a technical version online at www.translation-telephone.com that takes a little of the fun out of the process but proves a valuable point. The program takes whatever phrase you type in and translates it into 20 random languages and then back into English. If you type in Shakespeare's famous quote, "To be or not to be, that is the question," the final translation is, "To be or not to be a problem." This just goes to prove that even computers lose something in translation!

Whether you call it babble, tattle, wiggle-waggle, chatter, blether, blabbing, or bending an ear, gossip is gossip. Not all gossip is false, and not all of it is malicious (an attempt to hurt someone.) But all gossip has one thing in common: it is something that God frowns on.

Gossip is talking about someone in a negative way, and it often gets more and more negative the more it is repeated, just like the game. Even if you decide that you aren't going to gossip, it's hard to deal with other people who do. Telling them you don't want to hear it, walking away, or finding new friends are all firm strategies that work. Another way to deal with a persistent gossip is to respond with something positive after every remark they make. For example, if they say, "Hey, did you hear Beth got suspended?" You could respond, "Beth makes the best chocolate chip cookies *ever*." They'll get the point eventually. And if they don't, try one of the more drastic methods. But steer clear of gossip if you want to worship in God's sanctuary.

Ziggurwhat?

So the Lord scattered them abroad from there over
the face of all the earth, and they ceased building the city.
Therefore its name is called Babel,
because there the Lord confused the language of all the earth;
and from there the Lord scattered them abroad over
the face of all the earth. **Genesis 11:8, 9, NKJV.**

The people of Babylonia were all on the same page. They all spoke the same language, so they didn't have any pesky misunderstandings because of tricky translations. And they thought very highly of themselves. So highly, in fact, that they decided to build a great monument—a tower—to themselves to show the whole world how great they were.

Historians believe they built a ziggurat, which is a type of building made from bricks and tiles that has a wide base like a pyramid; it looks a bit like a stone mountain. There were steps on the outside so you could walk up to the top. It stood in stark contrast to the flat land all around and represented the brilliance of the people who built it. Some people believe that a ziggurat called Etemenanki, which means "house of the foundation of heaven on earth," was the Tower of Babel from the Bible.

It was a great human achievement. At the time it was probably considered one of the wonders of the world. Today it would take more than a pile of stones to impress us, but we might feel the same sense of respect and envy when we see someone wearing expensive clothes, living in a fancy neighborhood, driving a sleek car, or owning a top-of-the-line computer, gizmo, or gaming device. These status symbols can be monuments to ourselves.

Wait a minute, you're thinking, *are you saying we should go around in shabby clothes, living in tents, and using out-of-date technology so that we aren't building "towers" to show off to other people?* Not exactly. Whatever we use to call attention to ourselves and what we've achieved, no matter what it is, or how much it cost, or even how much of a deal we got on it, if we use that thing to take the place of God in our life, it's wrong. We can grow and develop in all kinds of ways in our lives, but they should never replace or exclude God. Remember, the Tower of Babel story didn't have a good ending.

Think About It: Have you built any towers in your life? How can you destroy them and put God back in His rightful place in your heart?

Billboard of Hate

Run from anything that stimulates youthful lusts. Instead, pursue righteous living, faithfulness, love, and peace. Enjoy the companionship of those who call on the Lord with pure hearts. **2 Timothy 2:22, NLT.**

Byron Widner, a rabid skinhead and cofounder of the Vinlanders, a gang of skinheads, was bad news. Anyone who saw him could read all about it, since his face and body were covered with racial tattoos: a blood-soaked razor, swastikas, and the word HATE engraved on his knuckles, to name a few. He was literally a walking billboard for hatred, and he had the life to go along with it.

And then his life changed. He got married, started a family, and wanted out of his life of violence and hatred. Only it wasn't as easy as that. First there were the death threats and the pig manure dumped on his car. Vicious Internet postings threatened his little family too, and there were hang-up calls in the middle of the night.

But for Byron all that paled in significance to the fact that he still wore all over his body the hatred he no longer felt, particularly on his face. He wanted it gone. But it's not easy to get rid of a tattoo. They may not be forever, but they are very difficult and extremely painful to remove. It also costs a lot of money to have tattoos removed—money Byron and his family didn't have.

Thankfully an anonymous donor learned about Byron and realized that the tattoos had to go if he was going to have any chance at a normal life. Now Byron's face is clean, clear, and smiling. But it cost him. Not money—the expenses for removal were covered by the donor. But the pain was excruciating, and he continues to have migraines and complications related to the surgeries. Today Byron's is a voice against hate. His surgeries were recorded in the documentary *Erasing Hate* in hopes that his story might change the course of an angry teenager who might otherwise join a gang. He's also given law enforcement important insider information about White supremacist gangs. But he lives in an undisclosed location because of the danger from those gangs.

Sometimes when God convicts us that something we're doing is wrong we try to turn a blind eye, thinking it would be too hard to give up. If you ever find yourself thinking like that, remember Byron and take courage. Is what you have to give up so hard after all?

Heart Guard

Put on the full armor of God, so that you can take
your stand against the devil's schemes. **Ephesians 6:11, NIV.**

A woman called in to a Christian radio show during a slot when the host (a man) promised to translate men's actions so women could under-stand them better. She said that she was a nurse, and her husband was a policeman, and for Valentine's Day he'd given her a bulletproof vest. Appar-ently she'd accepted it graciously but could not understand why she'd received such a gift.

The host suggested that her husband was symbolically (and literally) pro-tecting her heart and asked her if she'd worn it yet. The woman admitted that, no, she hadn't had the opportunity to wear a bulletproof vest anywhere, so the host encouraged her to wear it the next time she and her husband went out, to show him that she appreciated his protective sentiment. He was sort of kidding . . . I think.

Bulletproof vests are the younger cousins of full-blown plate armor, which was worn by soldiers beginning sometime in the Middle Ages. It was a type of personal armor designed to protect the person wearing it from all kinds of nasty things, such as swords, and spears, and pikes. Unfortunately it had weak points and could be penetrated by longer blades such as poleaxes, halberds, and long tapered swords.

In fact, the German school of swordsmanship taught students to concen-trate on the weak spots in the armor. Because of the weak spots, fighters began wearing mail shirts—mail was another type of armor created from little metal circles linked together—under their armor to protect them from weapons that managed to get through the plate armor.

The Bible tells us to put on the full armor of God so we can take our stand against the devil's schemes. Taking a stand isn't an offensive move. We aren't told to put on the armor of God and go out and hunt down the devil. There's no need; he prowls around like a roaring lion waiting to pounce on us and devour us. God will protect us with His armor. All we have to do is put it on before we take our stand, and it will keep us safe.

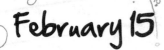

February 15

Take a Knee

Come, let us worship and bow down. Let us kneel before the Lord our maker, for he is our God. We are the people he watches over, the flock under his care. If only you would listen to his voice today! **Psalm 95:6, 7, NLT.**

You've been requested to appear before your brother the king today, so you'd better hurry and get ready so you can be there in time. Wait! You can't seriously mean to tell me you're wearing that! You just played soccer in it; it's splattered with mud. You've even got a spot of mud on your face, right there by your . . . oh, never mind. If you won't change, then you won't.

Do you have a gift? I know he's your brother, but he's also the king! You're still his subject. If you want to ask him to go jogging with you later, or to hang out and play games, you can, but this is an audience. You really should have a gift. Fine, then . . .

NO! You can't just run in there and high-five him! I know he's your brother, but he's still the . . . oh, what's the use . . .

You may be thinking this story doesn't apply to you because you don't have a brother who is a king. Ah, but you do. So do I. Jesus is our Brother, and He is also King of kings. The question is Which one do we treat Him like? Sure, the fact that He is our Brother as well as our King gives us special privileges, but He's still the King. Jesus is our Creator and our God; even if Jesus was only our earthly king, He'd deserve a certain level of respect. If you happened to meet the queen of England you'd be expected to bow (if you're a man) or curtsy (if you're a woman). Wouldn't the King of the universe deserve to be knelt before?

In Bible times Peter knelt to pray (see Acts 9:40), as did Paul (see Acts 20:36) and Jesus (see Luke 22:41). Kneeling used to be more commonly practiced than it is today. In our modern world we're comfortable praying while we walk, shower, or brush our teeth. And there's nothing wrong with praying in any and every position, but there's also something to be said for kneeling to pray. It puts us in a position of humility and submission, which may be why we avoid it. Makes you think, doesn't it?

Try putting yourself on your knees before your King and see if you more fully realize your complete dependence on Him.

Giving Props

No using the name of God, your God, in curses or silly banter; God won't put up with the irreverent use of his name. **Exodus 20:7, Message.**

The other day I heard a radio blurb, which was meant to be funny, refer to Jesus as "My Man J.C.," which is so not right I don't even know where to start. I almost e-mailed the radio station what I thought of that remark, but I got busy and forgot. Chances are they would have blown me off as some uptight legalist who couldn't take a joke. I guess when the joke is made about God's name, they'd be right about that.

We're all familiar with the Ten Commandments (and if you're not, you'll find them in Exodus 20), and the one listed above is number three. The way you may have heard that commandment is "Do not take the name of the Lord your God in vain." And people probably told you it meant: "Don't curse using God's name." But even that doesn't really cover what the commandment is talking about.

To take something "in vain" is to use it to no purpose; for instance, responding "God help us" when what you really mean is "Isn't that just awful." Another definition is to be disrespectful. For instance, responding "OMG" when someone tells you something incredible. (Yes, even the abbreviation counts—and OMGosh is no better.)

In the 1980s and 1990s rappers made the slang word "props" popular. It was short for "proper respect" and it means giving someone their due respect for something. The opposite of props is "diss," which is to disrespect someone. There are many levels of respect. You may respect your parents differently than you respect your friends, but in many ways respect is respect.

When I was in high school, my "best friend" called me Cat Chow because my last name, "Perrino," sounded to her like the cat food brand Purina. You'd better believe it didn't make me happy. Dissing my name was particularly hurtful because it was part of my identity.

In the same way, dissing God by using His name disrespectfully is disrespecting God Himself. God's name is who God is. When Moses asked God for His name so he could tell the people who sent Him, God replied, "I AM WHO I AM" (Exodus 3:14, NIV). We need to be particularly careful about how we use God's name and to use it only to honor Him and give Him props.

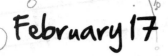

Secrets

And this is the message I proclaim—that the day is coming when God, through Christ Jesus, will judge everyone's secret life. **Romans 2:16, NLT.**

In 1940, during World War II, in the Katyn Forest in Russia, thousands of Polish officers, police, and civilians were brutally murdered. The executions were only part of a larger execution carried out at the same time. In all about 22,000 prisoners of war were killed by the Soviets. It took days to kill everyone, and they had to use German guns because the Soviet revolvers had such a hard recoil that it was painful to shoot more than a dozen people. When the killing was over, the Soviets buried the bodies in mass graves in the Katyn Forest, dusted off their dirty hands, and went on their merry way.

A group of Polish railroad workers later found one of the graves and reported it to the Polish Secret State. No one realized just how many people were buried in the graves until Joseph Goebbels, one of Hitler's right-hand men, found out about it. Since the Soviet Union and America were allies in World War II, Goebbels knew that if he could tell the world that the Russians had killed thousands of Poles in cold blood, he might be able to break up the alliance. So he had the graves dug up and brought in experts to prove that the Soviets had committed the murders. Then he told the whole world.

The Soviet Union denied it, of course. Britain and America didn't believe the Soviets, but since Hitler was the bigger threat, they stuck together and eventually won the war. And the Soviets? In 1990 Soviet president Mikhail Gorbachev finally admitted that the Soviet Union had committed the murders and expressed deep regret to the world. It took nearly 50 years for them to own up to what they'd done.

But what if the railroad workers hadn't found the graves? Those people might still be buried there and no one in the whole world would know Russia's secret.

There are secrets we've buried too. The world may not know them. Even our best friends may not know them. But God does. And one day He will reveal them, and we'll have to answer for them. Wouldn't you rather confess to God now, be forgiven, and not have anything hanging over your head for the day when all secrets will be revealed?

Pennies From Heaven

Then the Lord said to Moses, "Look, I'm going to rain down food from heaven for you. Each day the people can go out and pick up as much food as they need for that day. I will test them in this to see whether or not they will follow my instructions." **Exodus 16:4, NLT.**

My sister and I support a charity called the Smile Train (www.smile-train.org). Their mission is to repair cleft palates and cleft lips. Children born with clefts have trouble breathing and eating, and they are often ridiculed and rejected. Surgery to repair clefts has been around for a long time, but kids in poor countries can't afford it. So my sister and I donate money for surgeries to help these kids.

But that's just why. I want to tell you about how. We collect money all the time, and when we get enough to pay for a surgery, we send in a check and start over. We've paid for three surgeries so far. I keep a jar on the shelf to put my money in, and I call it the Smile jar.

One day I saw a penny on the ground and thought, *H'mm, it's just a penny, but Benjamin Franklin did say, "A penny saved is a penny earned." I'll pick it up and put it in the Smile jar.* So I did. Soon after that I saw more money on the ground and picked that up, too. I was finding small amounts of money, the kind you might be tempted to leave because it wasn't worth the bother of bending over to pick it up.

It finally dawned on me that maybe God was putting the money in my path because He knew what I would do with it. So I entered a partnership with God. I told Him that whatever money I found lying around, I would pick up, even if it was just a penny, and I'd put it in the Smile jar. I started finding money all over the place! Usually just small amounts, though I have found a few bills, mostly dollar bills. But it's a steady stream. I feel like one of the Israelites going out each morning to collect manna. It's like playing a game with God—a treasure hunt. Every day I wonder where He'll put the money this time.

When you're in a partnership with someone it's usually 50/50, but when we're partners with God, He gives 100 percent. If I was using that money to buy Starbucks coffee, do you think God would keep it coming? I don't think so. He trusts me with that money because I'm using it to help someone else. Can He trust you with extra money?

February 19

Accused!

The godly are directed by honesty; the wicked fall beneath their load of sin. The godliness of good people rescues them; the ambition of treacherous people traps them. **Proverbs 11:5, 6, NLT.**

Have you ever been accused of something you didn't do?

I once worked in the branch of a very small bank. There were only four of us working there, all women. The bank was near a ski area, and the other three women often went out partying after work. They asked me to join them, but I told them I didn't party. They knew I was religious, and I knew they also thought I was pretty dull.

One day a young woman came into the bank. She wanted money from her account, but there wasn't enough. She claimed that she'd met one of the bank employees at a bar over the weekend, and had given the employee her check to deposit in her account. That employee had stolen her money!

The bank manager didn't believe the woman, but like Solomon she asked the woman to point out the employee she'd given her check to. The young woman looked around the bank and pointed at me. Her own accusation condemned her. Everyone who worked at the bank knew that I was the only person there who wouldn't ever have taken her check. If she had chosen anyone else, she might have been able to convince the bank manager that she had really been robbed. But because she chose me, no one believed her.

It's easy to think that where we go, what we do, and how we act doesn't affect anyone but ourselves. We think that no one is watching us and forming opinions about Christ and Christianity based on how we act, what we do, and what we don't do. But that's not true. We are representatives for Jesus. What we do shouts to the world messages about Jesus. Make sure that the messages your life is shouting reflect what you truly believe, because what you do is your sermon to the world every day.

"We should take the greatest care to live a blameless life, and abstain from all appearance of evil, and then it is our duty to move boldly forward, and pay no regard to the reproachful falsehoods of the wicked. While the eyes of the righteous are fixed upon the heavenly priceless treasure, they will become more and more like Christ, and thus they will be transformed and fitted for translation" (Ellen G. White, *Testimonies for the Church*, vol. 1, p. 353).

Willing

Then I heard the Lord asking, "Whom should I send as a messenger to this people? Who will go for us?" I said, "Here I am. Send me." **Isaiah 6:8, NLT.**

A little boy heard a sermon about gifts in which the preacher told the congregation that they each had a special gift that they could use for Jesus. He encouraged them to find and use their gifts. The boy didn't know what his special gift was. When he asked the grown-ups, they told him that Jesus would tell him about his gift and show him how to use it. This didn't help, and every day the boy grew more discouraged. He prayed that Jesus would help him discover his gift so that he could use it.

One day he saw an old man sweeping the church parking lot. Since the man was old, the boy thought that Jesus must surely have told him what his gift was. He approached the old man and asked him, "Sir, can you tell me if you've discovered your gift? Has Jesus told you what it is?"

The old man leaned on his broom and said, "Son, I absolutely know what my gift is."

Excited, the little boy asked eagerly, "What is it?"

"I have one gift," the old man replied. "I'm willing." And with that he picked up his broom again and resumed sweeping the parking lot.

Spiritual gifts are a big deal; and rightly so. God gave us each talents, gifts, and abilities that we can use to serve and glorify Him. Some people know right away what their gift is; others have to search and ask God. There are even tests you can take to help you figure out what your spiritual gift is.

But the most important gift is to simply be willing. If more people were willing to do whatever work was available, a whole lot more of God's work would get done. Instead, they often wait for a grand work or a big mission project. What they don't understand is that there are a lot more small jobs to be done than there are great ones. Mother Teresa said, "Not all of us can do great things. But we can do small things with great love."

Ask God today to help you be willing to do whatever you find that needs to be done, or whatever someone asks you to do, no matter how small or insignificant it seems. And when you do it, put your whole heart into it, because you are doing it for God Himself. Tomorrow: repeat.

February 21

Forgiveness

And whenever you stand praying, if you have anything
against anyone, forgive him, that your Father in heaven may also
forgive you your trespasses. But if you do not forgive, neither will
your Father in heaven forgive your trespasses. **Mark 11:25, 26, NKJV.**

María Tañón* had a hard time making ends meet. Her husband, Juan
Carlos, had been unfaithful to her, and she had ended their marriage.
Now she was raising their five children alone. One day her former
mother-in-law called to tell her that Juan Carlos had been shot by his current girlfriend, who was pregnant with his child. He was paralyzed and in the
hospital.

María had forgiven Juan Carlos for his unfaithfulness and decided to show
him that she forgave him as well. Although her money, time, and energy were
limited, she gently helped nurse Juan Carlos back to health, constantly praying
for him to see Jesus and accept Him as his personal Savior. Juan Carlos eventually healed, although he remained a paraplegic. He pursued education and
careers, and lived well by worldly standards.

Nearly 30 years later Juan Carlos was struck down with aggressive cancer.
His ailing health caused him to become a quieter, more humble person. The
loving things that María had done for him so long ago began replaying in his
mind and eventually touched his heart. He saw that she had forgiven him for
all the pain and poverty he had caused her and their children, and in his own
way, he sought to be forgiven. The family had already forgiven him and still
loved him. He accepted Christ as his personal Savior and died peacefully less
than a month later, knowing he had been forgiven not only by María and the
children but by Christ as well.

Forgiving people can be hard, especially if they have hurt us badly. But it's
something we must do if we want God to forgive us. If you find it impossible to
forgive someone who has hurt you, consider how much you have hurt God by
sinning, and ask Him to give you the forgiveness you need for someone else's
sin against you.

---

* Names have been changed.
Submitted by Julián Anderson-Martín, M.A., L.L.P.C.

Your Father's Eyes

Christ chose some of us to be apostles, prophets, missionaries, pastors, and teachers, so that his people would learn to serve and his body would grow strong. This will continue until we are united by our faith and by our understanding of the Son of God. Then we will be mature, just as Christ is, and we will be completely like him. **Ephesians 4:11-13, CEV.**

I was once in a restroom checking my hair in the mirror while a woman washed her hands in the sink next to me. She smiled and said, "The older I get, the more I see my mother looking at me whenever I look in the mirror. You're probably too young to see your mother looking at you in the mirror."

"You're right," I quipped. "I don't see my mother. I see my father!"

It's true; the older we get, the more we start to resemble our parents. We're not exact replicas, of course, but there are elements of our parents' faces in our own, and those things become a lot more noticeable the older we get. I look like my father's side of the family, who take after the blond, blue-eyed Italian stock they came from, and the older I get, the more I look like my dad. Just, you know, girlier!

There is nothing we can control about these changes; they will happen whether we want them to or not. In a similar way, we as Christians become more like God with each year that passes. But how much we become like God is up to us; He won't change us without our permission.

The more we allow Him to change us, the more like Him we'll become. It's not always easy, but it's easier than you think it is, because we don't impose the changes on ourselves; He does. He changes us in ways that we don't even notice until someone says, "Hey, you look just like your dad."

"As we meditate upon the perfections of the Savior, we shall desire to be wholly transformed and renewed in the image of His purity. There will be a hungering and thirsting of soul to become like Him whom we adore. The more our thoughts are upon Christ, the more we shall speak of Him to others and represent Him to the world" (Ellen G. White, *Steps to Christ*, p. 57).

February 23

Open Mouth, Insert Foot

The human heart is the most deceitful of all things,
and desperately wicked. Who really knows how bad it is?
But I, the Lord, search all hearts and examine secret motives.
I give all people their due rewards, according to what
their actions deserve. **Jeremiah 17:9, 10, NLT.**

I read a joke the other day about a woman who brought her pet duck to a vet, who very sadly informed her that it was dead. The woman didn't believe him and wanted tests, so he called in a Labrador retriever and a cat to check out the duck. When he gave her the bill, it was very high, and the woman complained. The vet told her if that she'd taken his word for it, the bill would be lower, but he'd had to add in the "lab" report and the "cat" scan she'd requested to confirm his diagnosis.

I thought the joke was hilarious, and immediately fired it off to my friend Bob, who has animals. I thought he would find the vet's animal "colleagues" amusing. I mean, come on! Cat scan? Lab report? Too funny! Unfortunately, my joke backfired, because the same day it landed in his inbox, a mink attacked Bob's own ducks, and he'd just returned from the vet's office, where he'd had to have one put down.

I can't tell you how badly I felt. I apologized, of course, to Bob for being so insensitive, even if it was unintentional—I couldn't have known his ducks had just been attacked. Bob forgave me immediately, but it was a long time before I was able to forgive myself.

Have you ever done something hurtful without meaning to? It feels almost as bad as doing something hurtful on purpose. People looking at us from the outside might think we *did* do it on purpose. Aren't you glad that God judges us based on our motives instead of on what we did?

I'm sure Reuben was grateful for that after he discovered that nine of his brothers had sold their next-to-youngest brother, Joseph, to the Ishmaelites while he was gone. Even so, if you read the account in Genesis 37, Reuben seems more upset about what he's going to tell his father than the fact that his brother has just been sold into slavery.

God judges our hearts—our secret motives as well as the ones we freely admit. That's why it's so important that our hearts are right with God. We're not hiding anything from Him anyway. He knows everything in our hearts. Make sure yours is right with Him today.

Friendly Fire

For every kind of beast and bird, of reptile and creature
of the sea, is tamed and has been tamed by mankind.
But no man can tame the tongue. It is an unruly evil,
full of deadly poison. **James 3:7, 8, NKJV.**

Friendly fire occurs when an army accidentally fires on its own troops, or troops who are on the same side, during a battle. One recorded incident of the United States firing on its own troops by accident happened in Afghanistan in 2011. Two soldiers, Marine staff sergeant Jeremy Smith and Navy corpsman Benjamin Rast, were killed by a missile fired from a U.S. Air Force Predator—an unpiloted aerial vehicle. Marines on the battlefield were watching video feed from the Predator flying overhead and saw what looked like enemy "hot spots" moving toward them. They ordered the Predator to fire a missile at the hot spots, killing two of their own men.

Losses during a war are inevitable; it is war, after all. Some will be killed; some will desert; some will be injured and go home to recuperate. The enemy is fierce, and the losses can sometimes be high. But imagine how much harder those losses are to bear when they come at our own hands. Killing and maiming your own troops is not the way to win a battle!

We may not be in a physical battle, but we are in a spiritual battle. "Not without a struggle does Satan allow the kingdom of God to be built up in the earth. The forces of evil are engaged in unceasing warfare against the agencies appointed for the spread of the gospel" (Ellen G. White, *The Acts of the Apostles*, p. 167). This isn't just the fight of our lives; it's a fight for our souls.

Some of our comrades—our fellow Christians, people you see in school, in church, and in your own family—will fall. Some will simply fall away, and some will be injured. This is sad, but it's a lot more sad when they fall because we shot them down ourselves. Gossip, rumors, criticism, verbal abuse—these are all missiles we call down on the heads of our own troops, cutting them to ribbons. If you've ever felt the lash of someone's tongue on your reputation or your character, you know how painful it can be.

We need to be very careful about the things we say to, or about, someone in person, in a text, or online. Sometimes that's even harder because we aren't looking them in the eye and therefore can't see how much we've hurt them. Hurtful words can seem like such a little thing—a joke, even—but they can do harm to others that can never be completely repaired.

February 25

A Real Man

Most men will proclaim each his own goodness,
but who can find a faithful man? The righteous man walks
in his integrity; his children are blessed after him. **Proverbs 20:6, 7, NKJV.**

A young friend of mine once posted a status update that had all the qualities she thought made a "real man." For example, a real man calls you "beautiful" instead of "hot" or "sexy." He calls you back if you hang up on him. He holds your hand in front of his friends. He stays awake just to watch you sleep. He constantly reminds you how much he loves you and how lucky he is to have you.

Do "real" men do these things? Maybe, but there's a lot more to a real man than his romance skills. A real man is, above all things, *real*. He's doesn't just look like a Gap model with the tech skills of a poster geek who plays in a rock band in his spare time. And he's not a candy-box-and-flower-carrying figment of the imagination. By all means, accept and/or offer the flowers and candy, but when the rubber hits the road, accept and/or offer no-holds-barred love that endures illness, poverty, and other less-than-desirable situations.

Real men have real love, and that means taking responsibility seriously. God made men to protect their loved ones; guys are hardwired for this. Real men provide for their families; they put food on the table. They are leaders even if they don't always get the opportunity to lead, and they know how to lead without trampling people in the process. Real men have courage and guts; they don't scare easily. They don't wimp out when life gets hard.

But real men also know who is in charge. They recognize authority. They know where to go when they need help. And when they need to get something done, they don't stand around and complain; they go straight to the top. They are captains in God's army, and they take orders directly from Him.

Gents, are you real men? The world needs godly, committed men, men who care about the women they love, men who respect themselves and others. The world is a better place because of men who fulfill the role God has given them.

Ladies, do you know a real man? Tell him so. Give him respect for being the man God made him to be. (And if he forgets the flowers now and then, forgive him. Real men have a few rough spots—they're human, after all!)

A Real Woman

Charm is deceptive, and beauty does not last; but a woman
who fears the Lord will be greatly praised. Reward her for all she has done.
Let her deeds publicly declare her praise. **Proverbs 31:30, 31, NLT.**

Quick, off the top of your head, list five women you admire. Write down their names, and next to each name, write why you admire that woman. Is she smart? Is she beautiful? Is she godly? Is she kind? Is she funny? What makes her special in your opinion?

I wouldn't be surprised if at least one of the women made it onto your list because she is beautiful. In America we tend to glorify beauty. Why? Because beautiful people seem to have it better than average or homely people. They get better jobs, seem better educated, and go on more dates. This perception is called the halo effect because of the perfection associated with angels. "Research shows attractive people also have more occupational success and more dating experience than their unattractive counterparts. One theory behind this halo effect is that it is accurate—attractive people are indeed more successful," writes Charles Feng in an article titled *"Looking Good: The Psychology and Biology of Beauty."*

Want to appear more beautiful without Botox or cosmetic surgery? Be nice to others. It's true what your mother told you: beauty is as beauty does. Feng says, "In one study, 70 percent of college students deemed an instructor physically attractive when he acted in a friendly manner, while only 30 percent found him attractive when he was cold and distant. Indeed, when surveyed for attributes in selecting a mate, both males and females felt kindness and an exciting personality were more important in a mate than good looks."

Physical beauty doesn't last; look around you. Hollywood may be able to prolong the appearance of beauty, but eventually everyone gets old. You could rely on charm: flattering people and making them feel special. But eventually you'll get tired of it, and they'll get wise to you and know you're not sincere. The one thing that creates real beauty that will never fade is the genuine love radiating from someone who is close to God. Even their feet are beautiful! "How beautiful upon the mountains are the feet of him who brings good news, who proclaims peace, who brings glad tidings of good things, who proclaims salvation, who says to Zion, 'Your God reigns!' " (Isaiah 52:7, NKJV).

February 27

Free at Last

So, since we're out from under the old tyranny, does that mean
we can live any old way we want? Since we're free in the freedom of God,
can we do anything that comes to mind? Hardly. You know well enough
from your own experience that there are some acts of so-called freedom
that destroy freedom. Offer yourselves to sin, for instance, and it's your
last free act. But offer yourselves to the ways of God and the freedom
never quits. All your lives you've let sin tell you what to do. But thank
God you've started listening to a new master, one whose commands set
you free to live openly in his freedom! **Romans 6:15-18, Message.**

When my friend Susan had major surgery, she asked me to take her chickens because she could no longer care for them. Of course I said yes. We have 10 chickens and a rooster, so I didn't think another six would be any trouble. What I hadn't counted on was that Susan's chickens had never been free before.

Our chickens roam around during the day and come in at night to sleep in their coop. The first day I left the coop door open, Susan's chickens looked at me as if I'd lost my mind. It was a couple days before they'd venture past the open door to the big world outside.

Even after they began to wander a little way from the coop, they didn't always come back. They would end up in a feathered huddle somewhere, and I'd have to go find them and carry them back to the coop two at a time so they could be safe inside for the night.

It's important that they stay in the coop at night. The chicken coop keeps them safe. Foxes, coyotes, opossum, skunks, and weasels can't get in and eat them. But if they keep trying to do their own thing and roost outside the coop, some predator will eventually get them. Does it seem unkind that I make the chickens go inside at night so they won't get eaten?

Think carefully about your answer; we often feel "cooped up" by God's rules. Is there a difference? God's rules are meant to keep us safe so we can keep enjoying freedom. How much freedom do you think my chickens would have if they slept outside and were eaten by a predator? How much freedom do you think you'd have if you chose sin and were trapped by Satan?

Are any of God's rules making you feel caged right now? Write them down on one side of a piece of paper, and on the opposite side, write how that same rule keeps you safe.

Potty Mouth

Watch the way you talk. Let nothing foul or dirty come out of your mouth.
Say only what helps, each word a gift. **Ephesians 4:29, Message.**

The Bible says not to swear, right? I mean, it's in there somewhere. There's a list of swearwords and the command "Thou shalt not," right? No, not exactly. But first we need to define "swearing." There's a difference between blasphemy and profanity. Blasphemy is claiming to be God (Jesus got in trouble with the Pharisees for that) or taking God's name in vain (commandment number three). But profanity is swearing or cursing, using vulgar words. What makes a word a dirty word or a swearword is different depending on where you live, but you probably know which words I'm talking about.

McKay Hatch knows those words too, and he decided he didn't like hearing them all the time around his junior high school in South Pasadena, California. McKay was 14 years old at the time, and the cussing bothered him so much that he challenged his friends to stop! A lot of them accepted his challenge but told him they didn't know how to stop, so McKay created a No Cussing Club at his school. The kids in the club reminded one another not to cuss and supported one another. The club got so big it grew into a Web site (www.nocussing.com), where kids can take the No Cussing Challenge and get support for their decision to clean up their language.

McKay believes that you can clean up the world one word at a time and that people have a responsibility to leave others better than they found them by uplifting them through their words and actions. "We have received thousands of e-mails," says McKay. "Some say this is a waste of time because 'words have no meaning.' Some say our club goes against freedom of speech. But many, many of our e-mails are from people who see that this is a personal commitment to improve the level of language that we speak to each other throughout the world. Many of our e-mails are from people who say that they really do feel a difference in their lives because of a commitment to use polite, respectful, and kind language."

Now, if a teen can take the initiative to help his friends—and teens all over the United States—clean up their language and leave people better off than he found them, you can certainly find a way to improve your world, one word at a time. Take the No Cussing Challenge. Go to www.nocussing.com, sign the challenge, find support, or start your own No Cussing Club, and see how much better your life can be without foul language.

March 1

Destination: God's Will

Commit to the Lord whatever you do,
and he will establish your plans. **Proverbs 16:3, NIV.**

You're having the worst day on record. Your alarm didn't go off, which made you late for school. Some moron in the hallway dropped his books all over the place and you have to hurdle them to skid into class late, only to hear the science teacher cheerfully announce a pop quiz on material you haven't even looked at, much less studied. Your BFF isn't talking to you and won't tell you why. To top it all off, your parents have confiscated all your electronics because you forgot to do the dishes again. Seriously, this day could not get any worse.

Stop. Rewind. Replay.

Your alarm didn't go off, which made you late for school. But since everything that happens to one of God's kids happens for a reason, you set your GPS for the day "destination God's will." The first thing you do is refuse to panic: you're in God's will, so there's no reason for panic. Because you were late for school, you happen to be in the hallway when a kid you've seen around but don't know drops his books all over the place. You have two choices. You can pass him and get to class, or you can stop to help. You're in God's will, so you stop to help.

That's when you notice the kid is crying and trying to hide it. He's got a black eye and his shirt is torn. When you ask him what happened, he doesn't want to talk, but you're persistent, and he finally tells you that some kids were bullying him, threw him into the lockers, dumped his books, and ran off. They've been bothering him for a while and it's getting worse, but he is afraid to tell anyone. He begs you not to tell anyone either.

You, of course, know better. You talk him into coming with you to the principal's office to report the bullying. You decide you're going to help by keeping an eye out for him, and you tell him so. He gives you a weak smile and thanks you. By the time you get to class, it's almost over. The science teacher says you'll have to take your test the next day.

When you're a Christian and you are focused on doing God's will, you realize that no matter what happens, God can use it for good purposes. Does that mean you can do whatever you want and expect God to bless you? No. You have to be responsible. Study. Do your chores. But if something bad happens to you, don't react by demanding "Why me?" Stay in God's will and look for the lesson He's teaching you through any circumstances that come your way.

Giants

David answered, "You come at me with sword and spear
and battle-ax. I come at you in the name of God-of-the-Angel-Armies,
the God of Israel's troops, whom you curse and mock. This very day
God is handing you over to me. I'm about to kill you, cut off your head,
and serve up your body and the bodies of your Philistine buddies
to the crows and coyotes. The whole earth will know that there's
an extraordinary God in Israel. And everyone gathered here will learn
that God doesn't save by means of sword or spear. The battle belongs to
God—he's handing you to us on a platter!" **I Samuel 17:45-47, Message.**

The Bible doesn't say how old David was when he faced Goliath down, but we know that he was "a mere youngster, apple-cheeked and peach-fuzzed" (1 Samuel 17:42, Message). You know the story: all the grown men, including King Saul, were afraid of Goliath. They looked at that giant of a man and then looked for a place to hide. Even adults aren't always brave when they compare themselves to giants.

David was just a kid, but he didn't hesitate when he heard Goliath's challenge. He offered to fight Goliath, and Saul agreed. He loaded David up with his armor and pointed him toward the battlefield.

David didn't even keep the armor. It was too big for him and too heavy. He took it off and went to fight the giant with a couple of stones and a slingshot. But he had a weapon that Goliath didn't know about. And so do you.

What kind of giants are you facing in your life right now? Don't be afraid! The God-of-the-Angel-Armies is on your side. Think about that. Our God commands armies of angels. He *created the world*. He created *lots of worlds*. Tell me, what is bigger, stronger, or more powerful than God? Nothing!

One of the biggest mistakes we make is looking at our problems first and *then* looking at God. When we focus on the mountains in front of us, we panic and run for cover. But when we focus instead on how great our God is, the mountains disappear. David beat Goliath, and you can beat your giants too with God-of-the-Angel-Armies on your side.

March 3

Highly Favored

Shadrach, Meshach, and Abednego answered King Nebuchadnezzar, "Your threat means nothing to us. If you throw us in the fire, the God we serve can rescue us from your roaring furnace and anything else you might cook up, O king. But even if he doesn't, it wouldn't make a bit of difference, O king. We still wouldn't serve your gods or worship the gold statue you set up." **Daniel 3:16-18, Message.**

Sarah studies a lot. She gets the highest grades in class, and because of all her hard work, she's going to receive several awards when she graduates. She has a part-time job in the evenings as a short-order cook. She started as a dishwasher, making the lowest wage possible, but because she is such a hard worker, she was promoted quickly. She also excels in sports and was promoted to captain of her basketball team because of her constant practice. Sarah gives God all the credit for her accomplishments. God favors Sarah.

Wyatt studies very hard. He gets pretty good grades, but they suffer a little because his home life is difficult. Sometimes he has trouble concentrating at school. Everyone thought he was going to college on a baseball scholarship until he ripped a ligament in his shoulder and the doctor said he'd never play ball again. Wyatt thanks God that his shoulder injury wasn't worse and that he healed quickly. His patient cheerfulness is a constant reminder to people of where he puts his trust. God favors Wyatt.

Wait a minute, you say. God favors Sarah *and* Wyatt? How can that be? Sarah's got a lot going for her while poor Wyatt's had some pretty tough breaks. That's true. On the surface, to *us*, it looks as though Sarah is getting the better deal. But we aren't here on earth to have a good time, to find the easiest path, or to do what we want to do. We're here to glorify God with our lives. It's definitely a lot easier for Sarah to give God the glory for her blessings, but Wyatt praises God in his suffering, and that's a much stronger testimony for the power of God in our weakness.

Wyatt is committed to God, as were Shadrach, Meshach, and Abednego; he's going to trust God no matter what happens, even if what happens is awful. The real test for Sarah will be when things start going wrong. Will she be able to glorify God in the middle of trials? Will you?

Silent Witnesses

Though I am the least deserving of all God's people,
he graciously gave me the privilege of telling the Gentiles
about the endless treasures available to them in Christ. I was chosen
to explain to everyone this mysterious plan that God, the Creator of all
things, had kept secret from the beginning. God's purpose in all this was
to use the church to display his wisdom in its rich variety to all the unseen
rulers and authorities in the heavenly places. **Ephesians 3:8-10, NLT.**

The first time I went to a play I was in the fifth grade. I was in a new school and didn't know anyone. When they let us out of class and herded us all onto buses to go to the high school, I still didn't have a clue what was going on. I had never been to a "real" play before.

The auditorium was huge. We all shuffled into rows and scrunched down on the thin plastic seats. The lights went out, and the play started. It was *The Music Man*. I was mesmerized. I can still remember some of the songs. Years later, when I attended that high school, I joined the drama club and got to be part of one of the plays.

On opening night everyone was a mess of nerves. We'd peek out from backstage to see all the people in the audience. The plays were very well done, and the seats were always packed. On stage we knew that every move we made, every word we said, was contributing to the ultimate success or failure of the whole play. We couldn't afford to mess up, forget a line, or trip.

We don't often think about it that way, but life is like that too. We can't see the audience, but there is one. People we know here on earth are watching us, but Paul says that "unseen rulers and authorities" are watching us too. They are taking note of everything we do.

When we're suffering, either mentally or physically, our thoughts tend to turn inward. Everything is about me, me, me. That's natural. What's not natural is for our thoughts to turn to others and to God. When that happens, we prove that God is powerful and that He truly can take care of us through good times and bad times. We prove it by relying completely on Him no matter what happens. Did something great happen to you? Wonderful, thank God. Did something terrible happen you? Thank God then, too. Not for the terrible thing, but for what you learned from it: how to lean on Him for support, how to trust Him to lead you, how to stick with Him no matter what happens. This is the most important lesson you will ever learn, and the whole universe is watching you learn it.

March 5

Love/Hate Relationship

Let me give you a new command: Love one another.
In the same way I loved you, you love one another.
This is how everyone will recognize that you are my disciples—
when they see the love you have for each other. **John 13:34, 35, Message.**

You may have heard of the Westboro Baptist Church. They are well known for their "God hates . . ." theology. According to them, God hates a whole bunch of people. At least, that's what they'd like people to believe, and some people probably do. Many others are shocked and upset that anyone claiming to be a Christian could act the way the members of this church do, but either way, the Westboro Baptist Church claims they don't lose a nanosecond of sleep over anyone else's opinions or feelings.

Does God hate? There's only one thing God hates: sin.

God loves people, but He cannot accept sin. If people refuse to give up their sin, He still loves them, but if they won't let go of it when sin is destroyed, they will be destroyed right along with it. Think of it this way: If I held a big stick of dynamite while someone lit it and I wouldn't let go of it, what would happen? You could beg me to throw it as far away as possible, but is it your fault if I won't throw it and I get blown to smithereens? No, you did what you could. The responsibility for my death lies with me.

Most Christians would agree that the Westboro Baptist Church is extreme in their views. Most Christians do not believe that God hates the *people* who sin, but that He hates only the sin itself. But many Christians do the same thing in a smaller way and don't even realize it. We believe that God hates people who listen to *that* kind of music. We believe God hates people who dress *that* way. We believe God hates people who do *that*. We believe God hates them because we sure do—they're nowhere near as good a Christian as *we* are. If they were, they certainly wouldn't be doing *that*.

Do you see how it works? Where is the love in that attitude? God doesn't say we'll be known for what we hate. He doesn't say we'll be known for loving only the lovable, or only the people who have our approval. He says we'll be known by our love for *everyone*. That doesn't mean we have to accept and approve of sin—God doesn't either. It means that we love everyone in spite of their sin.

Now You See It;
Now You See It Everywhere

And now, dear brothers and sisters, one final thing. Fix your thoughts on what is true, and honorable, and right, and pure, and lovely, and admirable. Think about things that are excellent and worthy of praise. **Philippians 4:8, NLT.**

Have you ever noticed that when you become aware of something, suddenly it's everywhere? You can be completely oblivious to its existence until that moment, and then suddenly it's all over the place. For example, when I was thinking about buying a PT Cruiser, I had never seen one, but as soon as I starting looking for them they were all over the roads. I probably saw an example of every color there was within a week. Once I started looking for them, I couldn't *not* see PT Cruisers.

A few weeks ago I noticed a sticker on a car that had a symbol and the numbers "802." It meant nothing to me until I realized the symbol was actually the shape of our state (Vermont) and the number 802 is our area code. After I started noticing them, it seemed as if every other car in the state had that sticker on it. It was a sticker epidemic.

Try it for yourself and see if I'm right.

That's why God wants us to concentrate on good things: things that are true, and honorable, and right, and pure, and lovely, and admirable. If we concentrate on things that are excellent and worthy of praise, we will begin to see them everywhere. If we concentrate on bad things instead, we'll begin to see those everywhere. I don't know about you but I'd rather see the excellent and lovely things. The world has too many bad things as it is.

One of the best ways to keep our minds planted firmly on the good stuff is to surround ourselves with it. Think about the places you spend the most time, the people you see most often, the entertainment you enjoy most. Are these things that help you keep your mind fixed on good things, or do they get in your way?

Maybe you like rap music and you're thinking, *Well, I like the music, but the lyrics are not always so great.* Consider changing to Christian rap, which has the same style but lyrics that are about God and the Christian walk. Maybe it's your reading choices, your TV shows, or your friends that need to be changed, but the process of making those changes isn't easy to see or accept. Ask God to help you; He will. When He asks us to make a change, He's right there to help.

March 7

One of Those

> Peter fairly exploded with his good news:
> "It's God's own truth, nothing could be plainer:
> God plays no favorites! It makes no difference who you are
> or where you're from—if you want God and are ready to do as he says,
> the door is open. The Message he sent to the children of Israel
> —that through Jesus Christ everything is being put together again—well,
> he's doing it everywhere, among everyone." **Acts 10:34-36, Message.**

Julio was taking a cooking class. His friend Anne asked him if there were any other guys in his class. Julio thought for a minute. "There are five," he replied. "Well, I think one is gay, so I don't know if he counts."

"Of course he counts," Anne said indignantly. "How can he not count? He's a guy, isn't he?"

Julio said, "Not really. He's one of *those*."

Anne shook her head in disgust and walked away.

Julio and Anne are both Christians. They are both Christians, yet they don't have the same ideas about people who are different than they are. They should, though, because God has one idea about all of the people He created. He loves them all. Unconditionally. He didn't hand the soldiers who were crucifying Him a list of the people He was dying for and another list of people He wasn't dying for. The message He sent to the children of Israel is the same message He sent to the Gentiles and to each one of us today. He's sending that message everywhere and to everyone. It's not just a message for Christians or for straight people. It's for homosexuals, too.

Paul told the Corinthians that no one who practices homosexuality will inherit the kingdom of God. But neither will fornicators, idolaters, adulterers, sodomites, thieves, coveters, drunkards, revilers, or extortioners (see 1 Corinthians 6:9, 10). Then he went on to say that some of the Corinthians had been like that. "But you were cleansed; you were made holy; you were made right with God by calling on the name of the Lord Jesus Christ and by the Spirit of our God" (verse 11, NLT).

God doesn't play favorites. Anyone and everyone who wants to be made right with Him by calling on the name of the Lord Jesus Christ will be saved. It doesn't matter who you are—one of these or one of those, one of us or one of them—everyone becomes part of one family: God's.

Chosen

Then the Lord spoke to Moses, saying:
"See, I have called by name Bezalel the son of Uri,
the son of Hur, of the tribe of Judah. And I have filled him with the
Spirit of God, in wisdom, in understanding, in knowledge, and in all
manner of workmanship, to design artistic works, to work in gold,
in silver, in bronze, in cutting jewels for setting, in carving wood,
and to work in all manner of workmanship." **Exodus 31:1-5, NKJV.**

When you think of the "famous" people of the Bible, whom do you think of? Adam and Eve, Abraham, Joseph, David, Job, Daniel, Isaac, Jacob, Moses, Peter, and Paul are some of the first ones that come to my mind. Even if I had hours to come up with a more exhaustive list, Bezalel and his right-hand man, Aholiab, would never make it to the top 100. Not even if I had all day, a whole week, or months to come up with every name lurking in my subconscious.

And why is that? Until I read their names as I worked my way through the Bible, I had never heard of them before. Yet they did something truly amazing. Bezalel was the man God chose—God personally chose him!—to create all of the structures, furniture, and items for the sanctuary. He's the one who made the ark of the covenant, the altar of incense, the laver, the altar of burnt offering, and the list goes on and on.

He had help, of course. Aholiab was appointed his helper, and there were other creative workmen who God also filled with His Spirit so they could help Bezalel. Together these people created the place God's own presence would fill. Only two of them were even named in the Bible, and I'd never heard of either one. Had you?

So many people are afraid they'll never amount to much. They don't have any special skills or talents that they know of. They don't have any lofty goals or dreams. They don't feel like they have much to contribute.

Yet we all have something to contribute if we will do one thing. If we are willing to let God's Spirit fill us, we can do great and wonderful things. In fact, there's no limit to what we can do, because there's no limit to God's creativity and the opportunities He can provide if we are willing to let Him use us. Bezalel and Aholiab probably never aspired to be the leading craftsmen of Israel who would build God's house, but because they were willing, they were.

Playing With Fire

Can a man scoop fire into his lap without
his clothes being burned? Can a man walk on hot coals
without his feet being scorched? **Proverbs 6:27, 28, NIV.**

The National Fire Protection Association (NFPA) reports that between 2005 and 2009 about 56,300 fires set by children playing with fire were reported to local fire departments. As a result of these fires, about 110 people died per year and 880 were injured. The fires caused about $286 million worth of damage. The NFPA estimates that 69 percent of the fires were started by children playing with matches or lighters.

Playing with fire is dangerous. Just ask Smokey the Bear. He's been warning people to be careful with fire in the longest-running public service announcement campaign in United States history. Smokey the Bear was actually a real bear cub rescued in 1950 during a terrible forest fire that left him badly burned. After his recovery he was kept at the National Zoo and was the living symbol of the Smokey the Bear forest fire prevention program. He received so many letters each week (13,000!) that the post office gave him his own zip code.

Because fire is so devastating, the Bible gives us a word picture for sin of a man holding fire in his lap or walking over hot coals. We can't play with sin without getting "burned." Don't kid yourself that you can play with a sin a "little." There's no such thing as holding a little fire and not getting burned, and there's no such thing as sinning a little bit and not getting burned.

"All who willfully depart from God's commandments are placing themselves under the control of Satan. Many a man tampers with evil, thinking that he can break away at pleasure; but he is lured on and on, until he finds himself controlled by a will stronger than his own. He cannot escape its mysterious power. Secret sin or master passion may hold him a captive as helpless as was the demoniac of Capernaum.

"Yet his condition is not hopeless. God does not control our minds without our consent; but every man is free to choose what power he will have to rule over him" (Ellen G. White, *The Ministry of Healing*, pp. 92, 93).

It can be very tempting to play with sin. We think that if we do it a little, maybe our friends will accept us, or it'll be exciting but not dangerous. But you can't control sin. A little fire engulfs a forest in flames very quickly. If you feel as though the fire of sin is sweeping through your life, ask God to put it out.

Two Unlikely Missionaries

Then those who kept them fled; and they went away into the city and told everything, including what had happened to the demon-possessed men. And behold, the whole city came out to meet Jesus. And when they saw Him, they begged Him to depart from their region. **Matthew 8:33, 34, NKJV.**

When Jesus healed the demon-possessed men in the pagan country of Gadarenes, the demons begged Jesus to allow them to go into a herd of pigs. Jesus agreed, and the entire herd panicked and bolted off the side of a cliff. This, as you can imagine, did not make the residents very happy and they begged Jesus to leave. Satan figured that if he could drive Jesus away the people wouldn't hear His message of salvation.

That's where he was wrong. Satan might be in temporary possession of earth, but God is the real landlord, and He can turn Satan's raw deals into shining opportunities. Even though Jesus wasn't allowed into Gadarenes, there were two men who were—the formerly demon-possessed men. They lived there and knew everyone, and, boy, did they have a story to tell.

"The two restored demoniacs were the first missionaries whom Christ sent to teach the gospel in the region of Decapolis. For a short time only, these men had listened to His words. Not one sermon from His lips had ever fallen upon their ears. They could not instruct the people as the disciples who had been daily with Christ were able to do. But they could tell what they knew; what they themselves had seen, and heard, and felt of the Savior's power. This is what everyone can do whose heart has been touched by the grace of God. This is the witness for which our Lord calls, and for want of which the world is perishing.

"The gospel is to be presented, not as a lifeless theory, but as a living force to change the life. God would have His servants bear testimony to the fact that through His grace men may possess Christlikeness of character and may rejoice in the assurance of His great love" (Ellen G. White, *The Ministry of Healing,* p. 99).

You may not be a preacher, a teacher, or even an evangelist or missionary. It doesn't matter. You have a unique story to tell about how Jesus has changed your life, and how, because He's living in you right now, your life is different. Only you can tell people how His power changed your life, and if you don't tell your story, it will never be told. Tell it every chance you get. Your mission field awaits.

March 11

Heaven and Hell

Indeed Herod and Pontius Pilate met together with the Gentiles
and the people of Israel in this city to conspire against your
holy servant Jesus, whom you anointed. They did what your power and
will had decided beforehand should happen. **Acts 4:27, 28, NIV.**

Quick! What is the first thought that comes to you when something bad happens? If you're like 99.9 percent of the population, it's probably "Why does God let bad things happen to good people?"

That's certainly what Joni Eareckson Tada thought in 1967 when she dove into a shallow lake and broke her neck, which left her a quadriplegic, paralyzed from the neck down. At a time when the rest of her friends were heading off to college, Joni faced a major life change and struggled with the question, "Why do bad things happen to good people?"

One day when her friend Steve was visiting her, she admitted she was angry with God. How could He let this happen to her? She desperately asked him if he knew why. Steve admitted that he didn't, but he asked her whose will she thought the cross was: God's or Satan's? Joni brushed him off, telling him the cross was God's will, obviously, since Jesus came to save us by dying on the cross.

Steve said, "Joni, think it through, because you better believe that it was the devil who entered the heart of Judas Iscariot who handed over Jesus for a mere 30 pieces of silver. And you got to know that it was Satan who instigated that mob on the streets to clamor for Christ's crucifixion, and for sure, Joni, it had to be the devil who prodded those Roman soldiers to spit on Jesus and slap Him and mock Him. Even the devil inspired Pontius Pilate to hand down mock justice in order to gain political popularity. How can any of these things be God's will? Treason, injustice, murder, torture?"

That's when Joni began to see that God uses Satan's evil plans for His own glorious purposes. We may not be able to understand them right now but we have to trust that God knows what He's doing. Satan tried to crush Christ on the cross. He used every available means at his disposal to get rid of Jesus. Finally, he seemed to succeed. He had Jesus crucified. He won.

Or did he? Satan's victory was his ultimate defeat, because God used the very same event to provide a way for every person on earth to be saved. Heaven and hell were both active in the crucifixion, but for very different reasons.

Be About It

So when they saw Him, they were amazed; and His mother said to Him, "Son, why have You done this to us? Look, Your father and I have sought You anxiously." And He said to them, "Why did you seek Me? Did you not know that I must be about My Father's business?" **Luke 2:48, 49, NKJV.**

There are generally two kinds of people in this world: talkers and doers. The talkers like to check everything out before they make a move. They do all the prep work: they research, they get advice, they tell other people what they're planning to do, they make lists, they check things off—twice—and then they may or may not do anything at all. The doers just do it. They see what needs to be done, and they quietly go about it. No muss, no fuss, just quiet action.

Daniel Alexander Granderson, in his *Collegiate Quarterly* lesson titled "Living a Trinity-inspired Life," sums it up nicely. He writes, "Don't just talk about it; be about it." There's nothing wrong with getting all the facts before we take action. There's nothing wrong with getting advice or making a plan. But at some point, if we're going to act, we *must act*.

Jesus had a very short time on earth. He spent a lot of it just growing up, yet even while He was a kid, busy growing up, He was about His Father's business. He wasn't just talking about it, shooting the breeze with Mary and Joseph at the dinner table, texting His friends during the scripture reading at the synagogue. No, He was about His Father's business. He was all up in it, He was all about it. Jesus was focused. He knew what He had to do, and He did it. It was that simple.

Do you know what you have to do? What's your mission? Are you doing it, or are you just talking a lot about it? What is your Father's business? Is it helping out with the primary kids in Sabbath school? Is it offering to shovel snow or rake leaves for an elderly neighbor? Today, not tomorrow or next week, *today,* do one thing, and instead of talking about it, be about it.

Look Out!

And he ordered us to preach everywhere and to testify that Jesus is the one appointed by God to be the judge of all—the living and the dead. He is the one all the prophets testified about, saying that everyone who believes in him will have their sins forgiven through his name. **Acts 10:42, 43, NLT.**

Imagine this scene. You're waiting at a bus stop. It's raining and cold, and you're hunched up inside your coat wishing you were anywhere else. You look up and notice that there's a guy in the street. He's bent over tying his shoelaces. What he doesn't see is that there is a truck bearing down on him. It's raining so hard he can't hear the danger. In mere seconds he'll be crushed flat.

Do you look the other way? pretend you didn't see him? tell yourself that he probably already knows there's a truck coming and he just doesn't feel like getting out of the way? Or do you leave the shelter of the bus stop and tackle him to get him out of the truck's way? If he was about to be killed by a truck, you'd have to do *something,* wouldn't you? You couldn't just stand there and let him get run over and then go home and live happily ever after, could you?

How is that any different from sharing the gospel? It's not called the good news for nothing. Like a big old truck, eternal death is bearing down on people who don't know Christ. It's going to hit them, run over them, and squash them flat. That's bad news. The Good News is that Christ can save them and offers them eternal life instead of eternal death.

Christians have no business standing around in the shelter of the bus stop wondering if they ought to say something or take action. God has ordered us "to preach everywhere and to testify that Jesus is the one appointed by God to be the judge of all—the living and the dead."

This, I admit, sounds frightening, especially if you weren't born with the gift of gab. It's not always easy to tell someone you *know* about Jesus; forget about someone you don't know. So if the thought of preaching everywhere is scaring you silly, remember this: God doesn't expect us to go around tackling people on our own. Not only will He direct us to the people He wants us to speak to, but He'll also tell us what to say. That's a relief, isn't it?

Ask God to put you in the right position to push someone out of the devil's path today and to show you exactly how to do it.

Dark Nights

"Or let him take hold of My strength, that he may make peace with Me; and he shall make peace with Me. **Isaiah 27:5, NKJV.**

et's face it: life is not always a piece of cake. It's not even always a piece of pie. Sometimes life gets us where it really hurts. Young people are especially vulnerable to life's ups and downs because they lack the perspective that age brings. They haven't yet lived through a lot of situations in which something horrible happens and life goes on. In the face of hurt, or tragedy, it doesn't *feel* like it will go on. When pain feels unbearable, death seems like an attractive alternative.

Suicide is the third leading cause of death for adolescents and teens. But no matter a person's age, suicide is a permanent solution to a temporary problem. Eventually whatever is wrong will fade. It may never go away completely, depending on what it is, but it will feel like the skin over an old wound. Still sensitive maybe, but it doesn't actively hurt anymore.

Christians have a real reason for hope even when they're smack dab in the middle of despair, because they have a loving God who will be their guide, counselor, and friend. "Whatever our situation, if we are doers of His word, we have a Guide to direct our way; whatever our perplexity, we have a sure Counselor; whatever our sorrow, bereavement, or loneliness, we have a sympathizing Friend" (Ellen G. White, *The Ministry of Healing*, pp. 248, 249).

Sometimes getting through loss or pain on our own, even if we are relying on God, isn't enough and we need someone's help. There are always people in your life you can turn to, people who will put their arms around you and tell you that you are not alone. If the place where you are is so dark that you can't see God, they will hold your hand and walk you right up to Him so that even in the pitch blackness, even if you can't see Him, you can feel His presence and have assurance that you will come through to the light on the other side of your very dark night.

Only you know who these people are in your life. They may be parents, siblings, relatives, teachers, counselors, friends, a pastor, or church elder. Know that these people want you to ask for help if you need it. Bless them by letting them help you. And above all, cling to God. He is the only one who can help you find lasting peace and comfort here on earth, as well as the hope of an eternal place in heaven.

When a Plan Comes Together

All praise to God, the Father of our Lord Jesus Christ,
who has blessed us with every spiritual blessing
in the heavenly realms because we are united with Christ.
Even before he made the world, God loved us and chose us
in Christ to be holy and without fault in his eyes. **Ephesians 1:3, 4, NLT.**

In the dictionary failure comes before forgiveness, but in the Bible, forgiveness comes before failure. The Bible begins with an account of how God created the world and everything in it, including a man and a woman: Adam and Eve. Neither of them had sinned. God created them perfect, and they enjoyed the beautiful world He'd given them and all the animals and plant life in it. And they lived happily ever after. Whoops, wrong story.

No, sadly, by the third chapter of Genesis, Adam and Eve sin. "When the Woman saw that the tree looked like good eating and realized what she would get out of it—she'd know everything!—she took and ate the fruit and then gave some to her husband, and he ate" (Genesis 3:6, Message). "Wait," you say, "Jesus doesn't show up to save mankind until the New Testament." Yes, it looks like failure comes first. But it doesn't.

Before God even made the world, He planned how He would save us, because He knew we would sin and need saving. Before Adam, or Eve, or you, or I was even created, God planned to save us. The plan was that Jesus would come to earth, become a man, live with us and teach us, and then die for our sins because only a sinless, perfect person could redeem us, and only God is perfect and sinless. God—Father, Son, and Holy Spirit—created this plan of salvation before humanity was even *created*.

So in the Bible, forgiveness came *before* failure (sin). Now, that doesn't mean we have an open debit card on the Bank of Heaven so that we can sin as much as we want and put it on our heavenly account just because we know God will forgive us. When we blatantly sin, we are crucifying Jesus all over again. Ellen White says, "There are many ways in which human beings can crucify the Son of God afresh, and put Him to open shame" (*This Day With God*, p. 339).

Try This: Take a sheet of blank paper and write down your sins, shortcomings, and failures on it. Ask God to forgive each one. Fold the paper and then put the paper through a shredder. Thank God for forgiving you.

Judgment Day

Judge not, that you be not judged. For with what judgment
you judge, you will be judged; and with the measure you use,
it will be measured back to you. And why do you look at the speck
in your brother's eye, but do not consider the plank in your own eye?
Or how can you say to your brother, "Let me remove the speck
from your eye"; and look, a plank is in your own eye? Hypocrite!
First remove the plank from your own eye, and then you will see
clearly to remove the speck from your brother's eye. **Matthew 7:1-5, NKJV.**

You can't tell Becca anything. It goes in one ear and out her mouth. She couldn't keep a secret if her life depended on it. And whatever she says always sounds 10 times worse than what really happened.

Reggie is the loudest, most obnoxious guy around. It's no wonder everyone picks on him. He's such a loser that you wouldn't be caught dead hanging out with him.

Lydia lies. You know she does because you've caught her at it. And you're not sure, but you think she might steal too. It just seems weird that your memory stick went missing and a week later Lydia had one even though she couldn't afford one before. It sure looks the same, but there's no way you can prove it.

Have you ever noticed how easy it is to pick out other people's character flaws? It's like they have glaring neon signs flashing above their heads: Liar! Thief! Know-it-all! Indifferent! Bragger! Snob! Do you ever wonder what neon sign flashes over your own head? No, probably not. Humans tend to think they are perfect; it's the rest of the world that's wrong.

The Bible tells us that no one is perfect, "for all have sinned and fall short of the glory of God" (Romans 3:23, NKJV). So whether we realize it or not, there *is* a flashing neon sign above our heads. The question is, what does it say? Jesus called that fault a log and told us to get rid of it before we tried to help others remove their specks.

If we are honest, we have to admit that we are not perfect. We all have good points and bad points. The key is realizing what our bad points are so that we can ask God to remove them. And while we're doing that we need to remember to be patient with others who are still working on theirs. If we expect God to be merciful with us, we need to offer mercy to others.

March 17

Addicted

> The temptations in your life are no different from what others experience. And God is faithful. He will not allow the temptation to be more than you can stand. When you are tempted, he will show you a way out so that you can endure. **I Corinthians 10:13, NLT.**

I am so addicted to soda. I've gotta have my Dew every day."

"Those nacho chips are so addictive. I could eat them all day."

"I can't stop texting. I'm so addicted."

"This game is so addictive. I can't stop playing it."

It used to be that an "addict" was someone nobody wanted to be. An addict was the loser on the street corner who was strung out on drugs, hadn't showered in months, had baggy black circles under their eyes, rotten teeth, foul breath, hairy armpits, and lived only for the next hit of whatever they were addicted to. They didn't care about anything else in life except the drug they were addicted to. Who would want to trade their life, even if it wasn't very exciting, for that?

Now, it's common to claim that you're addicted to all kinds of things: food, games, activities, drinks, or other people. Scientists and researchers are even beginning to agree that we can become addicted to things such as games and social media. And a whole group of scientists are creating addicting flavors to add to foods on purpose so that people will eat (and buy) more of them.

Flavorist Dawn Streich told *60 Minutes* host Morley Safer that they are trying to create flavors with a burst in the beginning and a finish that doesn't linger so you have to eat more of the product to keep tasting the flavor. Streich, Safer, and Jim Hassel, another flavorist being interviewed, agreed that they were basically trying to create an addictive taste.

Finish this sentence: I'm so addicted to _____.

If you could fill in the blank, ask yourself: Am I really addicted to this? How does it affect me? Who can help me get some control over this?

Anything in your life that you think of as an addiction, whether it's real or just in your own mind, is not healthy. If you are addicted to something, it has control over you, which means that God doesn't. But God can have control over that area of your life if you'll let Him. Give it to Him and find someone you trust to help you make some changes in your life.

Turkeys and Eagles

Ahab reported to Jezebel everything that Elijah had done,
including the massacre of the prophets. Jezebel immediately
sent a messenger to Elijah with her threat: "The gods will get you
for this and I'll get even with you! By this time tomorrow you'll be as dead
as any one of those prophets." When Elijah saw how things were, he ran for
dear life to Beersheba, far in the south of Judah. He left his young servant
there and then went on into the desert another day's journey. He came
to a lone broom bush and collapsed in its shade, wanting in the worst
way to be done with it all—to just die: "Enough of this, God!
Take my life —I'm ready to join my ancestors in the grave!" Exhausted,
he fell asleep under the lone broom bush. **1 Kings 19:1-5, Message.**

Have you ever jumped on a trampoline? I have, and it was a lot harder than I thought it would be. First of all, I had to keep my balance so I wouldn't end up doing a face-plant onto the mat. Then I had to be sure I didn't bounce too high and go flying right off the side of the thing. And I had to control my jumping so I wouldn't lose my rhythm and land awkwardly. It was a lot of work.

Boy, did I have a rude awakening when I got back to solid ground again. When I tried to walk, it felt as if my legs were bolted to the ground. I ended up shuffling around stiff-legged for a while, trying to get used to the fact that the world didn't bounce any more. Gravity was riveting me to earth again.

Elijah had a similar experience in his spiritual life. After watching God put the prophets of Baal in their place at Mount Carmel (see 1 Kings 18), he ended up pouting under a broom bush, wishing he could die. One minute he was spiritually soaring on the wings of eagles, and the next he was wallowing with the earthworms. How do you go from such a spiritual high to such a spiritual low so fast?

One word: gravity. Not real gravity, the type that keeps us from floating off into space, but spiritual gravity. Elijah took his attention off God and listened to Jezebel instead, and *thunk!* Down to earth he plummeted.

We can't flock with the turkeys if we expect to fly with the eagles. Our thoughts need to be fixed on God and what He wants and what He says. We can't listen to negative thoughts and ideas spouted by Satan, or the people listening to him. We are God's children; we belong to God. Everything in our lives—*everything*—belongs to God and is His to keep and command.

More Fun Than a Barrel of Monkeys

*Whatever your hand finds to do, do it with all your strength.
For there is no work or planning or learning or wisdom in the place
of the dead where you are going.* **Ecclesiastes 9:10, NLV.**

I have a lot of hobbies. I mean, seriously, a *lot*. Here are just a few: watercolor painting, horseback riding, canoeing, hiking, spinning, weaving, knitting, crocheting, fiddling, singing, reading, sewing, quilting, biking, drawing, geocaching, mixed media artwork, playing handbells, designing knitwear, felting, cross-country skiing, cooking, snowshoeing . . . and I could go on but you get the idea. And there are lots more things I'd like to try: paddleboarding, rug hooking, rock climbing, metal work, Tunisian crochet, upcycling clothes, shape note singing, pottery, and writing worship music are just a few.

What do you like to do? I mean, what do you *really* like to do? What floats your boat? What makes you jump out of bed every morning? A hobby? A sport? An art project you're working on? A song you're practicing on your favorite instrument? An engine you're reconstructing? A piece of pottery you're throwing? What makes you happy just thinking about it?

God made each of us with different interests and abilities. You may find that you're drawn to something that your best friend could care less about. But that's OK. The important thing is that you have something you love to do and that you make the time to do it.

If you couldn't come up with anything that excites you, maybe you should take a look at your life and see if you're bored with life or with your activities. Maybe it's time for a change. Boredom can lead to all sorts of nasty things, such as depression and drug and alcohol use. People who are bored are often tempted to try stupid things they wouldn't have any interest in otherwise. And don't be fooled: Satan uses boredom to tempt people into trying dangerous activities because he knows they're easily led when they're bored.

What looks interesting but you haven't tried yet for whatever reason? What has kept you from trying new things? What would it take for you to overcome that obstacle?

Make a list of things that you would love to do but haven't tried yet. Try a new activity each month. If you love doing it, make it a part of your life. If it didn't live up to your wildest dreams, try something new next time.

Praise God

*I will praise you as long as I live, lifting up my hands to you
in prayer. You satisfy me more than the richest feast.
I will praise you with songs of joy. I lie awake thinking of you,
meditating on you through the night.* **Psalm 63:4-6, NLT.**

When I was a kid, we had a German shepherd named Baron. My dad spent a lot of time training him, and we brought him to some shows. My dad even taught me the basics of training and let me bring Baron in the ring for the kiddie round, in which we won a blue ribbon.

Praise, in dog training, means that you reinforce the behavior you want in order to get more of it. For example, if I wanted Baron to fetch a ball, every time he brought it back to me I would praise him, "Good dog, Baron, what a good boy. Good boy to fetch the ball." Because Baron wanted to make me happy, he'd repeat the performance in hopes that he'd get more praise, thus reinforcing his desire to make me happy.

Praising God is not like that. By praising God we aren't trying to reinforce His "good" behavior—or the behavior we want from Him—in order to manipulate Him into doing what we want. Instead, praising God is an expression of our gratitude and love for God. In Hebrew there are several words that mean praise, but each has its own particular meaning, from shouting and celebrating, to raising hands, to kneeling, to singing and making music. The thing that all those activities have in common is that they come from a grateful heart. Praise always comes from a deep sense that we are aware of what God does for us.

It's also an acknowledgment on our part that we know where all good things come from. We shouldn't ever take for granted the blessings in our lives; every one of them comes from God. We should thank Him and praise Him for them. If your dad handed you the keys to a brand-new car and you took them and went on your merry way, or worse yet, told your friend that the car just showed up in the driveway, how do you think your dad would feel? God won't get His feelings hurt as your dad would, but it's still disrespectful and shows that we don't care about Him.

Seven of the Hebrew words for praise are *halal, yadah, towdah, shabach, barak, zamar,* and *tehillah.* Look up the definitions of these words and notice the differences. When you are praising God, keep these words in mind and try to express your praise to God in as many different ways as possible. After all, we have a lot to praise Him for.

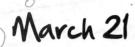

One Size Fits All

The world is unprincipled. It's dog-eat-dog out there!
The world doesn't fight fair. But we don't live or fight our battles that way—
never have and never will. The tools of our trade aren't for marketing
or manipulation, but they are for demolishing that entire massively corrupt
culture. We use our powerful God tools for smashing warped philosophies,
tearing down barriers erected against the truth of God, fitting every loose
thought and emotion and impulse into the structure of life shaped by Christ.
Our tools are ready at hand for clearing the ground of every obstruction
and building lives of obedience into maturity. **2 Corinthians 10:3-6, Message.**

They are everywhere: on the covers of every magazine, on every television show and movie. They've even taken over the Internet. Perfect people who have perfect faces and perfect bodies; everyone from authors to athletes to actresses tell us that we can look perfect too if we just eat this, or do that exercise, or try this beauty product.

Jesse Rosten, a filmmaker, was watching television late one night and saw an infomercial advertising a beauty product. When he saw the before and after pictures, he chuckled because it looked like the photos had been retouched in Adobe Photoshop. He decided to make a spoof commercial featuring "Fotoshop by Adobé" as the latest and greatest beauty product whose "pro-pixel intensifying fauxtanical hydro-jargon microbead extract infused with nutritive volumizing technology" will leave you "virtually unrecognizable." He used Photoshop to change the models' faces and even their bodies to show that the media distorts reality—what you see in the media isn't what's real. He says, "This commercial isn't real, and neither are society's standards of beauty."

The trouble is that a lot of damage has already been done. Despite being tech-savvy Photoshop users ourselves, we believe what we're seeing. We compare that to how we look and then starve, purge, binge, or exercise ourselves into unhealthiness trying to live up to the fraud.

This has to stop. According to the National Institute of Mental Health estimates, more than 5 million Americans are affected by eating disorders annually. That's 5 million people that Satan (with help from the media) has fooled. But we have powerful tools to fight the warped images of ourselves that Satan projects. While he's trying to get us to focus on the way we look, we need to ignore him and work with God to develop Christlike characters that are more pleasing to God than starved bodies or flawless faces.

All Grow and No Show

Even now the ax of God's judgment is poised, ready to sever the roots of the trees. Yes, every tree that does not produce good fruit will be chopped down and thrown into the fire. **Luke 3:9, NLT.**

Every Christmas my mom gives me and each of my sisters an amaryllis plant. It comes as a bulb in a box with some potting soil, a pot, and instructions. You're supposed to mix the potting soil with water, plant the bulb, water it well, and in a few weeks—voilà!—a big, spectacular, showy blossom will appear.

That's what's supposed to happen anyway. Sometimes when the shoots begin to grow, there is nothing on the end of them. There's no flower blossom, just leaves. They grow and grow until they get so heavy they topple over, but they never flower. The bulb is a dud. It's disappointing, all grow and no show. It's a bit like waiting for fireworks that just fizzle and don't explode.

The same thing can happen to us as Christians if we're not careful. All that learning we do in Sabbath school, in church, in school (if it's a Christian school), and at home can become one big buzz in our head. We can know a lot of facts *about* God. We'd be tough to beat in Bible trivia. But when it comes down to actual words, thoughts, and actions, our Christianity doesn't show up. We blend into the scenery and look just like everyone else.

God doesn't call us to blend in. He calls us to stand out, stand up, and make a difference. If we're doing that, it will show. People won't need to ask if there's something different about us, they'll see it. They'll see it in our fruit—the things we do, the things we say, the things we believe. Our fruit will be like the amaryllis' showy blossoms: big, bold, and breathtaking. People can't help but notice something that spectacular.

Growing fruit isn't something that happens overnight. It takes time for fruit to develop. It has to progress from flower to bud to tiny fruit to mature fruit. But at all stages you can see it growing there, ripening in the sun, perfuming the air with its fragrance even before it's ready to eat. The only way it can continue to grow is for the branch it's on to stay connected to the tree, and it's the same for us. The only way we can grow in Christ is if we stay connected to Him. Forget all the learning for just a minute. It's valuable, but for just this second, ask yourself, "Do I really *know* Jesus?" If you don't, get to know Him now and bear beautiful fruit for Him.

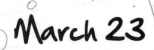

March 23

Remember Me?

*Their roots will dry up, and their branches will wither.
All memory of their existence will fade from the earth,
no one will remember their names. They will be thrust
from light into darkness, driven from the world.* Job 18:16-18, NLT.

I was once visiting a nursing home when their oldest resident, a woman who was 102 years old, received some visitors, an elderly couple who hadn't seen her in some time. The woman visiting was determined that the old woman remember them.

She kept asking, "Do you remember me? I'm Dr. Bedard's wife."

The old woman was hard of hearing, so the nurse, trying to be helpful, repeated everything, shouting in her ear. "Do you remember her? She's Dr. Bedard's wife."

The old woman kept shaking her head, but just before the visitors gave up, she perked up a little and said, "Dr. Bedard's wife?"

Everyone in the visitor's room got excited. Finally! She remembered! We all leaned closer to hear what she'd have to say.

"Dr. Bedard's wife," she proclaimed loudly, "was an alcoholic!"

The woman visiting blushed with embarrassment. "That was his first wife," she said a little testily. "I'm his second wife."

It didn't matter. The old woman had found a memory and she wasn't going to let it go. She went on and on about how Dr. Bedard's wife went to one treatment facility after another but couldn't stay off "the liquor" that finally killed her. The visitors eventually gave up and went home, but I couldn't stop thinking about Dr. Bedard's first wife. How sad that the only thing the old woman remembered about her was her failure to beat the addiction that finally killed her. What would she think about her life if she knew that after she was gone people would only remember her as an alcoholic?

Sooner or later we'll all be gone, and the only thing people will have to remember us by is their memory of how we lived our lives. Let's pray every day to live our lives in a way that's worthy of Jesus and all He sacrificed for us.

Think About It: How do you want people to remember you? What do you want them to remember you for?

Walking Billboard

> Joseph was a strikingly handsome man. As time went on,
> his master's wife became infatuated with Joseph and one day said,
> "Sleep with me." He wouldn't do it. He said to his master's wife,
> "Look, with me here, my master doesn't give a second thought
> to anything that goes on here—he's put me in charge of everything
> he owns. He treats me as an equal. The only thing he hasn't turned
> over to me is you. You're his wife, after all! How could I violate
> his trust and sin against God?" **Genesis 39:6-9, Message.**

You could say that Joseph had it pretty rough. His brothers were jerks who sold him into slavery. But he didn't get mad; he didn't even try to get even. He just quietly set about being the best slave he could be. Then he was betrayed by his master's wife and thrown into prison. Again, he didn't waste time shaking his fist over the injustice of it all. He just became the best prisoner he could be. His attitude was so remarkable that the prison warden made him into a junior warden, so Joseph was the best junior warden he could be. Eventually he was able to help the pharaoh, and Pharaoh made him his second-in-command.

No matter what circumstance Joseph found himself in, he tried his best. Why? Why be a good slave? Or prisoner? (Or student? Or employee? Or son? Or daughter? Or friend?) Because someone is watching. Sometimes it is someone who will really matter in your future, such as the person who will become your spouse. But God is always watching, as are the angels and the unfallen worlds. "We cannot show greater honor to our God, whose we are by creation and redemption, than to give evidence to the beings of heaven, to the worlds unfallen, and to fallen men, that we diligently hearken unto all His commandments, which are the laws that govern His kingdom" (Ellen G. White, *Our Father Cares*, p. 137).

That universal audience saw in Joseph someone who let God's spirit fill him and direct him. When Pharaoh needed someone to get the country ready for the coming famine, he said, "Isn't this the man we need? Are we going to find anyone else who has God's spirit in him like this?" (Genesis 41:38, Message). What will you do today that you can do only with God's spirit filling you? You are a walking billboard; what message will you send to others? Will you choose to send the message that the only thing that really matters in life is being full of God's Spirit and following Him? Your billboard is blank: write something awesome on it.

March 25

Servitude 101

But among you it will be different. Whoever wants to be a leader
among you must be your servant, and whoever wants to be
first among you must be the slave of everyone else.
For even the Son of Man came not to be served but to serve
others and to give his life as a ransom for many. **Mark 10:43-45, NLT.**

Wanted: Now accepting applications for slave position. No pay. Lousy treatment. Lots of overtime. No benefits. Must have positive attitude and good work ethic. Inquire within.

If you walked past a building with that sign on the door, how long do you suppose the line would be to apply for the job? You'd be first in line if you decided to apply. Who wants to be a slave? No one. In the whole history of slavery, I think I can say with confidence that no one stepped up and volunteered to become a slave. Can you imagine parents asking their kids, "What do you want to be when you grow up?" and the kids answering, "I'd like to be a slave."

It doesn't happen. Why? Because no one wants to be bossed around by someone else. Everyone wants to be the one *doing* the bossing. Or at least if they can't be the boss, they want to get paid for doing their job. And they want perks, such as a Christmas bonus, sick days, and vacations. Slaves don't get any of that. Yet Jesus told His disciples that not only did they have to serve one another, they had to be slaves to *everyone*.

That's easy for Him to say, you might think. *He doesn't know the kind of people I have to deal with. Not even Jesus would expect me to serve them, not if He knew what they were like.* Except that He would. However, Jesus isn't asking you to do anything He wasn't willing to do first. Even though He is the king of heaven, He came to be a servant. Serving others is what Christianity is all about. There's nothing natural about serving others. Our human natures want to seize honor, glory, and power, not to put everyone else before ourselves. But when we become servants we are placing ourselves in the position God designed for us. It may not look honorable from here, but when we look back from heaven it'll all become clear.

Take It to the Streets: Take a look at the different areas of your life. How can you be a servant at school? at home? at your job? with your friends? Ask Jesus to help you put others first.

The Nice and the Nasty

You're familiar with the old written law, "Love your friend," and its unwritten companion, "Hate your enemy." I'm challenging that. I'm telling you to love your enemies. Let them bring out the best in you, not the worst. When someone gives you a hard time, respond with the energies of prayer, for then you are working out of your true selves, your God-created selves. This is what God does. He gives his best—the sun to warm and the rain to nourish—to everyone, regardless: the good and bad, the nice and nasty. If all you do is love the lovable, do you expect a bonus? Anybody can do that. If you simply say hello to those who greet you, do you expect a medal? Any run-of-the-mill sinner does that. In a word, what I'm saying is, *Grow up.* You're kingdom subjects. Now live like it. Live out your God-created identity. Live generously and graciously toward others, the way God lives toward you. **Matthew 5:43-48, Message.**

People can be hard to deal with sometimes. They can be selfish, obnoxious, overbearing, needy, greedy, rude, insensitive, deceitful, foolish, grumpy, inconsiderate, jealous, lazy, deceptive, mistrustful, spiteful, self-centered, touchy, uncaring, and weak. And that's just us. The rest of the world is even worse. At least, it is according to us. It's easy to think we're not so bad compared to everyone else. But everyone else probably thinks the same thing about us!

The thing is, no one is perfect. Maybe that kid did just shove you on purpose and then yelled at you like it was your fault. Maybe your mother is in a really foul mood today and snapped your head off on the way to school. Maybe your little brother did kick you under the table and pretended you kicked him instead. Maybe your teacher singled you out for punishment when really it was someone else's fault.

You have two choices. You can either respond in kind—shove back, yell back, snap back, kick back—or you can think about how very much God has forgiven you, and you can act like *He* would act in your place. As my mother would say, you can be big about it. God calls it living like a "kingdom subject." We are so loved by God we can afford to be generous in our responses, to love people who aren't particularly nice to us, maybe even downright nasty. After all, we've got plenty of love to spare. We're like love millionaires. We don't need to be stingy with our love and forgiveness. God has an endless supply and showers it on us every minute of every day. Live generously and graciously toward others. Share the love, people!

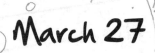

March 27

Parade of Daily Adventures

One of the teachers of the law came and heard them debating.
Noticing that Jesus had given them a good answer, he asked him,
"Of all the commandments, which is the most important?"
"The most important one," answered Jesus, "is this:'Hear, O Israel:
The Lord our God, the Lord is one. Love the Lord your God with all
your heart and with all your soul and with all your mind and
with all your strength.'The second is this:'Love your neighbor as yourself.'
There is no commandment greater than these." Mark 12:28-31, NIV.

Marla Cilley has been helping people deal with CHAOS (Can't Have Anyone Over Syndrome) for quite a while now. She has a Web site (www.flylady.net) where you can go to get help organizing just about every part of your life (yes, teens too!). Marla calls a to-do list a PODA (Parade of Daily Adventures), which sounds like a lot more fun than something you *have* to *do*. You've probably got a similar list full of items such as "clean your room," "study for science test," "load new iTunes songs," and "fill out job application." One school I know of, gives each student a personal agenda at the beginning of the school year and encourages them to write down all their homework assignments, projects, and so on each day to help them stay organized.

The fun part about making lists is that as you do each item, you cross it off the list. I keep a PODA, too, and it gives me a great feeling to put a check mark in the box next to each item. I've even been known to add to my list things I've already done just so I can have the satisfaction of checking them off.

Listmakers such as you and me have come up with different systems to decide which items on the list are the most important so that they can be done first. Some people write down everything they need to do and number them, starting with the most important thing on the list and going down to the least important. Some people use different colored ink to show whether something is important or just needs to be done whenever.

Jesus gave us two items to put at the very top of our PODAs. They were so important that even if we did these two things and didn't get anything else done all day long, we'd still have had a successful day: (1) loving God—spending time developing our relationship with Him; and (2) loving our neighbors as ourselves—making their needs as important as our own. If we will do those two things today, we will have our priorities in the right place.

Abandon Ship?

Don't be afraid, for I am with you. Don't be discouraged, for I am your God. I will strengthen you and help you. I will hold you up with my victorious right hand. Isaiah 41:10, NLT.

C aptain Francesco Schettino was piloting a cruise ship off the coast of Italy when he made an unscheduled detour to go close to one of the islands. Apparently he zigged when he should have zagged, and crashed into a reef. He managed to turn the boat around and run it aground on the island so it wouldn't sink farther out at sea, which would make rescue difficult, but then he did the unthinkable: *he abandoned ship before everyone had been rescued.*

While bobbing around in the lifeboat, he was ordered by the coast guard to get back on the ship and tell them how much damage there was, organize the rescue from onboard the ship, and let the coast guard know what the passengers needed. Captain Schettino had one excuse after another for why he couldn't go back on the ship, and a short while later they found him on the island and arrested him. Captains aren't supposed to abandon their ships, especially when there are passengers still on board. Thirty-two people died in this disaster, and the media nicknamed him "Captain Coward." Not surprisingly, he was also billed as the most hated man in Italy.

There are people who think God is like Captain Schettino. They believe He created earth and then abandoned ship, leaving us twirling around in space all by ourselves, drowning in our own misery. They think He's up in heaven somewhere shaking His head over what's happening down here, but like Captain Schettino, He's powerless to help, wringing his hands on land while his passengers drown.

I'm so glad they're wrong. I'm glad that when I feel weak and discouraged I can lean on God for strength. I'm glad that when I need to talk He's there to listen. I'm glad that when I need an answer to a question He gives it to me, and I'm always amazed at the many ways He finds to be present in my life even without a physical presence.

We don't have to be afraid of anything. God is with us. God is *always* with us. No matter what darkness you pass through, God is with you. He will give you strength and hold you up with His strong arm. He can do that because He's here, He's present, and He loves you. He will never abandon ship.

March 29

God's Laundry

Generous in love—God, give grace! Huge in mercy—
wipe out my bad record. Scrub away my guilt, soak out my sins
in your laundry. I know how bad I've been; my sins are staring me
down. You're the One I've violated, and you've seen it all, seen the full extent
of my evil. You have all the facts before you; whatever you decide about
me is fair. I've been out of step with you for a long time, in the wrong since
before I was born. What you're after is truth from the inside out. Enter me,
then; conceive a new, true life. Soak me in your laundry and I'll come out
clean, scrub me and I'll have a snow-white life. **Psalm 51:1-7, Message.**

If you dislike doing laundry, some chemical engineers in China have good news for you. They've created a cotton fabric that cleans and deodorizes itself; no more washing necessary. The only hitch is that it's activated by sunlight, so you have to actually go outside for a while in order for it to work. Still, all the work is gone out of cleaning your clothes. Just wander around outside for a while and presto! Clean clothes. Of course, no one's sure yet if it's actually safe.

I'm kind of old-fashioned myself. The thought of chemicals coating my clothes makes me nervous. I'd rather have a plain old T-shirt and wash it when it gets dirty. It's very satisfying to wash clothes and then hang them outside to dry. When you put them on, they smell like the outdoors, fresh and new.

Do you think God feels anything like that when He washes us? There we are, all filthy with our mistakes, sins, rebellion, wicked thoughts, cherished idols, and sneaky schemes. There's no self-cleaning chemical on earth that can cleanse us. The only way we can be spotless is if we let God wash us in the blood of Jesus. It's the only thing that will purify us.

In order to do that, we need two things: to be willing to let go of the stains, and to allow God to cleanse us. "By faith apply the blood of Christ to your heart, for that alone can make you whiter than snow. But you say, 'This surrender of all my idols will break my heart.' This giving up of all for God is represented by your falling upon the Rock and being broken. Then give up all for Him; for unless you are broken, you are worthless" (Ellen G. White, *Selected Messages, book 1,* p. 330). It is only when we are broken that God can hold us together, and when God is holding us together, nothing can break us ever again.

Reality Check

How then can you comfort me with empty words,
since falsehood remains in your answers? **Job 21:34, NKJV.**

For a long time, our television had four channels—if you included the Public Broadcasting Service, which was actually the one we watched most often because it had more educational content. We avoided having a satellite dish for years. Sure, there were a lot of interesting programs you could get, but who had time for more television? Not us. So we happily watched our four stations.

And then someone decided to make it impossible for people to get those four little stations without a satellite dish. We broke down and got one. The first thing we noticed after we were finished being dazzled by the hundreds of channels to choose from was that there was a whole lot of a new kind of programming. They called it reality television.

Now we could follow real people on ocean voyages, on makeovers, on their various dangerous—or dirty—jobs, to feasts in different countries, on survival adventures, or bidding on storage lockers. Wherever a camera could go, we the viewers could tag along.

I intensely dislike reality TV. When I found out that reality TV was actually staged, I disliked it even more. What's the point of calling something real if behind the scenes you're making up everything that happens so there's more drama for better ratings?

This fascination we have for unreality extends to all areas of our lives, even into church where we dress up in our best clothes, put a smile on our faces, and tell everyone what a great week we had, thanks, how about you? Inside we may be struggling with sin or despair. We may be hurting from circumstances beyond our control or consequences that we brought down on our own heads. But we *pretend* everything is fine because that's what everyone else does (and we don't want them to know that we're not OK).

What we need is to be real. First with God by opening up to Him about our problems, and then to others, when it's possible, to let them know what we're going through. That way they can *participate with God* by praying for us, they can *praise God* as we are helped, and they can *glorify God* by acknowledging His work in us. And that, my friends, is real.

March 31

Prescription for Disaster

Don't you realize that all of you together are the temple of God and that the Spirit of God lives in you? God will destroy anyone who destroys this temple. For God's temple is holy, and you are that temple. **I Corinthians 3:16, 17, NLT.**

True or false: Prescription drugs are perfectly safe to take even if it's someone else's prescription.

False. But if you answered "true," you wouldn't be the only one. Many people believe that prescription drugs are safe because a doctor has prescribed them. After all, why would a doctor prescribe something if it wasn't safe? What they don't consider is that doctors prescribe medication for individuals who are ill, have pain, or need certain drugs to correct a problem that *those* individuals have.

Doctors consider many factors before they decide what medication at which dose to prescribe for every single person. They have to take into account that person's medical history and any other problems they may have; they also have to factor in weight and any other medicines being taken. That's why prescriptions aren't one-size-fits-all. If you take someone else's prescription, even for *the same problem they have,* it could harm you.

People take medication to help with a certain problem, for example, pain. But even the most helpful medicine also affects other parts of the body. These are called side effects. For example, some people with ADHD take Adderall to help them focus. But Adderall also raises blood pressure and heart rate. Some teens are sharing (or selling) their meds as "study buddies" to help their friends stay awake and cram for tests. This can be dangerous. It's also illegal.

Taking prescription medications that haven't been prescribed for you can also lead to addiction. In the patient who is taking the prescribed medication, it counteracts a problem they're having and makes them feel better. But when someone who doesn't need a drug takes it, the brain can be affected in such a way that the person becomes addicted.

Abusing prescription drugs and over-the-counter drugs that are meant for someone else or for a different problem is still drug abuse. It's no different than buying illegal drugs; they have the same effect on the body. Christians are temples for the Holy Spirit. Abusing drugs destroys that temple one high at a time.

Tricked

"You won't die!" the serpent replied to the woman.
"God knows that your eyes will be opened as soon as you eat it,
and you will be like God, knowing both good and evil." **Genesis 3:4, 5, NLT.**

Long ago, on April 1, 1957, before you or I were even born, a British television show called *Panorama* had a special news report on the bumper spaghetti harvest in southern Switzerland. It reported that the success of the crop was due to the mild winter and disappearance of the awful spaghetti weevil. The audience was shown video footage of a Swiss family pulling spaghetti off trees and laying it out to dry in the sun.

The show ended with the host saying, "Now we say good night, on this first day of April," which was a clue to folks that the segment had been a joke. As soon as the program was off the air, the phones started to ring. Some people called in because they got the joke, others to complain that the show shouldn't tell stories that weren't true, but most called to settle an argument about whether or not spaghetti actually grows on trees. (It doesn't.)

The Swiss Spaghetti Harvest made it to the top of the Museum of Hoaxes' "Top 100 April Fool's Day Hoaxes of All Time" list but it wasn't the worst practical joke played, not by a long shot. The worst mischievous trick in the history of the world is the one Satan played on Adam and Eve. When Satan tricked Eve into eating the fruit of the tree of the knowledge of good and evil, he did it by telling her that God wasn't being truthful with her. God said she would die if she ate it; Satan said she wouldn't die. In fact, he told her that not only would she not die but she would become like God and know everything He knows.

You know the rest of the story: Eve fell for the trick. April Fool's!

But does Satan's trick sound familiar to you? It should; he uses the same one on us all the time. Whenever we want to do something we know God doesn't want us to do, Satan is right there saying, "It's OK; you won't surely die. In fact, if you do this, you'll feel great. I promise."

And maybe we even do feel great . . . at first. But the Bible tells us that sin *always* has the same result: "For the wages of sin is death" (Romans 6:23, NKJV). Don't listen to Satan the trickster; he's full of nothing but lies. In the end the joke will be on you.

Instead, listen to, obey, and love God, who will only tell you the truth. He will never pull a prank on you, never lie to you, never lead you on. God always delivers what He promises.

April 2

Your Honor

*But they didn't answer, because they had been arguing
about which of them was the greatest. He sat down,
called the twelve disciples over to him, and said,
"Whoever wants to be first must take last place and
be the servant of everyone else." **Mark 9:34, 35, NLT.***

You've probably never been hauled into court, and I hope you never will be. It's a very solemn thing to stand before a judge who has full authority over you and feel your knees knock while you wait to find out what they will say about your future. There are several positions of power in the community that command respect from citizens: mayors, police officers, and judges are a few. If you were standing in line at the Quik Stop to buy a pack of gum and one of them stepped into line behind you, chances are you'd stand a little straighter and become very polite all of a sudden. People in authority have that effect on others.

For a long time one of the volunteer positions I had was cooking dinner for people who had been released from jail and were living in a halfway house. Staff members helped them get new jobs, they received counseling, and the community was invited to show they cared by cooking and eating dinner with them each night. When I first started cooking there, before I could tell staff members from released prisoners, I noticed that one man always stepped right up and did the dishes. This was unusual because men don't usually volunteer to wash dishes. It was also unusual because dishwashing was the dirty work. Cooking was fun, but who likes to clean up afterward? Later I found out that this man who washed dishes was even more unusual. It turned out that he was a judge, probably the same judge who had sentenced many of these prisoners to jail in the first place. Yet he was a regular visitor at the halfway house, where he humbly and cheerfully did the dishes.

It's human nature to want to do the fun stuff, get the easy jobs, and be the top dog. No one wants to do the cleaning up, the serving, the hard work. Even the disciples argued over who was the greatest. Jesus told them that if they wanted to be first, they had to be last. He said that the way to greatness was in service to others. That was *not* what they wanted to hear.

How about you? How do you feel about serving others? Does it come easy to you, or do you find it hard to swallow? Pray for God to give you the humility you need to serve others cheerfully.

Oh, How He Loves

From noon until three in the afternoon darkness
came over all the land. About three in the afternoon Jesus cried
out in a loud voice, *"Eli, Eli, lema sabachthani?"* (which means "My God,
my God, why have you forsaken me?"). **Matthew 27:45, 46, NIV.**

When I was growing up, Good Friday was a very solemn day. We spent it remembering what Jesus was going through the day He was crucified. During the hours He hung on the cross—from noon until 3:00—we didn't even talk unless it was absolutely necessary. I still feel this solemnity on Good Friday when I think about what hung in the balance during Jesus' trial and crucifixion. At any time He could have said, "That's it! Humanity isn't worth this kind of pain." It would have been all over for us: no freedom from sin, no salvation, no eternal life.

When they talk about the Crucifixion, people often focus on what Jesus suffered physically: the beatings, the scourging, the crown of thorns, the nails. But it was not His physical wounds that caused His greatest suffering. "All His life Christ had been publishing to a fallen world the good news of the Father's mercy and pardoning love. Salvation for the chief of sinners was His theme. But now with the terrible weight of guilt He bears, He cannot see the Father's reconciling face. The withdrawal of the divine countenance from the Savior in this hour of supreme anguish pierced His heart with a sorrow that can never be fully understood by man. So great was this agony that His physical pain was hardly felt" (Ellen G. White, *The Desire of Ages*, p. 753).

In fact, Jesus "feared that sin was so offensive to God that Their separation was to be eternal" (p. 753). Yet He was still willing to go through that indescribable agony in order to save us. Think for a minute what that means. Think about how much He loves us, how much He loves *you*.

When you *really* think about it, are any of the small sacrifices He asks us to make actually sacrifices at all? The next time you face a temptation that is hard to walk away from, remind yourself how very much Jesus loves you.

Walk with Jesus today, through His trials, through His scourging, through the mocking, along the road to Calvary. Stand at the foot of the cross while He hangs there loving us so much that He was willing to risk losing His Father forever so that we could be with God in heaven where *He*—not we—belonged. Think about that and thank your Savior.

April 4

Sabbath Rest

Now the first day of the week Mary Magdalene
went to the tomb early, while it was still dark, and saw that
the stone had been taken away from the tomb. **John 20:1, NKJV.**

A friend of mine recently got an eReader device. He has the entire Bible on it—in multiple versions—all of Ellen White's writings, and the Sabbath school quarterly. The first time he opened it up in Sabbath school, he felt as though people suspected that he was playing games on it. In the end the pressure was too much, and he broke down and explained to the class that he was using the device to follow along with the lesson.

"When you think about it," he said, "it's probably as amazing to have all this information at our fingertips on one small device as it was for the first person to have the entire Bible in one book instead of many scrolls."

There's no doubt about it; technology has come a long way. But sometimes it goes too far. If you scan the sanctuary at your church on Sabbath, you'll likely see a variety of people using electronic devices, and most of them aren't reading the Bible or studying their Sabbath school lessons. People text, surf the Web, check Facebook, and play games during the church service, right there in their pews.

"What's the problem?" you might ask. "A conversation is the same whether it's texting or in person. And hanging out on Facebook isn't breaking the Sabbath." Maybe not, but is it the *best* way to spend the Sabbath? Anything that keeps you from paying attention to the service is a distraction. Can you think of anyone who might want to distract us from paying attention to God? (Hint: His name starts with an S.)

Think about it: Sabbath is so important that Jesus didn't even rise from the dead until after Sabbath; instead, He rested in the grave during Sabbath hours. The Sabbath is so important that God specifically instructed us to remember it: "Remember the Sabbath day, to keep it holy" (Exodus 20:8, NKJV). Why might He do that? Probably because it's so easy to get caught up with worldly things and forget how important and sacred the Sabbath is.

If you usually use electronics in church, try putting them away for one Sabbath. Get your Bible out and look up the verses. Take notes. Sing the hymns. Participate. Challenge yourself to find the *best* way to observe the Sabbath. Notice anything different?

The Great Blondin

Listen to me, family of Jacob, everyone that's left of the family of Israel. I've been carrying you on my back from the day you were born, and I'll keep on carrying you when you're old. I'll be there, bearing you when you're old and gray. I've done it and will keep on doing it, carrying you on my back, saving you. **Isaiah 46:3, 4, Message.**

The Great Blondin was a French acrobat named Jean François Gravelet. On June 30, 1859, the Great Blondin walked across Niagara Falls on a tightrope safely to the Canadian side. After a short rest he came back, this time carrying a camera. Not a little digital camera, mind you. He had a large, clunky Daguerreotype camera strapped to his back. Part of the way across, he stopped and took a picture of the crowd on the American side before finishing his walk.

The more times Blondin crossed the tightrope, the crazier his stunts were. Once he came back from the Canadian side carrying his manager, Harry Colcord, on his back. He told Harry, "Look up, Harry. . . . You are no longer Colcord, you are Blondin. Until I clear this place be a part of me, mind, body, and soul. If I sway, sway with me. Do not attempt to do any balancing yourself. If you do, we will both go to our death."

In many ways our relationship with God is like Blondin carrying Colcord. God carries us every step of the way in our lives. We are crossing a gaping cataract with water foaming and boiling beneath us. We can't do anything on our own. Clinging to God's back, we must look up. We must be part of Him—mind, body, and soul. If He sways, we must sway with Him. We can't attempt to do anything on our own. If we do, we will fall. Fortunately for us, God will give us a second chance that Blondin and Colcord would not have had.

Blondin relied on Colcord's obedience. He gave the instructions, but if Colcord had suddenly started trying to help him balance, or if he'd panicked halfway across, Blondin himself would have suffered as well as Colcord. In a similar way, God suffers when we don't trust Him and obey His commands.

If we want to make it across the Niagara Falls of our life, above the boiling falls of sin below, we must let God carry us. We must trust Him. We must believe that He will save us. As long as we cling to Him, we will never be lost.

April 6

Crack-the-Whip

My sheep listen to my voice; I know them, and they follow me. I give them eternal life, and they will never perish. No one can snatch them away from me, for my Father has given them to me, and he is more powerful than anyone else. No one can snatch them from the Father's hand. **John 10:27-29, NLT.**

Have you ever played crack-the-whip? It's a game that kids play either on grass or on ice. Someone is the leader, or "head," and everyone else joins hands in a long line following them. The leader starts running, or skating, in random directions. Everyone following goes in the same direction. But the closer you are to the "tail," the harder it is to hang on, because the force of the "whip" flings you around. Eventually the players on the end can't help letting go and falling off the whip. Players who fall off can rejoin the whip if they can grab onto the new tail. If they're faster than other players who have fallen off, they can get into a more secure position closer to the head.

Does life ever feel like a game of crack-the-whip? Everything moves so fast. You hold on tight, but suddenly you get flung off course. The ground is hard, and you sit there for a while catching your breath, feeling bruised and embarrassed. When you're ready, you get back up and catch the tail, and off you go again on another wild ride.

The trick to not being flung off is to stay close to the leader. The closer you are to the leader, the less action there is and the easier it is to hang on. Life is like that too. The closer we can stay to God, the more stable we are, the less we get tossed around, and the easier it is to stick to our walk and follow Him.

That's because God won't let us go. As long as we are near Him, we can rest in Him even if life is swirling all around us. We can trust Him and know that He won't let us go, no matter what. When you find that you're falling a lot, check to see where you are in line. Are you close to the head? Or are you whipping around at the tail?

An Act of God

The Lord merely spoke, and the heavens were created.
He breathed the word, and all the stars were born. He assigned the sea
its boundaries and locked the oceans in vast reservoirs. Let the whole world
fear the Lord, and let everyone stand in awe of him. **Psalm 33:6-8, NLT.**

An "act of God" is a legal term used to describe a natural disaster such as a flood, hurricane, or tornado that causes damage to people's property. It means that no one can legally be held responsible for the damage because no one could control what happened. Personally, I'd call that an "act of nature," or if you want to be precise, an "act of Satan."

I like to think that acts of God are those little things that happen all day long that God uses to communicate with us when we're paying attention. They are the kinds of things that you'd miss if you didn't look for them. Were you praying for an answer about something and suddenly the same thought keeps popping up everywhere? Maybe in your Sabbath school quarterly, and then again in your Bible reading, and then you see a quote echoing the same thing on a friend's Facebook page? Those are not random things happening for no reason. That is God responding to your prayer and guiding you. The question is: Are you listening?

We're often guilty of halfheartedly praying for something, and then forgetting all about it. It's as if we don't expect God to answer us. It's not as though He's going to text us or post on our Facebook wall, but He *will* answer us. Maybe He won't send a plane to skywrite a message across the heavens, but He often uses people, songs, books, His Word, and circumstances to communicate with us.

Still, sometimes if it looks like a duck, it walks like a duck, and it quacks like a duck, it might only be a duck. Because God can't sit down across a table from us and say, "Now look, here's what I want you to do," it *is* possible to think we're getting a message from God when it is really just something we want to see. That's why it's important to test what we believe God is telling us against the Word He's given us: the Bible. God will never tell us anything that can't be backed up with Scripture.

It's also important to be honest with ourselves and God. We need to be careful that we don't put our own spin on the answer He gives us so that it sounds more like the answer we *want*. When God speaks to us, we need to be willing to hear what He has to say.

Bibling

I observed everything going on under the sun, and really,
it is all meaningless—like chasing the wind. **Ecclesiastes 1:14, NLT.**

What do planking, teapotting, owling, Batmanning, Tebowing, Gronking, and now cat breading, have in common? They are all Internet memes. A meme is a type of behavior, idea, or style that spreads from one person to the next. These particular memes rely on people participating and then posting pictures of themselves participating. They spread like wildfire across the globe. Here is a brief description of a few Internet memes that are popular as I write:

Planking: lying face down with both arms at your sides.

Teapotting: posing with your arms creating a teapot's spout and handle.

Owling: Squatting like an owl.

Batmanning: Hanging by your feet.

Tebowing: Taking a knee in prayer position like quarterback Tim Tebow.

Gronking: Spiking anything handy the way Rob Gronkowski spikes a football.

Cat breading: Poking a hole in a piece of bread and stuffing your cat's face in it.

Most of these memes are just silly, but some can get dangerous. In an attempt to one-up one another by taking the meme to a new level, some people get more and more outrageous. A 20-year-old man plunged to his death when he tried to plank on a seventh-story balcony in Australia.

Solomon said there was nothing new under the sun, and although people keep trying to come up with original crazy things that will become the newest meme, they are still only coming up with a new variation of a fad, something silly that won't last and won't amount to anything. Christians are called to something higher, something meaningful.

We could start a new meme called Bibling, with people submittiing pictures of themselves reading the Bible in odd places, but what would that accomplish? Wouldn't it be better to encourage them to actually read the Bible? Memes start because someone has an idea and tells someone else about it. They tell someone else, and before you know it, everyone wants in on the action. Use your meme power for good and not evil. Instead of participating in the latest pointless meme, try sharing God instead.

Secret Agent Christian

Therefore, when you do a charitable deed, do not sound a trumpet before you as the hypocrites do in the synagogues and in the streets, that they may have glory from men. Assuredly, I say to you, they have their reward. But when you do a charitable deed, do not let your left hand know what your right hand is doing, that your charitable deed may be in secret; and your Father who sees in secret will Himself reward you openly. **Matthew 6:2-4, NKJV.**

I had to get up early today, so early that the moon was still in the sky, so early that the early birds still had their beaks tucked under their wings, so early that my alarm clock took one look outside and said, "It's too early. Go back to bed." OK, so it didn't really say that, but if the moon is still out when you get up, chances are *somebody* should say it.

I got up early because I was on a mission, a *secret* mission. It's so secret that I can't even tell you what it was, but I can tell you why I did it. You see, I have a friend who's had a rough time the past few months. She lost someone very dear to her, and today is a special occasion that I knew would be hard on her. I'd like to say that I came up with a supercreative idea to comfort her, but that's not what happened.

What happened is that God impressed me to do something nice for her that involved all kinds of sneaking around, strategic planning, and stealth maneuvers. It was awesome! I really had to think on my feet (take it from me, always have a backup plan!) when I hit a glitch in the delivery. God even had a message for her, which I printed out on a tag and put with my special delivery.

I may never find out what she thought about her surprise, but it doesn't matter. What matters is that I carried out my part of the mission. I made the delivery. The rest is up to God.

Has God ever impressed you to do something nice for someone? Did you do it, or did you put it off and later wish you'd done it? When His Spirit speaks to your heart, it's important to listen. You may be the only one able to deliver the message of love God has for that person.

When you act as God's secret agent, remember the operative word is "secret." I didn't tell my friend what I'd done, and she'll never know unless she guesses. That means I won't get a thank-you for my effort, and that's OK. The important thing is that God's message gets through. I'm just the delivery person. My reward will be waiting for me in heaven, and God Himself will give it to me. What could be better than that?

Seek and Find

When you call on me, when you come and pray to me,
I'll listen. When you come looking for me, you'll find me. Yes, when
you get serious about finding me and want it more than anything else,
I'll make sure you won't be disappointed. **Jeremiah 29:12-14, Message.**

Today is my birthday, and if I could have just one wish, it would be to grow even closer to God before my next birthday. Unlike other wishes, I don't have to wonder if mine will come true; it will. God has promised that "when you get serious about finding me and want it more than anything else, I'll make sure you won't be disappointed." Isn't that an awesome promise?

I only wish I'd been serious about finding God much earlier in my life. I thought I was, but I looked in the wrong places. I looked everywhere I could to find out *about* God. I didn't spend a lot of time trying to *know* God Himself. I was interested in what other people had to say about Him, but I wasn't as interested in knowing what He had to say about Himself.

Praying was boring (are we done yet?), and I would rather have read any other book—or the back of a cereal box—than the Bible. I didn't understand it; it was confusing; it was boring. I enjoyed doing things for others, but my works weren't coming from a heart that wanted to please God and do everything I could for Him. I just enjoyed the warm fuzzies I got making people happy. Even Labrador retrievers do that.

What I finally discovered is that in order to know God you have to spend time with Him, real quality time. You have to talk to Him and mean it; you can't just mumble a few phrases and get on with your day. You have to ask Him to talk to you, and then you have to listen to what He says. God talks to us in many ways, but we aren't always listening. One of the ways God talks to us is through the same Bible I used to think was boring. I still don't understand everything in the Bible, but God speaks to me through the parts I do understand, and He teaches me more about Himself and how to live for Him and with Him.

"There is nothing more calculated to strengthen the intellect than the study of the Scriptures. No other book is so potent to elevate the thoughts, to give vigor to the faculties, as the broad, ennobling truths of the Bible. If God's Word were studied as it should be, men would have a breadth of mind, a nobility of character, and a stability of purpose rarely seen in these times" (Ellen G. White, *Steps to Christ*, p. 90).

April 11

Can You Hear Me Now?

And the prayer of faith will save the sick, and the Lord will raise him up. And if he has committed sins, he will be forgiven. **James 5:15, NKJV.**

Have you ever felt that God was speaking to you? I don't mean through your conscience telling you that something you're doing is wrong. I mean an actual answer to prayer; as in you asked God for something in prayer and He answered you through a Bible verse, through something you read, through a person, or through a circumstance. In some way God answered you, and you saw the answer and knew it was from God.

"God speaks to us through His providential workings, and through the influence of His Spirit upon the heart. In our circumstances and surroundings, in the changes daily taking place around us, we may find precious lessons if our hearts are but open to discern them. The psalmist, tracing the work of God's providence, says, 'The earth is full of the goodness of the Lord.' 'Whoso is wise, and will observe these things, even they shall understand the lovingkindness of the Lord.' Psalm 33:5; 107:43.

"God speaks to us in His Word. Here we have in clearer lines the revelation of His character, of His dealings with men, and the great work of redemption" (Ellen G. White, *Steps to Christ*, p. 87).

I've had that experience a lot lately. In fact, it's happened so often that I've started to keep a notebook with my prayer requests and God's answers. Sometimes there is just one answer, but often there are more than one. God will impress me with a verse, but also someone will speak to me, or I'll read something else that supports God's answer in another way, or I'll hear something on the radio. I write down all the answers.

Last week a young friend of mine had a snowboarding accident and tore his spleen. It's a very serious injury and often results in surgery to remove the spleen. As I prayed for him, God impressed me to pray that he wouldn't lose his spleen, even though I didn't think that was even an option. As I prayed, God gave me today's verse. I believed God was saying that He was going to heal my friend and that he wouldn't need to have his spleen removed. And you know what? He didn't! The doctors decided to wait, and he got better so they didn't operate.

When you pray, one of the most important things you can do is to wait for an answer. Don't just ask for something and then rush off. Take the time to listen for God's answer. And be sure to thank Him for hearing your prayer and being involved in your life.

103

I Geek God

Attention, Israel! God, our God! God the one and only!
Love God, your God, with your whole heart: love him with all that's in you,
love him with all you've got! **Deuteronomy 6:4, 5, Message.**

According to a public awareness campaign for libraries, the word "geek" is a verb. It means: (1) to love, to enjoy, to celebrate, to have an intense passion for; (2) to express interest in; (3) to possess a large amount of knowledge in; and (4) to promote. This campaign, Geek the Library, gets people interested in their library by showing that no matter what you "geek," you can find out more about it at the library. Since the campaign was started, hundreds of libraries have participated.

There is even a Web site where you can go and share what you geek. For example, Becki geeks origami: "Folding paper into art forces you to slow down, breathe deeply, create, and solve. It's the ultimate therapy." Isabel geeks math: "I always get [A's] in it, plus it's fun!" Millie geeks physics: "I love physics. I started liking it when I was really young, about 8-9 years old, and I never stopped trying to learn new things." And Obuchi geeks gum: "I love gum and the library. I can check out all the books that I want for free."

I geek a lot of things, but I geek God most of all. Every day I learn something new about God, something I couldn't even have dreamed about the day before. When I read the Bible, God talks to me through what I'm reading. When I ask Him for help with a problem, He shows me a new way to solve it. He leads me to people I can help, and sometimes He gives me messages of encouragement for them.

God wants to be involved in every area of our lives. He wants to be the one to give us everything we need. We don't need to go begging with our hands out to other human beings when we have a God who is longing to supply our every need. "Do not depend upon human aid. Look beyond human beings to the One appointed by God to bear our griefs, to carry our sorrows, and to supply our necessities. Taking God at His word, make a beginning wherever you find work to do, and move forward with unfaltering faith. It is faith in Christ's presence that gives strength and steadfastness. Work with unselfish interest, with painstaking effort, with persevering energy" (Ellen G. White, *The Ministry of Healing*, p. 153).

No matter how much we geek God, He geeks us even more. There is nothing that is for our good that God wouldn't give us or do for us. Ask Him for what you need today.

Unplugged

*So the Lord spoke to Moses face to face,
as a man speaks to his friend.* **Exodus 33:11, NKJV.**

Jake Reilly, 24, decided to do something bold. Something unheard-of. Something crazy. He decided to unplug from all his social media; no Facebook, Twitter, LinkedIn, cell phone, e-mail, or texting for *90 days*. Three whole months without so much as a tweet or a status update. Jake was hanging out with a bunch of his friends when he realized that every single one of them was either on their laptop or phone. They weren't actually talking to *one another*. He decided he wanted to be with people in real time again.

At first it was frustrating. Jake was unplugged, but the rest of the world kept right on tweeting and IMing without him. Some of his friends dropped him because they couldn't reach him digitally any more, but some of his relationships got even better because he was able to spend time with people face to face.

There's no doubt about it: technology is here to stay. Not only that, but it will get better and better as people find new ways to connect with one another digitally. But there's something to be said for spending one-on-one time with people too.

Can you imagine, for example, if Jesus had come to earth today instead of 2,000 years ago? Do you think He'd have His whole ministry online at www.Jesus.com? Would He "friend" His followers, text the disciples, and Skype His sermons? It might be fun to think of Jesus being tech savvy, but Jesus was all about the people 2,000 years ago, and He'd be all about the people today. He'd want to meet them face to face. He'd want to talk to them in real time. He'd want to be there to lend a helping hand, offer a shoulder to cry on, or just beam a thousand-watt smile to brighten their day.

There's nothing wrong with technology. Like any other useful thing, there's a time to use it and a time to turn it off. But don't neglect your human connections. Spend more time with actual people and living your real life than you do online with virtual friends.

Jake unplugged for 90 days. That's a long time in today's digital world. Try to unplug yourself from all your technology for seven days. Or if that seems like a lot, try one day, just 24 hours. (Hint: Sabbath would be a convenient 24-hour time frame to try it out.)

April 14

Attacked!

*For we are not fighting against flesh-and-blood enemies,
but against evil rulers and authorities of the unseen world,
against mighty powers in this dark world, and against evil spirits
in the heavenly places.* **Ephesians 6:12, NLT.**

You're walking along, minding your own business, when suddenly from out of nowhere you're attacked! Your assailant jabs an elbow in your ribs, knocking the wind out of you. You grunt and stagger, gasping for breath. His fist slams into your face, blinding you. You can feel his knuckles crushing the bone of your temple. The pain sends stars shooting across your field of vision. His knee slamming into your stomach finishes you, and you crumple to your knees.

Stop. Rewind. You're walking along, minding your own business, when suddenly from out of nowhere you're attacked! Your assailant tries to jab an elbow into your ribs, but you whip out a Taser and stun him. He falls to the ground twitching and incapacitated. You calmly walk on and go about your business.

Which of these two scenarios would you rather experience? You may not realize it, but you face this situation every morning the moment you open your eyes. You may not realize it because the assailant you face is crafty and experienced. He sneaks up on you and before you realize it, *bam!* You've been attacked. Not with fists but with temptations.

You lie about where you were or what you were doing. You cheat on a test, just a little bit. You kill someone's character with gossip. With each epic fail, you are a little more wounded until by the end of the day you're a bleeding, broken mess.

The assailants you'll face can come from anywhere at any time; in order to defeat them you must be prepared. Satan isn't going to give you a warning when he's about to attack. You have to be smart. You wouldn't walk in a dangerous neighborhood at night, because you'd be risking an attack. In the same way, you shouldn't walk in dangerous spiritual neighborhoods, either; avoid them.

Be aware of your surroundings all the time. Keep your guard up. And don't get cocky; just as soon as you think you're untouchable, Satan will fiercely attack you. Arm yourself with prayer, Scripture, and buddies who will support you spiritually. Stay anchored in God so Satan won't be able to touch you.

Jump Already

So Jesus answered and said to them, "Have faith in God." **Mark 11:22, NKJV.**

Tell me: If you can't see something, does that mean it doesn't exist? Take God, for instance. You can't see Him. Does He exist?

There's a joke about a teacher who was instructing her young students about evolution. She asked a little boy if he could see the sky, grass, and trees. Each time he said he could. Then she asked him if he could see God. When he admitted that he couldn't see God, the teacher made her point: "You see, class? We can't see God because He isn't there. He doesn't exist."

A little girl piped up and asked the boy if he could see the sky, grass, and trees. He said that he could see them. Then the little girl asked if he could see the teacher. Yes. The teacher's brain? No. "Then, according to what we learned," the little girl said, "she doesn't have one."

Believing in something you can't see takes faith. You can't see air, yet you would die without it. Imagine that you are going skydiving. The instructor helps you strap on your parachute. He checks to be sure all your equipment is in order. He opens the hatch of the plane. You look down. It's a *long* way down. He asks, "Do you believe your parachute will open when you pull the cord?" You say, "Absolutely!" He asks, "Will you sign a paper saying you believe your parachute will open?" You say, "Absolutely!" He asks, "Will you jump and see if your parachute will open?"

You can *say* you believe something all you want to. You can even sign a legal document acknowledging that you believe something. But until you actually put your trust in it, all you have are words. They're nice. They're comforting. But they're just words. In order to exercise faith, you've got to take it around the block a few times. You've got to use it, just like a muscle. That's how it grows.

Every time you go to God with a problem or a concern *and* you trust Him to help you, that's exercising faith. When He answers you and you act on that answer, that's faith. The more you use your faith, the stronger it will get. Because you believe Him, you won't wonder if God will do something He said He would. That's faith.

Exercise your faith this week. Bring your prayer requests to God, listen for His answer, and then act on it. Be persistent. Don't stop asking until you get an answer.

A Song in the Night

They were severely beaten, and then they were thrown into prison.
The jailer was ordered to make sure they didn't escape. So the jailer
put them into the inner dungeon and clamped their feet in the stocks.
Around midnight Paul and Silas were praying and singing hymns to God,
and the other prisoners were listening. **Acts 16:23-25, NLT.**

'm sure there are plenty of times you feel like singing. On a beautiful spring day, or on the first day of vacation, or when you're driving in the car with the windows down, the radio cranked up, and the wind blowing through your hair. Maybe you like to sing in the shower. Or solo—so low no one can hear you!

But when you're hurting? When you've just been beaten and thrown into prison? When the jailer has clamped your feet in stocks so you can't lie down, you can't stand up, you can only sit there and feel miserable, scared, and exhausted? That does not strike me as an ideal time to burst into song. It seems more like an awesome time to start howling with misery.

Paul and Silas, however, did exactly that. The Bible says they were praying and singing hymns to God. Do you know how amazing that is? First of all, they were singing. In the dark. In prison. After a beating. All chained up. Wow. Only someone who is 100 percent committed to God could do something like that.

On top of that, it was midnight, which means it was dark. Even if they'd had hymnals, and they didn't, they couldn't have seen them, so that means they were singing songs they knew by heart. The songs they had back then were the Psalms, which means they had memorized them.

My friend Chris says, "One of the greatest things about music is its ability to carry to our hearts and minds great thoughts about God. This makes it a powerful weapon against fear in the night. When I'm all alone, I can still sing—as long as the song itself has a place in my heart and mind already. And how does it get in my heart and mind? Repetition. We should sing great songs often so they can come to mind easily. So that when the darkness comes . . . the truths about God found in the songs in your heart, and the presence of the One it describes, are there to settle you; . . . the music is merely a carrier."

Try memorizing spiritually uplifting songs that will bring you into God's presence the next time you're hurting—in the night or at any time.

You, Me, and Notorious Bandits

God's grace has saved you because of your faith in Christ.
Your salvation doesn't come from anything you do. It is God's gift.
It is not based on anything you have done. No one can brag
about earning it. **Ephesians 2:8, 9, NIrV.**

"You there," a rough voice barks. The sound of metal grating on metal makes the rats scurry back to their holes. Bearded men with gaunt faces and hollow, haunted eyes brace themselves warily against the rough stone of the prison cells. "You!" the guard spits out again. "The one they call Barabbas. Move along."

A disbelieving man staggers to his feet. "Me? Are they going to kill me already then?" He swaggers to the doorway so no one will know how scared he is at the prospect of dying, but the fear shows in his eyes.

"Kill you? Nah, they're letting you go."

Barabbas stops abruptly. "Letting me go? Me? A notorious bandit? They're letting me go? Why?"

The guard shrugs. "A man has taken your place. They're going to kill him instead."

"Is he guilty?" Barabbas asks.

"Innocent. Completely innocent."

"But they can't do that," Barabbas gasps. "I deserve my punishment. I know, let me wash dishes in Pilate's kitchen for a few years. Or I could muck out stalls in the stables. Or maybe money. I could pay for my freedom. Or I could donate a kidney—does anyone need a kidney?"

"Get out of here," the guard roars. "I said you were free. No strings attached. Now go; live like a free man."

OK, so maybe the Bible story didn't happen exactly like that. But the story of Barabbas has an important point to make. We are all like Barabbas. Maybe not murderers, thieves, or notorious bandits, but we have all committed crimes of one sort or another that make it impossible for us to go to heaven on our own. Only because Jesus died in our place can we go free. And like Barabbas, there is nothing we can ever do that will pay that debt; no work of ours will pay for any part of our salvation. It's a free gift; all we need to do is accept it and go live like grateful, free men and women.

April 18

Betrayed

And while He was still speaking, behold, Judas, one of the twelve, with a great multitude with swords and clubs, came from the chief priests and elders of the people. Now His betrayer had given them a sign, saying, "Whomever I kiss, He is the One; seize Him." Immediately he went up to Jesus and said, "Greetings, Rabbi!" and kissed Him. **Matthew 26:47-49, NKJV.**

Have you ever been betrayed? Maybe your best friend stole your boyfriend, or your friends all went off to have a fun time without you and you found out later, or a parent left your family, or someone close to you committed suicide. There are a lot of ways people can betray you. Sometimes they do it on purpose, and sometimes they are so focused on themselves they aren't even thinking about you. Either way, betrayal hurts.

Judas betrayed Jesus. He had what he thought were good intentions; he wanted to see Jesus take over as earthly king and defeat the horrible Romans. But his intentions were selfish too. He didn't really care what Jesus was actually on earth to accomplish. He just wanted Jesus to do what he—Judas—thought He ought to do.

Can you imagine how Jesus must have felt when Judas betrayed Him? Judas was one of the inner twelve, the people closest to Jesus and His ministry. Judas wasn't someone who watched Jesus from far off and got the wrong idea. He was someone who lived, worked, ate, and walked with Jesus every day. But he didn't want Jesus to change his heart; he wanted to fit Jesus into his own agenda.

Does that sound familiar?

How many times do we try to fit God into a box that *we* made? God doesn't care about *these* people, God doesn't do *those* things, God doesn't work like *that*, God can't be in *that* situation. Writer Anne Lamott said, "You can safely assume that you've created God in your own image when it turns out that God hates all the same people you do."

When we try to make God the way we want Him instead of becoming more and more like God, we turn God into a version of ourselves. It's the ultimate betrayal, and it hurts God as much as Judas' kiss.

Try This: Make a list of things you think God can't do. Then find scriptures to support your ideas about God. Are they correct? Or have you made God into an image you made up yourself? Ask God to give you a correct picture of Himself.

Write Now

Now go and write down these words. Write them in a book.
They will stand until the end of time as a witness. **Isaiah 30:8, NLT.**

Most children are taught to read and write in the first or second grade. Some kids are even bilingual, speaking more than one language. And IDK, but I think most kids over the age of 6 speak at least some form of "texting." You probably take all that reading and writing for granted. In fact, you probably wish you didn't have to read and write as much as you do.

Things were different for a Cherokee silversmith named Sequoyah. The Cherokees knew about writing. They saw the Whites do it, but it mystified them. They figured it had to be some sort of witchcraft. Still, Sequoyah wasn't so sure. He began to understand that writing represented spoken words.

He started working to create symbols to represent words in the Cherokee language. First he tried to create a symbol for every word, but there were too many. Next he concentrated on listening for the syllables and found there were 85 unique sounds that were combined to form different words. When he had come up with symbols for each of the sounds—called the Cherokee Syllabary—he taught them to his daughter, A-Yo-Ka.

Unfortunately Sequoyah's invention was greeted with suspicion, and he and his daughter were charged with witchcraft. They were brought before their town chief, George Lowery, for a "sorcery trial." Lowery invited a group of warriors to be judges. The warriors separated Sequoyah and his daughter and had them write messages to each other until they were finally convinced that the symbols on the paper were a method of talking.

The warriors were so impressed with writing that they asked Sequoyah to teach them the skill. These guys were so fierce that because they accepted writing and learned to read and write, literacy spread like wildfire throughout the Cherokee nation. The best part was that because of the syllabary, the Bible and hymnals could be translated into Cherokee.

Try reading your Bible upside down—the words look like gobbledygook, don't they? Imagine if you couldn't read them. How would you feel? Now be honest and answer this question: How often do you read your Bible? Do you appreciate the fact that you have a Bible to read and the ability to read it? Thank God for that ability.

April 20

Who Are You Really?

Laugh with your happy friends when they're happy; share tears when they're down. Get along with each other; don't be stuck-up. Make friends with nobodies; don't be the great somebody. **Romans 12:14-16, Message.**

I can still remember the phone call. It came early in the morning, and I didn't get to the phone in time. I replayed the message and stared at the machine in horror and disbelief. One of my students had been in a terrible car accident. She'd been taken to the hospital and had died. I stood there shouting at the phone, "No, no, no!"

What made it all worse was that there was no one there to share my pain. It was a full week before the funeral, a full week of suffering alone. When I got to the funeral, one of her classmates, Eric, met me as I walked toward the crowd gathered near the church and folded me in a bear hug, letting me cry all over his shirt. It was one of the kindest things anyone has ever done for me. Finally I was able to have my grief validated by someone who felt it too.

We've all gone through sad times. Some of them were sadder than others. Losing your dog (or your hamster, or your cat, or your parakeet) isn't as life-altering as losing a parent, grandparent, or sibling, but it still hurts. It can be very tempting to try to stuff that grief down inside somewhere, or drown it, or ignore it, or pretend nothing is wrong, but that's the worst thing you can do. Grief must be felt and expressed. Cry, vent, wail; let it out.

If it's a friend who hurts, the best—but hardest—thing you can do for them is to be strong enough to let them experience their own feelings of loss, no matter how uncomfortable it makes you feel. Don't try to talk them out of their grief. Eventually there will be a time to talk, usually when grief isn't so fresh. Time will help you heal. God will help you heal too, if you let Him.

As hard as it was to lose Chris, I know that I'll see her again someday. Just before she died, she completed a school assignment answering the question "Who am I?"

"Who am I really?" she wrote. "Well, most important, I am a Christian, a believer in Jesus Christ as my Savior. That one quality affects every other aspect of who I am; it is my one defining characteristic."

Grief is always a surprise visitor. We never expect it to arrive until suddenly it's there. There's only one way to get ready for it, and that's to stay as close to God as possible.

Letter to X

Wine is a mocker and beer a brawler; whoever is led astray by them is not wise. **Proverbs 20:1, NIV.**

Dear X,

I was so disappointed to hear you've been getting drunk with your friends. I know it may seem fun and exciting now. Maybe it makes you feel grown-up. Or maybe it helps you forget your problems. Maybe you like the way it makes you feel before the headaches and puking start. But I've been down the road you're on, and I can tell you that it's worse than a dead end.

Right now you decide when you want to drink. You set it up with your friends. You get the alcohol from someone who is old enough to buy it. You're in control. But what you may not realize is drinking changes your brain. It makes new pathways for coping with problems.

Right now when you have a problem you may get mad, go for a run to blow off steam, or talk it out with someone. Drinking will change that; the alcohol will begin to control you. Imagine that every time you get upset, or have a bad day, or disagree with someone, the first thing you want to do is have a drink to make the feeling go away. Every time. For the rest of your life. It never goes away.

It's like having an itch you can never safely scratch, as if you would lose fingers if you tried to reach it. Even though you may want to drink, hopefully you won't, because eventually it'll lead to worse problems than just cravings. People have lost their families, their jobs, and even their lives because of alcohol. Compared to that, living the rest of your life ignoring cravings every time you experience an emotion you don't want to feel is not so terrible.

But do you really want to live like that? Wouldn't it be better to stop now and avoid the headaches, the puking, the hangovers, the cravings? Wouldn't you rather save your brain for better things, such as curing cancer, or creating a wildly popular app that makes you a gazillion dollars, or even just loving people a whole bunch? Nobody ever did anything worthwhile when they were drunk.

If you're drinking because you have problems and you want to talk, I'm here. So is God. And we both care about you very much.

April 22

Litterbugs

O Lord, how manifold are Your works! In wisdom
You have made them all. The earth is full of Your possessions—
this great and wide sea, in which are innumerable teeming things,
living things both small and great. **Psalm 104:24, 25, NKJV.**

It's hard to imagine what earth looked like before the Fall, and then later the Flood. Nature is beautiful now; it must really have been something when it was brand-spanking new, fresh from the Creator's hand. Everything that God created, from the grandest mountain to the smallest living organism, has the stamp of God on it; nature itself is God's second book telling everyone on earth how awesome and great God is. Paul says, "For ever since the world was created, people have seen the earth and sky. Through everything God made, they can clearly see his invisible qualities—his eternal power and divine nature. So they have no excuse for not knowing God" (Romans 1:20, NLT).

So what I want to know is this: If nature is God's second book, why aren't we more careful with it? Would you appreciate it if someone borrowed one of your books and then wrote all over it, stuck wads of gum between the pages, and trampled it in the dirt? But that's what people do with God's book of nature all the time. Seventy-five percent of people admit they've littered in the past five years. Nine billion tons of litter is dumped in our oceans every year. What does that tell you about how people value the earth God gave us?

It tells me that a whole lot of us don't care. There are a few things you can do to keep God's second book clean so that others can read it. First, don't litter. Find a trash can when you have something to dispose of, or bring it home with you and throw it away there. Second, look around your neighborhood. If it's dirty, get to work and clean it up; we need to take responsibility for our surroundings. Third, help others become aware of littering. Many people just don't think before they toss something out the window of their car or drop it on the street. Use humor if you can, but speak up. If we each do our part, we can keep God's second book open for reading.

Today is Earth Day. Find out what's going on for Earth Day in your community and lend a hand. We should all do our part to keep God's creation beautiful.

Separate

For how then will it be known that Your people and I
have found grace in Your sight, except You go with us? So we shall
be separate, Your people and I, from all the people who are
upon the face of the earth. **Exodus 33:16, NKJV.**

On the way to school in the mornings, my kids and I read a devotional. *I* don't read it, of course; I'm driving. My son reads it to us. And then we go over my daughter's vocabulary words for biology to help her learn them. I don't need to learn biology; I studied it in school. What I've noticed, though, is that because we go over the words every day, I'm learning them right along with her. I'm learning them because I'm *exposed* to them.

That's how it works in life. We learn what we are exposed to. That's how you learned the ABCs, your numbers, and everything else you know right now. It was all around you, people repeated it all the time, and finally it started to sink in and you could recall it on your own.

Over time we become desensitized to what's around us as well—things don't seem strange or different to us, they seem normal. For instance, when I went to public high school there was a lot of swearing. At first I was shocked. I didn't hear that kind of language at home. But after I'd been there awhile, I barely noticed it anymore.

That's why God didn't want the Israelites hanging out with the pagans who lived in the countries around them. He knew they would start picking up pagan habits, thoughts, and ideas. He wanted to protect them for their own good. They weren't supposed to marry the pagans, get involved in their idol worship, or participate in the same activities the pagans did, even though the pagans lived all around them.

How about you? What's going on around you? What are you exposed to all the time? Whom are you hanging out with? All these things will affect you unless God goes with you. Only God can protect you from outside influences that Satan will use to try to change you, erode your standards, and weaken your boundaries. It was God going with Jesus that allowed Him to rub elbows with tax collectors and sinners every day. They spun around Him like satellites, but they couldn't penetrate the shield God placed around Him with His presence. We need that same shield when we go out in the world, separate from all the people on the face of the earth.

April 24

Prophecy App

> Daniel replied, "There are no wise men, enchanters, magicians, or fortune-tellers who can reveal the king's secret. But there is a God in heaven who reveals secrets, and he has shown King Nebuchadnezzar what will happen in the future. Now I will tell you your dream and the visions you saw as you lay on your bed." **Daniel 2:27, 28, NLT.**

King Nebuchadnezzar was having a temper tantrum. He'd had a very vivid, very disturbing dream the night before, and he wanted to know what it meant. What does a king do when he wants to know something that's humanly impossible to know? If he's not a Christian, he calls on all his wise men, enchanters, magicians, and fortunetellers to wave their magic wands and come up with the answer.

But interpreting a dream isn't like doing a card trick. No amount of sleight of hand in the world was going to make the explanation of the king's dream appear. King Nebuchadnezzar was so mad that he ordered all the wise men to be killed. When the commander of the king's guard reached Daniel's house to kill him and his friends, Daniel asked what was going on. As soon as he found out, he immediately asked the king for more time so he could talk to God. Daniel knew something very important: only God could tell him something that is humanly impossible to know.

All four of the friends prayed, but the Bible says that God revealed to Daniel the meaning of the dream. The men were saved, the king had his answer, and God pulled back the curtain and showed us all a glimpse of the future.

Knowing what is going to happen is important. For one thing, it's hard to be tricked if you know what's coming. For another, you can get prepared if you know what to prepare for. God gave us prophesies in the Bible so we wouldn't be in the dark about what will happen as the world comes to an end. As Seventh-day Adventists, we have even more information about how it's all going to turn out through the writings of Ellen White, which can now be found on the Internet at www.whiteestate.org. There's even an app that lets you read them on your digital device. You can also find modern language versions written by my friend Jerry Thomas at www.adventistbookcenter.com.

Deadly Party Trick

Forsake foolishness and live, and go
in the way of understanding. **Proverbs 9:6, NKJV.**

If I gave you a glass of water and said that there was something in it that *could* kill you if you drank it, would you? I mean, it *might not* kill you, right? Would you risk it? Would you chug it down and wait to see what would happen to you? Or would you hand it back to me and say, "No, thanks"?

What if I gave you the same glass of water—it still *might* kill you—and you were with a group of your friends? Would you drink it then? What about if some of them were crazy enough to try it? They tried it, and they didn't die. But you still *could* die if you drank it; would you drink it then? What if they pressured you to drink it? Would you cave in and try it, even if it could kill you? Would it be worth the risk?

How about if I told you that it would make you talk funny for a few seconds, although of course it still *might* kill you. Would you drink it then? Would that make it seem interesting enough to try? Your friends are all around saying, "Go on! What are you, some kind of baby?" Should you do it? You *might* die . . .

Fourteen-year-old Ashley Long probably wasn't too concerned about dying, or even about trying something that could kill her. She was already in the wrong place. She told her parents she was going to sleep over at a friend's house, but they moved on to a party in a condo where there was alcohol and pot. The kids were all taking turns inhaling helium from a tank to make their voices sound funny. When it was Ashley's turn, she probably didn't think twice; her system was already numb from the alcohol. She inhaled and died shortly afterward at the hospital.

Inhaling helium is an old party trick. It makes your voice sound funny, like Donald Duck. Dying from it is rare, but it *can* happen. Frank Pegueros, executive director of Drug Abuse Resistance Education (DARE), says, "It's important to remind kids that ingesting any substance—for the sake of getting high or just changing their voices—can be dangerous."

In Ashley's case one bad decision (leaving the sleepover to go to the party) led to another (drinking), which led to another (inhaling helium), which led to her death. It's important to stop and think about where decisions will lead you *before* you make them. The closer you stay to God, the easier it will be to make safe, sane, God-honoring decisions.

117

The Boss of Me

And the Lord our God commanded us to obey
all these decrees and to fear him so he can continue to bless us
and preserve our lives, as he has done to this day. **Deuteronomy 6:24, NLT.**

One thing that happens as you grow up is that you get more responsibility, especially over younger kids. You may be the older one put in charge of the "little kids" at a family, church, or school gathering. You might babysit for your own brothers and sisters, or for the children of families you know.

Once you're put in charge of someone, you figure things out pretty quick. Something you'll probably learn right away is that no one, not even a little kid, likes to be told what to do, even if it will keep them safe. It doesn't matter that you are older and wiser, and that you know it's absolutely not a good idea. Kids still want to try it for themselves. They will plant their little fists on their hips, jut out their chins, glare at you, and say, "You're not the boss of me!"

What they mean is that *you* can't control *them*. They'll do *exactly* what they want. *Nothing* you can say or do will change their mind. And sometimes it can't. If little Johnny decides to lick the metal post of the swing set one frosty January morning to see what will happen and his tongue sticks there, well, at least he will have learned an important lesson about cold and metal objects, hopefully a lesson he will not choose to repeat. Some things we have to learn for ourselves.

God knows this; He gave us free will. We can choose who's the boss of us. We can choose what we will do, who we will follow, and whose advice we will listen to.

Throughout the Bible the Israelites often acted like little children, stubbornly doing what they wanted to do and ignoring God. They basically thumbed their noses at God and said, "You're not the boss of us." They often chose to go their own way and always regretted it.

Like little Johnny with his tongue stuck to the metal pole, they learned their lesson *after* making a mistake. That's why having a relationship with God is so important; He can and will direct us *if* we allow Him to be the boss of us. Having that connection to God, the communication that goes both ways, the humility to take direction, and faith that God knows more than we do and wants what's best for us, will always keep us from making mistakes and getting hurt.

Who will be the boss of *you* today?

Fountain of Knowledge

If any of you lacks wisdom, you should ask God, who gives generously to all without finding fault, and it will be given to you. James 1:5, NIV.

When someone asks me a question and I don't know the answer, I go to the source of all knowledge, aka the Internet. It's amazing what you can learn from the Internet. For instance, my friend shared this helpful information with me that he picked up on Twitter: "Cigarettes are a lot like hamsters, perfectly harmless until you put one in your mouth and light it on fire." I never thought about that before, have you? But it makes perfect sense.

Of course, you can't believe everything you see on the Internet. People who think they are experts post incorrect information. If you don't check it out, you could end up looking foolish when you state that "John Seigenthaler, Sr. was the assistant to Attorney General Robert Kennedy in the early 1960s. For a brief time he was thought to have been directly involved in the assassinations of both John and his brother Bobby. Nothing was ever proven." Mr. Seigenthaler, who really *was* the assistant to Attorney General Robert Kennedy in the early 1960s, was outraged to read this false information about himself in his biography on the Internet. So you can't believe everything you see.

There are also many questions the Internet has no answer to. Only one Person can answer the hard questions, the ones too tough for the Internet. He doesn't hang out online or get e-mail, but you have access to Him 24 hours a day, seven days a week through prayer, and He has promised to give us wisdom if we'll ask for it.

There are two kinds of wisdom: worldly wisdom and divine wisdom. Worldly wisdom is the kind you get from anywhere, from books, tutorials, or your own experience. Worldly wisdom can make men proud, and sometimes it hurts people. Divine wisdom only comes from God. It helps us to be humble and give glory to God because it is from Him.

Wisdom was so important that when God told Solomon he could ask for whatever he wanted, Solomon asked for wisdom. God was pleased that he didn't ask for money, or the death of his enemies, or even a long life. Solomon wasn't selfish; he asked for wisdom so that he could judge God's people fairly. Because Solomon wasn't greedy, God gave him all the things he didn't ask for as well. His wisdom honored and glorified God. Seek God's divine wisdom today.

April 28

Water Walking

But Jesus spoke to them at once. "Don't be afraid," he said. "Take courage. I am here!" Then Peter called to him, "Lord, if it's really you, tell me to come to you, walking on the water." "Yes, come," Jesus said. So Peter went over the side of the boat and walked on the water toward Jesus. But when he saw the strong wind and the waves, he was terrified and began to sink. "Save me, Lord!" he shouted. Jesus immediately reached out and grabbed him. "You have so little faith," Jesus said. "Why did you doubt me?" **Matthew 14:27-31, NLT.**

We were supposed to be meeting a group of friends from our new church. We were joining them for a weekend of camping on a lake in the Adirondacks. We had to cross the lake in our canoe to get to the other side where the camping spot was.

At first it wasn't too bad. We enjoyed canoeing, and we were pretty good at it. But once we came out of the sheltered bay where we'd launched the canoe, we suddenly realized we were in over our heads—literally. The farther we got from shore, the larger the waves were. The rough water tossed the canoe up and slammed it back down. The canoe was loaded with camping supplies, which made it ride lower in the water. It would take only one good, big wave crashing down on us to swamp the canoe and we'd go under. We paddled as fast as we could, praying all the way. Finally we escaped the waves and we were able to hug the shoreline until we reached the safety of the camp.

When we were in the middle of all those waves, and they were small waves compared to what could kick up in a larger lake, there is no way I would have wanted to waltz out of that canoe and try to walk on water, but Peter did. Not only did he leap onto the waves, but he was also busy patting himself on the back as he did it.

"Peter had taken only a step upon the surface of the boiling deep, when he looked back proudly toward his companions to see if they were watching his movements, and admiring the ease with which he trod upon the yielding water.

"In taking his eyes from Jesus, they fell upon the boisterous waves that seemed greedily threatening to swallow him; their roaring filled his ears, his head swam, his heart failed him with fear. . . .

"When he took his eyes from Jesus in order to note the admiration of others, he lost guidance, and doubt and fear seized upon him. So it is in the Christian life; nothing but an eye firmly fixed upon the Savior will enable us to tread the stormy billows of the world" (Ellen G. White, *The Spirit of Prophecy*, vol. 2, pp. 269, 270).

What's Your Word?

And he said, "What is the word that the Lord spoke to you?
Please do not hide it from me. God do so to you, and more also, if you hide
anything from me of all the things that He said to you." **I Samuel 3:17, NKJV.**

My daughter's friend Carly was 12 years old when she lost her mom to cancer. The next year, for his birthday, her grandfather requested that everyone in the family send him a Bible verse that had meaning for them. After asking if the whole Bible could be her "favorite verse," Carly managed to narrow it down to a few that really stuck with her.

She wrote, "My verse for this year is Hebrews 12:1: 'Therefore, since we are surrounded by such a great cloud of witnesses, let us throw off everything that hinders and the sin that so easily entangles, and let us run with perseverance the race marked out for us.' This verse has really come to mean a lot to me, because I realized that I haven't really been doing my part in the Great Commission. So I am trying to look for opportunities that God has most certainly been providing me with. The question is just whether I see them. That is my verse for this year."

Yesterday I thought of Carly and her verse for the year when the host of the radio show I was listening to started talking about her "word from God." She said that God often gave her a word for the year, and throughout the year would give her insight into how that word affected her and would help her grow in that area. She asked if listeners who had the same experience would call in and tell others what word or verse God had put on their hearts.

I wanted to call in and tell her that God had recently given me a life verse: Isaiah 26:3. That wouldn't take into account all the other verses He's given me, though. Like Carly, I could almost name the whole Bible as my favorite verse; so many of them are God's responses to my questions, searching, and prayer requests.

Doesn't it amaze you that God interacts with us constantly? We don't have to wait to hear from Him until we're warming our pew at church each week, or even for our daily prayer time. He talks to us *all the time*. It blows my mind that God's word is interactive, that it's living, that it can and does change our lives.

What about you? What is God's word for you today, or for the year? What is your favorite Bible verse? Why is it your favorite? What does it mean to you?

April 30

Frenemies

But I say to you who hear: Love your enemies,
do good to those who hate you, bless those who curse you,
and pray for those who spitefully use you. **Luke 6:27, 28, NKJV.**

"Frenemy" is the combination of two words: friend and enemy. It may sound like a recent invention, but actually it's been around since 1953. A frenemy is someone who acts like your friend to your face but turns into your enemy behind your back. A frenemy might hang out with you, say nice things about you, invite you places, or stick up for you—that's the friend part. But when you're not around, they'll tear you down, spread rumors about you, or set you up—that's the enemy part.

Even though you can combine the words "friend" and "enemy," it's impossible to *be* both a friend and an enemy. A frenemy is really an enemy. But, of course, the Bible tells us to treat our friends and our enemies exactly the same way!

We love our friends, right? Great, because we should love our enemies, too. We do good things for our friends, and we should do good things for our enemies. We should bless them even if they curse us, and pray for them even if they mistreat us. If that sounds like a lot to swallow, think about how Jesus treats us.

We have all sinned. Technically every one of us should be banned from heaven for all eternity. We don't have one good bone in our bodies. We're all natural born enemies of God. We were lost at birth, and it all went downhill from there. Consider the bad things (sins) you've done in the last week alone. Our rebellion makes us enemies of God.

But that doesn't stop God from loving us and treating us well even while we're sinning. God is generous with His love; He's not stingy. He doesn't dole it out a smidgen at a time; He pours it out, great oceans of it. Since we have so much of God's love, how can we not share it? Even with our enemies? Maybe they do want to hurt us, but God loves us so fiercely, so abundantly, and so joyfully that we have plenty left over to go around. We could love whole armies of enemies just with the love that's left over from what God heaps on our head every day. Why be miserly with it? Give it to friends *and* enemies. Who knows—if you do, the enemy might just drop out of your "frenemy," and you'll be left with a friend.

May 1

Oneness

You were all called to travel on the same road
and in the same direction, so stay together, both outwardly and inwardly.
You have one Master, one faith, one baptism, one God and Father of all,
who rules over all, works through all, and is present in all. Everything you are
and think and do is permeated with Oneness. **Ephesians 4:4-6, Message.**

When you think of the church, how does it make you feel? Does it feel like family, always there to support you? Or does it feel more like a judge and jury, ready to condemn you and your ideas? Or does it seem like a collection of friends who want to hang out with you? Or is it more like a group of people who irritate you with their rules and treat you like a kid? Or is it a combination of all those things?

"Church" may be a collective thing, a big group that is by itself the Seventh-day Adventist Church. But it is also an individual thing, because a group of individuals makes up the church. And individuals are . . . well, individual. Just like sometimes you don't get along with the members of your family, sometimes you won't get along with members of your church family either.

It's not just because you're a teen and you don't think the same way people older than you think; they have their differences with one another, too. The reason people don't always get along, even in the church, is that we aren't all clones, or even robots. We have unique personalities, individual wills, free choice. We all have bad days and problems we're struggling with. Sometimes we take those things out on others. We also have our own ideas about how to do things "correctly," and if your ideas aren't like ours, we will disagree with you.

The bad part of this is that sometimes people, especially teens who want to be valued as individuals with important contributions to the church, allow disagreements with others to drive them from church. This is sad because God wants His church to represent His "oneness" on earth. He wants us to show the world that people do not have to live selfishly and concerned only with their own happiness. God wants His church to be a working model of the Christian life.

The good part is that God hasn't left us stranded down here to figure it out on our own. God is one; His church is one through Him. Because of this, it can't be permanently broken.

How do you feel about your church? Why? Do you need to work with God to change your feelings or ideas about your church so that you can be "one"?

Walk On

For we walk by faith, not by sight. **2 Corinthians 5:7, NKJV.**

D o you like optical illusions? An optical illusion is something that's not real but because of a quirk in human vision *looks* real. For instance, if you stare at a swirling spiral for 20 seconds and then look at your hand, or the wall, it will seem as though your hand, or the wall, starts to bulge. If you don't believe me, you can find this illusion, "motion aftereffects," and other optical illusions at www.at-bristol.org.uk/opticalillusions.html.

On the other hand, a mirage, while also not real in the sense that it is an image of something that doesn't really exist, is an actual phenomenon of atmospheric optics, and because of that, it can be photographed. The mirage of a lake you see when you're stumbling across the desert desperately wishing for water? You can take a picture of that and send it home to your folks. But that lake still won't exist.

We live on earth, a fallen planet, ruled by Satan, prince of demons, who is responsible for all the nonsense we live with every day: poverty, decay, death, destruction, illness, pestilence, disease. We can see this; it's right in front of our eyes. No one, no matter how rich, powerful, successful, or protected, can escape the effects of Satan's sticky fingers in their lives.

No one except Christians.

Unbelievers walk by sight; they believe what they see. Christians have faith in God to supply what they *can't* see. For example, one of my homeschooled students stopped coming to my handbell class recently. When I called to find out why, her mom told me that one of their cars had broken down and the father had taken their only operational vehicle to work. I could have said, "Oh, well. That's too bad. Guess they can't have two vehicles."

But because I'm a believer and I walk by faith, I don't have to believe what I see: an empty driveway and no way to fill it. Instead, I see a parking space God can fill. So I started praying. I also offered to give my student a ride for as long as she needed one, which was about a week ago. Today, when I stopped by to pick her up, she told me that they'd gotten her dad's car to start and she wouldn't need a ride home. Praise God!

Before you take one more step in life, decide right now whether you're going to walk by faith or by sight. Your choice.

Just Do It

Do you not know that your bodies are temples
of the Holy Spirit, who is in you, whom you have received from God?
You are not your own; you were bought at a price. Therefore honor
God with your bodies. I Corinthians 6:19, 20, NIV.

Back in the 1980s the Nike company came out with an ad campaign that was so successful it practically made history. They coined the advertising phrase "Just do it." Their campaign begged people to start exercising for their health, and made exercising look cool and exciting. People wanted to exercise, or at least they wanted to *look* like they *planned* to exercise, so they started buying exercise shoes even if they never used them. Nike is now so popular they have only to show their swoosh symbol and people recognize their brand.

The trouble is that most of the people buying Nikes aren't actually exercising in them, and that's a shame, because a lot of people in this country are getting, well, quite padded, if you know what I mean. The latest figures for obesity show that 17 percent (that's 12.5 *million*) kids age 2-19 are obese. That doesn't even factor in the ones who could just stand to lose some weight. By the time you read this, the figure will most certainly be, uh, bigger. Experts are calling obesity an epidemic in this country.

I'm not so sure about that since epidemics are spread by contagious viruses and not by a lack of exercise and too many potato chips. But one thing I do know: God created us with an intricate, delicate, incredible design meant to be His temple, and we're not taking very good care of that temple. Some things, such as the laws of health, can't be ignored without consequences. If we want to be healthy, we need to eat healthy food and exercise regularly.

Listen to Nike: just do it. Don't wait until you want to eat healthy and exercise; you could be waiting a long time. Instead, make a decision to honor God with your body and keep it clean and fit to be His temple. Find an exercise you like—there are tons to choose from—and find an exercise partner. Look at a few healthy food blogs and get some ideas to clean up your diet. It may not be easy, but it will be totally worth it.

May 4

Clean Enough

"Come now, let's settle this," says the Lord. "Though your sins are like scarlet, I will make them as white as snow. Though they are red like crimson, I will make them as white as wool." **Isaiah 1:18, NLT.**

I never had to do laundry until I went away to academy for a year during high school. My house mother brought me down to the basement, where the washer and dryer were. She handed me the laundry detergent and left. She must have thought I knew what I was doing. I didn't. That's how I ended up turning all my white clothes pink. I learned pretty quickly what the word "colorfast" meant, and I learned to separate my white and colored loads so I wouldn't accidentally dye more clothes.

The one thing I knew my clothes would never do, though, was try to wash themselves before I put them into the washing machine. No one expects to go down to the laundry room and find their clothes jumping out of the basket, knocking over the laundry detergent, and trying to scrub themselves up before being tossed into the washing machine.

Doesn't happen, right? Those clothes can't clean themselves any more than we can clean ourselves from sin. The only difference is the clothes aren't silly enough to try. But sometimes we are.

We feel really bad about things that we've done and think, *God won't be able to forgive me. I'm not good enough. I have to get my life in shape before I can let Him look at it and clean me up.* Then we try to clean up our act. The trouble is we're trying to do it on our own, and on our own we have no more power than one of the shirts in your laundry basket.

God says that though our sins are like scarlet, He'll make them white as snow. *He* will make them as white as snow; not *we* will make them as white as snow. Not even we will *together* make them as white as snow. *He* will do it; *only* He can do it.

Have you ever considered telling the children's story at your church? Here's your chance to volunteer. Bring a laundry basket full of clothes as a prop and demonstrate this illustration for the kids, showing how the clothes can't wash themselves. Tell them how much we can learn from a basket full of clothes if we will remember that nothing we can do will clean us up; we need to turn ourselves over to God for washing.

Revengance

Don't seek revenge or carry a grudge against any of your people.
Love your neighbor as yourself. I am God. **Leviticus 19:18, Message.**

I couldn't believe my ears. Apparently Cinco de Mayo (May 5) is known on the *Wally Show,* a Christian radio show I like to listen to, as Cinco de Betty, since it's the birthday of Betty Rock, one of the regulars on the show. Because Wally picks on Betty all year, he gives her a chance to hurt him on her birthday. She says she looks forward to that day all year long. This year Betty was going to get to tase Wally.

And she did.

They gave her five questions and for each question she answered correctly, she was allowed to add one second of tasing time. Betty ended up with the privilege of tasing Wally for four seconds. On the air. While he screamed and yelped.

Now, I can imagine tasing someone who was attacking me, although I'd probably apologize while I did it. But I can't imagine tasing someone I was friends with. I can't even imagine tasing someone I didn't really like. But Betty couldn't wait.

Of course, on the show it's all done in fun. No one tied Wally up and let Betty tase him; he offered to submit to the tasing (and lots of other punishments). But can you imagine what would happen if we were allowed to hurt people when we felt we'd been wronged? In the musical *The Fiddler on the Roof* a villager says, "An eye for an eye, and a tooth for a tooth!" Tevye replies, "Very good. That way the whole world will be blind and toothless."

It's not our place to take revenge. For one thing, where would it all stop? We could hurt others, and then they could hurt us right back because we had hurt them. There would be no end to the cycle of revenge, because there would be no limit to how many times we could hurt one another. Sometimes we hurt people accidentally, but would they know that? Would they believe it if we told them? Maybe; maybe not. But they might still be hurt enough to want to get back at us.

God calls us to something higher than that. He calls us to love one another and to forgive them when they hurt us. We're to leave revenge to God. He knows what's in our hearts. He knows if we meant to hurt someone or if it was an accident. Only He is capable of judging correctly, and we can always trust His justice.

May 6

Eye Trouble

I have made a covenant with my eyes; why then should
I look upon a young woman? For what is the allotment of God
from above, and the inheritance of the Almighty from on high?
Is it not destruction for the wicked, and disaster for the workers of iniquity?
Does He not see my ways, and count all my steps? **Job 31:1-4, NKJV.**

O*h, be careful, little eyes, what you see; Oh, be careful, little eyes, what you see. There's a Savior up above, and He's looking down in love; Oh, be careful, little eyes, what you see.*

Do you remember that cute song from beginners? You probably didn't think much about it at the time, but now that you're older, do you ever hear the little kids singing it and think, *Whoa, how true?*

Maybe not. But you should. For such a simple song, it packs a whole lot of truth.

Guarding your eyes is hard work—things we shouldn't look at are everywhere. Men and boys have the harder time, because Satan has convinced the world that sex is not a gift from God but an opportunity to make money. Therefore, people in ads, on television, and in magazines are often dressed in provocative clothing. The Internet does not make things any easier. The average age of first exposure to Internet pornography is 11. And the number of 15- to 17-year-olds exposed more than once to hard-core pornography (the most explicit kind) is 80 percent.

Fortunately, God didn't leave us without weapons against viewing evil. If you are having "eye" trouble, try these suggestions:

1. Make a covenant with your eyes, as Job did. Decide you will not look at things you know are bad.

2. Avoid temptation. Don't hang out where you are likely to be tempted, whether it's in the locker room or on the Internet.

3. Ask God for help. When you are tempted, pray immediately that He will give you His strength to resist the devil's snare.

4. Fire scriptural missiles. Jesus always met temptation with Scripture. Memorize scriptures that you can fire at the devil when he tempts you.

5. Confess, don't obsess. If you fall, don't use it as an excuse. Confess your sin, get up, and move on.

6. Find friends who are committed to being pure. You can support and encourage one another.

Would Your Majesty Like Fries With That?

The Word became flesh and blood, and moved into the neighborhood. We saw the glory with our own eyes, the one-of-a-kind glory, like Father, like Son, generous inside and out, true from start to finish. John 1:14, Message.

There are some things royalty just doesn't do. If they are traveling somewhere, they don't ride the subway; they take a limo. If they are dining, they don't get fast food from the take-out window; they eat a sit-down dinner at a fancy restaurant, and the chef sweats bullets hoping they like the food. They don't do much visiting; they expect approved visitors to come see them—by appointment. And they definitely don't "hang out"; they "attend" functions.

The paparazzi like to follow them around and report on every little detail of their lives: what they're wearing, where they're going, whom they're with, when they're going somewhere else, why they are out and about. Pictures are taken and distributed everywhere that show them in every possible situation and pose. It must be exhausting to be royalty, don't you think?

Jesus was probably glad the paparazzi hadn't been invented yet when He was on earth. Can you imagine some of the headlines? "King of Heaven Born in Manger While Royal Family on Trip." Or "Young Prince of Peace Lost in Jerusalem, Found in Temple." Or "King of the Jews Dies Traitor's Death on Calvary." They would have hounded His every move.

But then, even though Jesus is royalty, He didn't act as though He had special privileges when He was here. We wouldn't expect Prince William or Prince Harry, England's young princes, to walk around on foot if they were visiting our country, but Jesus walked everywhere He went. You could never say the princes didn't have a place to lay their heads; people would outdo one another to offer them a room if they needed it, maybe even put an entire house at their disposal. They would never go hungry; Jesus relied on the kindness of little boys who shared their lunches and dinner invitations from people no one else wanted to talk to.

When Jesus lived on earth, He walked and talked and rubbed shoulders with the poorest of the poor. He didn't expect any special treatment, even though He deserved it. Although very few people realized who He was, no one who knew Him could ever doubt who He really was.

So . . . how do you treat Jesus?

May 8

Still Small Voice

Samuel got up and went to Eli and said, "Here I am; you called me."
Then Eli realized that the Lord was calling the boy. So Eli told Samuel,
"Go and lie down, and if he calls you, say, 'Speak, Lord, for your servant
is listening.'" So Samuel went and lay down in his place. The Lord came and
stood there, calling as at the other times, "Samuel! Samuel!" Then Samuel
said, "Speak, for your servant is listening." I Samuel 3:8-10, NIV.

Yáuco Manbuzee* had a busy day of homework deadlines and class projects that had to be finished the next day by noon, but had no idea how to finish them. He hadn't been irresponsible, as some of his other classmates had. He came home every day after school and worked hard to complete what his parents and teachers expected him to do.

As nighttime approached, he prepared his humble cot in his corner of the family's dirt floor hut. His father prayed with the family, and everyone went to bed. Yáuco tossed and turned and tried to sleep, but couldn't; he was worried about school. One hour, two hours, and then three hours passed, and still no sleep.

Finally in frustration he began to pray. As he did he remembered the story of young Samuel in the Bible. He stopped praying and silently breathed, "Speak to me, Lord; I'm listening to You." As Yáuco listened for the Lord to speak to him, he drifted off to sleep. When he woke up, his mind was full of ideas about how to finish his homework assignments and class projects, and he was able to complete them on time.

Your sleepless nights may be a way the Lord is trying to spend some special quiet time with you. Sometimes life gets so busy or confusing that we have trouble hearing God when He speaks to us. Your mind may race with ideas and thoughts that you have trouble making sense of. At night they may keep you awake, busy thinking and worrying.

When you're overwhelmed, it's hard to take the time to find a quiet spot and spend some time asking God for help, but it's important. The Bible says that God speaks with a "still small voice" (1 Kings 19:12). Find a quiet place where you can listen, and then sleep peacefully.

---

* Names have been changed.
Submitted by Julián Anderson-Martín, M.A., L.L.P.C.

The Big Test

All of us, like sheep, have strayed away. We have left God's paths to follow our own. Yet the Lord laid on him the sins of us all. **Isaiah 53:6, NLT.**

Have you ever faced a big test? I mean a really, really big test. A whopper of a test. Did you know about the test ahead of time? Would it have made a difference? Would you have studied harder? What if the teacher told you that if you made one mistake, even just a spelling or grammar mistake, you'd fail? Oh, and you have to write your answers backward and upside down and still not make a mistake.

Before you took that test, how do you suppose you'd feel? You certainly wouldn't be calm and happy. No doubt you'd be a nervous, scared, shaking wreck. I mean, who could pass with those rules? Everyone makes grammar mistakes; no one could possibly pass that test.

As Christians, we know there's a big test coming; a gigantic, humdinger of a test. It's the kind of test that will decide our future and where we'll spend it. We call it the judgment.

Unlike a pop quiz, this test has been announced ahead of time. But we can't study for it. In fact, we can't do much of anything at all to get ready for it. Oh, and did I mention that only one person has ever (ever!) passed the test? What are the odds that we'll pass? They aren't even as good as a million to one. They aren't even as good as a gazillion to one! There is no chance whatsoever that we can pass this test.

But do you know what? The one person who did pass the test has volunteered to take it in our place. What a relief! Next to our name in the gradebook will be a big fat A+. One hundred percent. A perfect score.

The word "judgment," like the word "test," is scary. We've got this idea that God is up in heaven like a big mean judge just itching to pass sentence on us, and only because of the goodness of Jesus does He put up with us at all. But that's not true. God loves us just as much as Jesus does. But He's actually not going to be our judge. The Bible says: "In addition, the Father judges no one. Instead, he has given the Son absolute authority to judge" (John 5:22, NLT).

Isn't that awesome news? Jesus, who loves us and died to save us, is our judge. That's like having your best friend grading your test! We don't need to be afraid or nervous. We just need to trust our Best Friend to take the test for us. We have to accept His test results as our own.

131

May 10

Mama Mia

The father of godly children has cause for joy. What a pleasure to have children who are wise. So give your father and mother joy! May she who gave you birth be happy. **Proverbs 23:24, 25, NLT.**

My grandmother was not always the easiest person to get along with. She could slice a brick with her tongue sometimes. But let her start talking about her kids or her grandkids and you'd see her entire face light up. There wasn't much she enjoyed more than bragging on our accomplishments; just the fact that we were breathing was enough to make her proud.

After I had kids of my own, I understood why she was so proud of us for doing nothing more than existing. It's natural for a parent to be proud of their children. As children you are literally part of your parents. Your parents can see themselves in you. They have a stake in you and a claim on you for the rest of your life. Naturally they want you to do wonderful things, become wonderful people, and live amazing lives, because in a way, as your parents, they will too.

Making your parents proud isn't always easy. What they want you to do and what you want to do might not be the same thing. In fact, their idea of life and how to live it might be nothing like yours. That will cause some tension for sure. But one way you can always make your parents proud is by making wise choices.

At this time in your life you are moving toward adulthood and gaining independence. It can be very tempting to rely on your own ideas or on your friends' ideas and advice rather than your parents'. However, your parents have a lot of experience and really do want you to be a happy, well-adjusted individual. You can save yourself a lot of unnecessary heartache by asking your parents for advice.

Just because you ask for advice doesn't mean that you have to take it. But you may find that you have more options just by being open to listening to your parents' advice. Who knows? They may have ideas you hadn't even thought of yet. One thing is for sure, though: If you ask your parents for advice, they'll respect you. And your openness to their ideas and opinions might even make your life better.

There's no secret to making your parents happy and proud; they already are. They just want to continue to have a good relationship with you. Isn't that what you want too?

Transformers

Whenever, though, they turn to face God as Moses did,
God removes the veil and there they are—face-to-face!
They suddenly recognize that God is a living, personal presence,
not a piece of chiseled stone. And when God is personally present,
a living Spirit, that old, constricting legislation is recognized as obsolete.
We're free of it! All of us! Nothing between us and God, our faces shining
with the brightness of his face. And so we are transfigured much like the
Messiah, our lives gradually becoming brighter and more beautiful as God
enters our lives and we become like him. **2 Corinthians 3:16-18, Message.**

D o you want to know a secret? What you see affects what you do as well as who you become. There's a saying that the eyes are the windows to the soul. Apparently whatever your eyes see goes straight in and starts making changes. For example, a study found that when kids were exposed to pro-tobacco ads, movies, and media, they were more than twice as likely to start smoking themselves. Just from *seeing* people smoke! They found that kids who didn't see people smoking in movies were less likely to start smoking themselves.

What you see gives you ideas, and your mind starts playing with those ideas. Eventually the ideas become part of who you are and what you believe about yourself. You are like the little girl who saw a statue that changed her life.

"A beautiful statue once stood in the marketplace of an Italian city. It was the statue of a Greek slave girl. It represented the slave as tidy and well dressed. A ragged, unkempt little street child, coming across the statue in her play one day, stopped and gazed at it in admiration. She was captivated by it. She gazed long and lovingly. Moved by a sudden impulse, she went home and washed her face and combed her hair. Another day she stopped again before the statue and admired it, and got a new idea. Next day her tattered clothes were washed and mended. Each time she looked at the statue she found something in its beauties to admire and copy, until she was a transformed child. By beholding we become changed" (*Bible Readings for the Home Circle,* p. 98).

We can use this power for good or for evil. If we let evil things into our minds, guess what will happen to us? But if we keep our minds on God, we will become more and more like Him. The only way to do that is by spending time with God, getting to know Him personally. When we see Him, in all His awesome power and glory, we will be changed forever.

May 12

The God Channel

Watch therefore, and pray always that you
may be counted worthy to escape all these things that will
come to pass, and to stand before the Son of Man. **Luke 21:36, NKJV.**

On April 17, 1917, the president of the United States ordered nearly all private radio stations to stop broadcasting. In fact, one city manager announced that it was treason to have operational radio equipment. Why? Because the United States had just entered into World War I. All radio was reserved for the war effort.

This was a terrible blow for amateur radio operators. Radio was just beginning to be developed, and hobby radio operators all anxiously awaited each new issue of *The Electrical Experimenter* magazine so they could read about all the newest developments and test them out on their own radio sets.

You could probably care less about radio; it's so last century. But what if the government shut down the Internet so they could use it for government transmissions and research? Think about radio silence. This was at a time when there was no Internet. There wasn't even television, if you can believe that. All that quiet would be practically deafening. With no good way to get information in from outside, how would you know what was going on? Someone could tell you that Germany had won the war, and how would you know it wasn't true?

But what if you had a secret radio signal? You could contact the outside to give them news and find out what was happening in the world.

In a way, that's exactly what's going on here every day. Planet Earth is at war, and Satan has shut down every means of communication he can so we won't get any news from heaven. He makes it hard for us to send communication too by distracting us and redirecting us. He knows we have a secret signal, but he can't hijack it because he can't read our minds. Ellen White says, "The adversary of souls is not permitted to read the thoughts of men" (*Selected Messages,* book 1, p. 122).

Having a secret radio signal to God is like having your very own God channel. You can broadcast to God, and He can broadcast back to you. I can tell I'm tuned in to the God channel when I wake up in the middle of the night with Scripture going through my head, or a hymn, or a prayer before my mind is even in gear. You can tune in to the God channel too. Keep it open and running 24/7 and watch your back. Our enemy is on the prowl.

The Edge of the Cliff

My child, don't lose sight of common sense and discernment.
Hang on to them, for they will refresh your soul.
They are like jewels on a necklace. They keep you safe on
your way, and your feet will not stumble. **Proverbs 3:21-23, NLT.**

Henry and Larry decided to go walking one day. The path they took brought them far up into the mountains. As they climbed higher and higher above the tree line, the view became spectacular. The air was perfectly clear, and they could see for miles. At last the path disappeared. To the left was a steep cliff. Henry looked at the cliff and decided he didn't want to get too close, so he moved farther away from it and continued hiking. "There's no way I want to fall off the edge of that cliff," Henry told Larry.

But Larry wanted to see how close he could get to the edge of the cliff. He moved closer and closer until he had to be very careful where he placed his feet. One wrong move, and he would plummet over the edge. "You don't know what you're missing," Larry hollered over to Henry. "The view is amazing."

Suddenly one of Larry's feet slipped, and his heart leaped into his throat. *That was close*, he thought. *I almost went over the side that time.* Just then a fierce wind kicked up and raced across the unprotected top of the mountain. Henry staggered before recovering himself, but Larry, with a yelp of fear, went right over the side of the cliff.

Have you ever asked yourself if you could get away with something? Maybe it was something that wasn't really *bad*, just not so great. Maybe it wasn't so much that you shouldn't do it, but that there were other, better things you could do instead. This is what they call a "slippery slope."

We need to stop and think about where our hearts are whenever we start asking ourselves "Is this really so bad?" The point isn't to get as close to the cliff as we can without falling off; the point is to walk safely away from it. The moral of the story about Larry and Henry is: When you're walking on the edge of the cliff, it doesn't take much effort to fall off; but if you're walking a mile from the cliff, it's rather difficult to fall over the side.

Try This: Replace the question "Is this really so bad/wrong?" with "What is the very *best* thing I can do?" The answer will make all the difference.

The Gimp Squad

For this very reason, make every effort to add to your faith goodness;
and to goodness, knowledge; and to knowledge, self-control;
and to self-control, perseverance; and to perseverance, godliness;
and to godliness, mutual affection; and to mutual affection, love.
For if you possess these qualities in increasing measure,
they will keep you from being ineffective and unproductive
in your knowledge of our Lord Jesus Christ. **2 Peter 1:5-8, NIV.**

Every team has a Gimp Squad. These are the unfortunate folks on the injured and disabled list. They often still come to games to lend their support. They sit on the sidelines and cheer, but they can't participate in the game, because they're injured. They may resent the fact that another player is taking their place while they're forced to rest and heal. Or they might look at their injury as a good excuse to be lazy for a while.

Christians have a Gimp Squad too. Sometimes people end up on the Gimp Squad because they got stabbed by someone's sharp tongue. They bandage up the wound, but they're still out of the game. Even after it heals they're often too frightened to join the team again. Other people imagine they have all kinds of problems that keep them from playing. There's nothing really wrong with them, but they believe it so strongly that they can't participate.

There are many ways to end up on the Gimp Squad. Some of them are legitimate, and some are just excuses, but there is no reason for any of us to be injured or disabled. Everything we need for our healing, whether it's real or only in our heads, we can get from Jesus if we just ask. Ellen White says, "Let us no longer talk of our inefficiency and lack of power. Forgetting the things that are behind, let us press forward in the heavenward way. Let us neglect no opportunity that, if improved, will make us more useful in God's service. Then like threads of gold, holiness will run through our lives, and the angels, beholding our consecration, will repeat the promise, 'I will make a man more precious than fine gold; even a man than the golden wedge of Ophir.' All heaven rejoices when weak, faulty human beings give themselves to Jesus, to live His life" (*Messages to Young People*, p. 108).

You can make all of heaven rejoice today by giving all your weaknesses, all your injuries, all your faults, to Jesus. Instead of hobbling around today under your own steam, why don't you try living Jesus' powerful life and score a touchdown for the team?

Good Deed Doers

Then a despised Samaritan came along, and when he saw the man,
he felt compassion for him. Going over to him, the Samaritan soothed
his wounds with olive oil and wine and bandaged them. Then he put the man
on his own donkey and took him to an inn, where he took care of him.
The next day he handed the innkeeper two silver coins, telling him,
"Take care of this man. If his bill runs higher than this,
I'll pay you the next time I'm here." **Luke 10:33-35, NLT.**

I saw it when I pulled up to a stoplight on the busiest street in town. Right in front of my car was a tiny little chickadee sitting dazed on the road. Just as I saw it, the light turned green. It would have been suicide to jump out of my car and try to save it. Even pulling over would have been dangerous and impossible. There were cars, buses, and semis all tearing pell-mell down that road. No one was going to stop while I ran out in the middle of the road to rescue a bird that, in all probability, was going to flap away at the last instant. And that was *if* the woman behind me (and the five people behind her) hadn't already squashed the little guy flat.

No, it would have been suicide to try, but I couldn't get it out of my mind, so I turned the car around and went back, sure that the bird would be a pancake by the time I arrived. But it wasn't. There it sat, blinking, waiting for death. The light turned green again just as I got to the side of the road and wondered if I would really get hit by a car if I made a dash for it. No one stopped so I could try. I had to watch as cars, trucks, and buses all passed over that little bird, each one just inches from crushing it, until the light finally turned red again. As soon as the traffic stopped, I ran into the road, scooped up the bird, and ran back to my car.

I was shaking. I released the bird when I got home, and it flew away immediately, happy, I'm sure, to be alive. As I watched it, I cried in gratitude to God that He allowed me to save it. I know it was a small thing, but it meant a lot to me.

We like the story of the good Samaritan—or any hero, for that matter—because it makes us feel all warm and fuzzy inside. There's a good reason for that. Doing good deeds puts us squarely on God's side; can you imagine Satan doing anything nice? Hardly. When you're on the winning team, you naturally feel good about it. When you spread love, joy, and happiness, you're spreading God's messages. Those messages matter; they have eternal value.

May 16

Complain, Complain

When you complain about Aaron and his sons,
you're really rebelling against the way the Lord
has set things up. **Numbers 16:11, Clear Word.**

D o you know anyone who complains all the time? Maybe even, ahem,
you? Let's face it, sometimes it's a whole lot easier to complain about a
situation than it is to find anything good to say about it. Some people
would claim that complaining is really just a way of expressing your opinion
about something or someone you don't like. That would be awesome because
then there would be nothing wrong with it; and complaining can seem like a
lot of fun.

But as Christians we believe that everything in our lives comes from God.
That means everything, good and bad. When Job's wife told him to curse God
and die, he said, "You talk like a foolish woman. Should we accept only good
things from the hand of God and never anything bad?" (Job 2:10, NLT). So . . .
if we accept both good and bad, *what are we complaining about?*

I never thought about it this way before, but if we complain about something, we're really rebelling against God and the way He's running things.
That's what some of the Israelites were doing when they complained to Moses,
claiming that he and Aaron were hogging all the glory of managing the sanctuary. God was the one who set up the sanctuary service and assigned jobs, so
what they were really complaining about was how God was operating things.
They were rebelling against God's authority and His leadership.

There are a lot of ways to rebel against God's authority in your life without
actually coming out and saying, "God, I don't like the way You're doing things."
Complaining is only one of them. When you blame anyone else for circumstances in your life, you're really blaming God—if you believe that God is in
control of your life.

When you understand that everything that happens to you, every circumstance, every person you meet, every situation you encounter, is either sent by
or allowed by God, it changes the way you see *everything*. For one thing, it will
be easier to accept bad things, because you won't be going through them alone.
There's a popular expression that says God won't give you more than you can
handle. Sure He will! But He will never give you more than you and He can
handle *together,* and that is the important difference.

Prayer Pail

Don't fret or worry. Instead of worrying, pray.
Let petitions and praises shape your worries into prayers,
letting God know your concerns. Before you know it,
a sense of God's wholeness, everything coming together for good,
will come and settle you down. It's wonderful what happens when
Christ displaces worry at the center of your life. **Philippians 4:6, 7, Message.**

You know when you hear an idea and it just sounds so bizarre you can't help laughing and scratching your head? I was sitting in Sabbath school class one day when I heard an idea like that. The teacher asked if anyone kept a prayer journal. A bunch of hands shot into the air, but one woman said, "No, but we keep a prayer pail."

When the teacher asked her to explain, she said, "It's a plastic pail that we keep on our dresser. All week we put in prayer requests and praises. Because God knows all of them, we just pray that He'll take care of all the requests."

There are a lot of ways to talk to God, but I had never heard of putting your requests into a prayer pail. It just goes to show that there are as many ways to talk to God as there are people who talk to Him. You can have a prayer list, or a prayer journal, or even, apparently, a prayer pail. You can talk to God out loud or in your mind. You can write your prayers like letters, and if you want to, you can mail them to God through the United States Postal Service, who claims they are receiving a lot more mail addressed to heaven these days. Addresses vary, but God, streets of gold, heaven, will probably work. You can even e-mail God at sendemailtogod.com, or send Him a text at 463 (God).

Do these methods of communication with God really work? Well, we know that postal employees can't actually deliver letters to heaven. A text to "463" will probably bounce back as an invalid number, and the e-mail will likely end up in cyberspace somewhere. But Gary Sawtelle, a spokesperson for the post office, said, "I'm not a religious person, but I have to believe that you don't need the Postal Service for these. The minute you put your pen to paper, and address a letter to God, it gets delivered."

Sawtelle says he isn't religious, yet even he knows that God is so compassionate and concerned for His children that any cry of our heart immediately gets His full attention.

There are many ways to talk to God. Pick a few and start a conversation today.

May 18

Kidnapped!

For even the Son of Man came not to be served but to serve others and to give his life as a ransom for many. **Matthew 20:28, NLT.**

Charles Lindbergh was the first solo pilot who ever flew across the Atlantic Ocean. He became an instant celebrity, of course. But something happened to Charles five years later that made him even more famous and a whole lot sadder. On March 1, 1932, someone kidnapped his little boy. Baby Charles was only 20 months old when he was swiped from his room. His parents, Charles and Anne, found a ransom note for $50,000 in his room.

A lot of people offered to help the Lindberghs find their kidnapped baby. Even Al Capone, a famous gangster who was behind bars at the time, offered to help. When an imprisoned gangster offers to help, you know things are pretty bad. It was three days before the Lindberghs heard from the kidnapper again, this time asking for $70,000.

They got the money together, and after it was delivered, they received word that their little boy was in a boat called *Nelly,* which was anchored off the coast of Massachusetts. Unfortunately, the police couldn't find any trace of the boat or the little boy. Not on a boat, anyway, but they did find him soon afterward. It turns out that Baby Charles had been killed the night he was kidnapped; his body was found less than a mile from his home.

Poor Charles and Anne. They were so heartbroken they gave their mansion to charity and moved somewhere else. They really loved their little boy. When the kidnappers asked for $50,000, they were willing to give it. When they were asked for $70,000, they were willing to give that. And they did. Some of that money was later recovered when a man was arrested for the crime. Although he was convicted and sentenced to death for it, some people believe he may not have been the real kidnapper.

Have you ever stopped to think about the fact that we could have suffered the same fate as Baby Charles? We've been kidnapped, every last one of us. Satan kidnapped us and sent a ransom note to heaven. Only he didn't want $50,000, or even $70,000. He wanted the life of God's Son. God could have said, "That's too much! I won't do it. Not to save human beings."

But He said, "Yes!" Jesus gave everything to pay our ransom. If *we* are worth so much to *Him,* how much should *He* be worth to *us*?

Before and After

Jesus asked them, "Am I some dangerous revolutionary,
that you come with swords and clubs to arrest me?
Why didn't you arrest me in the Temple? I was there among you
teaching every day. But these things are happening
to fulfill what the Scriptures say about me." Then all his disciples
deserted him and ran away. **Mark 14:48-50, NLT.**

Have you ever seen before and after pictures? Someone loses weight, and they show a picture of them before, and then a picture of them after. Hair growth formula, before and after. A complete makeover, before and after. A bedroom remodel, before and after. Wrinkle remover, before and after. Some of the pictures are amazing: the person is so changed that you can't even believe it's the same person in both pictures.

If you had taken before and after pictures of the disciples, you'd find it pretty hard to recognize them in their after shots, too. At Gethsemane, when the soldiers came to arrest Jesus, they took off crying like little girls because they didn't want to die. The crowd nabbed one poor guy who ran right out of his clothes and escaped wearing nothing but his birthday suit (see Mark 14:51, 52).

That was the "before" picture—before the Holy Spirit descended on the day of Pentecost and filled them. After that you couldn't shut them up. They preached, healed, got thrown into prison, traveled, and endured hardships. Many died. The Bible doesn't tell us how they all died, but historians do. Many of them died as martyrs. For instance, church tradition says that Peter, who ran away and then claimed he didn't even know Jesus, opted to be crucified upside down because he didn't feel worthy to be crucified in the same position as Jesus.

What makes that kind of difference in people? There is only one force capable of changing the disciples from fraidy cats into roaring lions: the Holy Spirit. God's Spirit is a bit mysterious to us; we're not quite sure what to expect. Think of it this way: if God was an electrical outlet and we plugged into Him, the Holy Spirit would be the electricity. The moment we "plug in," the Spirit courses through us. If we were toasters, we'd be able to pop toast out all day, just as long as we were plugged in. The Holy Spirit is much more than that, of course, but more than anything the Holy Spirit is a power-filled, life-giving, energizing force that will change us into the very likeness of God.

May 20

God's Yes-Man

Death and life are in the power of the tongue,
and those who love it will eat its fruit. **Proverbs 18:21, NKJV.**

According to the Merriam-Webster dictionary, which should know about such things, a yes-man is "a person who agrees with everything that is said; *especially:* one who endorses or supports without criticism every opinion or proposal of an associate or superior." If you say the sky is blue, the yes-man will agree with you. "Yes, sir, it is blue. It sure is blue." You may be right, you may be wrong, but that doesn't matter to the yes-man, because all he wants is to impress you, especially if you're his boss or teacher.

Agreeing with someone important may earn you reward points because people like to have others agree with them. Words are extremely powerful: they can hurt people, help people, make people feel better, cut them down to size, make them go weak in the knees, even start wars. But just because you say something does not make it true, no matter how hard the person agreeing with you, well, *agrees.*

Watch. I'll demonstrate. "The sky is pink with green polka dots." Go ahead, check. Is it? No. I can insult someone with my words and cause them to feel bad, but I can't cause the color of the sky to change. But God's words are way more powerful than ours. The Bible says that "the word of God is alive and active" (Hebrews 4:12, NIV). God's words are living words. They are powerful. They are active. Because they are active, they *can* change things.

This is important because it means that when we agree with God—when we agree with something He said—His alive and active words can make changes in our lives. For this reason it is important to watch what you say, making sure that you're agreeing with God and not with Satan.

It is very easy to agree with Satan because he puts negative thoughts in our heads all day long. We do it without even realizing it. We might say, "I can't do _____[fill in the blank]. I'm not _____ [fill in the blank]." But what does God tell us? "For I can do everything through Christ, who gives me strength" (Philippians 4:13, NLT). Everything, that's *all* things. When you agree with God and say, "Hey, I *can* do *all* things *through Christ,* who gives me strength," then you will find that—guess what?—you *can* do all things. Say no to Satan and yes to God. Become God's yes-man; it'll change your life.

Why Me?

*Now I take limitations in stride, and with good cheer,
these limitations that cut me down to size—abuse, accidents,
opposition, bad breaks. I just let Christ take over! And so the
weaker I get, the stronger I become.* **2 Corinthians 12:10, Message.**

What's holding you back? Keeping you down? Getting in your way? We're only human; a lot of things can get us down and keep us stuck in the mud, whether they are physical, mental, or spiritual. And it's true that some of us have more to bear and higher obstacles to hurdle than others. If you have to grow up in a broken home with a parent who doesn't care about you, who deals and abuses drugs, your life is going to look a whole lot different than the kid who grows up with two parents who dote on him. But even that kid goes through hard times.

And when those tough times come, it's easy to catch ourselves thinking, *Why me? Why is it always me?* Sometimes when it seems like nothing is going right, or you're tired of living with a problem, it's easy to forget that God never gives us anything we can't handle *as long as He's carrying us.*

Joni Eareckson Tada, who has been confined to a wheelchair for many years, realizes this. In fact, she says she'd kind of like to take her wheelchair to heaven with her. "In a way," says Joni, "I wish I could take to heaven my old, tattered Everest and Jennings wheelchair. I would point to the empty seat and say, 'Lord, for decades I was paralyzed in this chair. But it showed me how paralyzed You must have felt to be nailed to Your cross. My limitations taught me something about the limitations You endured when You laid aside your robes of state and put on the indignity of human flesh.' At that point, with my strong and glorified body, I might sit in it, rub the armrests with my hands, look up at Jesus, and add, 'The weaker I felt in this chair, the harder I leaned on You. And the harder I leaned, the more I discovered how strong You are. Thank You, Jesus, for learning obedience in Your suffering. . . . You gave me the grace to learn obedience in mine.'"

Having a lot to overcome seems unfair when we look at it from the surface; it's only natural we should want things to be easy. But the secret is to let our problems drive us to God, and He will help us in ways we can't even imagine. When we are obedient to God in our suffering, He will carry us through every heartache and over every obstacle, and that makes all the difference.

May 22

Step Aside

The angel answered, "The Holy Spirit will come on you, and the power of the Most High will overshadow you. So the holy one to be born will be called the Son of God." Luke 1:35, NIV.

Do you have a little brother or sister who always wants you to watch what they can do? Whenever they try something new, they want an audience. "Watch me! Look at me! See what I can do!" And they wait until you are watching before they show you the same thing again and again. It doesn't matter to them that you can do it a thousand times better than they can. They aren't interested in how well *you* can do it; they only want you to watch while *they* do it.

We tend to do the same thing with God. We want Him to watch us and see what we can do for Him when He's just aching for us to let Him work through us. Remember when the angel appeared to Mary to tell her that God had chosen her to give birth to Jesus? What did Mary have to do? Nothing! Nada. Zip. She only had to be willing to carry God's Son.

God didn't put her on a diet. He didn't send an angel to be her personal trainer so she could get in shape and have a gym-toned body worthy of carrying the Savior of the world. And He didn't make her go to college and get a degree in child psychology so she could be the best mother the world has ever known.

When Mary asked how she could do something so impossible as carrying the Son of God, the angel told her that God would do everything: the Holy Spirit would come on her and the power of the Most High would overshadow her. And here's the best part: *He does the same thing for us today!*

But, you say, I'm not carrying God's Son. Oh, yes, you are! Every Christian is. The whole process of being a Christian is dying to ourselves and what we want, and letting Jesus live in us instead. In a manner of speaking, we give birth to Jesus' life in us with God's help.

God wants to give us tremendous power and work out great things in our life—He wants to live out Jesus' life in us—but we've been too busy trying to show Him what *we* can do instead of standing back and watching what *He* can do.

Let Mary's words be yours each and every day: "Behold the maidservant [or manservant] of the Lord! Let it be to me according to your word" (Luke 1:38, NKJV).

Walk This Way

Dear brothers and sisters, pattern your lives after mine,
and learn from those who follow our example.
For I have told you often before, and I say it again with tears
in my eyes, that there are many whose conduct shows they
are really enemies of the cross of Christ. **Philippians 3:17, 18, NLT.**

You never know who is watching you. For example, I've been watching some of the teens I know who left a small Christian school to go off to the big public high school in town. They all left confident that they could maintain their Christianity and their principles out there among the "heathen." They were all sure that rubbing elbows with non-Christians wouldn't affect them. They were going to be the examples, not the other way around.

For the most part . . . epic fail. These kids used to post Bible verses and messages on Facebook about how much they loved God. Now a quick scan through their time lines reveals not even a mention about God. Are they bad kids? Probably not, although some of them are experimenting with dangerous substances or behaviors that could get them into serious trouble down the road. But I know if you had asked them, before they left the safe harbor of being completely surrounded by Christians, if they thought they'd be any different in a couple years, all of them would have said no . . . and laughed at you because the idea was so ridiculous.

The trouble is that it *is* always dangerous to spend a lot of time around people who don't have the same values you do. There's always the chance you'll get pulled down into their world. Ellen White says, "The great lesson to be given to the youth is that, as worshipers of God, they are to cherish Bible principles, and hold the world as subordinate. God would have all instructed as to how they can work the works of Christ, and enter in through the gates into the heavenly city. We are not to let the world convert us; we are to strive most earnestly to convert the world. Christ has made it our privilege and duty to stand up for Him under all circumstances" (*Fundamentals of Christian Education*, p. 470).

The only chance we have to convert the world and not be converted by it is to stay so close to God that Satan can't pry us away. And the only way we can do that is to have the sort of relationship with Him that is constant all day, every day. If we let go, we'll get sucked down onto Satan's turf. But if we hold on to Jesus, we may become the bridge He uses to lift the people we meet out of the pit and into His arms.

Penny Dreadful

And we are instructed to turn from godless living
and sinful pleasures. We should live in this evil world with wisdom,
righteousness, and devotion to God, while we look forward
with hope to that wonderful day when the glory of our great God
and Savior, Jesus Christ, will be revealed. **Titus 2:12, 13, NLT.**

Back in the nineteenth century the British published a type of story for teens called the penny dreadful. It only cost a penny to buy; that was the "penny" part. The "dreadful" part came from the fact that they were cheap, sensational fiction. The stories were continued, so each week you had to buy the newest one to find out what happened next.

Adults believed the penny dreadfuls had a bad influence on kids. One man, Alfred Harmsworth, wanted to change that. He created a half-penny paper with inspiring, moral, and true tales. But it wasn't long before the stories got worse. Soon they were just as bad as the penny dreadfuls.

It's easy enough for us to stay away from the penny dreadfuls because they aren't published any more, but finding good reading material can still be hard. It's important, though, to read material that challenges your brain. Imagine if all you chewed throughout the day was bubble gum; no food, just bubble gum. Pretty soon you'd starve to death. It's the same with your brain. Feed it empty fluff all day, and it will starve.

"With the cultivation of an appetite for sensational stories the mental taste is perverted, and the mind is not satisfied unless fed upon this unwholesome food. I can think of no more fitting name for those who indulge in such reading than mental inebriates. Intemperate habits of reading have an effect upon the brain similar to that which intemperate habits of eating and drinking have upon the body" (Ellen G. White, *The Adventist Home*, p. 414).

A mental inebriate is a mental drunk. In other words, reading sensational stories lowers your brainpower and makes it difficult for you to understand deeper thoughts, such as the kind you find in the Bible or other Christian books that teach about God. Instead of craving God's Word, your mind will want only easy, exciting stories. If you want to grow in your spiritual life, you need to be careful what you read. Of course, of all the books you could read, the Bible is the best. They don't call it the Good Book for nothing.

Pause and Remember

It was there at Gilgal that Joshua piled up the twelve stones
taken from the Jordan River. Then Joshua said to the Israelites,
"In the future your children will ask, 'What do these stones mean?'
Then you can tell them, 'This is where the Israelites crossed the Jordan
on dry ground.' For the Lord your God dried up the river right before
your eyes, and he kept it dry until you were all across, just as he did at the
Red Sea when he dried it up until we had all crossed over. He did this so
all the nations of the earth might know that the Lord's hand is powerful,
and so you might fear the Lord your God forever." **Joshua 4:20-24, NLT.**

What will you be doing today at 3:00 p.m.? Today is Memorial Day, and many people around the United States will pause for a moment of silence to remember the great sacrifices our military personnel have made so we could remain a free nation with the ability to believe and worship as we choose. The first Memorial Day was observed on May 30, 1868. Flowers were placed on the graves of Union and Confederate soldiers buried at Arlington National Cemetery.

Nowadays many people aren't really sure what Memorial Day is supposed to be for. Some honor and remember all who have died, and others honor only those who died serving our country. In order to help people remember what the day is all about, the United States government passed the National Moment of Remembrance resolution. The resolution asks that Americans pause for one minute at 3:00 p.m. on Memorial Day to remember and reflect on the sacrifices made by so many while protecting our freedom, and to recognize the families of those who made the ultimate sacrifice for freedom.

Remembering is important, not only for patriotism to a country, but for Christians too. When the Israelites finally crossed over the Jordan River to take possession of the Promised Land after wandering around in the desert for 40 years, God told them to make a pile of 12 stones to help them remember what had happened. The sight of the stones triggered questions from their children, which gave them an opportunity to tell the story of God's amazing guidance years later. The next time God helps you in an amazing way, consider making some kind of monument (even if it's finding a single stone to use as a doorstop) as a reminder to thank Him.

Consider expressing your appreciation to our nation's fallen soldiers and their families for the gift of freedom they fought and died for. Thank God for your freedom, too.

May 26

House Rules

Rule-keeping does not naturally evolve into living by faith,
but only perpetuates itself in more and more rule-keeping,
a fact observed in Scripture: "The one who does these things
[rule-keeping] continues to live by them." **Galatians 3:12, Message.**

Rules are not much fun. You have to remember them, and you have to be careful you don't break them, either on purpose or by accident. I don't know about you, but I have never really liked rules.

When I was growing up, one of the rules in my house was that if you were going out, you had to call and let someone know you'd arrived safely. And if you stayed out longer than you planned, you had to call and let someone know. I always forgot that rule until one night when my parents went to a party at my aunt's house.

I stayed home watching television, and it got later and later. They weren't home at the time they'd said they would return, and I started to worry. Had they had an accident? Were they lying in a ditch somewhere bleeding to death and no one knew? Did they need help? I was so worried that I called my aunt's house. My parents were still there, and they never let me forget that I was so worried that I called to find out if they were OK. I still wonder if they weren't just trying to teach me a lesson. If so, it worked.

The next time I went out and stayed later than I planned, I called home, because I realized that the rule was there to protect me and to keep my parents from worrying about where I was. Before I learned that the hard way, it was just a rule.

A lot of Christians have trouble with God's "rules." All they see is "Don't do this" and "Don't do that." What they can't see is the love behind the rules . . . until they break them. Then they realize all of God's rules are motivated by one thing: love. God wants us to have the best lives possible and He knows that for that to happen we have to be protected from ourselves and from other people who want to harm us.

When we can see that God's rules are really about love, we can stop worrying about them and start living a life of love for God and others. We'll still obey the rules, but we'll be obeying because we understand where they come from and why they are important, rather than just because we have to. God's rules won't just be in our heads where we can forget them. He will write them on our hearts so we can live them.

You've Got Mail

Let such a person consider this,
that what we are in word by letters when absent, such persons
we are also in deed when present. **2 Corinthians 10:11, NASB.**

You may think getting mail at the speed of light is pretty awesome. Well, it is. But it's still not as thrilling as the Pony Express was. At a time when civil war was looming on the horizon, there were 2,000 long, lonely miles between the east and west coasts. It was wild country, inhabited mostly by Native Americans who were none too happy about all these White people swarming over their lands.

Riders for the Pony Express had to be brave and have all their wits about them. That's probably why riders had to sign an oath pledging "before the Great and Living God" that they would not swear, drink alcohol, or fight with other riders, and that they would be honest and faithful.

Buffalo Bill made the longest ride without stopping in the history of the Pony Express. He carried the mail from Red Buttes to Rocky Ridge and back because his relief rider had been killed. In all, he rode 322 miles along one of the most dangerous parts of the trail, and he made it in 21 hours and 40 minutes using a total of 21 horses. Getting a letter from one side of the country to the other took an average of eight to 10 days.

Can you imagine how you'd feel if you received a letter that had traveled 2,000 miles across hostile Indian country? A letter that men had risked their lives to deliver, traveling day and night, sometimes without rest or food? If you received a letter like that, do you think you'd read it? Or would you toss it on the table and ignore it?

We've each received a letter that Someone risked His life to deliver—gave His life to deliver, in fact. It's the Bible, God's love letter to us. It's an incredible privilege to own a copy of God's Word. Sometimes we don't appreciate that. Through the ages, men, women, and children have risked their lives to share God's Word at a time when Bibles hadn't even been printed yet. They had to copy the words on pieces of paper to share. There are still countries today where a person would consider themselves blessed to own a Bible. What about you?

Do a Google search on how the Bible came into existence, then thank God for His love letter—by reading it.

May 28

Dog Vomit

As a dog returns to his own vomit,
so a fool repeats his folly. **Proverbs 26:11, NKJV.**

Not far from my house is a field. Every year in the fall geese stop at that field on their migration south for the winter. I'm not sure how many different types of waterfowl stop there, but I've seen Canada geese and snow geese. They circle the field like planes above an airport waiting their turn on the "runway," an empty strip of field where the flocks touch down and take off. At any given time there are flocks coming and going while other flocks graze in the field.

According to NASA, geese and other birds migrate thousands of miles each year. Some of them travel more than 7,000 miles one way. When they fly over the Gulf of Mexico or the Sahara, they fly up to 1,000 miles without stopping. While migrating, they must follow their food supply. They also go back to particular places in order to breed.

Geese are just doing what comes naturally. No one tells them to leave each year and return to a certain place. They just instinctively do it. It's something that's hardwired into their systems.

Unfortunately, we can be a lot like geese in that way. Because we were born in sin, our old sinful nature wants to return to it, like a dog returns to his vomit, as the proverb says. Even though we know it's disgusting, we naturally want to go back to it. This can be very frustrating because we end up doing the very things we don't want to do and then we feel bad about it.

But we don't have to! Jesus stands between us and our sin. He knows that the only way we can stop sinning is if He changes our sinful nature. And He will do that *if we ask Him to*. The change doesn't usually happen all at once. It takes place over time. So be patient and work with Jesus by listening and responding when He talks to you about things that you need to move away from in your life. Eventually you won't want to return to them anymore.

Interview some Christians you know. Ask them to share with you some of the ways that God has changed them. What kinds of things did they previously enjoy that they don't want to do anymore because of the changes God has made in their hearts? Don't forget to make your own list!

Bowwow-Meow

And now, in my old age, don't set me aside.
Don't abandon me when my strength is failing. **Psalm 71:9, NLT.**

Do you have a dog or a cat? (Or a hamster, or a rat, or a hissing cockroach?) If you do, chances are you come home after a bad day and spend some quality time with your pet. Pets always seem to make us feel better. They love us just the way we are and don't even care if we have bad breath.

Elderly people who have to live in nursing homes are forced to leave their pets behind when they move. Because people are starting to realize how hard this is for them, some nursing homes have a mascot dog or cat that lives in the nursing home. There are also people who volunteer to do pet therapy. They take dogs, cats, and other animals to nursing homes and let people visit with them.

I have done this with the Humane Society's puppies and kittens, as well as with my own dogs and bunnies. If you're shy, pet therapy is a great way to be involved in outreach without worrying about what you'll say to people. As soon as they see that you have an animal, they'll do all the talking. You can just answer questions and add whatever you like.

You'll also have funny stories to tell your friends. Once, when I had one of the Humane Society's puppies in my arms, a resident's face lit up and she exclaimed, "What a beautiful baby you have!" Every time I went back she said the same thing, and I was never sure if she thought the puppy was a *real* baby.

Sharing your pet, or even just your time, with elderly persons is a win-win situation. They are always so happy to see young people you can't help feeling appreciated. You may even strike up a friendship with an elderly individual and "adopt" them as a grandparent. God is honored when we help those who are elderly and don't forget about them.

Are you interested in pet therapy? There are a couple options if you want to get involved. You can contact your local Humane Society and see if they already have a program you can join. If they don't, you can contact nursing homes yourself and see if they are interested in letting you bring your own pets around for residents to visit with. If your pet is a dog, you can even take special classes to get your pooch certified as a therapy animal.

Lonely Hearts

Turn to me and be gracious to me, for I am lonely and afflicted. Relieve the troubles of my heart and free me from my anguish. **Psalm 25:16, 17, NIV.**

When I was in the third grade, my parents moved me to a new school. I was a shy kid, and I didn't know a soul. In third grade you live for recess, but I dreaded it. Not *one single kid* all year long asked me to play. Every day I spent the entire recess counting down how many more days were left of school before vacation. It was the longest, loneliest school year of my life.

You probably don't have to worry about being lonely. You're probably so popular that people have to stand in line just to talk to you. Or poke you on Facebook, text you, Skype with you, or tweet you. Or do you find that despite your numerous friends and followers you aren't *really* close to anyone?

An article in *The Atlantic* magazine claims that even though we're more virtually connected than ever, we're also lonelier than we've ever been—and that this loneliness is making us mentally and physically ill. In fact, they claim loneliness is reaching epidemic proportions across America. All this while we're developing super thumbs from texting and accumulating "friends" via Facebook at the speed of light. What gives?

Have you ever noticed that most of the time when people get together they aren't actually *talking* to each other? Instead, they're on whatever type of communication device they have, "talking" with someone who isn't actually there. They trade virtual memories—pokes, likes, and forwards—for actual memories—laughs and shared experiences that bond people together. Because those virtual experiences exist only on the surface, they aren't satisfying in the same way that an actual relationship with someone you can talk to and do things with can be. We have a front (like a cardboard cutout of our best selves) that we present to the virtual world. But it's not who we really are. We put forward our best, cleverest, most photogenic selves, because we want people to think well of us.

When you have real-time friends, they get to see you at your best, your worst, and every moment in between. They prove they are your friends by sticking with you. In return, you stick with them. You know each other because you spend time together doing things. Having *real* friends will help keep you from being lonely.

Now You See It

But when people keep on sinning, it shows that they belong to the devil, who has been sinning since the beginning. But the Son of God came to destroy the works of the devil. I John 3:8, NLT.

Have you ever watched an illusionist perform a sleight-of-hand trick? You know it's a trick. You know it's not real. But you just can't figure out how they're doing it. Sometimes that illusion persists even if you *can* see what they're doing. Early in their career now-famous magicians Penn and Teller were at a diner when Teller began practicing the cups and balls trick with some wadded-up napkins and clear glasses. In the trick, various-sized balls appear on top of and under various cups, but always in places you wouldn't suppose them to be.

Even though it was possible to see every move he made and track the napkins as he pulled them out and moved them around, the brain wasn't capable of grasping what was happening. "The eye could see the moves, but the mind could not comprehend them," Teller says. "Giving the trick away gave nothing away, because you still couldn't grasp it."

When Penn and Teller put the see-through cups and balls trick in their act, audiences loved it, but the magic community was horrified. They'd broken the "never show 'em how it's done" code. They even received threats of physical violence. Anyone who exposes deception and trickery can expect the same kind of treatment; if you rely on tricking people, you don't want them to "see how it's done."

Satan has an endless variety of tricks he can play on us, but just as in real magic there are only a few fundamental tricks that have endless variations, so Satan relies on the same basic tricks over and over. His most basic trick is to hold up something interesting and dangle it in front of us until we want it. It could be drugs, alcohol, tobacco, sex, wealth, or any number of other things. We're so focused on whatever he's holding up that we don't see his other hand as it reaches into our pocket and steals our health, relationships, brain cells, freedom, or sometimes even our lives. No matter how hard we study his trick, even if we know we're being tricked we'll never see how he does it, because he's a master magician. We can't outtrick him; we can only place ourselves in God's hands, because He came to destroy the works of Satan, and He will keep us safely in His hands.

The Damage or the Divine

Don't repay evil for evil. Don't retaliate with insults
when people insult you. Instead, pay them back with a blessing. That is what
God has called you to do, and he will bless you for it. **I Peter 3:9, NLT.**

My family has a tradition that on someone's birthday everyone else calls and sings "Happy Birthday" to them over the phone. On my nephew Zeb's birthday I wanted to call him but I didn't know his new cell phone number, so I called my sister—his mom—to get it. She was at the grocery store and gave me the number while she was distracted.

When I dialed the number she'd given me, a crabby woman answered. I couldn't imagine why a woman was answering my nephew's phone, but I politely asked if I could speak with Zeb.

"Who? There's no Zeb here. Who are you? Why are you calling me? How did you get this number? You know, I don't appreciate calls like this at all." Then she rudely hung up on me.

Eventually I reached my nephew's voice mail and sang "Happy Birthday" onto his machine. While I was singing, my phone beeped with an incoming call. It was the crabby woman! She left a snotty message on my voice mail, threatening to report my number if I called her again.

I was rattled. And angry. All I'd wanted to do was wish Zeb happy birthday. I didn't deserve to be chewed up one side and down the other for making a mistake.

As I stewed about that awful woman, God quietly pointed out to me how very miserable her life must be if she could treat a perfect stranger so terribly over a mistake. Then I felt so bad for her that I prayed God would send someone kind who could tell her how much He loves her. As I was praying, my mind jumped ahead and wondered if someday, when Jesus comes back, an angel will approach me leading a stranger who was saved because of a prayer for salvation that began because of a misdialed number. I still pray for that woman every time I remember that call. Sometimes I think about how embarrassing and awful that experience was, and I have to stop myself and concentrate not on the damage but on the divine intervention that keeps me praying for some desperately crabby woman I don't even know.

We all have opportunities like that. When people are rude to us or treat us unkindly, whether on purpose or by accident, we have a choice: we can focus on the damage or on the divine. Which will you choose?

The Story of You

Do not be afraid, for I have ransomed you.
I have called you by name; you are mine. When you go through
deep waters, I will be with you. When you go through rivers of difficulty,
you will not drown. When you walk through the fire of oppression,
you will not be burned up; the flames will not consume you. For I am the
Lord, your God, the Holy One of Israel, your Savior. **Isaiah 43:1-3, NLT.**

There was a group of kids (real kids; I'm not making this up) who were labeled "unteachable." People thought they were stupid, so the kids believed they were stupid. The communities they lived in were divided by race, and most of them had lost friends and relatives to gang violence. They carried their hatred into their classrooms. The school wouldn't even give them books to read, because they thought they were too stupid to read them.

And then a teacher named Erin Gruwell came into their lives. She believed in them and worked hard to help them believe in themselves. She gave them journals to write in so they could record their feelings and experiences. Eventually those "losers" wrote their own book, *The Freedom Writers Diary*, which became a movie, *Freedom Writers*, and those kids walked across the stage at graduation to receive their diplomas, something no one except Erin Gruwell thought they could do. Many of them have gone on to become teachers themselves in order to inspire a whole new generation of students.

Why did that happen? Because someone believed in them. Someone stood up for them against all the people who thought they were worthless and who had given up on them. Someone proved to them that they had value.

We each have "Someone" who believes in us no matter what—God. We belong to Him; we are His most valuable possessions, and He will never let us down. He'll stand up to anyone who tries to harm or belittle us. He knows our potential, because He created us, and when we follow Him, we'll walk across our own graduation stage someday and get our "diploma."

In the meantime we have a responsibility to let others know they have value in the sight of God, too. We must help them to realize that Someone believes in them, loves them, and wants them to reach their potential. It's up to each of us to support and inspire one another so that on graduation day we can all graduate together.

June 3

Fearless

Therefore, go and make disciples of all the nations, baptizing them in the name of the Father and the Son and the Holy Spirit. Teach these new disciples to obey all the commands I have given you. And be sure of this: I am with you always, even to the end of the age. **Matthew 28:19, 20, NLT.**

My daughter Rachel is 15, and she's fearless. She got a lift home one day with an older woman who works with her, and on the way she asked the woman if she wanted to come to church. The woman said no, not right now, but maybe sometime. At her brother's graduation she met one of his non-Christian friends and again extended an invitation to come to church.

When I asked her how she could be so bold, she said, "Do you know that it takes something like seven times people have to be asked to go to church before they finally say yes? What if no one ever asks them?"

I don't know how many times you have to ask someone to come to church before they say yes, but I do know that most people who accept Christ do it before they are 21 years old. Do you know what that means? It means the clock is ticking. I also know that one out of every five kids who accept Christ do so because of a friend. That means that teens are the main evangelists of other teens. Think of five of your non-Christian friends. At least one of them will come to know Christ because of a friend—maybe even you. But why stop with one?

I'm a big chicken; I'd be afraid that if I asked someone to come to church they'd say no. But so what if they do? Rachel didn't dry up and blow away because her friend didn't say yes. She didn't even let her disappointment stop her from asking someone else. If we expect to reach others for Christ, sometimes we have to be bold *and* relentless.

Chances are you have friends who don't know Jesus. In the back of your Bible (or on a spare scrap of paper), write down their names. Make a commitment to ask them to your church. You may want to wait for a special event at church that you think they'll be interested in, or ask them to come to your youth group, or just ask them off-the-cuff. But remember to do one thing before you ask: pray. We aren't responsible for people's reactions to us and God's message, but we are responsible for asking God's Spirit to prepare the way.

Sidetracked

We can make our plans,
but the Lord determines our steps. **Proverbs 16:9, NLT.**

I like lists. I like to check things off my list as I finish them. What I don't like is something unexpected coming along to mess up my neat little list. It's the control freak in me—I feel safe when my life is scheduled in advance.

Ah, but God often throws the unexpected into our day. I think He likes to do it to see how we'll handle it. You have to admit, it's a great way to keep us on our spiritual toes. Will we freak out (as I often do) and find some way out of the situation or away from the demanding person, or will we throw ourselves on God to get us through? Good question.

Here's a practice run: a classmate sees that you're online late at night. It's someone you know, but not well. They send you a chat message asking if you could help them with homework. You were just about to go to bed. You're tired. You've had a long day. You had a track meet after school and then a couple hours of homework when you finally got home. You were just logging on to check your e-mail. Do you ignore them, or do you help them?

It would be easy to ignore them. After all, they wouldn't *know* if you got their message. You could have been in the middle of logging off and not seen it. But, of course, *you* would know. But you're tired. You need your sleep. You aren't even good friends with them, so you're not really obligated by friendship to help them out. This was not a scheduled part of your day.

This is one of those situations that would benefit from the question "What would Jesus do?" Now, you don't need me to answer that question for you; I'm sure you know as well as I do what He'd do. The question is What will *you* do? Will you allow God to sidetrack you?

The great thing is that God never sidetracks you for nothing. He always has a reason. Maybe the person who sidetracks you needs to know someone cares about them, and this contact with you will eventually lead them to God, or maybe someone who hears about what you did will be affected. We may never know this side of heaven.

When God sidetracks us, He asks us to partner with Him in a celestial assignment. Isn't that exciting? Your mission, should you choose to accept it, is to (a) stop and pray for God to use you to accomplish His mission, (b) pray for the person who sidetracked you to be open to God's Spirit speaking to them, and (c) let God lead you to say and do His will. Oh, and enjoy the ride!

Music to My Ears

Listen, you kings! Pay attention, you mighty rulers!
For I will sing to the Lord. I will make music to the Lord,
the God of Israel. **Judges 5:3, NLT.**

Have you ever noticed that when people communicate they have different ways of expressing themselves that reveal their strengths? For example, someone may talk to get their point across. Someone else might write a letter or send an e-mail. They might post a picture that expresses how they are feeling. Or they might share, or sing, a song. They might even act out a response using body language. The method someone uses the most is probably their strongest, the one they are most comfortable with, and the one that makes them feel as though they are expressing their true feelings.

For me, it's a no-brainer; I communicate best through writing, which would explain all the books I've written. But music would come in a strong second. Christian singer Steve Green said it best: "There is great music to fit every ear and preference, every situation in life. Music is a companion in sorrow, an expression of joy, an articulation of the heart when words fail, a soothing balm to the aching heart and soaring strains that feed our longing for a beauty that will be realized only in the new heaven and new earth."

No matter which way you prefer to communicate, I think music is one method that all of us share. Even if someone can't carry a tune in a bucket, he or she can appreciate the music others make. If you don't believe me, ask Apple, which sold a total of 275 million iPods within 10 years of releasing the first one. We love our music.

King David and the other writers of Psalms loved music too. If iPods had existed in Bible times, those guys would have had the whole book of Psalms on their favorite playlist. The interesting thing about Psalms is that the songs aren't just any sort of music; they are songs that express an enormous range of human emotion, all written to be sung and played to music, and all directed toward God.

No matter what type of situation you're facing, chances are you can find a psalm that will express how you're feeling, whether you're depressed or so full of praise for God that you just want to burst. Even if singing's not your thing, try finding a psalm to match your emotions and speak it directly to God. If you're musical, you can even put it to a tune.

The Least You Can Do

Sitting across from the offering box, he was observing how the crowd tossed money in for the collection. Many of the rich were making large contributions. One poor widow came up and put in two small coins—a measly two cents. Jesus called his disciples over and said, "The truth is that this poor widow gave more to the collection than all the others put together. All the others gave what they'll never miss; she gave extravagantly what she couldn't afford—she gave her all." **Mark 12:41-44, Message.**

T hat's the least you can do."

Has anyone ever said that to you? The least you can do is the bottom of the barrel, the minimum effort possible. What they mean is "That much is expected. What else have you got?"

Some people get by all their lives on the least they can do. They never make a big effort to do anything more than they absolutely have to. Their motto is, as one television character famously quipped, "Never let it be said I didn't do the least I could do." They figure that if they do the least they can do, they've met the requirements; there's no reason to go beyond that.

That's the same attitude the rich people in the synagogue had the day Jesus was watching them put in their offerings. Only they weren't just doing the least they could do, they were patting themselves on the back for it, as if they were doing something really great.

"Way to go, Frank! Nice coin toss into the collection plate."

"Marv! That's a lotta sparkle you just threw in there. Sweet!"

Can't you just see them high-fiving it over the offerings? And while they're so busy congratulating themselves, the poor widow sneaks in, drops her mite, and scurries away before anyone can see her. The thing is, even though what she gave was not worth much in monetary terms, it was all she had. Maybe it meant that she was going to go without food the rest of that day. Maybe more than one day. Her offering was sacrificial; it cost her something.

How much would you have to give God before it cost you something? I mean, *really* cost you something? Most of the time we give out of our surplus—our extra—what we can afford to let go, but how often do we give out of our need? Think about how you can give God something this week that will really cost you something.

Puzzle Master

*We've been surrounded and battered by troubles,
but we're not demoralized; we're not sure what to do,
but we know that God knows what to do; we've been spiritually
terrorized, but God hasn't left our side; we've been thrown down,
but we haven't broken.* **2 Corinthians 4:8, Message.**

Do you like puzzles? I do, except for one thing: I'm no good at them. I get frustrated when I can't figure them out, and then I get impatient because I'm frustrated, and then I give up before I've gotten anywhere. One of the few puzzles I do enjoy working on is Sudoku, as long as they're rated "easy."

The thing about Sudoku is that you have to "work" the puzzle. You start in one section, and if you get stumped you move to a different section and work that part for a while. As you work through the puzzle, you eventually get the entire puzzle solved.

It would be nice if the only puzzles we ever faced were on paper so that we could give up and stuff them in a drawer when we got sick of trying to solve them. But the most common puzzles we'll ever have to face are the ones that happen in our lives. There will be tricky situations to navigate through, sticky misunderstandings between friends that we'll have to figure out, tangled decisions we'll have to make that will affect our lives, sometimes forever.

Whenever we face these daunting, twisting routes through which are no clear paths, we need to remember that God is a puzzle master. He can guide us through puzzles because He has the answer key. Imagine how easy it would be to complete a puzzle if you could see a diagram of exactly how to solve it! We can't see that ourselves, but God can.

He knows the outcome of every move we can make. He knows the end of every path we could take. When we don't know which course to take, or we get sick of trying to figure it all out, we need to go to God for advice and direction. Sometimes He'll tell us what step to take, and sometimes He'll lead us to people who can help us.

But God is no bully. He won't butt in where He's not wanted. Don't expect God to try to help you solve your puzzle if you haven't taken the time to ask Him for help. When we have a difficult puzzle to solve, doesn't it make sense to get direction from the One who knows how to solve it?

Spoiler Alert

He who testifies to all these things says it again: "I'm on my way! I'll be there soon!" Yes! Come, Master Jesus! **Revelation 22:20, Message.**

Have you ever been reading a book or watching a TV show when some-one walks up and carelessly tells you how it will end? That's just not right! They should have warned you that a spoiler was coming before giving the whole story away. Most of the time the suspense of wondering how it will all come out in the end is what keeps you reading the story or watching the show in the first place. It just wouldn't be the same if you knew how it was going to turn out, which is why I really have to stop skipping ahead when I read books!

Although that's true for books and movies, it's certainly not true in life. Most of us would gladly pay whatever it cost to know what the future held. "Spoil away," we'd like to say, "Just tell me what's going to happen. Will I get married? Will I have kids? Will I become a millionaire? Will I travel the world? Will I become famous? How long will I live?"

While it seems that knowing the future would be great, chances are it would be a real joy-killer. For instance, can you imagine knowing exactly when you were going to die? How could you enjoy anything while you watched the clock count down your years, months, days, and hours? You wouldn't be able to think about anything else. The time of your death would hang over your head like an executioner's sword.

There's only one thing about the future that's really worth knowing, and that's the fact that this old world is not going to last forever, and will continue to get worse and worse. In fact (spoiler alert), it's going to come to an end very soon. We know that, of course; it's even part of the name of our church. The word "Adventist" means that we believe God is coming back for us very soon. Aren't you glad we know that? Aren't you glad we don't have to guess about what's coming up? Aren't you glad we don't have to worry about whether or not sin will continue forever and ever?

The question is: How does our knowledge of the future affect what we do in the present? It should change everything about how we live *right now*. We know how the story ends! We need to work with God's Holy Spirit to get us to that ending as fast as possible. I don't know about you, but I can't wait for the part where Jesus says, "The end . . . and now, the beginning."

June 9

Spartan Death Race

God guards you from every evil, he guards your very life.
He guards you when you leave and when you return, he guards
you now, he guards you always. **Psalm 121:7, 8, Message.**

In the town next to mine they hold a mega race called the Spartan Death Race. The "death" part isn't an exaggeration. Racers have to sign release forms acknowledging that they could die during the race.

Participants have no way of knowing exactly what kind of challenges they'll face, because the race details are kept secret. They don't even know how long the race will last. They aren't sure how to train, because they don't know what sort of terrain they'll be in. Each year the course is completely different.

The only thing competitors know for sure is that the race creators will try to break them down physically and mentally. The race makers *want* them to quit. They *want* them to give up. They try real hard to force the racers to drop out. Most people do. In the 2012 Death Race 344 people registered for the race, and only 51 officially finished.

That sounded awfully familiar . . . and that's when it hit me. Aren't all Christians in a type of Spartan Death Race? We have no idea when it will end, the challenges and temptations are always changing so we have no idea what to expect, or how to prepare. We could die, and the race maker (Satan) doesn't want us to finish. Yup, that about sums it up, doesn't it?

When I read about the upcoming race in the newspaper, I was surprised to find that I know someone who entered. In fact, this will be his *third* Death Race. And I wondered, *Why?* Why would you put yourself through the agony? "For me," he said, "it's how much are you willing to suffer. Within five hours I'll be suffering, but it just becomes the way. . . . I know I won't find comfort until I'm done."

Neither will we. Some parts will be easier than others. A lot of us will drop out. Some will die. Some will be injured. And none of us will find real comfort until we're done, the race safely behind us, heaven firmly before us. But we have one thing Death Racers don't: we have Someone in our corner. We have Someone who will help us through whatever challenges we find in our race. We won't take one step or face one obstacle He won't help us overcome. And if we'll just trust Him completely and lean on Him absolutely, we *will* finish.

All Shapes and Sizes

Some were fools; they rebelled and suffered for their sins.
They couldn't stand the thought of food, and they were knocking
on death's door. "Lord, help!" they cried in their trouble, and he saved
them from their distress. He sent out his word and healed them, snatching
them from the door of death. Let them praise the Lord for his great love and
for the wonderful things he has done for them. **Psalm 107:17-21, NLT.**

I saw a cartoon the other day. Two little girls were looking at a scale. One told the other not to step on it, because it makes you cry. The cartoon is funny until you stop to think about how many (millions of) people struggle with overeating or, on the flip side, starving themselves. And it's not just girls; therapists say they are seeing 50 percent more men for these "women's diseases" than they were 10 years ago, and some think that could just be the tip of the iceberg. Everyone wants to have the perfect body.

The question is Why? Starving ourselves won't help us enjoy life. It won't make us stronger. It can't even add one single second of happiness to our day. Whether we starve ourselves into thinness or stuff ourselves into obesity, at the end of the day we will only be skinny or fat. Not happy.

Having a healthy body and a healthy mind are more important than meeting some standard of beauty set up by the world. Healthy bodies—*real* bodies—come in all shapes and sizes. What about you? Can your body carry you out into the world on adventures? Thank God for it. There are plenty of people who would love to be in your shoes. A friend of mine is paralyzed, yet she still thanks God that she can feed herself and drive her wheelchair. Be sure you take time each day to appreciate what your body can carry you through. Take care of it; don't punish it.

I challenge you not to let other people's idea of a "perfect" body rule your life. If you struggle with an eating disorder of any kind you can find help. God is ready to heal you; reach out to Him today, right now. Then confide in someone you trust and ask them to help you get the support you need to break free of Satan's unhealthy trap.

Bed of Roses

I am the Vine, you are the branches. When you're joined with me and I with you, the relation intimate and organic, the harvest is sure to be abundant. Separated, you can't produce a thing. Anyone who separates from me is deadwood, gathered up and thrown on the bonfire. **John 15:5, 6, Message.**

I'm a sucker for roses. It's not just the fact that they're pretty; they *smell* so good. And they seem romantic, don't they? Not only because guys like to give them to their sweethearts on Valentine's Day, but because rose gardens are quaint and romantic. Not that I've ever seen one, but they *sound* quaint and romantic. Imagine what a whole garden full of roses must smell like!

Unfortunately, my thumb isn't green enough to really do justice to the rosebushes I've bought over the years. My garden is the place plants come to die. It's not my fault, not really. After all, if the roses weren't so eager to die they might live longer.

Because I keep dragging rosebushes home, planting them, and watching them slowly wither away, I always feel a kind of bad when I see a new one at a store. I'll stand there for a while, inhaling the lovely scent, and think just how beautiful this rose would look by my back door. Or in the side garden. Or tucked over in the corner by the fencepost. Even as my fingers reach out to grasp the bucket of dirt it lives in, I feel like apologizing to it. It's a bit like snatching someone off the street and putting them on death row.

I bought my latest victim, er, rosebush just a few weeks ago. It had the most beautiful roses ever. They were two shades, kind of red and orangey. They were so different that when I brought one to church, someone asked me if it was fake. I like to buy my rosebushes when they've already got roses on them because sometimes those are the only roses they have before they die.

When I cut the roses off the bush that time, I got a little carried away and suddenly realized I'd just snipped off some new growth with two buds . . . buds that *would have been* roses. Cut off from the plant, they could only die. Jesus tells us that we're just like those roses. We have a lot of potential when we're connected to the bush (Him). We can bloom and people will smell our fragrance for miles. They'll stop and admire the beautiful flower He's made of us. But we have to stay connected to Him in order to bloom. Otherwise, like my rosebuds, we'll just droop, wither, and die.

No Pain, No Gain

"For I know the plans I have for you," declares the Lord,
"plans to prosper you and not to harm you,
plans to give you hope and a future." **Jeremiah 29:11, NIV.**

Right about now my dog Max hates me. This morning I had to bring him to the vet to get his yearly shots. It's his least-favorite thing in the whole world. He has no idea that the vet is trying to help him. He doesn't know that the needles the vet pokes him with are giving him medicine or vaccines that he needs in order to be healthy and feel good. All he knows is that he hates the tiny exam room with people he doesn't know manhandling him and poking him with sharp things.

What do you suppose would happen if I could sit him down in a chair and reason with him? I could say, "Now, Max, listen here. I know you don't like needles, and I know you're scared, but trust me. When this is all over, you'll feel a lot better."

Do you think he'd reply, "Really? You're sure there's nothing to be afraid of? OK, I'll try to be brave."

If you were Max, would you respond that way? As long as you knew ahead of time that something was going to hurt but that it was good for you, that it was necessary for you to either grow or get well, would it be easier to take the pain or discomfort?

Fortunately, we don't have to go to the vet, and you've probably had all the shots you're going to need for a while. Unless you break something, you probably won't even have to go to the doctor unless you need a checkup. But other parts of your life might hurt, and you may feel just like Max, scared and afraid.

Can you trust God? He wants to sit you down and explain that He has plans for you, special plans. And those plans aren't meant to harm you at all. They may hurt for just a little while, but in the end those experiences that hurt you will help you grow in your faith and closer to Him.

There's a saying that goes "No pain, no gain." It means that all growth takes some kind of pain. That's a good thing to keep in mind when you're feeling those growing pains. It's nice to remember that God's plans are to give you hope, a future, and incredible gains. If you realize that, it will be easier to be brave . . . like Max.

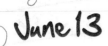

June 13

A Crack in the Asphalt

> There the angel of the Lord appeared to him in flames of fire
> from within a bush. Moses saw that though the bush was on fire
> it did not burn up. So Moses thought, "I will go over and see this strange
> sight—why the bush does not burn up." **Exodus 3:2, 3, NIV.**

I felt a bit like Moses seeing the burning bush. Driving down the road in the center of the city, I saw a beautiful viper plant blossoming in the middle of two lanes. It was covered with bright-blue showy blossoms that filled the paved road with color.

Nothing should have been able to grow there. The island of asphalt between two busy streets had no dirt, no nourishment of any kind for plants. It was baked by the sun all day and pelted by water when it rained. There was nothing for a plant to sink its roots into. Well, except for one crack in the asphalt. And in that crack a solitary plant had sprouted, grown, and blossomed.

Cars whizzed by in either direction. Maybe some of the drivers looked with wonder on that brave little plant blooming for all it was worth, but most of them probably didn't even take the time to notice. The plant doesn't care, though. It simply keeps blooming whether anyone notices or not. Why? Because that is what God created it to do. It doesn't need an audience in order to be obedient to its Creator, and neither should we.

Have you ever felt like that plant, trying to bloom where you were planted? Maybe you're in a tough public school, trying to stick to your Christian principles. Maybe you're the only Christian in your family and you're trying to be a good example for your younger brothers and sisters, or even for your parents. Maybe you're in a great church but the youth group is full of phonies. You look around and wish there were lots of other flowers to hang out with but it's just you alone on the asphalt. Sometimes you wonder if you should even bother.

The answer is yes, you should. You will never know whom your example of obedience to God will affect. You may never know. But you can be sure that people will see you blooming in the asphalt and they'll think, "I will go over and see this strange sight." That's when you can tell them the secret source of your strength.

If you are blooming in a tough place right now, it's important to keep your focus on God. Be sure to find your strength in Him each day so you won't wither.

Scavenger Hunt

But from there you will seek the Lord your God,
and you will find Him if you search for Him with all
your heart and all your soul. **Deuteronomy 4:29, NASB.**

This week we're going to go on a scavenger hunt. Usually the object of a scavenger hunt is to find all the items on a list and check them off before the other players or teams do. And the items are tricky to find, so you really have to look for them, although they're usually common enough that you have a chance of finding them, such as a red leaf, a ketchup packet, or a paper clip.

On our scavenger hunt, though, we're going to look for God. We know that if we search for God with all our might (all our heart and all our soul), we'll find Him, right? So that's what we're going to do. We're going to look in several places for God and record what we find. You'll need to come back to this devotional during the week to finish the scavenger hunt. Ready?

Here's your scavenger list; you need to "find" all these things:

Bible verse about God's plan for your future: _____

_____

Quote from a friend about God's love: _____

_____

Quote from a book that answers a question you have right now about God:

_____

Advice from someone about serving God:

_____

_____

One person to show God's love to this week.

_____

_____

One service opportunity in your community.

_____

_____

At the end of the week, answer this question: Where have I found God this week, and where else can I look for Him?

God's Shovel

But since you excel in everything—in faith, in speech,
in knowledge, in complete earnestness and in the love we have kindled in
you—see that you also excel in this grace of giving. **2 Corinthians 8:7, NIV.**

Tithe is one tenth of whatever comes into our possession, and it belongs to God, according to the Bible (see Deuteronomy 14:22-29). You're probably already familiar with tithe and have been tithing since you were small. If Grandma gave you $100, you'd fill out your tithe envelope for $10—that's 10 percent. But what if Grandma gave you $100 and you filled out your tithe envelope for $90? What if, instead of giving God 10 percent and keeping 90 percent, you gave God 90 percent and kept 10 percent? Could you do it? *Would* you do it?

Impossible, you say! No one could live like that, especially if they had bills to pay and groceries to buy. It couldn't be done. After all, you need money to buy things with, things necessary to live.

Well, it's a good thing you can't tell that to R. G. LeTourneau, but he wouldn't have listened to you anyway. Mr. LeTourneau was a bigwig Christian businessman during the early part of the twentieth century. He became a Christian when he was 16 years old, and he realized a very important fact: everything we have comes from God. That means that everything we own is really God's, not ours. We're just borrowing it. Mr. LeTourneau figured that if it was all God's, he should give it right back. So he gave a reverse tithe of 90 percent.

Poor man, you might think, *with hardly any money to live on, he really must have had it tough*. He didn't. He said, "I shovel out the money, and God shovels it back—but God has a bigger shovel." Mr. LeTourneau discovered that you can't outgive God.

Now, you don't have to give 90 percent of your income in order for God to bless you. What matters more than the amount you give is the attitude you have when you give. If you are stingy and your wallet creaks when you open it to give to God, why should He bless you with more? But if you "excel in this grace of giving," you might just find out, as Mr. LeTourneau did, that God's shovel is so big you don't have enough room for all His blessings.

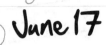

Follow Me

Walking along the beach of Lake Galilee,
Jesus saw two brothers: Simon (later called Peter) and Andrew.
They were fishing, throwing their nets into the lake. It was their
regular work. Jesus said to them, "Come with me. I'll make a new
kind of fisherman out of you. I'll show you how to catch men and
women instead of perch and bass." They didn't ask questions, but simply
dropped their nets and followed. **Matthew 4:18-20, Message.**

A group of cyclists biking through China had no idea they were about to make a friend for life. During a stop they noticed a little homeless dog wandering around on the side of the highway. One of the bikers offered the dog a piece of chicken, and she began to follow them. And she kept following them. Every day. For 24 days and more than 1,000 miles.

The cyclists met the dog in Yajiang, Sichuan province, on their way to Lhasa, Tibet. At first they thought she just liked them. But day after day she continued to follow them. She ran most of the way, although they strapped a cage onto the back of one of the bikes to carry the dog when they went downhill, because they traveled too fast for her to keep up. The bikers were so encouraged by the little dog's persistence that they started a blog for her. They decided to call her Xiao (little) Sa (short for Lhasa, where they were headed).

In less than two weeks the blog had more than 37,000 followers, and people started calling her the "dog with determination." Xiao Sa, the homeless dog on the side of the road who found kindness with a bunch of passing cyclists, was suddenly famous. The Internet was abuzz about her, inspired by her story. One of the cyclists wanted to adopt her.

All because somebody decided to act with kindness and give a homeless dog something to eat, which just goes to show that you never know where a little kindness will lead. What might happen, for instance, if you were kind to someone today? If you held the door for an elderly woman, or smiled back at the Walmart greeter, or stood up for someone being bullied, something wonderful could happen.

Jesus said simply, "Follow Me." The disciples followed Him and the world was inspired by their deeds. When we follow Him, the world will be inspired by our deeds too. More people will want to follow Jesus because He is kind enough to stop by the side of the road and offer them something to eat. They'll follow Him anywhere. So will we.

Warning: Attack Goose

When the seventy-two disciples returned, they joyfully reported to him, "Lord, even the demons obey us when we use your name!" "Yes," he told them, "I saw Satan fall from heaven like lightning! Look, I have given you authority over all the power of the enemy, and you can walk among snakes and scorpions and crush them. Nothing will injure you." **Luke 10:17-19, NLT.**

B elieve me when I tell you that you don't want to be bitten by a goose. Oh, sure, they seem all cute and peaceful waddling across a field as they honk softly. But it's a very different story when they're chasing you, beaks lowered and snapping at your tender calves. If they manage to nab you, they'll hang on, beating you with their strong wings, and kicking you with their powerful legs, which have talons on the back of their feet. I've learned to steer clear of geese.

If geese are scary to me, can you imagine how frightening they must have seemed to a little 5-year-old boy? When President Dwight Eisenhower was a kid, he visited a farm and decided he'd like to explore while the grown-ups gabbed. Unfortunately he found the barn guarded by a big goose that threatened to attack him. No matter how he tried to sneak past, the goose wouldn't let him.

By the time his uncle found him, he was in tears. Uncle Luther gave little Dwight an old broom, and he managed to thump the unsuspecting goose on the tail. It was so surprised it backed off. Dwight, who grew up to become the leader of the Allied armies during World War II and a president of the United States, said that he had learned from that encounter with a goose "never to negotiate with an adversary except from a position of strength."

What he meant is that you should attack enemies only if you are strong enough to defeat them. When Jesus sent out His disciples, His Spirit went with them. In His name they were able to cast out demons. They were thrilled. Satan fell at the mighty name of Jesus. He had no choice; he's a loser and he knows it.

But if the disciples had gone out and said, "In Fred's name I cast you out," the demons would have laughed them all the way back home. Fred has no power against satanic forces, and neither do we. Only Jesus has defeated Satan, and only He has power. In order for us to go out and fight Satan from a position of power, we need to have Jesus with us and in us. Then we too will be able to tell demons to get lost, and they'll have no choice but to obey.

Juneteenth

Therefore if the Son makes you free,
you shall be free indeed. **John 8:36, NKJV.**

On January 1, 1863, President Abraham Lincoln announced the Emancipation Proclamation. All African American slaves in the United States were now free. Can you imagine how the slaves must have celebrated their freedom? They were now free to do whatever they wanted. No one had control of them anymore. They couldn't be whipped, beaten, killed, bought, or sold. President Abraham Lincoln had set them free.

But some slaves living in the state of Texas didn't know about the president's announcement. No one is sure why the slaves weren't told they were free, but they weren't. The Civil War continued until April 1865, and it wasn't until June 19, 1865, that Major General Gordon Granger came to Galveston, Texas, and read the short version of the Emancipation Proclamation. The slaves realized that they had actually been free for more than two years!

The following year the freedmen gathered in Texas to celebrate, and the tradition continued. They called their new holiday Juneteenth and celebrated their freedom very much like we celebrate our freedom from Britain on the Fourth of July with parades, games, and special food and songs.

But what if Major General Granger had never arrived to give them the good news? It's a small country; they would have learned they were free sooner or later, right? Probably. But who knows how many years they would have suffered in slavery before they realized they were actually free? It's sad to think about, isn't it? They lived in slavery more than two years while they were actually free.

Our job as Christians is just as important as Major General Granger's. It's our responsibility to bring to all the people of the world the news that they are no longer slaves to sin. They have been set free by Jesus. They don't have to live degrading lives anymore; they aren't slaves to Satan. Jesus has set them free. It's time to celebrate! But if we don't tell them, how will they ever find out?

The Ants Have It

*My brothers and sisters, if one of you should wander
from the truth and someone should bring that person back,
remember this: Whoever turns a sinner from the error of their way will
save them from death and cover over a multitude of sins.* **James 5:19, 20, NIV.**

You probably think there's not much you can learn from something as small as an ant. I mean, come on . . . how small are their brains, anyway? Do they even have brains? I'm not sure. But I do know that you can learn something from just about any animal if you pay attention. I think Solomon must have thought so too. In Proverbs he tells us, "Take a lesson from the ants, you lazybones. Learn from their ways and become wise!" (Proverbs 6:6, NLT).

Austrian researchers studying ants did become wiser by watching them. They learned how all the ants in a colony managed to gain immunity when workers accidentally brought germs back to the colony. In order to figure it out, they infected some ants with glow-in-the-dark fungal spores.

The ants the researchers studied licked the spores off the infected ants. This act of grooming spreads the germs throughout the colony so that all the healthy ants get a little bit, which their immune systems are able to handle, and the infected ants get cleaned up so the germs don't kill them.

Wouldn't it be great if our churches worked that way? We all sin, even if we don't want to admit it—the Bible tells us we do (see Romans 3:23). When a sinner comes to church—either we or someone else—what if, instead of making sure they realize they've been really, really bad by judging them and ignoring them until they either start doing good or get discouraged and leave the church, we all supported them by praying for them and helping them come back to God? Imagine what a healthy "colony" we'd have?

Satan is exactly like those researchers infecting us with glow-in-the-dark sin, but we don't have to lose our brothers and sisters to his germs. We can help them straight back to God. God's Holy Spirit will strengthen our immune systems so that none of us will die.

He Loves Me,
He Loves Me Not?

See how very much our Father loves us, for he calls us his children, and that is what we are! But the people who belong to this world don't recognize that we are God's children because they don't know him. I John 3:1, NLT.

Did you know there's a surefire way to tell if someone loves you? It's true. I learned this when I was a kid. Step one, pick a daisy. Step two, start picking the petals off. Pluck the first petal and say, "[He or she] loves me." Pluck the second petal and say, "[He or she] loves me not." Repeat until you have only one petal left. Is it "loves me" or "loves me not"? There you go: now you know if you're loved.

All right, so maybe it's not a *scientific* method. And there is room for error . . . lots of room, in fact. Maybe it's not so surefire after all, but it *is* a method. Aren't you glad we don't have to resort to plucking daisy petals to know whether or not God loves us? We know He loves us because He has made us His children. He could have made us His slaves instead. He could have forced us to pretend to love Him no matter how we really felt about it. He could have made us work for salvation instead of giving it to us as a gift.

Do you realize that God loves you every day? You may wake up, go off to school, talk to your friends, argue with your family members, pet your dog, and all the time—every second that ticks by—God is loving you. Really think about that for a minute. Let it sink into your brain how very much God loves and cares for you. He watches over you every second, not just the ones during which you happen to be thinking about Him. He loves you even when you forget He exists.

That's the definition of a father. He loves you, protects you, helps you, takes care of you, looks out for you, and provides for you always. Earthly fathers may not live up to that definition. Sometimes they let us down. They're only human, and they can make mistakes. But God is perfect, and He loves perfectly.

Today is Father's Day. Don't forget to honor your earthly father. "Honor your father and mother. Then you will live a long, full life in the land the Lord your God is giving you" (Exodus 20:12, NLT). Try to think of some way to honor your heavenly Father, too. Write God a poem telling Him how much you love Him. Or give an offering just to say "I love you." Or do something nice for someone because you know it would make Him happy.

Heavenly Shock Absorbers

"Does Job fear God for nothing?" Satan replied. "Have you not put a hedge around him and his household and everything he has? You have blessed the work of his hands, so that his flocks and herds are spread throughout the land. But now stretch out your hand and strike everything he has, and he will surely curse you to your face." The Lord said to Satan, "Very well, then, everything he has is in your power, but on the man himself do not lay a finger." **Job 1:9-12, NIV.**

I just got a new bike, and the guy who sold it to me showed me how to adjust it so that if I'm riding on a bumpy road, the bike absorbs the shock. Instead of jarring my teeth when I hit a bump in the road, the bike (via the shock absorbers) takes all that beating for me so I get a cushy ride.

You may have noticed that life is not a cushy ride. There's a lot of bad stuff happening. Maybe it's happening to you or people you know, or even just people in general. You don't even have to watch the news to see bad stuff. You could unplug from the Internet, never listen to the radio, throw away your phone, and you'd still hear about it. It's everywhere.

That's because this planet is broken. Adam and Eve's sin cracked it right in two. God is on one side of the crack and Satan is on the other. Life is like a big tug-of-war. If we don't grab hold of God with both hands, our teeth, and our toes, Satan will pull us right into that big old crack in between both of them, and we don't want that.

That's what Satan tried to do to Job. When God pointed out that Job was His faithful servant, Satan said it was because God protected Job, that God was like Job's shock absorber, keeping him from having a bumpy ride through life. So God said He'd stop being Job's shock absorber so Satan could see that Job loved God even when things weren't going well for him.

How about you? It's easy to follow God when life is good, but it's not so easy when it starts to get bumpy. If God took away His protection today and bad stuff started happening to you, would you still follow Him? Do you love Him? Or just what He does for you?

Even though things got really bad for Job, do you know what he said? He said that even if God killed him he'd still trust God. His love for God wasn't about what God could do for him. He trusted that if things weren't going well for him, God was still there. For Satan, that was quite a shock. The next time things aren't going so great for you, why don't you try praising God anyway and give Satan a shock yourself?

Somebody, Anybody Else

For we are His workmanship, created in
Christ Jesus for good works, which God prepared beforehand
so that we would walk in them. **Ephesians 2:10, NASB.**

Have you ever wished you were somebody, anybody else? I have. When I wish I were smarter, there's always someone I can think of who is smarter than me. I wish I were them. When I wish I were better looking, there's always someone I can think of who is better looking than me. I wish I were them, too. There's someone who knows exactly what to say when I get tongue-tied. There's someone who always does the right thing when I can't figure out what I'm supposed to do. There's always someone who is better than I am at almost anything.

That's when I have to stop and remind myself that God made only one me. I'm not perfect and I don't always know what to say, but if I'm willing to let God use me, He doesn't need my words. He may just need my presence or maybe my smile. If I get hung up on what I think God needs from me, I'm just getting in His way.

Last week I went to visit a woman in the hospital who was dying. I really wanted to ask her if she was saved, but I didn't know how to ask, and she was on so much pain medicine I'm not sure she would have been able to answer the question. I felt helpless. I really wanted to be someone who could help that woman put her heart right with Jesus before she died.

But maybe that's not why God wanted me there. When we struggle to do what we *think* God wants us to do, we have to remember that we are not trailblazers. No one has asked us to hew a path through the wilderness. God prepared the path for us. He's gone ahead of us. If God had needed me to lead that woman to Christ before she died, He would have made it possible for her to concentrate on what I had to say, and then He would have given me the right words to say. He wouldn't let me fail Him if I was willing to do His work; He would have made it possible. So instead of wasting time wanting to be someone who knew exactly what to do, I should have concentrated on being willing to do what only I could do—the good work that God created me to do—and taken the path ahead of me that God had prepared.

You are unique, and no one can take your place. You have a work to do for God. If you don't do it, who will? The path has been prepared with you in mind. Only you can walk down it. The question is: Will you follow God on the path He has prepared for you?

YOLO

*Jesus said to him, "'You shall love the Lord your God
with all your heart, with all your soul, and with all your mind.'
This is the first and great commandment. And the second is like it:
'You shall love your neighbor as yourself.' On these two commandments
hang all the Law and the Prophets."* **Matthew 22:37-40, NKJV.**

Do you know what YOLO means? That's short for You Only Live Once. YOLO is a bit like *carpe diem,* which is a phrase from a Latin poem that means "seize the day." If you were afraid to give a speech but you were passionate about a cause—say, helping homeless pets—someone might encourage you by saying *"Carpe diem!"* You would find your voice, give your speech, and save lots of cute, cuddly pets.

YOLO, on the other hand, doesn't have the same noble goals as *carpe diem.* If someone didn't like their teacher and thought it would be a great prank to spill a can of vegetable soup on her desk and tell her it was puke, someone might say, "Dude, do it. YOLO." No, there's nothing noble about YOLO. Generally, teens use it to encourage one another to do stupid or risky things because, hey, YOLO.

The thing is, YOLO isn't for Christians. This world isn't even our home, as the old song goes: we're just a-passing through. We aren't living here; we're only taking a short, painful vacation. Our real home is heaven, and we'll *really* live when we get there. And once we're there it will be forever.

This little pit stop we're making on Planet Earth won't last forever, though. While we're here we have some responsibilities. Our most important priority is to make every day count. Christians don't have time to waste looking at the scenery; it's much better where we're headed than where we are. We need to keep our heads in the game and focus on what is important.

Someone interpreted today's verse this way: "The purpose of your time on earth is not primarily about acquiring possessions, attaining status, achieving success or even experiencing happiness. Those are secondary issues. Life is all about love with God and with other people. You may succeed in many areas, but if you fail to love God and love others, you have missed the reason God created you."

Mirror, Mirror

Your adornment must not be merely external—braiding the hair, and wearing gold jewelry, or putting on dresses; but let it be the hidden person of the heart, with the imperishable quality of a gentle and quiet spirit, which is precious in the sight of God. **I Peter 3:3, 4, NASB.**

Mirror, mirror, on the wall, who's the fairest of them all?"
No, it's not Snow White. It's not even that girl in your class with the sparkling white teeth, the designer clothes, and the expensive shoes. It might be you. Or it could be the guy who helped his friend move last weekend after his parents broke up. Then again, it could be that kid in the youth group, the one who volunteers for everything. You know, the girl who always has spinach in her teeth and looks like she got dressed in the dark?

It all depends on who is doing the judging. People usually judge by looking only on the outside. That's why you don't see any ugly celebrities. It's also why Miss America winners are always beautiful, never homely. Not that there's anything wrong with looking good or even with dressing nicely. The thing is, no matter how nice you look, no matter how many fashionable clothes you have in your closet, what makes you beautiful is something most people overlook completely: your personality.

I'm not talking about the personality you were born with, the traits you have that make you the life of the party, the class clown, or the kid voted most likely to become president. I'm talking about the part of your personality you've let God work on. We've all got unique character traits that make us who we are. Think about the disciples. Peter was impulsive; he acted before he thought things through. John was loving. Phillip was cynical; he didn't believe everything he heard. Judas was sneaky.

Most of them let Jesus change their personalities—except Judas—so that they became ambassadors for Him. He sanded down the rough edges of their characters and polished them to a shine so they could better reflect Him. He'll do that for us too. He'll create His character in us so that when we look in the mirror we'll see Him shining back at us.

Try This: Write down your character traits: the good, the bad, and the ugly. Then pray that God will create inner beauty in you that will shine out with such force that everyone who looks at you will recognize Jesus living in you.

Suffering

Endure suffering along with me, as a good soldier of Christ Jesus. **2 Timothy 2:3, NLT.**

How do you feel about suffering? I'm against it. But let's face it: Life is full of suffering. My friend Jai was picked up out of her crib and shaken when she was a baby. Now she's blind and paralyzed from the waist down. She says, "I hate being paralyzed. I didn't ask to be confined to a wheelchair. But there's nothing I can do to change that. I have to make the best of it."

Suffering is painful. It hurts. Some people make the mistake of trying to escape from it by drowning their pain in alcohol, numbing it with drugs, or distracting themselves from it with promiscuous or risky behavior. These things have one thing in common: they don't make the problem, or the pain, go away. In fact, they make things much worse, because now, on top of suffering from your problem, you'll also be suffering from addiction to something that can mask the pain but never make it go away.

We must remember that God can use our suffering to make us stronger Christians. When our faith in God is tempted by suffering, we often think, *God must hate me or He wouldn't let this terrible thing happen to me. Where is God? Why isn't He rescuing me from this pain?* If we think that, it's the first step to turning our back on God. We can't let Satan plant those thoughts in our head. Resist them.

If we don't question where God is in our suffering and instead lean on Him harder, clutching Him with both hands and refusing to let go, two things will happen. First, we will get stronger. Our faith won't just be lip service. We'll be living it. And second, we'll make Satan mad. I don't know about you, but I like to be the kind of girl who gets up in the morning ready to wreck Satan's day. I like him to see my feet hit the floor and know he's muttering, "Oh, great; she's awake."

When he was a young monk, Martin Luther struggled to believe that God had accepted him. But he wouldn't let go of God. Over and over he pleaded, "I am yours, save me" (Psalm 119:94, NKJV). When we are battered by suffering, we can claim that verse, too. You can never be lost while claiming that verse. Never.

Starting Over

This means that anyone who belongs to Christ has become a new person. The old life is gone; a new life has begun! **2 Corinthians 5:17, NLT.**

They called him the Forest Boy after he wandered in to the German capital saying he'd spent five years living in the woods with his father. He said they'd taken to the woods after his mother died in a car accident and had been wandering around ever since. Then his father died, and Forest Boy buried him in the woods and hiked out. He said he was 17 and wasn't able to give authorities much information about himself, only that his name was Ray.

They couldn't find his father's body and weren't able to locate any family, let alone figure out what country Forest Boy came from. He spoke English, but they could tell he wasn't American. Oh, and he didn't want them to release his photo.

Months dragged on before it all came out. Forest Boy was really Robin van Helsum, a 20-year-old Dutch man who was having personal problems and wanted to get away and start a new life. His father hadn't died in the forest either. Needless to say, authorities were not amused. In fact, they were so seriously displeased with Robin's little hoax that they decided to prosecute him for fraud and smack him with a big, fat legal bill for wasting their time.

Starting over can be very tempting. Everyone botches things at some point and wants to start again. Our God is a God of second chances, after all. If He wasn't, there'd be no point in any of us living even one more day, because we'd all be doomed before we even got started.

But there's no need to make up different identities for ourselves when we need a new beginning. God takes us just as we are; we don't even have to clean up first. All we have to do is ask Him for a fresh start. What we do need to do, though, is put the past behind us. We need to focus our attention on the future and let go of the habits and behaviors that have gotten us into trouble. We can't hang on to them with one hand and reach out to God with the other. We have to let go and be willing to become new people in Jesus. Our old life is gone, and our new life has begun.

Have you ever wanted just to step into a new life, as Robin van Helsum did? Many people have fantasized about it at one time or another, but they forget about all the people they'd be leaving behind. Robin's father actually did pass away before Robin was "found," and never knew what had become of his son. And Robin never had a chance to say goodbye.

Shake It Up

Sing for joy, you heavens, for the Lord has done this;
shout aloud, you earth beneath. Burst into song, you mountains,
you forests and all your trees, for the Lord has redeemed Jacob,
he displays his glory in Israel. **Isaiah 44:23, NIV.**

Do you need a makeover? A worship makeover, I mean. Has your worship gotten predictable? Is it boring? Do you do the same worship activities over and over? Are you in a rut? Do you yawn your way through devotions? nod off to sleep while you read your Bible?

Wake up! It's time to sing! It's time to shout! It's time to worship our great God! There's no time like the present to get started. Take one of these ideas each day and try them out. If you like them, keep using them. If you don't, try others. Make it your mission to find new and exciting ways to worship God each day. God isn't boring; why should worship be?

Idea 1: Make some noise. Sing your peppiest worship songs and bang things. The Israelites would have had tambourines and cymbals. Bang on a pot with a wooden spoon if you need to. Generate some enthusiasm.

Idea 2: Recite poetry to God. This one's even better if you can find a nice spot outside under the trees. The poetry, of course, is the Psalms. Some good ones to start with: Psalms 35, 91, 98, 99, 100, 111, 117, 136.

Idea 3: Paint or draw God a picture. Play some worship music on your iPod to keep your thoughts focused. Use bright, bold colors.

Idea 4: Run. That's right, run! As you run, list God's blessings. Say them out loud if you have enough breath.

Idea 5: Dance. King David danced before the Lord. Put on some worship music and dance for joy.

Idea 6: Sing to God. Choose a contemporary worship song, or for something interesting, sing one of the psalms to your favorite tune.

Idea 7: Make a list of all the things you love about God. See if you can come up with 100. Read them aloud to God.

Remember, worship isn't something you do; it's a gratefulness that starts inside you. It's a genuine desire to get closer to God and love Him more.

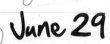

June 29

All-Rounder

Let the message about Christ, in all its richness,
fill your lives. Teach and counsel each other with all the wisdom he gives.
Sing psalms and hymns and spiritual songs to God with thankful hearts.
And whatever you do or say, do it as a representative of the Lord Jesus,
giving thanks through him to God the Father. **Colossians 3:16, 17, NLT.**

An all-rounder is someone who is good at many things. If they play on a baseball team, they can pitch as well as they hit, they can run as well as they can catch. You can put them in any position and they'll do a great job.

As Christians we need to be all-rounders. Then, no matter what situation we find ourselves in, God can use us. We must take advantage of any chance to learn something new. Ellen White says, "Let the youth who need an education set to work with a determination to obtain it. Do not wait for an opening; make one for yourselves. Take hold in any small way that presents itself. . . . Be determined to become as useful and efficient as God calls you to be. Be thorough and faithful in whatever you undertake. Procure every advantage within your reach for strengthening the intellect. Let the study of books be combined with useful manual labor, and by faithful endeavor, watchfulness, and prayer, secure the wisdom that is from above. This will give you an all-round education. Thus you may rise in character and gain an influence over other minds, enabling you to lead them in the path of uprightness and holiness. . . . Let every student take his Bible, and place himself in communion with the great Teacher. Let the mind be trained and disciplined to wrestle with hard problems in the search for divine truth" (*Messages to Young People*, pp. 174, 175).

Right now you probably feel that you've learned as much as school can possibly stuff into your head. And chances are at least half of what you've learned isn't even interesting to you; you just learned it because you had to. But the brain is an amazing organ. It has the ability to grow and learn, but you have to exercise it. If all you ever do is sit in front of the television, your brain will be a mental couch potato. In order to strengthen it, you have to stretch it.

Believe it or not, you can learn all sorts of things. Why not find something you're truly interested in and learn more about it? Learn an interesting language, a new sport, or a challenging game. Memorize scripture. Above all, never stop learning.

Two-faced

*You're hopeless, you religion scholars and Pharisees!
Frauds! You're like manicured grave plots, grass clipped
and the flowers bright, but six feet down it's all rotting bones
and worm-eaten flesh. People look at you and think you're saints,
but beneath the skin you're total frauds.* **Matthew 23:27, 28, Message.**

Ethan graduated from a Christian high school. He'd been inducted into the honor society and had done well in school. He had a bright career ahead of him, and everyone spoke well of him at his graduation, saying what a fine Christian young man he was. If you didn't know him, you would have no reason to suspect that he wasn't.

Most of the audience at his graduation had no reason not to believe all the wonderful things the teachers were saying about Ethan. But his friends, who were also sitting in the audience, knew that lately Ethan had been doing things that Christian young men didn't do. He'd been lying to his parents, drinking, smoking, and other things that would likely get him into trouble someday. Ethan looked one way on the outside, but inside he was very different. He was a fraud; he was pretending to be a Christian but really wasn't committed to Christ and His values.

When Jesus was on earth, there was a whole group of these people. They were called Pharisees. They acted as though they were religious and thought they were better than everyone else, who were just lowly sinners. But Jesus knew what was in their hearts. He knew that in spite of their polished outsides, they weren't so shiny on the inside. And it's the inside that matters.

Jesus called the Pharisees hypocrites. Today we'd say they were two-faced, showing one face in public and another in private. It was their pompous confidence that got them into trouble, and it can get us into trouble too if we're not careful. What we have to remember is that it's a level playing field. God doesn't have favorites. We're all equal; we're all sinners. We're all saved by the same sacrifice.

We can't earn salvation. Nothing we can do will ever save us. When we truly understand that, we'll become humble. Our hearts will break from having hurt Jesus so badly. We'll have only one face to show the world. It'll be a face that's grateful for God's mercy and eager to share it with others.

Love Hunger

*This is my commandment: Love each other in the same way
I have loved you. There is no greater love than to lay down one's life
for one's friends. You are my friends if you do what I command. . . .
This is my command: Love each other. John 15:12-17, NLT.*

On my way home I saw a man with a cast on one leg, propped up near a stop sign holding a piece of cardboard with the words "Anything will help." He looked very dejected. His head drooped down, his chin practically on his chest. As I sat there, I wondered if I should help. After all, he sure looked as though he needed help. Should I give him some money? Or shouldn't I? While I was trying to make up my mind, the light changed color, and I was forced into the flow of traffic. I never did answer my question, because I'm still not sure what I should have done.

On one hand, there are several places in the city that care for homeless individuals. If he really needed a square meal or a bed to sleep in, it was there. They would not, however, give him drugs or alcohol. Maybe he was sitting at the corner with a sign to get some money to buy those things. I'll probably never know, and it bugs me.

Mother Teresa, who did a lot of work with poor people and ought to know, said, "The greatest disease in the West today is not TB or leprosy; it is being unwanted, unloved, and uncared for. We can cure physical diseases with medicine, but the only cure for loneliness, despair, and hopelessness is love." If we followed Jesus' command, love hunger wouldn't be a disease at all.

We all have an obligation to love others, but we must find ways to do it safely. Working with a group from church or school is a great way to be able to reach out to others and show them God's love. Mission trips also give us a good way to reach out to people we wouldn't normally be exposed to. But we shouldn't forget that some of the hardest loving we may have to do is right in our own backyards. We should start by loving those we know, and grow our love from there.

If you passed a homeless person with a sign, what would you do? How does your own personal safety influence whether or not you get involved? Are there safe places in your town where you can volunteer to help the less fortunate?

High Seas Hero

Shortly before dawn Jesus went out to them,
walking on the lake. When the disciples saw him
walking on the lake, they were terrified. "It's a ghost,"
they said, and cried out in fear. **Matthew 14:25, 26, NIV.**

The Wedge in California is a super-duper-wave-producing beach that is world-famous. Surfers come from miles around to tackle the enormous waves, which are created partly because of improvements people have made to the rock jetty at the Newport Harbor entrance. When the water hits just right, the waves can reach 30 feet high. Dude, that's a lot of wave!

Of course, this makes the Wedge a great place for surfers to catch some hang time. It's exciting and also very dangerous because the other thing the Wedge features is a steep, sandy shore that creates a really strong backwash that can drag people out to sea. If you watch a video of the waves at the Wedge, you can see that the power of the ocean in that spot is intense.

Needless to say, when you combine huge waves, strong pull, and people both on and off skinny surfboards, you end up with a high probability for disaster. Lifeguards are often called on to drag people back to shore when they get pulled out by accident or lose their boards. Of course, lifeguards aren't bobbing around in the water waiting for people to rescue. They're on shore watching the water. When they see someone in trouble, they race down the beach, jump into the water, and swim out to pull the person to safety.

And just because they're lifeguards doesn't mean they have superhuman strength. Lifeguards get bashed by the waves too—they're only human, after all. It's just as dangerous for them to be out in the pounding surf as it is for the surfers.

Aren't you glad we have a Lifeguard who can walk on water? When we're drowning in the sea of life, we don't have to wait for someone to swim out and save us. We have only to lift our hands and grab the Lifeguard. He's always there; He's ready to save us whenever we need Him.

If we want, we don't even have to swim in the water where the sea tosses us around. We can take His hand and walk on water, too. When we do that, it doesn't matter how many storms are raging or how high the waves are. The only thing that matters is that we don't take our eyes off Him. As long as we do that, we don't have to fear drowning.

I Give Up

He went on a little farther and fell to the ground.
He prayed that, if it were possible, the awful hour awaiting him
might pass him by. "Abba, Father," he cried out, "everything is possible
for you. Please take this cup of suffering away from me.
Yet I want your will to be done, not mine." **Mark 14:35, 36, NLT.**

Have you ever been in the middle of a difficult experience or project and wanted to throw up your hands and say, "I give up"? Beginnings are full of energy and excitement. Endings leave us satisfied with accomplishment. But middles are painful. We've lost the energy and optimism that got us started, and we're beginning to get tired of the work. In the middle is where people most often give up. When you give up in the middle, you always wonder if you could have finished eventually.

If you've ever wondered why it's tempting to give up, you don't have to look far. Satan loves to discourage us. He will tell us anything in order to get us to give up. If we listen to him and he sees that he's winning, he'll even give us excuses so that we feel better about giving up, because he knows that if we can feel good about ditching our project, we'll surrender even faster.

That's what he tried to do to Jesus in the Garden of Gethsemane. He told Jesus that there was no point in going through with Calvary, because the people He came to save didn't even love Him. They wouldn't even appreciate His sacrifice. Satan said, "One of Your own disciples, who has listened to Your instruction, and has been among the foremost in church activities, will betray You. One of Your most zealous followers will deny You. All will forsake You" (Ellen G. White, *The Desire of Ages,* p. 687).

Looking ahead to the darkness of Calvary, feeling God's presence leave Him as He carried our sins, knowing not one single earthly friend would comfort Him, Jesus faced Satan's temptation to give up. And even though He asked that God allow Him not to go through Calvary, He surrendered to God's will, and that's the key to facing any tough situation. Only God knows the ultimate outcome. While quitting isn't always a good thing, it's not always a bad thing, either. It depends on the situation, and only God knows how your particular situation will turn out. If you stay firmly planted in God's will, then no matter what happens, you'll be where you're supposed to be. And when the going gets tough, He'll support and comfort you and give you the strength to keep going.

Old Glory

Do not be misled: "Bad company corrupts good character."
Come back to your senses as you ought, and stop sinning;
for there are some who are ignorant of God—I say this
to your shame. **I Corinthians 15:33, 34, NIV.**

Today patriotic Americans will salute a flag we affectionately call Old Glory at picnics, parades, and firework displays. The flag received its nickname from William Driver, an early-nineteenth-century sea captain. It's the same flag we salute in schools and at sports events.

There's another flag that's well known in the South. It's called the Southern Cross, and it was the Confederate battle flag. Depending on whom you talk to, the Southern Cross is either a proud symbol of Southern heritage or a shameful reminder of slavery and segregation. In fact, because of its past, the Confederate flag symbol has been used by the Ku Klux Klan and more than 500 other racist hate groups.

So why did 19-year-old Byron Thomas, a Black student at the University of South Carolina at Beaufort, display the Confederate flag in his dorm room window? He said that when he looks at the flag, he doesn't see a symbol of racism and hate. He sees a symbol of respect and Southern pride. A lot of other people didn't see it that way, and Thomas was asked to remove the flag. The college reconsidered its decision, however, and told him that he was free to put it up. But he admitted that flying the Confederate flag is "kind of weird" because he's Black.

Thomas had a sense that all was not quite right, but he chose to fly the flag anyway because he wanted to see it as something different than a symbol used to promote hateful ideas. In the same way, Christians are lured into supporting Satan's ideas that may be mixed with some good or may even have some merit, or that may be downright bad but seem exciting or interesting.

Our attention is caught and we try to rationalize that this particular thing is harmless—it's not so bad, it's misunderstood, and so on. We have many excuses to convince ourselves and others that whatever we want to do, see, or experience is not a sin. If you suspect that something you are dabbling in is a sin but you're not sure, ask someone you trust who knows their Bible to help you understand God's position about it.

How Tempting

Blessed is the man who endures temptation;
for when he has been approved, he will receive the crown of life
which the Lord has promised to those who love Him. Let no one say when
he is tempted, "I am tempted by God"; for God cannot be tempted by evil,
nor does He Himself tempt anyone. But each one is tempted when he is
drawn away by his own desires and enticed. **James 1:12-14, NKJV.**

Have you ever fallen for a temptation? I won't believe you if you say no. Everyone has been tempted and given in at some point in their life. In fact, you probably can't count the number of times you've done a face-plant into temptation. I know I can't. That's why I appreciate God's forgiveness so much. I know I don't deserve it, but I'm grateful for it.

Still, I'd rather not let temptation get the better of me. There's a saying that goes something like "You can't keep the birds from flying around your head, but you can keep them from making a nest in your hair." Satan is going to tempt us; that's practically his job description. But we don't have to fall. We can endure temptation, as James says.

"How?" you ask. First, we have to remember God isn't the one who is tempting us. This is great news because that means God is on our side. He wants us to endure temptation even more than we do. Second, we need to re-member that temptation is not sin. It *leads* to sin, but it isn't sin.

It's like this: If it's midnight and I wake up hungry, I might be tempted to eat the chocolate cake I know is in the refrigerator. Have I eaten it? Not yet. I've only been tempted. The chocolate cake is still in the fridge. If I get out of bed, shuffle to the kitchen, put the cake on a plate, find a fork, start shoveling the cake into my mouth, and chew and swallow it, then I've eaten the cake.

Satan can bombard us with as many temptations as he wants to (and he does), but he can't make us *act* on them. Only we can decide to do that. That's our free will kicking in. But one thing is for certain. When we get the idea of the temptation, that's when we need to stop it. Don't play with it. Step away. Pray. Ask God to redirect your thoughts. Recite scriptures to get your mind firmly focused on God. If you pray every time Satan tempts you, he'll start to leave you alone.

I Need a Hero

The Lord is near to all who call upon Him, to all who call upon Him in truth. He will fulfill the desire of those who fear Him; He also will hear their cry and save them. **Psalm 145:18, 19, NKJV.**

You're having a bad day. No, worse than a bad day. It's a rotten day, and it's just gotten worse. Not only did you miss your ride to school, dump your books trying to put them in your locker, then accidentally lock yourself *out* of your locker, but now that gang of bullies who has been pestering you is headed over, and this time it looks as though they mean business. Has that one gotten even bigger since yesterday?

Great, there's not even anyone around to hear you scream. You clutch your books tighter, close your eyes as tight as you can, and . . . but wait! What is that?

It's a bird! It's a plane! No, it's Superman!

Yeah, you wish. Wouldn't it be great if every time you got into a rough situation there was someone to call on for help? Well, guess what: there is! Our Superhero makes Superman look like the cartoon character he is. Superman and all his superhero buddies are only fiction. They can help other comic characters, but they can't help us. God, on the other hand, is the ultimate superhero. Not only is He waiting to save us from whatever trouble we've gotten ourselves into but He wants to save us for eternity, which is even more important.

God already knows your situation. He's waiting for you to ask for help. It doesn't matter what is happening in your life. He can help you now and prepare you for heaven, too. But don't wait until you get into trouble to call on Him. Do it now. Right now, even if everything in your life is going well. God isn't just a help line for when we get in trouble. He's not just around to snatch you out of whatever jam you've gotten yourself into this time. He wants to walk with you all day, every day. That's how He teaches you to lean on Him, to trust Him, to rely only on Him and not on yourself.

Today, take God along with you wherever you go, no matter where it is. Pretend you're His tour guide. Narrate for Him what you're doing, and if you need help, ask Him for it. When something happens that's a blessing, thank Him. Talk to Him as if He's really there. He is.

Christians Without Borders

And the Good News about the Kingdom
will be preached throughout the whole world, so that all nations
will hear it; and then the end will come. **Matthew 24:14, NLT.**

Imagine if you were living in a country in which the closest doctor or hospital was more than 100 miles away. If you got hurt or sick, it would take a long time to get to help. Things would be even worse if there was a war going on in your country that made it dangerous even to travel to the closest hospital. Oh, and you don't have any transportation; you'll have to walk. You could be dead by the time you ever got anywhere near a doctor.

Sadly, that's not a situation that exists only in our imagination. It's what a lot of people in the world are actually living with. Back in 1971 a group of doctors and journalists decided that they wanted to do something to change that, so they formed an organization called Doctors Without Borders. They travel around the world wherever they are needed. If they have to go into a country at war, they don't take sides. They simply go into the country and treat the sick and injured. In 1999 they received the Nobel Peace Prize for their humanitarian work.

As Christians we tend to hang out in our safe churches. It's as though there's an imaginary border around the property that we're afraid to cross. It's us and them. But what if we decided to get rid of our border? What if we considered the whole neighborhood, the whole city or town, the whole state, the whole country, the whole world, as part of our church? Doctors Without Borders does wonderful work, but they don't share the good news with their patients. They can offer only temporary help. We can offer eternal help: the hope of salvation through Jesus.

We may not win a Nobel Peace Prize for our efforts, we may not even get a thank-you, but we will be helping to reach everyone in the world so that finally we can see the day when the end will come and the beginning will start. Is life here so great that you want it to go on and on? Wouldn't you rather join Christians Without Borders and bring the gospel to all the world so Jesus can come home and take us to heaven?

The next time you're at church, pretend the walls don't exist. Look outside and think of the neighborhood all around as part of the church. Would you act any differently to the people outside if there were no walls separating you from them?

i-Dosing

*May God himself, the God who makes everything holy and whole,
make you holy and whole, put you together—spirit, soul,
and body—and keep you fit for the coming of our Master, Jesus Christ.
The One who called you is completely dependable.
If he said it, he'll do it! I Thessalonians 5:23, 24, Message.*

They call it digital dosing, or i-dosing. Some people claim it's digital drugs, while others say at the most it'll just relax you, so what's the big deal? What's all the fuss about? Just what *is* i-dosing? It's the use of sounds to re-create the feeling of being on drugs. The technical term is binaural beats. A tone of one frequency is played in one ear while a tone of a slightly different frequency is played in the other ear. Supposedly, these beats alter brain waves to make it feel as if you've been doing drugs. "Doses" are named after the particular drug they are supposed to copy, such as marijuana or cocaine. YouTube videos that show teens acting silly document their "trips."

A lot of teens are interested. Parents and teachers are seriously freaked out. But is there anything to really be worried about? Is i-dosing really all that bad? In a word, yes. Whenever you look at any behavior, substance, or action and evaluate it by asking, "Is this really all that bad for me?" you've already started off on the wrong foot.

Christians aren't supposed to measure their behavior or activities by whether or not something is "really that bad" but by whether or not it brings them closer to God. If you wonder whether or not something is "all that bad," then you can be sure it's taking you further away from God, not bringing you closer. The trouble with "not all that bad" things is that they lead to worse things, until eventually you find you're on the wrong path altogether.

There's a difference between having fun and doing something destructive, or even something that has the potential for being destructive. Maybe i-dosing isn't really all that bad, but we know it's not all that good. And if it isn't all that good, we should leave it alone.

There will always be a latest and greatest new thing coming along. The next time something new catches your attention, start your evaluation by asking, "Will this bring me closer to God?" If you can't answer that question with a "Yes!" then walk away and find a better alternative.

July 9

Gimme a Break

After He had sent the crowds away,
He went up on the mountain by Himself to pray;
and when it was evening, He was there alone. **Matthew 14:23, NASB.**

Last weekend I went on a camping trip with my family. I got to bike, canoe, play games, make music, chat, read, eat camp food, watch fireworks, and if only I had remembered my bathing suit, I would have been able to swim. When I got home, I spent a fun day splashing around at a nearby dam, swimming, reading, and just sitting around appreciating the sunshine. When I got back to work, I felt like a new person.

Everyone needs a break. That's why schools schedule vacations into the school year, and employers give employees paid time off. They know that if you don't rest now, you'll burn out and not be able to do a good job. That's why God gave us Sabbath. He didn't design our bodies to work nonstop, and knew that if we tried we'd wear ourselves out. During His ministry Jesus took frequent breaks from the crowds—and sometimes even His disciples—and went up into the mountains by Himself to pray and just be still and rest for a while.

Overscheduling is a problem not just for adults but for teens, too. In fact, teens are busier than ever between college prep classes, community service, sports, clubs, and keeping in touch with their friends on multiple social media sites.

How about you? Is there any downtime in your schedule? If not, it may be time to sit back, take a look at your activities, and decide what to cut out, especially if your busyness is causing rushed or skipped devotions. It may be time to make some hard decisions.

If you're not sure what to cut out, try talking to your parents. That's what Lauren Biglow did. She said, "I would come home overflowing with stress over the fact that I had so many things to do simultaneously. And they would say, 'This is crazy, listen to yourself. You need to take a breath, reevaluate, and decide what you need to cut down on.'" Lauren ended up taking fewer AP classes and dropping a sport in order to get her schedule under control.

You may feel as if you're getting a lot done by jamming your schedule full to overflowing, but most of the time you'll actually get less done. Why? Without rest, your brain and body won't be able to function optimally. Follow Jesus right up onto the mountain to rest for a while. Then you'll be able to conquer the world. Or maybe just your homework.

Going Up

For the heart of this people has become dull,
with their ears they scarcely hear, and they have closed their eyes
lest they should see with their eyes, and hear with their ears,
and understand with their heart and return,
and I should heal them. **Matthew 13:15, NASB.**

Have you ever been in a crowd of strangers, looked around, and thought, *I wonder how many of these people know Jesus and are going to heaven?* I have. My next thought is always *How can I help them be saved?* I imagine I feel a bit like someone on the ship *Titanic* felt as it was sinking, peering down into the icy water at all the thrashing bodies. But while the *Titanic* had only enough lifeboats to save about half the people aboard, there are endless lifeboats to save the inhabitants of earth. There are enough lifeboats for everyone to have their own. The problem is convincing people to get *into* the lifeboats.

One man, John Harper, who was aboard the *Titanic* when it sank, knew he had an important work to do while there was still time to do it. After seeing that his little daughter was placed on one of the lifeboats, he gave his life jacket to another man and said, "I don't need this. I'm not going down; I'm going up!" As he floated in the icy water with other passengers who hadn't made it onto the lifeboats, Harper swam from one to another asking, "Are you saved?" He pleaded with them to accept Christ.

One young man managed to climb onto a piece of debris when Harper swam by. He called out to him, "Are you saved?" The man said, "No." Harper shouted, " 'Believe in the Lord Jesus Christ and thou shalt be saved.' " The current carried the two men apart but later brought them back together. Again, Harper repeated his question. Again the man replied, "No." With his dying breath, Harper told the man to believe in Jesus and be saved, and then he sank beneath the water and drowned. The man decided then and there to turn his life over to Christ.

John Harper was a man who understood the value of salvation. It's the only thing in life that really matters. Without salvation we are lost, not only here, but forever. With salvation, on the other hand, it doesn't matter what happens to us here. We don't have to worry. We're not going down—we're going up.

Make it your mission this week to ask at least one person if they are saved. If they aren't, lead them to Christ, where they'll be safe.

Crash Bang

Don't be selfish; don't try to impress others.
Be humble, thinking of others as better than yourselves. Don't look
out only for your own interests, but take an interest in others, too. You must
have the same attitude that Christ Jesus had. **Philippians 2:3-5, NLT.**

Would you believe me if I told you that your phone was a deadly weapon? Sure, you might have some friends you think might talk or text you to death, but that's not the kind of dead I'm talking about. I'm talking about really dead. Dead dead. Funeral dead. Never-see-someone-alive-again-here-on-earth dead.

What? You don't believe me? Would you believe Ashley's big sister? She pointed her phone at Ashley and killed her dead. She didn't mean it, of course. It was an accident. She was just texting. The text that cost Ashley her life said, "Yeah." It was the last thing Ashley saw before she flipped her car and was killed on impact.

Take a look at the most recent text you've sent. What does it say? Is it the cure for cancer? the formula for world peace? the solution to famine? Write it here:

_____

_____

Now ask yourself: Would I trade my life for this? Would I trade anyone's life for this? The truth is that no text is worth someone's life. There is nothing so important—even if it *is* the cure for cancer—that it can't wait until you get home to read or send.

You wouldn't get behind the wheel of a car, close your eyes, and drive the length of a football field, would you? That's how far you'd travel in just 4.6 seconds while reading the average text if you were driving 55 miles per hour. Think of all the things you could hit in that length of road: bikers, joggers, animals, oncoming cars, people walking their dogs, babies being pushed in strollers. Yet almost half of American teens say they've been in a car with a driver who used their cell phone in a way that put everyone's life in danger. The other half are probably the ones driving and doing the texting.

We can't look out for others while our thumbs are busy texting and our eyes are supposed to be on the road. Driving is serious business. Make it a rule that you won't talk on the phone, text, or search for music on your iPod while you're driving. The life you save could be your own. Or it could be the life of someone you love.

It's Your Choice

But if you refuse to serve the Lord, then choose today
whom you will serve. Would you prefer the gods your ancestors
served beyond the Euphrates? Or will it be the gods of the Amorites
in whose land you now live? But as for me and my family,
we will serve the Lord. **Joshua 24:15, NLT.**

There are lots of things you could choose to do today. Here are just a few:
- You could ride your bike down a busy freeway and risk getting run over by a semi.
- You could visit an elderly person.
- You could write a letter to someone who lives far away.
- You could plan a fund-raiser for a mission project.
- You could run away from home.
- You could stay in bed all day long.

You could do any of those things. But that doesn't mean they're the best things you could do, or even that they would be a good choice. The point is that you *could* do them. The reason you could do them is that you have free will—you decide what you will and will not do. God gave every human being free will.

God didn't have to give us free will. He could have forced us to love and serve Him. After all, He's bigger and stronger than we are. But God didn't want people to love Him because they were afraid of Him or because they had to. That wouldn't be real love. You can't actually *make* anyone love you. You can only make them *act* like they love you. And God isn't interested in an act. He only wants our love if we give it freely.

You may think that the decision to love and follow God happens just once. Some people call this "being saved" or "accepting Jesus as your personal Savior." But real Christianity is based on a choice you make to follow God (or not) *every* day. During that day you have many more choices about following God. As long as you live, you'll be able to decide every minute whether or not to follow God. You can do that because you have free will. You can follow God or follow someone else. The choice is yours. Today, whom will you follow? Can you say with Joshua, "As for me and my family, we will serve the Lord"?

Is That Legal?

Just because something is technically legal doesn't mean that it's spiritually appropriate. If I went around doing whatever I thought I could get by with, I'd be a slave to my whims. **I Corinthians 6:12, Message.**

In Culpeper, Virginia, it is illegal to wash a mule on the sidewalk. In Norfolk, Virginia, you may not spit on a seagull.

In Reno, Nevada, it is illegal to lie down on the sidewalk, and you may not drive your camel down the highway.

In Alaska it is legal to shoot bears, but it is unlawful to wake them up to take their picture. It is also illegal to push a live moose out of a moving airplane. In Juneau, pet flamingos are not allowed in barbershops.

In Texas, criminals must give their victims 24 hours notice either orally or in writing to explain the nature of the crimes they are about to commit.

These silly laws are, or were, on the books of these states. Most of them seem ridiculous to us. (OK, let's face it, most of them *are* ridiculous.) Way back when they were written they probably made sense to whoever voted them into law. But most laws exist for good reason and should be obeyed in order to keep everyone safe and keep society working properly.

There are some things, though, that are technically legal—you won't get arrested for doing them—but they're not good for us spiritually. You can lie to a friend, and a police officer won't slap handcuffs on you. You can keep your mouth shut and pocket the extra change the clerk gives you accidentally, and no one will drag you to jail. You can cheat on a test, and no one will book you and lock you in a cell.

But just because these things are technically legal doesn't mean they are the actions of a Christian. Humans naturally want to take the easy route, not the difficult one. But Jesus isn't calling us to walk on the easy road. He calls us to the difficult one and offers to help us. He says, "But the gateway to life is very narrow and the road is difficult, and only a few ever find it" (Matthew 7:14, NLT).

Today, look for the narrow gate and the difficult road and ask Jesus to help you walk it.

One Big Happy Family

*If it is possible, as much as depends on you,
live peaceably with all men.* **Romans 12:18, NKJV.**

Dan's parents were separated. They didn't even live in the same state anymore, and he knew they would probably never get together again. Sometimes Dan lived with one and sometimes with the other. He felt like a soccer ball being kicked between homes, and he hated trying to explain his family situation to anyone. He didn't understand it himself; how could he explain it to someone else?

If Dan's parents divorce, there's a good chance that one or both of them will get remarried within two years. About 75 percent of couples who divorce do just that, blending their original families. The new family is made up of children from both previous families, and the children often live between two homes, one with their mother and her new spouse and his kids, and another with their father and possibly his new spouse and maybe even her kids.

All this blending can get confusing. It's estimated that more than 50 percent of church members are either in or related to a blended family, so chances are, if you're not in one or related to one, you have friends in a blended family. These families face a lot of challenges trying to adjust to new circumstances, new people, and new rules.

At times the challenges may seem overwhelming. No matter what your family situation is, it can help to remember that this family isn't the first you've been blended into. "God wants every child of tender age to be His child, to be adopted into His family. Young though they may be, the youth may be members of the household of faith and have a most precious experience" (Ellen G. White, *The Adventist Home*, p. 486). We are God's children first, and as God's children we've all been adopted into the same big, blended family. Yes, it's hard, and there are growing pains. We may not always agree with one another, but there is something we can do that will help us get along with everyone: we can put all our relationships into God's hands.

If you are part of a blended family and you're having trouble adjusting, remember that psychologists say it can take anywhere from four to eight years for a blended family to "gel" and feel like a family. Be patient. Be forgiving. And as much as it depends on you, live at peace with all men (and family members). You never know what effect your faithful witness in this way will have on others.

A Shot in the Dark

Brothers and sisters, I do not consider myself yet
to have taken hold of it. But one thing I do: Forgetting what
is behind and straining toward what is ahead, I press on toward
the goal to win the prize for which God has called me
heavenward in Christ Jesus. **Philippians 3:13, 14, NIV.**

Today we're going to do a little target practicing. I had a slingshot made for you that is a replica of the one David used when he fought Goliath. I mean, this baby is awesome! I call it the Goliathater 2000. It will shoot a pebble 2,000 yards with complete accuracy. Here are the pebbles; grab a handful. Now load the Goliathater with a pebble, pull back on the doohickey, close your eyes, and hit the bull's-eye in that target.

What do you mean you can't see the target with your eyes closed? Oh, right, I understand. Yeah, you should have your eyes open. So open your eyes, turn around, and face away from the target. Now shoot.

What do you mean you can't see the target if you're facing away from it? Oh, yeah, I can see how that might be a problem. All right, this time face the target, pull back on the doohickey, let go, and see if you can hit the target. Wow! A bull's-eye. Hey, you're good at this. I guess it really helped to be able to see the target, huh?

Targets are a bit like goals in that way—if you can't see them, you can't reach them. That's why it's important to know exactly what you're aiming for. The best way to do this is to write down your goals and review them often. That way you'll keep working toward them.

As great as the Goliathater 2000 is, it does have some disadvantages. Once you shoot your pebble, you can't change the direction it's traveling. If you have bad aim, you're not going to hit the target. When trying to hit a goal, however, you have an advantage. As you work toward your goal, you may find yourself getting a little off course. When that happens, simply make an adjustment so that you're headed toward your target again.

The Christian life is full of setbacks. We make mistakes and fall down even when we're trying to reach our goal of pleasing God and obeying Him. What we need to realize is that as long as we keep our eyes on Jesus and continue to make small corrections in our behavior and attitude when we go off course, we will eventually reach our goal: the prize for which God has called us heavenward in Christ Jesus.

Half-baked

Then God said, "Let there be light"; and there was light.
And God saw the light, that it was good; and God divided the light
from the darkness. God called the light Day, and the darkness He called Night.
So the evening and the morning were the first day. **Genesis 1:3-5, NKJV.**

The sun is the largest star in our solar system. And is it ever hot! The sun's core is about 15.6 million kelvin. (A kelvin [K] is a unit the scientific community uses to measure heat, the way we measure the temperature using Celsius or Fahrenheit.) By the time that heat reaches the surface of the sun—called the photosphere—it's cooled down to a balmy 5800 K. Sunspots are cooler areas on the sun and are about 3800 K, which would still make our hottest days on earth seem icy.

The sun's power comes from nuclear fusion reactions. Every second approximately 700 million tons of hydrogen are converted to about 695 million tons of helium and 5 million tons of energy in the form of gamma rays. The sun warms us, helps our plants grow, and even gives us vitamin D.

It's also a fashion statement. Depending on when and where you live, you will have different ideas about the sun. My Filipino friends tell me that people in the Philippines lighten their skin so they won't be so dark, while in the United States we flock to tanning booths or bake in the sun to darken up.

God gave us the sun to light our days and to keep us and our planet healthy. A little sunshine is healthy for us. Although experts argue about whether or not we should use sunscreen, the safest thing is to spend a reasonable amount of time in the sun, which will also get you outdoors into the fresh air. If you're careful, you can prevent sunburns by not staying in the sun too long, covering your skin up so the sun can't reach it, and going outside during the hours of the day when the sun isn't strongest.

Just because the sun is a powerful force doesn't mean we shouldn't enjoy it. But like all other good things that God gives us, we need to enjoy it in moderation. Ellen White wrote that "sunlight is one of the best tonics and beautifiers in the world; therefore, men, women, and children, one and all, should seek it as one of the great natural agencies which help to form the 'elixir of life' " (in *The Health Reformer*, Apr. 1, 1871).

July 17

No Such Thing

It's in Christ that we find out who we are
and what we are living for. Long before we first heard of Christ
and got our hopes up, he had his eye on us, had designs on
us for glorious living, part of the overall purpose he is working
out in everything and everyone. **Ephesians 1:11, 12, Message.**

A coincidence is when two things happen that appear to be related. It's very random, like finding money on the ground when you forgot to bring any money to buy your lunch, or meeting someone by chance who can give you a ride somewhere you need to go. In other words, a coincidence is a happy circumstance that just happened for no reason. Boom. Just like that.

So here's the question: Can a Christian believe in coincidence?

You first. What do you think?

I used to believe in coincidence until I realized that if I believed in coincidence, it meant that I didn't believe in God, or at least I didn't believe that He was involved in my life, my whole life, and every part of my life. Think about it: if you believe that things happen by chance, then what exactly is God doing in your life? Some things? A few things? Occasional things? And how can you tell exactly which things God is doing so you can thank Him?

It's not easy believing there is no such thing as coincidence, because if you believe that God is behind all the good things that happen to you, then you also have to accept that He is responsible for allowing all the bad things that happen to you as well. Did your bike get a flat tire just when you really needed it to get to class on time? It's not a coincidence. God allowed that to happen. Your job is to accept whatever God lets into your life, good and bad, and learn from it.

There's no such thing as a coincidence, there are only circumstances that God allows. It helps to remember this the next time something goes wrong. Instead of thinking *Why is this happening to me?* realize that God is allowing this into your life, and whatever God allows in, He will help you overcome. You may never know why some things happen to you; understanding how and why God works isn't part of the package. What's important is to learn to trust Him, and when we can do that, we'll see everything that happens in our lives as opportunities to learn, whether they seem like coincidences or not.

So Not Laughing

Who has anguish? Who has sorrow? Who is always fighting?
Who is always complaining? Who has unnecessary bruises?
Who has bloodshot eyes? It is the one who spends long hours in the
taverns, trying out new drinks. Don't gaze at the wine, seeing how red it is,
how it sparkles in the cup, how smoothly it goes down. For in the end it
bites like a poisonous snake; it stings like a viper. **Proverbs 23:29-32, NLT.**

I overheard a conversation a couple teens were having. It went like this:
Guy: "So, like, I was at this party, and some dudes wanted me to have a drink, but I kept on saying no until finally I was sick of it, and so I took a drink. Ha-ha."

Girl: "Ha-ha. That's funny. You are so busted. Go right back to NA [Narcotics Anonymous]."

Guy: "Ha-ha. I know. Seven months of rehab down the toilet in one party. Ha-ha."

Girl: "Ha-ha. You mean to tell me they didn't cover peer pressure in rehab? I don't believe that. Ha-ha."

Guy: "Yeah, sure, they covered it. I blew it. I know. I so blew it. Ha-ha."

I was the only one not laughing. I couldn't believe this guy blew seven months of rehab at one stupid party just because someone nagged him into taking a drink he didn't even want. Obviously he knew he had a problem; he'd just spent all that time in rehab. Obviously he'd worked hard to get clean and learn how to deal with his addiction. And all it took for him to waste all that time and effort was a couple people putting on some pressure.

Peer pressure is definitely hard to resist. After all, who doesn't want to look cool, smart, or funny in front of their friends? That's why it's important to have safeguards in place to prevent you from doing something stupid just because your friends pressure you into it.

First, it's important to choose your friends wisely. If you hang out with people who have the same standards you do, you'll spend a lot less time trying to avoid doing something you don't want to do. Second, stay away from places where you're likely to be pressured into compromising. Having adults around might sound like a drag, but they can save you from a lot of embarrassment. Third, pray that God will open your eyes so you can avoid bad situations in the first place. Sin is no laughing matter.

July 19

It Can't Happen to Me

And so, dear brothers and sisters, I plead with you
to give your bodies to God because of all he has done for you.
Let them be a living and holy sacrifice—the kind he will find acceptable.
This is truly the way to worship him. **Romans 12:1, NLT.**

Do you like chocolate doughnuts? Family legend has it that my grandfather, Peter Perrino, invented them during the Great Depression. He was a teen working in his father's bakery in Winooski, Vermont. He sold the recipe for $100 because times were tough and the family needed the money.

You can't thank him, though, because he passed away on May 30, 1996. He died of lung cancer. You see, Grandpa was a smoker, although he quit before I was old enough to remember ever seeing him smoke. He was seeing someone off at an airport when he started coughing and couldn't stop. He was smoking a cigarette at the time and got so disgusted he threw it in the trash and never smoked again. But he didn't stop early enough to save his life.

Most of the people in my family smoked, but they all quit when I was very young, and I don't remember it. Back then people didn't know smoking caused cancer or other health problems. Now the law requires tobacco companies to put warning labels on their products so you know they can kill you.

Unfortunately, this doesn't stop people from using them. That's because of the "it can't happen to me" myth. It goes something like this: "Other people might get cancer from smoking, but it can't happen to me." But it does happen to someone. Every year 443,000 people in the United States die from smoking or exposure to secondhand smoke. Another 8.6 million live with diseases caused by smoking. Despite this, about 46.6 million adults smoke, and that number doesn't even include teens.

As Christians we are stewards of our bodies. We're supposed to keep them clean so they will be a place where God's Spirit can live and work. This is a message God wants us to take to others, too. As members of the Seventh-day Adventist Church, we have a strong health message to share with the world. By sharing it, we can save lives, here and for eternity.

Find out if your church is running a stop-smoking program. If they are, offer to help. If they aren't, see if they will let you run one.

Ghostbusters

For the living know they will die; but the dead
do not know anything, nor have they any longer a reward,
for their memory is forgotten. **Ecclesiastes 9:5, NASB.**

I went to a memorial service for a woman I had just met who had died of cancer. She was a Christian, and the memorial service was at a Christian church. People were invited to stand up and talk about their memories of her. One man told a story about how just minutes after she passed away, the television in her hospital room, which had been playing soothing landscape scenes, suddenly had a scene of donkeys in a meadow. The woman had loved all animals, but especially donkeys. Her husband believed the donkeys were a message his wife had sent from heaven saying that she'd gotten there safely and that she was happy. The man telling the story said, "I never believed in ghosts or the afterlife before, but I believe now."

I felt a chill go down my spine as people gasped in awe all around the room.

I knew that if the woman's "ghost" suddenly appeared in the room, I would be the only person there who knew it was an evil angel impersonating her. I'm convinced that no matter what "she" said, everyone in that room would have believed it. Why wouldn't they? She was someone they had known and loved and trusted. They believed she was now in heaven. If she had a message, they would have handed her a microphone to make sure everyone could hear what she had to say.

Maybe you've never thought about this before, but take a minute to thank God for the light He's given the Seventh-day Adventist Church about the state of the dead. Because we know the truth, Satan can never deceive us with "ghosts." He's been busted, and that trick won't work on us. But there are many people who believe in an afterlife for spirits of the dead. We have to be very careful that we don't let them sway us from our beliefs, no matter the stories people tell or what our eyes see. Now, more than ever, you can't believe everything you see and hear.

In the last days Satan will use spiritualism more often to deceive people. Take some time to memorize verses to explain the biblical position about what happens after we die. If you have some friends who are interested in this subject, stage a debate, with one half taking the position that we go directly to heaven or hell after death and one taking the biblical position. What did you learn about how to discuss this subject with people who have different views than we do? Why is spiritualism such a dangerous deception?

Got God?

Like newborn babies, you must crave pure spiritual milk so that you will grow into a full experience of salvation. Cry out for this nourishment, now that you have had a taste of the Lord's kindness. **I Peter 2:2, 3, NLT.**

It's your standard-issue nightmare. You're a history nut. You're eating a peanut butter sandwich when a radio station places a random call to answer a history question on their trivia show. Your phone rings. You answer it. For the $10,000 prize, the DJ wants to know who shot Alexander Hamilton in his famous duel.

"Aaron Burr!" you exclaim triumphantly. You don't even have to think twice, because you know so much about history. Unfortunately, because your mouth is glued shut by peanut butter, it sounds more like "Auun Buuh." The DJ can't understand you. You become frantic. You spy the milk container and try to pour yourself a glass to wash down the peanut butter. But you're out of milk! You're also out of time, and the DJ hangs up. You stare sadly at the phone, still trying to say "Aaron Burr." At the end of the commercial the announcer asks, "Got milk?"

And that, my friends, was the commercial that made drinking milk popular again. The ad was called "Aaron Burr," and was one of six ads created to boost the milk industry's sagging sales and turn milk into a cool drink. It wasn't long before people started making the slogan their own by substituting their own word for the word "milk." The top 10 listed by the Got Milk? people themselves: Got energy? Got cheese? Got virtual? Got love? Got money? Got protein? Got wrinkles? Got promotions? Got rice? Got taste?

Got Jesus? is actually listed at number 12, but it's my favorite because it's actually asking an important question. Cow's milk may be the best food for baby cows, but spiritual milk is the best food for baby Christians. The Bible tells us that we should crave it. Have you ever had a craving? It starts as a thought in your mind. *Boy, I'd really like some* _____ (fill in the blank). It doesn't go away. It just gets stronger and louder until you finally go looking for whatever you are craving. That's how we need to crave our spiritual food: Bible reading, prayer, getting together with other Christians to talk about God, listening to spiritual music that helps us feel closer to God. All those things are our spiritual milk. Ask the Holy Spirit to help you crave them.

Got God?

TKN?

You shall not go about as a talebearer among your people; nor shall you take a stand against the life of your neighbor: I am the Lord. **Leviticus 19:16, NKJV.**

"That Sonia thinks she's so clever," Monica said sourly, slamming her locker shut. "She sweet-talked Mrs. Lambson into giving her an extra day to finish her history assignment. I guess some people get special privileges." Stop! Is that TKN (true, kind, or necessary)?

That's how one school tells students to test what they're saying to see if it meets God's standards. For everything you are about to say, you must ask yourself if what you're about to say is true. Is it kind? Is it necessary? If you can't answer yes to those questions, then what's about to shoot out of your mouth shouldn't be said. It would be best to keep it to yourself.

It's easy to get caught up in talking badly about others. Sometimes we even trick ourselves into thinking that when we talk about someone we're doing it for Christian reasons if we are bearing tales in order to let people know about someone's situation so that they can pray for that person.

For instance, if Brian got in a drunk driving accident and you're dying to tell someone but you realize that is gossip, it's easy to feel as if you can put God's blessing on the news if you tell a few people who know Brian so they can *pray for him*. But telling others about Brian's trouble might not be the wisest thing to do. It could damage his reputation, embarrass him, and hurt him. We can think we're doing something for good reasons, but if we examined our hearts, we'd see that our reasons are actually very selfish. If we stop to ask that one simple question—is this TKN?—we can save ourselves and others from a lot of grief.

The Bible tells us that we should speak only words that will build up others (see Ephesians 4:29). Our words should benefit, not hurt, the people who hear them as well as the people we're talking about. Our words are a reflection of our hearts. When we truly love others as God loves them, we will try very hard not to hurt them. If this is an area you struggle with, ask God to place a guard around your mouth to help you think before you speak.

July 23

Bonking

If anyone thirsts, let him come to me and drink.
Rivers of living water will brim and spill out of the depths
of anyone who believes in me this way,
just as the Scripture says. **John 7:37, 38, Message.**

Ask any athlete what bonking is, and they'll probably wince remembering a time in the not-too-distant past when they've done just that. Bonking is how athletes describe "hitting the wall," that point in their training or race when they've expended all their energy and their second wind hasn't kicked in yet. It's the part of the run, or swim, or bike ride, or skate when energy levels are at their lowest. It feels as if you can't take one more stride or you'll fall flat on your face. When you reach that spot, you've bonked.

There are two reasons to be grateful for bonking. The first is that you can't bonk if you never exercise. The fact that you're bonking means that you're exercising. Congratulations! You go, dude! Exercise, no matter what kind you do, is great for your health—both physical and mental. In a world with so many couch potatoes, you should celebrate being active.

Second, if you're bonking it means that you've reached a place where you need help, and recognizing that fact means that you're ready to get help. When exercising, many athletes fend off bonking by drinking a lot of water to stay hydrated. They may also carry with them quick energy foods to get them over the wall and into the homestretch.

Sometimes we bonk in our Christian life too. That kind of bonking is a warning sign. It means that we've been traveling under our own steam and not relying on God's power. We're just human beings. Our own power has a limit, and we can only get so far with it before we run out. But that's not the kind of race God wants us to run. Not when He's got all the power we need to run without ever getting tired at all! Just like a physical athlete has to stay hydrated with water, we need to drink spiritual water: Bible study, prayer, time with God.

Our spiritual energy foods are those things that bring us closer to God, our source of power. For some people that might be listening to Christian music. For others it may be prayerwalking. Still others might feel closest to God when they are prayer journaling. God has different ways of filling each of us because we're all different. What are some of your spiritual energy sources? What does God use to really speak to you and fill you up?

Boundaries

It is God's will that you should be sanctified: that you should avoid sexual
immorality; that each of you should learn to control your own body
in a way that is holy and honorable, not in passionate lust like the pagans,
who do not know God; and that in this matter no one should wrong
or take advantage of a brother or sister. The Lord will punish all
those who commit such sins, as we told you and warned you before.
For God did not call us to be impure, but to live a holy life. Therefore,
anyone who rejects this instruction does not reject a human being but God,
the very God who gives you his Holy Spirit. **I Thessalonians 4:3-8, NIV.**

Boundaries mark off what belongs inside a specified area and what needs to be kept outside. They protect and define what is mine and belongs to me, and what is yours and belongs to you. We're encouraged to keep our personal boundaries safe and secure from being violated or harmed.

At school Katrina* struggled with fitting in with her friends while at the same time keeping herself sexually pure. Her friends didn't share her values and sometimes made life difficult for her. One day, after an incident at school, she burst into the kitchen in tears as she fell into her father's arms. She told him that her classmates had made fun of her because she was a virgin, and she didn't know what to say to them.

"Oh, honey," Katrina's father said, "I love you so much. Would it help you to know that any day you could become like your friends but you're choosing to keep yourself sexually pure like your mom and I did for each other?" Katrina looked up at her father and, wiping her tears, smiled, realizing that it was OK to set and keep her sexual boundary. One day it would be a precious benefit to her and her future husband.

Sexual abstinence—not having sex before marriage—seems like a decision you make by yourself, for yourself. But in reality it's a decision that affects you and the person you will one day marry. Think of it as a wedding present for your future spouse. If you're going to give someone you love a gift, would you rather give them a new gift or a used one?

---

* Names have been changed.
Submitted by Julián Anderson-Martín, M.A., L.L.P.C.

Second Virginity

Don't you realize that those who do wrong will not inherit
the Kingdom of God? Don't fool yourselves. Those who indulge in sexual sin,
or who worship idols, or commit adultery, or are male prostitutes,
or practice homosexuality, or are thieves, or greedy people, or drunkards,
or are abusive, or cheat people—none of these will inherit the Kingdom
of God. Some of you were once like that. But you were cleansed; you were
made holy; you were made right with God by calling on the name of the
Lord Jesus Christ and by the Spirit of our God. **I Corinthians 6:9-11, NLT.**

What if you've already lost your virginity? Once it's gone, it's gone, right? Yes and no. Physically if you did it, you did it. There's no getting that first time back, or any other times that came after it. There may be consequences—damaged reputation, health, future, or emotions—that you might not be able to change. You may struggle with feelings of low self-esteem, shame, or guilt. Physically what's done is done.

But spiritually you can start with a new slate, a second virginity. If you confess your sin and repent (tell God you are sorry and make a commitment to stay sexually pure), God will forgive you, and you can start over. The past won't change, but the future will.

That doesn't mean you'll never be tempted again, but if you let God be in charge of your life, He will always save you from giving in to any temptation. Always. He promised (see 1 Corinthians 10:13). Any successful general will tell you that to win a war you have to be prepared. You have to know your enemy. That means being smart, using your head. Don't put yourself in the middle of temptation and expect God to work miracles to get you out. Stay far away in the first place.

Make rules for yourself. Don't put yourself into a position in which you're alone with your date. Surround yourself with other people. Make dating a social occasion: go out with groups of people. Know your physical boundaries, and even more important, know what you will say and do if your date tries to violate them. If you begin dating someone special, let them know where you stand on the issue of sex outside of marriage.

Be firm. If you date someone who continues to try to encroach on your boundaries, break up with them. If they do not respect you, they do not love you. You must respect yourself. You belong to God.

Bragging Rights

God said to Gideon, "You have too large an army with you.
I can't turn Midian over to them like this—they'll take all the credit,
saying, 'I did it all myself,' and forget about me. Make a public
announcement: 'Anyone afraid, anyone who has any qualms at all,
may leave Mount Gilead now and go home.'" **Judges 7:2, 3, Message.**

When Gideon looked across the camp of the Israelites and saw the 32,000 soldiers he would soon be leading into battle, he felt pretty confident. At least as confident as you *can* feel facing a battle. There was plenty of manpower, and they had God on their side. What more could they want?

When God looked across the camp of the Israelites and saw 32,000 soldiers, He knew they all felt confident. In fact, they felt so confident that if they won the battle, they'd be doing little victory dances and patting themselves on the back. So He started sending them home. When He finished picking the ones who would stay, there were only 300 left. Now they didn't feel so confident.

Gideon was understandably nervous. Maybe he even wondered if God had counted wrong because now they were greatly outnumbered. Before they had had all the manpower they needed. Now they were down to just a bare-bones crew, and it would take a miracle to win.

And that is the point God was making not only with Gideon but with every battle you face today. We're outnumbered, outgunned, and outsmarted, but *we're still going to win.* And we're going to win because we have God on our side. Not because we are so clever. Not because we are so strong. Not because we are so good. Not because we have any special superpower of our own. We are going to win because *God* is on our side and *He* fights our battles and He is bigger than *anything* the enemy can throw at us.

We won't be able to brag that we did anything special, but we will be able to brag that God did something special. And that is your testimony: it's your story about what God is doing in your life to fight your battles and overcome your enemies.

Gideon and the 300 men God sent with Him won their battle that day, and the only weapons they fought with were ram's horns and clay jars. Curious? Check out Judges 7 for the rest of the story.

I Want Your Jesus

*Whatever you do, work at it with all your heart,
as working for the Lord, not for human masters, since you know
that you will receive an inheritance from the Lord as a reward.
It is the Lord Christ you are serving.* **Colossians 3:23, 24, NIV.**

They're called slackers, and you'll see them in any job you ever have. You'll also see them in your classroom. In school the slackers are the ones who never have their homework done. They don't study for tests. They write the shortest answers they can get away with. They show up late for class, and they leave early if they can. They take all their sick days and usually a few more besides.

They act pretty much the same way once they graduate from school and go out in the world to get a job. Since the boss can't be everywhere, slackers learn to "slack off" when the boss's back is turned. They stretch out their break time and lunch hour. They don't work as hard as they can, and they waste a lot of time doing things that aren't really necessary.

It can be tempting to ease up when you see others goofing off, especially when they seem to get away with it. They don't get in trouble. They get a paycheck every week, same as you. The only difference is that you worked your tail off and gave it all you had while they got by doing as little as possible. Sometimes they'll even try to get you to stop working so hard because it makes them look bad.

But you can't do that. No, sir, you can't. *You aren't working for a human boss.* You're working for Jesus Christ Himself. In the same way that you watch the slackers, other people will watch you. They'll know something is different about you because of the way you work. When they find out what it is, they may want your Jesus, the one who inspires you to be such a hard and honest worker. Maybe you'll even have the chance to tell them about your retirement plan and the mansion your Boss is building for you in Paradise. You can tell them that the work may seem hard now, but the benefits are out of this world.

Take a minute to consider how you usually work, whether it's in school or at a job. Do you give it your all? Are you aware of the fact that you're working for Jesus? If you've been guilty of slacking off, talk to your Boss and ask Him to help you give your job or your schoolwork everything you've got so that others will want your Jesus.

The Good Rapper

Then a despised Samaritan came along,
and when he saw the man, he felt compassion for him.
Going over to him, the Samaritan soothed his wounds with olive oil
and wine and bandaged them. Then he put the man on his own donkey
and took him to an inn, where he took care of him. **Luke 10:33, 34, NLT.**

Once upon a time there was a classical violinist who was on a journey to Carnegie Hall (where the really famous people go to perform). But while he was trying to hail a taxi, he was run over by a bike messenger. He crashed onto the sidewalk on his back, the wind completely knocked out of him because he fell right on top of his violin case. (We won't even talk about what happened to his priceless violin.)

As he lay there gasping, positive he'd broken a rib or three, the conductor of the orchestra came bustling along. He was late for the performance. When he saw the violinist all sprawled out on the sidewalk, he knew he'd be late if he stopped to help, so he darted across the street. He didn't even wait for the "walk" sign to light up, and he didn't use a crosswalk.

The violinist couldn't believe it, but he was too stunned and injured to say anything. A few minutes later when the concert master came hustling down the sidewalk, he figured his troubles were over. Surely the concert master would stop to help. But the instant the concert master saw him, he too ran across the street . . . and nearly got hit by a bus.

After that the violinist gave up. If the people in his own orchestra wouldn't help him, there was no hope anybody else would stop. Sure enough, the next person to come by was a rapper. And he wasn't even a *Christian* rapper.

The violinist couldn't believe his eyes when the guy stopped and said, "Hey, dog, 'sup? Lookin' a little rough, you feel me?" He helped the violinist stand up, and he picked up all the pieces of the smashed violin. Then he took him to the emergency room and paid all his bills. He even got him a teddy bear and some balloons for his hospital room.

According to Jesus, that rapper was a real neighbor to the classical violinist. When we step in to help someone who's been knocked flat by a bike messenger—or just some gossip—we're being real neighbors too. It doesn't matter if the victim is someone we even have anything in common with. Our responsibility as Christians is simply to help. (A teddy bear and balloons would be nice too.)

July 29

The Kidney Off His Back

In everything, therefore, treat people the same way you want them to treat you, for this is the Law and the Prophets. **Matthew 7:12, NASB.**

You've heard the expression "He's so nice he'd give you the shirt off his back." If you need something and he can give it to you, he will. You probably feel that way about some people in your life. Your parents, siblings, your best friend, your boyfriend or girlfriend, maybe even a couple other people you really like. But what about that kid who works at the Quik Stop with you? You're just friends. You shoot the breeze during break, maybe even buy each other sodas. But would you give him your coat if it was the only one you had and it was freezing outside? How about the shoes off your feet? Or what about a kidney? Would you give him one of your kidneys? You only need one to live, you know.

That's what Jermaine Washington did for his work buddy Michelle Stevens. Some people thought he was nuts. Michelle had been on a kidney donor waiting list for 11 months, and she had lost all hope. Her mother couldn't donate a kidney for her because she had high blood pressure. Michelle had two brothers, but they were both too scared to give her a kidney.

Jermaine wasn't even related to her; they were just friends. He says, "I saw my friend dying before my eyes. What was I supposed to do? Sit back and watch her die?"

Even though you can live without one of your kidneys, they aren't meant to come out. Jermaine had to go through some painful procedures just to find out if he could donate his kidney to Michelle. Once doctors determined that his kidney was suitable, he had another painful surgery to remove the kidney; it left him with a 15-inch scar from his belly button to his back.

Today both Michelle and Jermaine have recovered from their ordeal. Three times a month they get together for what they call a "gratitude lunch." When one admirer asked Jermaine where he found the courage to give one of his kidneys away, he said, "I prayed for it. I asked God for guidance, and that's what I got."

There's (usually) no need to go as far as Jermaine Washington did to follow Jesus' command to do unto others as we'd like others to do unto us, but when you have the opportunity to do something, follow Jermaine's example and ask God for the courage. You can be sure He'll give it to you.

Second Mile Club

If anyone forces you to go one mile, go with them two miles.
Give to the one who asks you, and do not turn away from
the one who wants to borrow from you. **Matthew 5:41, 42, NIV.**

Hello, and welcome to the Second Mile Club! Here's your membership card and a decal for your bike or planner, and this is your handbook. Meetings are once a week. Members will gather and talk about the activities they participated in the previous week. We'll encourage one another, laugh together, maybe cry together, and share refreshments after the meeting.

What do you mean you didn't know you were a member of the Second Mile Club? Didn't anyone brief you before the meeting? Oh, well, let me tell you a little about the history of the club you've just joined. The Second Mile Club has been functioning since about A.D. 30. It was started by Jesus, who is the president of the club. Our motto is "Don't go one when you can go two!"

It all started back when Jesus was giving a little talk. Back then the club members were living under the authority of the Romans, and there were a lot of laws no one liked. One of them was that if a Roman soldier asked you to carry his gear, you had to carry it for one mile. Imagine! Carrying a soldier's heavy load for a whole mile! Everyone hated it. In fact, some people tried to get out of it, and some tried to skimp on carrying the load for the whole mile. But Jesus said, "If a Roman soldier, or anyone for that matter, makes you carry their gear for a mile, don't stop there. Carry it for two miles!"

Some people thought He was nuts, of course. Two miles? One was more than enough. The Roman soldiers were pretty impressed, though. All that walking gave us a good chance to tell them about the club. We got some new members that way. And it gave the ones who weren't convinced right away (the ones who thought we had ulterior motives) something to think about.

So welcome to the club! I hope you take advantage of all it has to offer.

Since there is a scarcity of Roman soldiers to force you to carry their gear, you'll have to find other people to go the second mile for. Make it your mission this week to go the second mile for someone every day. At the end of the week, talk with other club members (church members or Sabbath school members) about your experiences. What did you think about your Second Mile Club experience?

There Goes the Neighborhood

For the authorities do not strike fear in people who are doing right, but in those who are doing wrong. Would you like to live without fear of the authorities? Do what is right, and they will honor you. The authorities are God's servants, sent for your good. But if you are doing wrong, of course you should be afraid, for they have the power to punish you. They are God's servants, sent for the very purpose of punishing those who do what is wrong. **Romans 13:3, 4, NLT.**

Not far from where I live is a trail system through the woods. It's on the edge of my city, which can be a problem because gang members who live in the city hang out on the trails to make their drug deals. I learned that because not long after I started hiking there, I found the gates locked. A group of women were just leaving the parking lot, so I asked them if they knew why the gates were locked and if we could still hike the trails. They told me gangs had been hanging around dealing drugs so the police locked the gates and were patrolling regularly.

They said that as far as they knew, we could still use the trails. The question was Did I want to take the chance of running into drug dealers? After all, they aren't exactly known for their easygoing, pleasant natures. I did end up hiking that day, and I did see a shady character who could very easily have been waiting around to make a drug deal, and I've never been able to hike those trails since then without being just a little scared.

We know drugs ruin our health. We know drugs ruin the lives of people who deal them and people who take them. We've seen their stories on the news, or maybe we even know them. They end up in jail, sick, or dead, all because of drugs. But what we sometimes forget is how drugs affect us even when we *don't* take them. They make the places around us dangerous: my hiking spot, your neighborhood or school, our favorite park. Drugs ruin things: neighborhoods, people's lives, towns, cities, even homes.

Fortunately there are people in authority who work tirelessly to stop the violence and destruction caused by drugs and the people who choose to use them. Aren't you grateful that God supports these defenders of our safety? Tell them so!

Even if drugs don't affect you or your neighborhood, find out what actions are being taken by authorities and see what you can do to support them. If you don't want to get that involved, bake cookies or make a card to give to your local police station as a thank-you for all their hard work keeping your space safe.

Disqualified

The master will return unannounced and unexpected, and he will cut the servant to pieces and assign him a place with the hypocrites. In that place there will be weeping and gnashing of teeth. **Matthew 24:50, 51, NLT.**

Nadzeya Ostapchuk of Belarus was the first Olympian to lose her gold medal after the 2012 London Olympic Games. Her whole life had been poured into the Olympics. She'd trained, worked, sweated, and probably cried as she tried to be the best shot putter in the world and to prove it at the Olympic Games. Who knows how many sacrifices she and her family made for her to represent her country before the world? We can only imagine. But what the entire world now knows is that although she won the gold medal in shot put, she lost it because of one bad choice: drugs.

She was stripped of her gold medal because she tested positive for steroids before and after her competition. The International Olympic Committee expelled her from the games and removed her victory and medal from the books after the test results came back. Nadzeya was sent home in disgrace. All the hard work, all the money spent, all the hours devoted to practice, everything Nadzeya had went into trying to win that medal, but none of that, including her victory at the games, meant anything when she was disqualified.

Obviously Nadzeya didn't tell anyone she was taking steroids; it was a secret. But even though she thought she could get away with it and she made it all the way to the Olympics, her secret, like all secrets, was eventually revealed.

We are all like Nadzeya. We have secrets that we're hiding from the people around us, but there is Someone who knows all secrets. And there is a day coming when every secret will be revealed.

Pretending to be Christians won't get us into heaven. One day the whole world will know whether or not our faith is genuine. That's why it's important for us to be honest with ourselves and God all the time. If we are ready for Jesus to return right now, then we will be ready whenever the day comes. And we'll be able to stand by the grace of God when "by the all-seeing God, men will be judged by what they are in purity, in nobility, in love for Christ" (Ellen G. White, *Counsels on Stewardship,* p. 162).

The Clock Is Ticking

Therefore be careful how you walk, not as unwise men but as wise, making the most of your time, because the days are evil. **Ephesians 5:15, 16, NASB.**

What if I told you that you have a bank account into which someone has been depositing $86,400 *every day of your life?* Pretty awesome, huh? I'll bet you're already thinking of how you can spend all that wonderful money. But wait! There's something else you need to know.

At the end of every day, whatever money you haven't used disappears. *Poof!* Gone, just like that. But every day you start again with $86,400. Now, I'll bet you're speeding down the road to the bank to withdraw whatever's left of today's money before it's all gone. Well, you can slow down. You don't have to go to the bank to withdraw the money. You only have to spend it.

It's not real money; I was just kidding about that part. But I wasn't joking about your account, or about the 86,400. Every day you get 86,400 *seconds* to spend any way you want. If you think about it, time really is more valuable than money. If you don't believe me, ask a millionaire breathing their last breath. They would spend every cent they own if it would give them just a little more time on earth.

If time is so valuable, why don't we appreciate it? Part of the reason might be that we think there will always be more. Every day when we wake up, we find that God has given us another 86,400 seconds and we didn't even have to lift a finger. Maybe we want to waste 10,000 (that's close to three hours) of them watching TV or playing a video game. *Why not?* we think. *We'll get more tomorrow anyway. We can afford to waste some right now.*

No matter what you spend your time on, in the end you're spending it on life because you're trading your life for whatever you spend time on. When your life is over, it will have been made from everything you chose to do with your time. Time = life.

We can choose to spend our life on whatever we want, but we need to remember that someday we're going to have to account for every second that we've been given and exactly how we used it. Time should be our most prized possession. How will you spend yours today?

Pray for Me

And pray in the Spirit on all occasions with all kinds of prayers and requests. With this in mind, be alert and always keep on praying for all the Lord's people. **Ephesians 6:18, NIV.**

People say that prayer changes things, but I don't believe that. Prayer changes *people*; God changes *things*. Do you remember the last time someone asked you for prayer? Maybe it was your grandmother who was having a cataract operation, or your friend who broke an ankle, or someone from your church who just found out they have cancer. When you prayed for them, the Holy Spirit joined with you in your prayer. Maybe the Spirit impressed you about how you should pray, or what exactly the person you were praying for needed. Or maybe God's Spirit helped you to accept the fact that what the person you prayed for was going through was not going to change. Prayer, even for others, doesn't just make a difference to *them*. It also makes a difference in *us*. You can't unite with God and come away unchanged.

All the prayer in the world won't change some things, but it will change us and our ability to trust God for the things we don't understand. We can tell God what we'd like, but only God knows what we need. It's important for us to trust Him, and prayer will help us do that.

Just knowing that someone is praying for them is often very comforting to people who are facing a crisis. Praying for someone is also a way that we can open up a conversation about God with people who might not know Him, which gives us the chance to tell them about our faith. They might brush you off, but it's just as possible they'll thank you. People are often the most open to hearing about God when they are facing serious situations.

When you don't know exactly how to pray for someone, you can always pray Scripture for them. The Psalms are a good place to search for Scripture that will apply to most prayer requests, because the Psalms cover a wide range of emotions. Try Psalms 61, 70, 71, and 121. Replace the pronouns in the psalm with the name of the person you're praying for.

The Bible tells us to pray for one another. It doesn't matter if we're not quite sure what they need, because God knows. If we pray in the Spirit, we know we're asking for God's best for them. And if we pray the prayer that never fails—Thy will be done—then the answer to our prayer will *always* be God's best for them, no matter how the situation turns out.

Tip of My Tongue

I have hidden your word in my heart that I might not sin against you. Praise be to you, Lord; teach me your decrees. With my lips I recount all the laws that come from your mouth. **Psalm 119:11-13, NIV.**

Every week your Sabbath school lesson includes a memory text. When you were younger, your Sabbath school teacher probably gave you a sticker each week if you could recite the verse. Maybe at the end of the quarter he or she offered a prize if you could still recite all that quarter's verses. When you were younger, it was probably fun. Now, maybe not so much.

Well, it's time to change that! We need to have Scripture firmly planted in our minds because it's the sword of the Spirit. What kind of spiritual warriors would we be if we left home to go into battle and forgot to bring our swords? What are you going to attack the enemy with if you have no sword? You can't hurl a peanut butter sandwich at him and expect a victory. And because the Word of God is living and active, it can change us. But it can't change us if we never use it.

Try these tips for learning your weekly memory verse. But don't stop there. Find other great verses that you can use to praise God or find encouragement when you're facing a challenge.

1. Ask God to help you. Hiding His Word in your heart is something He wants you to do, and He'll help you do it.

2. If you want to memorize a Bible verse, you have to look at it more than once. Write it out and keep it where you can see it. Or get an app. Yes, there's an app for that!

3. Join a club. Get together with friends to practice memorization. Or involve your family. Make it a game or play in the car on trips.

4. Start easy. Begin with easy verses and work up to longer passages so you don't get discouraged.

5. Make it a habit. If you work on memorization every couple of days, you won't make any progress. Spend a little time every day. Find the time of day that works best for you.

6. Put it to music. My daughter learned all her times tables that way. If you can put something to music, you'll learn it faster and remember it longer.

7. Have fun! Learning Scripture should be a joy; using it should be one too.

A Person of Trust

Whoever can be trusted with very little can also be trusted with much, and whoever is dishonest with very little will also be dishonest with much. So if you have not been trustworthy in handling worldly wealth, who will trust you with true riches? And if you have not been trustworthy with someone else's property, who will give you property of your own? **Luke 16:10-12, NIV.**

Mackenzie was excited. She had a boyfriend, and no one else knew about it. It was their secret, and it felt good to have a secret. She saw him every day in school and texted him when she was home. Her mom suspected something was up, but no one really knew anything until her boyfriend told his parents. And then Mackenzie had to tell *her* parents before they found out from someone else. By the time she told her parents, she'd had her first boyfriend for a month.

Her parents were cool about it. They weren't crazy about the boyfriend, but they didn't make her break up with him or anything. But they weren't very happy that she'd kept the relationship a secret from them. All in all, Mackenzie thought everything had gone pretty well until a few months later when she wanted to do something and her parents said no. Hurt, she accused them of not trusting her.

"No, we don't trust you," her mom agreed. "In order to be trusted, you have to be someone that people can trust. If you expect people to trust you than you have to be open with them and not sneak around behind their backs. Trust is something you earn."

That was a hard lesson for Mackenzie to learn; it's a hard lesson for anyone to learn. Trust is very fragile, and once it's broken it can be hard to get back. It has to be earned, and that takes time.

Are *you* trustworthy? Really think about that for a minute. Just because you don't do some of the things your peers do doesn't mean that you are trustworthy. "I'm not as bad as those guys" isn't the same as "Yes, I can be trusted." Can you really be trusted to do what you say, be open about your activities, and stay out of trouble? It's natural to want some privacy, but remember that Christians are above all open and honest. We are the light of the world, not the darkness of it. We should have nothing to hide. Whatever you do, do it in the open and not in secret, and then you'll have nothing to hide and you'll truly be trustworthy.

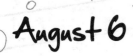

Nuclear Meltdown

Go ahead and be angry. You do well to be angry—
but don't use your anger as fuel for revenge.
And don't stay angry. Don't go to bed angry. Don't give the Devil
that kind of foothold in your life. **Ephesians 4:26, 27, Message.**

Nuclear power is very strong. It's used to make energy in nuclear power plants, and it's been used in some of the most powerful bombs ever exploded on earth. Because it's not very stable, it's hard to use. In 2011 a nuclear power plant in Japan had a major meltdown after a tsunami. More than 100,000 people had to leave their homes because of the radiation the plant released. It will take many years for the Japanese to clean up that area. Nuclear power is so powerful that when it goes wrong it destroys countless lives. You can't control it; you just have to try to clean up the mess afterward.

Do you know anyone with a nuclear temper, the kind that just spews onto everyone around when it goes off? When some people are mad, they don't care who they hurt. They rip, cut, and tear with their words and actions and leave a lot of wounded people behind them. Often they're sorry afterward, but then it's too late to do anything except damage control. It would be easier to stuff all the lava back into a volcano that erupted than it would be to heal some of the wounds caused by anger.

Anger is a tough one. On one hand, it's an emotion that God gave us. It's no better or worse than any other emotion. How we deal with anger, though, is what can lead us to sin. Anger is a sign that something in our life needs to change. If we feel angry, the first thing we should ask is "What is making me angry?" Once we identify the problem, the next question is "How can I change this?" You may not know how to change what is making you angry. If not, talk to your parents or other trusted adults and, if necessary, seek professional help.

Anger becomes a sin when we release it on others, even if we feel they deserve it because they made us so mad. Christians never have an excuse to have a nuclear meltdown and lash out at others. And if we've been burned by the anger of others, we'll find healing only if we forgive them. But if you're exposed to unhealthy anger, seek help from someone in authority.

The next time you are angry, pray. Ask God to show you how to deal with your anger in a Christian way and to keep you from sinning.

Promises, Promises

And because of his glory and excellence, he has given us great and precious promises. These are the promises that enable you to share his divine nature and escape the world's corruption caused by human desires. **2 Peter 1:4, NLT.**

promise I will." Has anyone ever said that to you and then broken their promise? Sometimes people make promises they have no intention of keeping. Other times they make promises they fully intend to keep, but something happens to prevent them. No matter what causes a broken promise, it's disappointing when someone doesn't keep their promise. And it makes you distrust the person who promised—next time you might not believe them.

Aren't you glad that you can believe every one of God's promises? Here are just a few:

God has promised to give us hope and a future: " 'For I know the plans I have for you,' declares the Lord, 'plans to prosper you and not to harm you, plans to give you hope and a future' " (Jeremiah 29:11, NIV).

God has promised to carry our burdens: "Come to me, all you who are weary and burdened, and I will give you rest. Take my yoke upon you and learn from me, for I am gentle and humble in heart, and you will find rest for your souls" (Matthew 11:28, 29, NIV).

God has promised to supply all our needs: "And my God will meet all your needs according to the riches of his glory in Christ Jesus" (Philippians 4:19, NIV).

God has promised to give us peace: "But all who listen to me will live in peace, untroubled by fear of harm" (Proverbs 1:33, NLT).

God has promised to give us freedom from fear: "Don't be afraid, for I am with you. Don't be discouraged, for I am your God. I will strengthen you and help you. I will hold you up with my victorious right hand" (Isaiah 41:10, NLT).

God has promised to heal us: "And the prayer offered in faith will make the sick person well; the Lord will raise them up. If they have sinned, they will be forgiven" (James 5:15, NIV).

These are just a few of God's many promises. How many more can you find?

I just heard about a neat art idea. Every day you take one index card and use it as a canvas to create art. Simple, right? Using index cards, write one of God's promises on each card. Then shuffle them up and choose one to read (and decorate, if you want) every day.

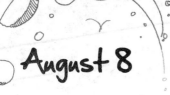

Bee-lieve It

For nothing is impossible with God. **Luke 1:37, NLT.**

You've probably seen plenty of bumblebees. Hopefully you haven't been stung by one. Have you ever stopped to think about how it can fly? "Everyone, except the bumblebee itself, knows that a bumblebee can't fly. Its body is too big for such small wings and furthermore it isn't particularly streamlined like the wasp," wrote Robert W. Husband in his article on bumblebees for *Entomology Notes.*

He isn't the first person to point out the impracticality of bumblebees and flight. In fact, there's an ongoing debate over who first said the bumblebee can't fly (when, obviously, it can). Several people are credited with making the statement, but no one knows for sure. What everyone seems to agree on is that there's no way anything as bumbling as the bumblebee ought to be able to fly based on mathematical models. A submarine would have about as much chance at flight if you clapped a pair of glider wings on it.

Yet the bumblebee flies. Quite well, in fact. It travels about 10 feet (three meters) per second and beats its wings 130 times per second. This ought to tell us something. First, it should tell us that we shouldn't look only at the outside of something when we are drawing our conclusions. We should never size up a problem and write it off. If we do that, we aren't taking into consideration that God is involved in everything in our lives and that nothing is impossible with God.

Second, we should never underestimate God. Just because our minds are large enough to know God does not mean that we should limit God by the size of our minds. God is so much bigger, wiser, and more complex than we are able to grasp. Rather than pulling God down to our level, let's open our minds and hearts and reach up to Him.

The researchers and scientists who weren't able to prove that a bumblebee can fly were working with mathematics and calculations, not with a real bumblebee. Their "model" wasn't alive and powered by God. They didn't really prove that a bumblebee can't fly; they proved that there is a big difference between the way something behaves on paper (in theory) and in real life (in reality). Just because something looks impossible to us does not mean that it is. Things may *look* one way, but God can make them turn out another. We have to remember that when God is in our lives, *nothing* is impossible.

Strong and Courageous

Be strong and courageous. Do not be afraid or terrified because of them, for the Lord your God goes with you; he will never leave you nor forsake you. **Deuteronomy 31:6, NIV.**

My mom teaches computer classes at a high school. Not long ago they had a lockdown. It wasn't a drill; someone spotted a guy walking around the school grounds with a gun. The kids were locked down for a couple hours before school officials decided it was safe.

School ought to be one of those places where you can feel safe, but that's not always the case. Sometimes unhappy or mentally ill people bring guns to schools, malls, theaters, and other places and start shooting. It's nothing personal. They don't care who they hit; they just want to express their anger or misery. Because school shootings and other kinds of violence like this are so random, it can make us feel unsafe and scared.

When I was a teenager, I remember being worried that I would die or Jesus would come back before I had a chance to really live. There were so many things I wanted to do. As I got older, I realized there was nothing to be worried about. There wasn't a single thing I wanted to do that wouldn't be a whole lot more fun in heaven.

Everyone is going to die someday; we start dying the day we are born. Some will die early; others when they are old. But everyone will die. Paul calls this "gain" (Philippians 1:21). It's like graduation day. We'll graduate from earth to heaven.

I'm not saying death is not a sad thing. It absolutely is. God created us to form attachments to one another. There are family members and friends you can't bear to think of living without. That's as it should be. But Christians shouldn't mourn the same way non-Christians do, because we have something they don't have: hope. We will see our loved ones again. They will see us. We will all spend eternity in heaven. Yes, it's sad that we can't see them here anymore, but we *will* see them again.

No matter what, we should not live in fear. Our God goes before us. We don't need to cower and quake because we can live with absolute assurance that wherever we go, whatever we do, our God will never leave us or forsake us. He will stay with us until the end. Even then He won't desert us. Our spirits will return to Him (see Ecclesiastes 12:7), and when He comes back to earth the final time, He'll raise us from the dead. Wherever you go today, be strong and courageous.

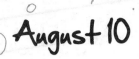

Encrusted

The land you're taking over is a polluted land,
polluted with the obscene vulgarities of the people who live there;
they've filled it with their moral rot from one end to the other.
Whatever you do, don't give your daughters in marriage to their sons
nor marry your sons to their daughters. **Ezra 9:11, 12, Message.**

Artist Jason deCaires Taylor is probably as famous for his sculptures as he is for sinking them into the sea. Concerned about fragile coral reefs, Taylor wanted to do something to help preserve them. He decided to create an underwater attraction that would draw divers and other tourists away from the delicate reefs. He created sculptures from a marine-safe cement that has a near-neutral pH so it doesn't harm marine life, and placed them into the ocean, creating an underwater museum. But the sculptures weren't meant to stay as they were created; they were designed to host sea life and to change as creatures began to use them as homes, covering them in the process.

Taylor documented the evolution in short films that show seaweed and other life forms covering the sculptures; some even appear to be part of the original idea, like seaweed flowing from a sculpture's head as if it were hair. Despite the sea life covering the figures, you can see the vague outlines of the original sculptures underneath. At the time of writing, Taylor has sunk 65 statues, 500 more have been commissioned, and thousands are planned. Once the sculptures enter the ocean, all of them will eventually be covered with sea life.

The same thing happens to us when we put ourselves into environments in which sin is considered normal. God warned His people many times not to marry pagans and other people groups who did not follow Him, because He knew that over time the things that those people considered OK would seem OK to His people, too, and it would lead to their destruction.

This principle of cause and effect is of vital importance when choosing a person to marry. Right now you may be thinking, *Whoa! Marriage? I'm not ready for that yet.* But if you are dating, or even thinking about dating, than you are basically interviewing possible candidates for marriage, which is the end purpose of dating. You should carefully and prayerfully consider the kind of environment you're thinking about sinking yourself into. Make sure that anyone you contemplate spending a lifetime with loves your God as much as you do and won't cover you with "seaweed."

Tale of Peter the Rabbit

I had to feed you with milk, not with solid food,
because you weren't ready for anything stronger.
And you still aren't ready, for you are still controlled by your sinful nature.
You are jealous of one another and quarrel with each other.
Doesn't that prove you are controlled by your sinful nature?
Aren't you living like people of the world? **I Corinthians 3:2, 3, NLT.**

Last week I took in some orphaned baby cottontail rabbits. They were tiny little things. There were four of them: three big ones and a tiny little runt. I named them after the rabbits in the Beatrix Potter story you might remember from when you were little: Flopsy, Mopsy, Cottontail, and Peter. Peter was the runt.

The three bigger rabbits did very well on the kitten milk replacer, and they had big, round tummies. But poor little Peter just couldn't seem to gain any weight. No matter how much formula he drank, he didn't get any bigger or stronger. Soon the other babies were three times his size. When Peter would start to feel bad, he'd cry, and he wouldn't stop until I picked him up and held him. When he felt better, he'd try to hop around, but he just couldn't seem to make any progress.

This story doesn't have a happy ending. Peter finally died. His body just couldn't grow on kitten milk replacer.

You may think you have nothing in common with a little brown cottontail rabbit, but you do—we all do. When we first become Christians, our spiritual food is like milk: it's easy to digest; it's baby food. We're babies; we can't handle anything stronger than that. Some of us grow big and strong on milk, and then we're ready for solid foods. Others, like Peter, get weaker and weaker. We cry, and God holds us until we feel better. But we never get stronger, we never move past drinking milk. Eventually our spiritual life simply dies from lack of nourishment.

That's what happens if we don't give up our sinful nature. Paul tells the Corinthians that their behavior proves that they are still spiritual babies and aren't ready for solid food. They're living like people of the world. We can't have it both ways. We can't grow spiritually while we hang on to the world. We've got to let it go in order to keep growing as Christians. Only then can the spiritual milk we're drinking make us stronger.

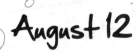

August 12

One Little Lamb

Celebrate God all day, every day. I mean, *revel* in him!
Make it as clear as you can to all you meet that you're on their side,
working with them and not against them. Help them see that the Master
is about to arrive. He could show up any minute! **Philippians 4:4, 5, Message.**

Not far from where I live is a little flock of sheep. I happen to know the people who own them, so I know that a pack of coyotes often stops by for a sheep dinner. Sheep aren't especially friendly, and if you reach out to pet them they usually turn tail, kick up their little black heels, and bounce away across the meadow. Sheep are, after all, a prey animal. And that's what makes them so skittish. If you're a sheep and you're overly friendly, some nice coyote might invite you over for dinner . . . as the main course.

You've heard the saying "There's safety in numbers." It wouldn't surprise me if I found out that a shepherd came up with it. When you're a prey animal, it's better for your health if you hang out with all the other prey animals. That way if an animal with big teeth happens by, you can blend in and you might even get away if it starts chasing you.

So when I walked past this little flock of sheep the other day, I was very surprised to see one little lamb off by itself. At first I thought it was sick or injured. But no, it was almost smiling because it was so happy. It was just chewing its cud and enjoying the beautiful weather, not at all concerned that it was alone halfway across the meadow from the rest of the sheep. I almost laughed when I saw the look of complete happiness on its little face.

In the Bible, Jesus often compares His people to sheep. It's a pretty accurate description. We like to flock together. We're scared of everything, even our Shepherd, who just wants to help us. We're apt to follow the flock even if it's going in a dangerous direction. That's why one lone sheep not acting like a sheep can turn heads.

We each have the opportunity to be the sheep everyone notices when we celebrate God every day. When we don't go with the crowd and yet we're happy and confident, people will want to know what makes us different. They'll notice that we don't depend on those around us to decide what to do and how to act, and they'll want to know why. Do it today; don't wait. The Shepherd could show up at any minute. Let's bring as many of the other sheep with us as we can.

Friend Me

The righteous should choose his friends carefully,
for the way of the wicked leads them astray. **Proverbs 12:26, NKJV.**

Jillian's older brother had a friend, Patrick, about whom he was always telling stories. Jillian heard so many stories about Patrick that she felt as though she knew him too. And he *was* her brother's friend, after all, so that made him her friend too. Except that it didn't. When Jillian ran into Patrick at the mall, she started following him around. She thought it was fun, hanging out with her brother's friend; he was older, which made him automatically cool.

What Jillian didn't know was that Patrick was texting her brother such things as "Your little sister is following me around." He told her brother she was a "pest" and a "punk kid." Patrick told Jillian she ought to go back and hang out with the group she'd come to the mall with. Eventually Jillian did, but she still thought of Patrick as her friend because she *wanted him to be*, not because he was. Inventor and mathematician Blaise Pascal said, "If all men knew what each said of the other, there would not be four friends in the world."

How would you define the word "friend"? The Merriam-Webster dictionary says that a friend is "one attached to another by affection or esteem; one that is not hostile; a favored companion." "To friend" has now become a verb that means a person is willing to connect with someone on a social networking site such as Facebook. People you may or may not know ask you to friend them, and then their friends ask you to friend them, until soon you're "friends" with a lot of people you don't really know.

Friends are important because we allow them to be close to us. What they believe and how they act tends to rub off. That's why it's vital that we choose good people to have close to us, to be our friends. It's also vital that we know which people are *not* our friends. When we're blinded by our own need to be noticed and appreciated, we can sometimes make the same sort of mistake Jillian made.

Take a good, long look at your friends, all of them. Are they really friends? Or are they simply people in your life? Think about the ones you consider your closest friends, the ones you really trust. Really think about whom you've chosen and whom you haven't. How does this affect what you will share with either group?

227

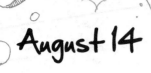

I Volunteer

This is a trustworthy statement; and concerning these things
I want you to speak confidently, so that those who have believed
God will be careful to engage in good deeds. These things
are good and profitable for men. **Titus 3:8, NASB.**

Without looking it up on Google, can you tell me your state's nickname?

The nickname of my state—Vermont—is the Green Mountain State. We got our nickname, not surprisingly, because of our beautiful green mountains.

Tennessee is called the Volunteer State. It got that nickname because during the War of 1812 the volunteer soldiers from Tennessee showed great bravery under General Andrew Jackson during the Battle of New Orleans. Everyone likes a volunteer, but I'm sure General Jackson wanted to high-five every one of his soldiers. What made their bravery so remarkable? No one had to twist their arm to force them to defend their country. They willingly put themselves in harm's way.

Volunteering is a selfless act; you give your time to benefit someone else. Volunteers help in many ways, from cleaning out dog pens at the pet shelter to selling tickets for a fund-raiser. In this show-me-the-money world, volunteering can be a hard sell. But Christians should be first in line to volunteer and to engage in good deeds.

There are probably as many ways and opportunities to volunteer as there are people in the world. One girl I know has learned how to trim horse's hooves and now volunteers to trim the horses at a horse rescue center. I groom rabbits at the shelter. A friend of mine who is confined to a wheelchair volunteers at an after-school center. You won't get paid for volunteering, but you'll get a sense of satisfaction that money can't buy.

Would you like to engage in a good deed by volunteering? To find a good fit, think about what you like to do. Enjoy animals? Help at the local shelter. Like kids? Mentor at a Boys and Girls Club. Shy? Sort clothes at Goodwill. Chatty? Stamp hands at a fund-raiser. Somewhere out there is a volunteer position you'll love and an organization that would love to have your help.

If Looks Could Kill

A cheerful heart is good medicine,
but a broken spirit saps a person's strength. **Proverbs 17:22, NLT.**

D o you see those two people over there? The one on the left has her head in her hands, she's scowling, her eyes are dull, and she's got a dejected slump to her shoulders. You can almost see a rain cloud forming over her head. That girl on the right, though: she's smiling. Her whole face is lit up. She looks as though she might start laughing any minute.

Which one would you rather get to know? Before you answer that, think about this: We don't know why the girl on the left (we'll call her Lefty) looks so gloomy. Maybe her dog just died. And we don't know why the girl on the right (let's call her Righty) looks so happy. Maybe she just pulled a really nasty prank on someone she doesn't like. As we all know, looks can be deceiving. But based on looks alone, which girl would you rather strike up a conversation with?

Since I have a 50-50 chance of guessing which one you'd choose, I'm going to say Righty. And what does that tell you about how important it is for Christians not to simply know the good news but to let their faces know, too? "When Christians appear as gloomy and depressed as though they thought themselves friendless, they give a wrong impression of religion. In some cases the idea has been entertained that cheerfulness is inconsistent with the dignity of the Christian character, but this is a mistake. Heaven is all joy; and if we gather to our souls the joys of heaven and, as far as possible, express them in our words and deportment, we shall be more pleasing to our heavenly Father than if we were gloomy and sad" (Ellen G. White, *The Adventist Home*, p. 430).

Your smiling, happy face might be the only "religion" some people ever get. Your cheerfulness could be the thing that gives them the courage to ask the reason for your hope. If instead we drive others off with a sullen scowl, they will miss the opportunity to hear anything we might tell them about Jesus. I know it's not possible to be cheerful 24/7, but we must try to keep in mind the great hope that we have, and the limitless forgiveness God gives us to cover our sins. God has given us every reason to rejoice.

You are a billboard for Christianity. What message do you want others to see when they whiz by you in life: "Go away" or "Come here"? Which message do you think Jesus wants the world to see in His people?

August 16

Got Your Back

*A person standing alone can be attacked and defeated,
but two can stand back-to-back and conquer. Three are even better,
for a triple-braided cord is not easily broken.* **Ecclesiastes 4:12, NLT.**

Are you an introvert or an extrovert? If you're an introvert, you enjoy spending time alone. Not talking to people for long stretches of time doesn't bother you. You like doing activities by yourself and you don't need company to go somewhere. You are the kind of person who looks happy when eating alone at a restaurant. If you hear something interesting, you might share it with one or two close buddies.

If you're an extrovert, you're exactly the opposite. You love spending time with people, and if you can't be with at least one other person, you're unhappy. If something cool happens to you, you share it with a hundred of your closest friends. You've never met a stranger, and your contact list is as tall as you are. You don't like going places alone; in fact, you prefer to be in a crowd of people.

Extroverts don't have any trouble making friends, but it can be difficult for introverts. They tend to isolate themselves, spending long periods of time alone playing games, reading, or doing projects. They don't feel the need to be around other people as extroverts do.

While one personality type isn't better than another, introverts can get into trouble without meaning to because no one is watching their backs; no one is looking out for them. The Bible says they are like a single cord, weak and easily broken. But if they have at least one friend, they'll double their strength. And if they have two friends, they won't easily be broken. If that third friend is Jesus, then they really can't fail.

It's not easy for an introvert to make the effort to find friends, but it's important. Because this level of being social goes against your nature, it's especially important to ask God to help you in this area. He made you, after all; He knows exactly where to direct you in your search for friends.

If you are an introvert, make an attempt every day this week to reach out to someone who could become your friend, even if it is just to offer someone a smile. If you are an extrovert, seek out an introvert and invite them to join your circle of friends.

Russian Roulette

The thief does not come except to steal, and to kill,
and to destroy. I have come that they may have life, and that
they may have it more abundantly. **John 10:10, NKJV.**

Fifteen-year-old Neal Hammond wasn't trying to kill himself; he was just having fun at a sleepover. He and a couple of his friends had gotten together, and one of them had brought a gun, a .38-caliber Smith & Wesson. The boys were joking around. Cole McConoughey, Neal's best friend, put a couple bullets in the chamber and then suggested they play Russian roulette. He pointed the gun at Neal and pulled the trigger, expecting to hear a click, and instead, shot a bullet into Neal's head. Neal died the next morning.

Russian roulette is the name of a game in which players put one bullet in the chamber of a gun, point it at their head, and pull the trigger. If the gun can fire six bullets, they have a one-in-six chance of shooting themselves. You could say the odds are in their favor, but I don't think Neal Hammond would agree with you—that one bullet makes all the difference in the world.

In popular myth this game got its name from a similar game played by bored Russian soldiers who wanted to demonstrate their bravery, but the story hasn't been verified by any actual evidence. It's unclear exactly how it got started, but even today the game is claiming victims.

Maybe you're thinking this doesn't have much to do with you because you don't have any intention of playing Russian roulette. I'm certainly glad to hear that. But you don't actually need a gun to play Russian roulette. Many people play Russian roulette without even realizing that's what they're doing when they experiment with drugs or other toxic substances. The first time might not be deadly, or the second, or third. Or it might. You just never know.

It often starts out innocently enough, just playing around like Neal and his friends were. It's natural to be curious about what it would feel like to take a pill or huff fumes. Some drugs do make you feel good for a while. But each time you use them, the feeling lasts for a shorter and shorter amount of time, until soon you're using drugs just so you don't feel horrible . . . unless they kill you first. Healthy people can die inhaling fumes for the first time, something so common it has a name: sudden sniffing death syndrome.

But just as in Russian roulette, drugs won't always kill you. At least not right away. But they sure will make you wish you were dead.

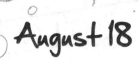

The Donkey and the Well

Then he said, "Is there anyone here who, if a child or animal fell
down a well, wouldn't rush to pull him out immediately,
not asking whether or not it was the Sabbath?" They were stumped.
There was nothing they could say to that. **Luke 14:5, 6, Message.**

I once read a parable about a farmer who had a donkey. One morning he found that during the night the donkey had fallen into an old abandoned well on his property. He looked down into the dark well, and there it was. As soon as the donkey saw him, it started to cry. The farmer scratched his head and wondered what to do. The well was deep, and the donkey was heavy, and he couldn't think of any way to haul that donkey out of the well.

Finally he decided that there was no help for it. The well was old and he never used it; the donkey was old, too, and it just wasn't worth it to rescue him. He'd simply fill the old well with dirt and bury the donkey at the same time. So he invited all his neighbors to bring their shovels, and they began throwing shovelfuls of dirt onto the donkey's back.

When the donkey realized what was happening, he cried even harder, but soon he stopped. Thinking the poor beast was dead, the farmer looked down into the well and saw an amazing thing. Every time a shovelful of dirt hit the donkey's back, he shook it off and stepped up a little higher in the well. Before long he was able to step out of the well, and he happily trotted off.

Sooner or later we will all fall into a well. It's when we're down there looking up at that little circle of sunshine somewhere high above our heads, knowing there's nothing we can do to get out on our own, that the first shovelful of dirt lands on us. We have two choices. We can stay there and get buried, or, like the donkey, we can shake it off and take a step up.

Sometimes the worst thing about being in a deep, dark place is the feeling that we are alone. This is especially true when it's our friends or family above us throwing the shovelfuls of dirt down on top of us. But the truth is that no matter who hurts us or deserts us in life—and people *will* eventually desert us or let us down—God will never desert us. He's the only sure thing we can count on. Jesus says, "I will never leave you nor forsake you" (Hebrews 13:5, NKJV).

When you're alone and hurting, cling to Jesus' promise, shake off the dirt, and take a step up. And after you leave the well behind and trot out into the sunshine, remember what you've learned from the experience.

Cart Before the Horse

Seek the Kingdom of God above all else, and live righteously, and he will give you everything you need. **Matthew 6:33, NLT.**

If someone (like me) asked you, "How much time do you spend with God every day?" what would your answer be? If you're like most people, you'll probably respond, "Not enough." Life is busy and full of projects, church, and other commitments. We're often busy working *for* God and too busy to spend any time *with* Him.

Where I come from we have a saying for that. It's called "Putting the cart before the horse." If you hitch a horse to a cart, expecting him to pull it, the cart better be behind the horse. There isn't a horse in the world that can pull a cart from behind; he could push it, but horses don't push carts. If you've got your cart in front of your horse, you're going nowhere.

That's precisely where you're going if you put life as your first priority before God. God is the ruler of the universe, the Creator, the Redeemer, the God of the angel armies. He doesn't follow behind the cart or push it from back there. He pulls our cart through life.

Let's try an experiment. The results might scare you, so be prepared. You'll need a paper plate and a marker; you're going to make a pie chart. There are 24 hours in every day, so divide your pie into 24 pieces. In each hourlong slot, write what you're doing. If you get eight hours of sleep per night, write "sleeping" in eight sections of pie. If you're at school or work for eight hours every day, write "school/work" in eight pieces. That will leave you with about eight hours. Fill in what you do for those remaining eight hours. Sports? Eating? Playing games? After-school job? Homework?

When you finish take a look at your pie and see how much time you spent with God. How much is it? Are you scared or pleased? Which is first in your life, the cart or the horse? This can be a shocking exercise because often we *think* we spend a lot of time with God when in reality we don't. Thinking *about* God and going to church are wonderful but don't count. If your spiritual life is going to grow, you need to spend actual, serious, one-on-one time with God, not just now and then, but every day. We need to seek God first, and everything else will follow along behind.

August 20

Christians Are Boring?

How blessed are the people who are so situated;
how blessed are the people whose God is the Lord! **Psalm 144:15, NASB.**

I was talking to a 15-year-old (Seventh-day Adventist) girl the other day. She was feeling bored with her friends and her life and wanted some excitement. When I asked her what she thought about visiting some new churches and meeting some new kids, she wrinkled her nose. "No offense," she said, "but Christians are boring."

Boring? Since when did Christians get boring? We should be the most exciting people on the planet! Who else has been saved by a God who rose from the dead? Who else can talk to the One who made the entire earth and everything in it, the universe, and all the galaxies? Who is going to be rescued one day soon by a Savior coming back in the clouds with an army of angels?

If there was a knock on your door right now and God Himself was standing there, would you be excited? I would! This is God we're talking about, after all. Who could possibly be more exciting than God? He created us, He saved us, He's coming back for us. Any way you look at it, that's not boring.

So why do so many people think Christians are boring? Do *you* think they're boring? The fact is, sometimes we are. We get stuck in ruts. We focus on the "thou shalt nots" until we completely forget the "thou shalts." We pile rules onto ourselves until we're scared of making a move in case someone else gets offended.

Chances are, no matter how well meaning you are, you're going to offend someone sooner or later. But wouldn't you rather offend them by being excited about God than by being uptight and boring about being a Christian? What kind of witnesses are we when we act like being a Christian is a dull experience full of obligation and duty? Would you be drawn to someone like that?

If you feel like your Christian walk is tired and boring, go straight to the Source and ask God for ways to fill it with excitement. Talk to others who might also be stuck in a rut and plan a new ministry or small study group. Get energized by spending time with other Christians who are on fire for God. Prove to the world that Christians are many things, but they're *not* boring.

Past, Present, and Future

Nation will go to war against nation, and kingdom against kingdom.
There will be famines and earthquakes in many parts of the world.
But all this is only the first of the birth pains, with more to come.
Then you will be arrested, persecuted, and killed. You will be hated all
over the world because you are my followers. **Matthew 24:7-9, NLT.**

A long, long time ago, when Christianity was brand-new, the early Christians faced really bad persecution. I'm not talking about bullying; they didn't get shoved into their lockers and beaten up at the bus stop. They were killed for their faith. In one country any man, woman, or child who wouldn't swear an oath that the king was like God on earth could be killed. At other times people could be killed if they believed Jesus was the Son of God. Early Christians were fed to hungry beasts, burned at the stake, and killed in other ways too gruesome to mention.

We're sure glad that those things aren't happening anymore. Or are they? If you live in America, the worst persecution you'll probably have to endure for your faith is to be made fun of or shunned. People might think you're odd and want to have nothing to do with you. Or they might think you make a great target for their jokes because of your beliefs.

If, however, you live in other parts of the world, you can still be killed for believing in Jesus. Authorities can beat you up, throw you in prison, and even kill you. Organizations such as the Voice of the Martyrs keep Christians informed about situations around the world where believers are being persecuted so they can pray for them and help by writing letters of support and encouragement.

The Bible tells us that before the Second Coming no Christian will be safe from persecution. We must be prepared now for what's ahead. If you were preparing for something hard, a test or race, you'd practice, right? Well, the test ahead for Christians will be hard, but practicing to endure persecution won't help. The only way we will be able to keep our faith when the going gets really tough is to be so close to Jesus now that nothing will ever separate us. We have to trust Jesus for the rest. "I give them eternal life," He says, "and they shall never perish; no one will snatch them out of my hand" (John 10:28, NIV). We can trust Jesus with our past, our present, and our future.

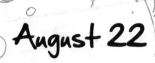

Mine, All Mine

David was furious. "As surely as the Lord lives," he vowed,
"any man who would do such a thing deserves to die! He must repay
four lambs to the poor man for the one he stole and for having no pity."
Then Nathan said to David, "You are that man!" **2 Samuel 12:5-7, NLT.**

Dave was one of those guys who had everything. His laptop was the newest one on the market. His phone could do everything except drive a car. He had an e-book reader, the latest iPod, and even a digital watch full of gadgets. His gaming system was in 3-D, his television took up half the wall, and his digital camera was even waterproof. Whenever anything new came out, he had to have it.

His neighbor Corey didn't have a lot. He couldn't afford a computer, so he used the public computers at the library. He was still listening to his music on a CD player, and the only phone he could afford was a prepaid phone that only worked when he had enough money to buy some minutes. Corey's family wasn't rich either, but when his grandfather passed away, he left Corey one thing in his will. It was a prototype for the world's smallest computer—a real working model. It wasn't worth much, because it would cost too much to manufacture, so the computer companies wouldn't make it. But it was really cute, and it was the only one of its kind in the world.

As soon as Dave saw it, he had to have it. In fact, he wanted it so badly he would have traded every electronic gadget he had in order to get it. Of course, he offered to buy it from Corey; said he'd pay whatever Corey wanted for it. But Corey wouldn't sell, because it reminded him of his grandfather, a man he'd respected and loved. Dave was so desperate to get what he wanted that he hired some bad men. He sent some to murder Corey as he walked home late one night after work, and he sent others to steal the little computer from Corey's house. In the dark, all alone, Dave held the tiny computer in his palm and admired it. Finally, it was his, all his.

Dave had many things, but they didn't make him happy. Instead, he only wanted the one thing he couldn't have, and when he couldn't get it, he simply destroyed the obstacle in his path and took it. Nice guy, huh? Sadly, this sort of thing happens all the time. Maybe we don't go around killing people to take their stuff, but we ignore all the blessings God has heaped on us and focus only on what we don't have. Instead of always looking for what's newer, brighter, and better, thank God for everything He's given you today.

One of These Things

Don't copy the behavior and customs of this world,
but let God transform you into a new person by changing the way
you think. Then you will learn to know God's will for you,
which is good and pleasing and perfect. **Romans 12:2, NLT.**

When I was a kid, one of the children's programs I watched had a game called One of These Things. They would show you a picture of four items and play a song saying that one of these things was not like the other and you had to figure out which one it was. There might be a knife, a fork, a spoon, and a slipper. Even though it was never very hard to figure out which of the things didn't belong, I considered it a point of personal pride to choose the correct item.

As I grew up, I was frequently moved around to different schools. Every time I had to try to find new friends and figure out a way to fit in. I felt like a square peg trying to fit into a round hole, and I began to think I was stuck in a version of that game I liked so much when I was little. I started to think that maybe *I* was the thing that was not like the others.

I fit in even less once I became a Seventh-day Adventist. Now I couldn't work on Sabbath, I didn't party like the other people my age, and I went to church on a perfectly good Saturday instead of getting together with non-Christian friends. There were things I didn't do and food I didn't eat, and all of it made me stick out. I was definitely not like the others.

Have you ever felt as though you just didn't belong? It's a pretty lonely feeling. I'm so glad Jesus knows how that feels, because He's the one I go to when the loneliness becomes overwhelming. If anyone didn't fit in down here, it was Jesus. Even His own disciples didn't get Him most of the time. When He was going through horrible experiences, such as the Garden of Gethsemane, they couldn't even be bothered to stay awake and pray. When He was arrested, they headed for the hills; they didn't want anything to do with Him.

There's an old hymn that says that this world is not our home, that we're just passing through on our way to heaven. If you were in a foreign land, would you feel at home? No. And this world is so foreign to Christians that we can't expect to feel at home here either. We're going to look different, talk different, and act different. But when that makes us lonely, and it will, we can talk to Jesus. He knows exactly how we feel, and He can't wait for us to come home for good.

August 24

Making Friends

A friend loves at all times, and a brother is born
for a time of adversity. **Proverbs 17:17, NIV.**

When you don't "fit in," having some real friends can help. Except that if you're like me, making friends might not be easy. I always dread getting e-mails that ask you to "forward to 20 of your friends." Are they joking? Who on earth has 20 friends? It's not that I don't want to have friends; I just seem to have trouble making them.

If that sounds like you, or if you just want to add to your existing number of friends, try some of these suggestions:

1. To have a friend, you must first be a friend. Have you ever had the kind of friend who always wants something but never does any giving? Friends have to do some of both. It's OK to ask friends for help and support, but be sure to return the favor.

2. Consider friends who might not be your own age. People who are older have a lot to offer. Not only can they help you with life issues that come up, but they can teach you all kinds of great stuff, too.

3. To find people who like the same things you do, hang out in those places. People who like to do the same things tend to get together somewhere to do them. It doesn't matter what your interest is—chances are you aren't the only one. Check to see if there is a club or other gathering in your town of people who like the same things you like.

4. Buddy up. If you work on projects with someone, you'll accomplish two things: you'll get the work done faster, and you'll have more fun. If you find a friend to share the job with (and help when it's their turn), you may discover you have a lot more than work in common.

5. Say hello and smile. Having trouble making friends is very common. A lot of people are shy and afraid to make the first move. That guy in your class who is full of curiosity and has great ideas might turn out to be a great friend with a little encouragement. It can be hard to take the first step, but someone has to do it. Try smiling and saying hello and see where that leads you.

Friends are important. Even Jesus had His disciples and other friends such as Lazarus, Mary, and Martha; they came from all walks of life. Who knows where you'll find your next friend?

World of Regret

For the sorrow that is according to the will of God
produces a repentance without regret, leading to salvation,
but the sorrow of the world produces death. **2 Corinthians 7:10, NASB.**

Life is full of choices. Should I go right or left? forward or backward? attend college or get a job? get married or stay single? stay in my hometown or move away? For every choice we make there is at least one choice we didn't make. As time goes by and the choice we did make doesn't turn out well, we may have regrets and wish we'd chosen something else instead. Sometimes it's not too late to make a change and do things differently. Other times the choice is more permanent, and there's nothing you can do except live with it.

At the end of life when people look back over all their choices and decisions, they tend to regret some things more than others. When asked what they regret the most, dying people have listed such things as not spending more time with their families, not keeping in touch with friends, not living the way they wanted to live instead of living the way other people expected them to live, and not having the courage to tell people how they really felt, among other things.

The thing about regret is that it's pretty useless unless it makes us change something. The thief on the cross next to Jesus who asked to be remembered when Jesus came into His kingdom probably regretted the crimes that had brought him to that cross. His regret caused him to repent and believe in Jesus for salvation. It was *godly* regret. If he'd been allowed to live, he would have become one of Jesus' followers.

The thief on the other side probably regretted his crimes too, but only because he got caught. His regret was *worldly*; it didn't lead to repentance, only frustration and anger that he'd been caught. If he'd been allowed to live, he would have continued to live the same way he always had, committing crimes that would eventually put him back up on a cross if he was caught.

Hopefully you don't have many regrets. Dedicate your life to God and ask Him to direct your decision-making so that you won't have many regrets when you reach the end of it. And if you do regret choices that you have made, let them lead you to God.

August 26

Good Enough?

Jesus is "the stone you builders rejected, which has become the cornerstone." Salvation is found in no one else, for there is no other name under heaven given to mankind by which we must be saved. **Acts 4:11, 12, NIV.**

A speaker at my church distributed a questionnaire that had these questions on it: "If you die tonight, will you go to heaven? Why or why not?" He was conducting a survey and we had to mark our answer and turn in the paper. I admit I panicked a little. It's all right thinking you'll go to heaven someday, but this was a concrete question: If I die tonight, will I go to heaven? Not "if I die in a few years, or a long time from now," but "if I die *tonight*."

As we were marking our sheets, the speaker read some responses he'd collected previously, mostly from teens. He said the majority of teens either said they would go to heaven, because they were good people and better than most of the people they knew, or they said they wouldn't go to heaven, because they sinned too much and they weren't good enough, although some of them added that God was still working on them so they hoped someday to be good enough to go to heaven.

What about you? If you die tonight, will you go to heaven? Why or why not?

Before you answer that, you should know that all of the teens gave the wrong reason for whether or not they'd go to heaven. They were all wrong, because they based their salvation on themselves, not on Jesus. They won't go to heaven on their own goodness or for being better than most people they know, and they won't *not* go to heaven because they have sinned too much, unless they aren't willing to confess and give up their sins.

Those teens, and you and I, will be able to go to heaven for only one reason, and it's the same reason for all of us. The *only* way to God is through Jesus: "There is no other name under heaven given to mankind by which we must be saved (Acts 4:12, NIV). Trying to reach God any other way is like needing to cross an ocean and Jesus offering you a boat that He gave up everything to purchase so you could make the journey safely and you saying, "No, thanks. I'd rather swim."

We can confidently answer today's question only when we accept Jesus as our Savior. Our only contribution is to hang on for the ride of our lives.

The Next Big Thing

When Barnabas and Paul finally realized what was going on,
they stopped them. Waving their arms, they interrupted the parade,
calling out, "What do you think you're doing! We're not gods!
We are men just like you, and we're here to bring you the Message,
to persuade you to abandon these silly god-superstitions and embrace God
himself, the living God. We don't make God; he makes us, and all of
this—sky, earth, sea, and everything in them." **Acts 14:14, 15, Message.**

I saw a video the other day of a girl with an amazing voice. She was on one of those shows that search for talented people, and she blew the judges away. One of them climbed up on top of the table to give her a standing ovation. All the judges agreed that she had extraordinary talent and that she'd be the next big thing.

Nowadays it's easier than ever to get "famous." And with so many people climbing the ladder to insta-stardom, it's easy to idolize them. The problem is that humans aren't meant to be idolized. Even in Christian circles it can be tempting to be too impressed by Christian "celebrities": singers, radio personalities, writers, speakers, or even pastors or youth leaders. Whenever we look up to another human being, we're looking in the wrong direction.

Ellen White says, "The Bible has little to say in praise of men. Little space is given to recounting the virtues of even the best men who have ever lived. This silence is not without purpose; it is not without a lesson. All the good qualities that men possess are the gift of God; their good deeds are performed by the grace of God through Christ. Since they owe all to God the glory of whatever they are or do belongs to Him alone; they are but instruments in His hands. More than this—as all the lessons of Bible history teach—it is a perilous thing to praise or exalt men; for if one comes to lose sight of his entire dependence on God, and to trust to his own strength, he is sure to fall" (*Patriarchs and Prophets,* p. 717).

We all have talents that God gave us, and that's the important part: *God gave them to us.* We need to be careful that we don't start thinking we developed them on our own somehow, all by ourselves. With our talents comes a responsibility to use them in a way that honors God. There is no limit to how far our talent can bring us when we're firmly anchored in God and depending entirely on Him, honoring Him completely with the gifts He's given us.

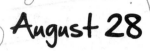

No Holds Barred

*We know that God's children do not make a practice of sinning,
for God's Son holds them securely, and the evil one cannot touch them.
We know that we are children of God and that the world
around us is under the control of the evil one.* I John 5:18, 19, NLT.

No-holds-barred fighting, also known as mixed martial arts or ultimate fighting, means that pretty much everything goes. It's been compared to gladiator fights because of how violent it is. People have called the fighting brutal and inhumane. The organizers themselves called it the "bloodiest, most barbaric show in history."

But even in this type of fighting there are a few rules. No gouging someone's eyes, for instance, which means that the "most barbaric show in history" is tamer than the spiritual battles we face every day as Christians, because there are no rules in that fight. Satan can use every means available to him to attack us. He's cold, calculating, and endlessly patient. He will wait for the moment we're at our weakest and most vulnerable to pounce on us.

Did you fail your math test today? Were your parents fighting this morning before you left the house? Do you have a cold? Did you break your ankle in gym class? take too many classes and are now buried under heaps of homework? join one too many after-school activities? go to bed late? get up early? have no time for devotions? fail to crack open your Bible except when you're in Sabbath school?

That's perfect for Satan. That's when he'll strike. Not when you're reading your Sabbath school lesson every day, participating in class, digging into your Bible, going to prayer meeting, and talking with God. He won't come after you when you're strong. He'll wait until you slip up and relax your grip on God before he tries to take you down. You're on Satan's hit list in the most vicious and most important fight in history.

Fortunately, as long as God is our coach and we stay in our corner with Him, Satan can't touch us. He can try, but unless we walk away from God and climb into the ring with him, Satan can only shout insults from his corner. Yeah, he can make us mad. Yeah, he can be really annoying. But he can't win the fight if we stay with God, because God already won the championship round. We've got nothing to prove except that we support our Champion.

I'm Bored

Besides, they get into the habit of being idle and going about from house to house. And not only do they become idlers, but also busybodies who talk nonsense, saying things they ought not to. I Timothy 5:13, NIV.

'm bored.

I challenge you to count the number of times you hear those words coming out of your mouth. I've heard them most often over the weekend or during a school vacation when my kids were around the house more. I've even had friends text them to me hoping I had time to chat with them.

Boredom is an invitation to Satan to present us with possibilities. One of the most public sins on record in the Bible happened because King David was bored. He was supposed to be with his men, fighting the Ammonites. Instead he left his commander in charge and moseyed on back to the palace where he dawdled around with nothing to do. He was bored, bored, bored.

That's when he saw a pretty girl. Ellen White says, "It was now, while he was at ease and unguarded, that the tempter seized the opportunity to occupy his mind. The fact that God had taken David into so close connection with Himself and had manifested so great favor toward him, should have been to him the strongest of incentives to preserve his character unblemished. But when in ease and self-security he let go his hold upon God, David yielded to Satan and brought upon his soul the stain of guilt" (*Patriarchs and Prophets*, p. 718). You can find the full story in 2 Samuel 11; 12.

When my sisters and I were bored, we would make a list of all the possible things we could do and then we'd vote on them. It would probably be even more helpful if you had a list ahead of time so that when boredom snuck up on you, it would be ready and waiting to give you direction. What have you always wanted to do? Write it down! The next time you're bored, instead of waiting for Satan to suggest something, you'll be all ready to set off on an adventure instead.

Try This: Throughout the week, keep a tally of the number of times you say "I'm bored." Score yourself with the following points: 0-3 = 10 points; 4-8 = 20 points; 9-12 = 30 points; 13-17 = 40 points; 18-25 = 50 points. If you get 20 points or more, keep score again in the next weeks until you get down to 10 points a week. Follow up: How many weeks does it take?

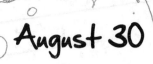

August 30

Airmail

Then Samson went and caught three hundred foxes;
and he took torches, turned the foxes tail to tail, and put a torch
between each pair of tails. When he had set the torches on fire,
he let the foxes go into the standing grain of the Philistines,
and burned up both the shocks and the standing grain, as well
as the vineyards and olive groves. **Judges 15:4, 5, NKJV.**

I don't share today's Bible verse because I like that story. I don't; I feel bad for the poor foxes. But it does illustrate an interesting point: When you send something out into the world that you have no control over, it can affect the world in ways you couldn't even imagine. Samson let the foxes go in the fields of grain, but they also ended up burning down the vineyards and the olive groves. Clearly Samson had a message to send.

Too bad Samson didn't use bottles or balloons, two traditional ways to send messages off into the world. The first message in a bottle was launched way back in 310 B.C. by a philosopher named Theophrastus, who wanted to prove that the Mediterranean Sea was filled by the Atlantic Ocean. In the sixteenth century the English Navy used bottles to send messages about enemy positions. To be sure the right people saw the messages when they were found, Queen Elizabeth I created an official position, "Uncorker of Ocean Bottles." If you found a bottle and opened it yourself, you could get the death penalty.

People who can't put their messages into bottles and throw them into the ocean sometimes use balloons to send messages. Through the years I've found two of these balloon messages. It's fun to write back to the person who released the balloon and find out how far it traveled. Most often the messages simply have contact information from the person who launched the balloon, but in South Korea, Christians have launched balloons carrying New Testaments, Scripture verses, and other gospel messages that they hoped would land in North Korea and spread the good news since Christianity isn't welcome in North Korea.

You don't need foxes to send messages that will spread out into the world. You can attach some sharing tracts (you can find many different kinds at www.adventistbookcenter.com) to helium balloons and have your own missionary balloon launch. Be sure to put the literature inside plastic baggies in case it gets wet before someone finds it. To make sure the finder can locate a local Seventh-day Adventist church, you can include our church's Web site address: www.adventist.org.

Hazed

Instead, be kind to each other, tenderhearted, forgiving one another, just as God through Christ has forgiven you. **Ephesians 4:32, NLT.**

What's that? You want to join our church? Hey, that's great! First you need to go through an initiation, you know, just to prove you have what it takes to be part of our group. Don't worry, all of us have gone through the same thing. It's hard, I won't lie to you, but you've got to go through it if you want to join. Are you sure you want to join? Are you sure you've got what it takes?

"OK, then, here's where we start. Come right on in this room. It's kind of chilly down here, isn't it? Here are some of the other members. They're going to force you to drink gallons of water. And you'll have to pour some on yourself; you're going to get pretty cold. Don't worry, though—people don't die . . . usually. Matthew Carrington died of water intoxication during a hazing, but no one has died this week."

Do you think many people would join the church if they had to go through a hazing ritual like this in order to become a member? I wouldn't have believed it, but statistics show that almost all (91 percent) high school students belong to a group, and nearly half of those groups (48 percent) have some kind of hazing ritual, so hazing clearly doesn't deter teens from joining groups. You could argue that those kids weren't Christians, but you'd be only partly right. Twenty-four percent of the students were involved in church groups. What's worse is that almost half of the kids hazed were subjected to humiliating activities, and nearly a third had to perform acts that were illegal or bordering on illegal. The hazing I described actually happened—not to join a church, but a fraternity—and one of the pledges, Matthew Carrington, really died of water intoxication. Seven members of the fraternity were charged in connection with his death.

Matthew's friend Michael, who had also gone through a hazing ritual, said, "Hazing seemed to me to be stupid and harmless; however, I know now that it is serious and deadly, and I want more people to be aware of that. I feel if this could happen to us it could happen to anybody." Even as serious and deadly as hazing is, chances are it will continue. But you don't have to be part of it. Don't cave in to hazing pressure, and if you learn about hazing activities, report them. You could save someone's life. Maybe even your own.

September 1

Edumission

For this is what the Lord has commanded us:
"I have made you a light for the Gentiles, that you may
bring salvation to the ends of the earth." **Acts 13:47, NIV.**

Any time now (or maybe it was last week) it will be That Day: the first day of school. It's a day you've probably dreaded all summer long unless you've recently graduated and aren't going to college, in which case you're probably feeling pretty smug right now. At least until you remember that instead of getting ready for a day of school you're off to your new job.

No matter whether you are going to school or work one thing stays the same: you leave the comfort of home and enter your mission field each and every day. You will need all the help you can get, and that's exactly what Jesus wants to give you. He says He has made us a light for the Gentiles.

When you think about it, if we are the light, let's say a flashlight, Jesus is the batteries in our flashlight. Without Him we can't shine. We may have good intentions. We may want to shine very much. But unless He gives us the power, we're just going to get sucked up into the darkness. And there's plenty of darkness to get sucked up into in this crazy world.

You may think you're going to school only for an *education*, but that's not true. Because school is also your *mission* field, you could say that school is your *edumission* because you'll have opportunities to get an education *and* witness as a missionary.

Don't think you're off the hook if you happen to go to a Christian school. You'll find plenty of posers there who don't really know Jesus, but pretend to. It can be just as hard to hang on to your faith when you are around fake Christians all day as it is to be surrounded by non-Christians.

Before you head out into your mission field, wherever it may be, make sure your batteries are charged. Get your marching orders for the day from Jesus and then turn on your light. Remember, your mission field lies wherever you travel beyond your own door.

Bunny Overboard!

Are not two sparrows sold for a penny? Yet not one of them will fall to the ground outside your Father's care. And even the very hairs of your head are all numbered. So don't be afraid; you are worth more than many sparrows. **Matthew 10:29-31, NIV.**

John Byrne is a homeless man who lives in Dublin, Ireland. He can't stay at a shelter, because they won't accept his animals, a small dog, Lily, and a rabbit named Barney, so he sleeps in a tent at night. During the day he begs around the city. As he sat on O'Connell Bridge one day, an 18-year-old passed him and saw his pets. The teen grabbed poor Barney by the ears and flung him over the side of the bridge into the rushing River Liffey below. Not only is the river filthy, but it is cold and its strong currents result in deaths every year.

John didn't hesitate. He didn't think about the fact that he could be killed jumping over the side of the bridge. He didn't think about the fact that he could drown trying to save Barney. He just leaped off the side of the bridge and into the water.

John said Barney swam toward him. With the rabbit in his arms he climbed onto a piling beneath the bridge where they waited for rescue by the Dublin Fire Brigade. Later John was honored as a hero in a ceremony and given the compassionate citizen award by an animal welfare charity. When asked why he risked his life to save his pet, John said, "Because he is my child, I love him, and I just wanted to save him. I didn't think; I just jumped."

This story touched a lot of people. According to some comment chatter following the story's posting, John and his animals may even have been given a place to live off the streets. It's easy to see why people are impressed at the way he saved a small, defenseless animal. It strikes a chord in us, and it should because it's a small version of a bigger story that we all know but don't always appreciate.

When humanity fell, Jesus jumped right over the bridge to save us. He didn't think of the risk to Himself; He didn't look over the side and say, "Oh, well, I'll just make some more." We're His children and He loves us, so He came to earth to save us. Like Barney, we may be small and helpless, but that doesn't mean that we don't matter to God.

Think About It: How could working with the homeless help us to understand our relationship with God better? Are there ways you might minister to the homeless in your city?

September 3

Potty Talk

But immorality or any impurity or greed must not
even be named among you, as is proper among saints;
and there must be no filthiness and silly talk, or coarse jesting,
which are not fitting, but rather giving of thanks. **Ephesians 5:3, 4, NASB.**

You may have noticed that little children are easily amused by bathroom talk. This is partly because some words associated with bathroom activities such as "tinkling," "tooting," and "pooping," sound funny, and partly because they are not old enough to be embarrassed by such words. They won't understand for a few more years that talking about bathroom stuff is not something you do in front of a crowd of people.

The trouble is that as soon as they figure out it's not polite to talk about bathroom activities, they start seeing children's movies and television programs in which there are plenty of jokes made using bathroom humor or potty talk. The jokes are often funny; we might as well admit that. Cute little animals making rude sounds or getting caught with their pants down in the outhouse make us laugh. We might be a little embarrassed about laughing at such things, but we still laugh. After all, that's what bathroom humor is all about: making people laugh.

Unfortunately what starts out as silly jokes about the bathroom then grows up into worse jokes about other things that are meant to be private. Because one fairly innocent thing leads to the next slightly less innocent thing, it's easy to get caught up in it, thinking that it's really harmless. Except that it's not. Not really. The Bible calls it filthiness, silly talk, and coarse jesting, and it has no place coming out of the mouth of a Christian.

Why? Because our whole purpose here is to raise people's thoughts up to God, not drag them down to the sewer. You can be sure the angels don't sit around heaven telling bathroom jokes, and neither should we. You might think that sounds a little fanatical. After all, there's usually no cursing or swearing in bathroom humor. Most of the language is cleaned up because it's meant for kids. But the principle is still the same. If it comes out of our mouths, it should point to Jesus, and bathroom humor never points to Jesus. It points to someone else entirely, someone who doesn't mind having a dirty mind and a gutter mouth. Leave him to it and make a commitment to keep your mouth and mind clean so you can praise Jesus with them.

Home Alone

His master replied, "Well done, good and faithful servant!
You have been faithful with a few things; I will put you in charge of many
things. Come and share your master's happiness!" **Matthew 25:23, NIV.**

Have you ever been left in charge of something? A younger sibling? The family dog? A goldfish? Your parents' house? Have your parents ever decided to go away for the weekend and leave you in charge? If they haven't, it's probably something you dream about: the control, the power, the thrill, sole possession of the remote control. If they have, it's probably something you dread: the responsibility.

What if something goes wrong? What if the house burns down? What if your friends hear that you are home alone and crash your place to have a wild party? You may have perfectly good intentions: "No one is coming in this house while Mom and Dad are gone except for my best friend, Bill." But what if Bill tells his older sister that your parents are out of town, and she tells her boyfriend, and he brings three friends? Suddenly you have a houseful of people, and you don't even know half of them.

If you're in charge, then you are also responsible if something happens on your watch. It's your responsibility as caretaker to stand up for your parent's wishes and be their representative in their place. That means you get to be the bad guy and spoil everyone's "fun" by making them stop doing things your parents wouldn't approve of. Being in charge is a serious thing.

Jesus once told a parable about a master who left servants to care for some of his property. All of the servants wanted to hear "Well done, good and faithful servant" when their master returned, but not all of them did. In the parable Jesus is the master and we are the servants. We've been entrusted with His property; how are we caring for it while He's away? Jesus didn't simply leave us in charge of the house: we've got a whole planet to care for and protect.

It's important that we care about our planet, because the health of the planet will affect our own health. We can't leave that job to someone else; it matters too much.

Think About It: What are some ways you can care for the environment? This week, find out how you can help in your own community.

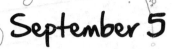

September 5

Dead That Quick

> But God said to him, "You fool! This very night your life will be demanded from you. Then who will get what you have prepared for yourself?" **Luke 12:20, NIV.**

Carly Ferro was 17 years old. She worked a couple jobs, was active in school, and never dreamed when she woke up on September 26, 2012, that she'd be dead that evening. It was a normal day, an ordinary day. There was nothing special about it. She went to school, and then she went to work.

Her dad came to pick her up that evening and was waiting in his car. Carly came out of the store and as she walked around her dad's car, another vehicle driving down the street at 80 miles per hour struck her father's car, pinning it, and Carly, against the building. Paramedics tried to save her, but she died later at the hospital.

The car that hit Carly was driven by Alex Spanos. It's no wonder he lost control of it; police discovered he'd been inhaling Dust-Off just before the crash. Passengers in his car said that he was making no sense when he tried to speak just before the accident.

This happened about a mile or so from where I live, outside a store I shop at. It could have been me, or my daughter, or my son, or one of their friends, or even you if you had come to visit. How many times have you walked out of a store, laughing, minding your own business, never dreaming that you could be mere seconds from being crushed by a car?

People sometimes think Jesus is taking an awfully long time to come back. Have you ever thought so yourself? They wonder if He will come back in their lifetime. The answer is yes. Yes, He will. Because the very next thing you'll be aware of the moment after your life is over is Jesus coming back. There may be 50 or 100 years between your death and His return, but to you it'll seem like you just closed your eyes and opened them again.

How important is it, then, that we're ready for that day? Some people put it off. They think, *I've got plenty of time before Jesus comes back. I don't have to get to know Him now. I can give Him my heart later. What's the rush?*

But you won't necessarily know when your time is up. Just because you're young does not mean you can't die. You could walk out of a store and be crushed by a car. There's no time to wait. Thank God that's He's given you today, this minute, and use it to get to know Him.

Burden of Unforgiveness

*All this is from God, who reconciled us to himself
through Christ and gave us the ministry of reconciliation:
that God was reconciling the world to himself in Christ,
not counting people's sins against them. And he has committed
to us the message of reconciliation.* **2 Corinthians 5:18, 19, NIV.**

It's April 1939. A young African American man in Tennessee gets into a fight with White store owners who claim he stole merchandise from their store. He's later found lynched and thrown into a river. No one is ever charged with his murder, and his death certificate claims that he drowned accidentally.

When his brother, Charlie Morris, hears what happened, he's in school. All he wants is revenge. He goes home and gets a .38 revolver and brings it, crying, to his grandmother's house. "Son, don't do this," she tells him. "I've got one grandson dead. I don't want the burden of another grandson being dead."

So Charlie buries his anger, his hurt, and his grief. But he doesn't forget it. And he doesn't forgive. He carries that burden of unforgiveness with him for 10 years, and it makes him sick. Not sick inside, but really, actually sick. He has aches and pains and feels awful. He goes to the doctor, but they can't find anything wrong with him.

The doctor asks him to bring his wife along on the next visit, and she says that Charlie has been having nightmares and calling for his brother in his sleep. The doctor knows then what is causing Charlie's physical pain. "When I began to forgive," says Charlie, "there was all the answers to my illness. I didn't have to go to the doctor anymore. I didn't have those pains."

Are you carrying a burden of unforgiveness that's making you sick? Has someone posted an unforgivable picture of you on Facebook? Stolen your best friend or your boyfriend or girlfriend? Told everyone terrible lies about you? Someone once said, "Not forgiving someone is like drinking poison and expecting the other person to die." You have two choices when you face an unforgivable situation or person. You can hang on to your anger, which will eventually poison you. Or you can ask God to help you forgive and let it go.

Think About It: Would you like God to forgive you the way you forgive others?

September 7

Who Cares for You?

Therefore humble yourselves under the mighty hand of God,
that He may exalt you in due time, casting all your care
upon Him, for He cares for you. **I Peter 5:6, 7, NKJV.**

Today I broke my Internet connection. I don't mean that it just discon-nected. I mean that I dropped it and it broke, literally. The little thingy-whatsit in the back of the thingamabob was all loose, and by the time I got to the store it had fallen out completely. There wasn't a whisper of a signal, nothing, nada, zilch. That may be only an inconvenience to some people who just use the Internet for playing around on Facebook, but I use it for work. Without the Internet I can't do the research I need for the projects I'm working on. I'm dead in the water.

Now, I didn't have enough money to replace that Internet device. I mean, I *had* it, I just couldn't justify spending it to replace something I'd accidentally broken. That felt like being careless with God's resources, since He provides me with my living and all my money is His. So I told God, "I'm putting this in Your hands. I can't do a thing about it. Maybe You want me to pay all that money to replace this device. Or maybe You've got something else in mind. I accept Your will *no matter what it is*. It's Your money, and I'll accept however You want to spend it."

The women at the store were very sympathetic, maybe because I was prac-tically in tears. I'd already called ahead and been told it was going to cost hun-dreds of dollars to replace, and they assured me that was correct and my only other options were even more expensive. I left the store without deciding what to do. I felt strongly that I should wait. When I got home, I decided to explore other ways to get on the Internet. The first company I called informed me that not only could they give me way more Internet options than I'd been getting, but they could do it for a third of the price!

I always have a sense of God's presence in my life as long as I'm spending time with Him, but situations like these make me realize that He's not just *in* my life the way the sun is in the sky, but He *cares* for me. He cares for me so much that He makes a difference in a practical way. My life would be differ-ent—it would be much worse—if He wasn't in it, directing it, and showing me every now and then just how much of a difference He makes.

Who cares for you? Is God an active presence in your life? If He's not, ask Him to care for you today.

Rembrandt's Crayon

We are all infected and impure with sin. When we display our righteous deeds, they are nothing but filthy rags. Like autumn leaves, we wither and fall, and our sins sweep us away like the wind. **Isaiah 64:6, NLT.**

Danny was 5 years old, and he'd just gotten a brand-new box of crayons. His mom gave him a sheet of paper from the printer tray, and he sat down at the kitchen table to draw a picture for his father. Dad would be home any minute now. Danny knew his father liked art, because he had several paintings on the wall of his study. So Danny decided to draw one of those pictures. Surely Dad would like his picture better, because he made it himself. Maybe his father would even take the real painting off the wall and put Danny's picture up instead.

He colored feverishly until he heard the front door open. Just in time; he'd finished his masterpiece. He put his crayons away, and carrying his drawing, he met his father in the living room. "Here, Daddy, I made this just for you."

What do you think Danny's dad said? Do you think he compared it to the masterpiece in his study and pointed out all the flaws in Danny's picture to him? Or do you think he looked at the picture as the very best his son could do and praised his efforts?

I can't tell you, because I made Danny up. But I believe Danny's father would have loved his son's drawing. The way you think the story ends could tell you a lot about how you think God feels about the things that you do for Him. The Bible tells us that nothing good that we do amounts to anything in God's eyes. He sees it all as filthy rags. We're all so polluted with sin that nothing we do is any good.

That doesn't mean we should stop doing good things, though, any more than Danny should stop coloring just because he can't produce a masterpiece at the age of 5. Danny drew his picture out of love and offered it to his father, who loved it not because it was a masterpiece of artistic skill, but because his son loved him enough to make it. Just because we aren't capable of creating anything good on our own doesn't mean we shouldn't. God loves us and accepts the flaws in our offerings when we create them out of love for Him. If we're just trying to impress Him with our great behavior, we can stop trying. But if we're loving Him with our good works, then He'll accept our gift as though it was drawn by a Master—Jesus.

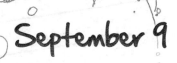

September 9

You and Your SSB

Jesus said, "Everyone who drinks this water
will get thirsty again and again. Anyone who drinks the water
I give will never thirst—not ever. The water I give will be an artesian
spring within, gushing fountains of endless life." **John 4:13, 14, Message.**

You. Yeah, you. Put down that SSB and step away from the table. Slowly. Keep your hands where I can see them. That's it. Nice and easy, and no one will get hurt.

What's a nice person like you doing hanging around with SSBs in the first place? Didn't anyone ever tell you what bad characters these dudes are? They're on the FBI's (Federal Bureau of Impostors) Most Wanted List. They are sly, sneaky, and up to no good. They are not what they pretend to be. Who are these nefarious characters? Sugar-sweetened beverages, that's who.

You know the ones: sodas, fruity-tasting drinks that only pretend to have anything to do with real fruit, beverages with colors that aren't found in nature, all those cans and shiny, bright bottles lining the cooler shelves at the local convenience store. They whisper to you as you walk past the cooler, "Psst! Hey, you, pick me." What chance has a bottle of plain old water got with those colorful characters around?

The Centers for Disease Control and Prevention (CDC) reported that sugar-sweetened beverages are the biggest source of added sugar in the diets of U.S. teens. They discovered that the calories from all that sugar are a big reason teens are struggling with obesity. Not to mention that sugar is terrible for your health in general. See? I told you those guys were bad news.

No matter how old you are, the trouble with all those sugary drinks is that they are pretending to be something they're not: healthy. Once your taste buds get used to all that sugar, it's hard to go back to drinking plain water even though it's healthier and what our bodies need to really function at their best. The same thing can happen to us spiritually: we get hooked on all kinds of exciting worship experiences that may be great in their own way but can't take the place of the simple, powerful presence of the Holy Spirit in our lives.

When we drink water, our bodies will function better, we'll get sick less, and we'll have more energy. We will get thirsty again, though. When we drink the water Jesus offers us—the Holy Spirit—we'll never be spiritually thirsty again.

September 10

Risky Business

Don't pick on people, jump on their failures, criticize their faults—unless, of course, you want the same treatment. That critical spirit has a way of boomeranging. It's easy to see a smudge on your neighbor's face and be oblivious to the ugly sneer on your own. **Matthew 7:1, 2, Message.**

In the mornings I like to listen to a Christian radio program called *The Wally Show,* hosted by, you guessed it, a guy named Wally. I don't always agree with what Wally says or what he has on his program, and when I don't, I just switch the station. But for the most part when I'm driving around, he amuses me, plays some awesome contemporary Christian worship music, and often gives me something to think about until I get home.

This morning Wally read an e-mail a listener had sent him that slammed him for the way he looks—his physical appearance. That is probably something no one has ever done to you, but I have plenty of (stinging) experience in that area, and I felt really bad for Wally.

The thing that amazed me, though, is that not only did Wally read the e-mail on the air—he actually asked for feedback on the criticism from his cohosts. He didn't just blow it off, get mad, slam the person back over the air—all things I would have been tempted to do myself. He actually considered the criticism thoughtfully and said that he hoped the person who wrote the e-mail wasn't as mean-spirited as they came across.

Criticism is risky business. It's like using a grenade to perform surgery: it makes a big mess, and when you're done, there's not much left of the patient. It also makes a lot of shrapnel, and you're likely to get hit yourself when it's flying around.

Although they share some letters, there is no "Christ" in "criticism." But did you notice what letter is in there three times? I. When you criticize someone, you are placing yourself above them. Whenever we make judgments or criticisms, we invite them back on our own heads.

"He who takes upon himself the work of judging and criticizing others, lays himself open to the same degree of judgment and criticism. Those who are ready to condemn their brethren, would do well to examine their own works and character. Such an examination, honestly made, will reveal the fact that they, too, have defects of character, and have made grave blunders in their work. If the great Judge should deal with men as they deal with their fellow workers, they would regard him as unkind and unmerciful" (Ellen G. White, *Christian Leadership,* p. 59).

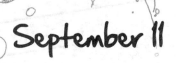

September 11

Famous Last Words

When he had received the drink, Jesus said, "It is finished." With that, he bowed his head and gave up his spirit. **John 19:30, NIV.**

Not everyone has the chance to say one last thing before they die, but those who do prefer that it be something meaningful, something profound, something quotable. Pancho Villa, the Mexican revolutionary, for example, reportedly said, "Don't let it end like this. Tell them I said something." Not very memorable, but his heart was in the right place. Some people, such as novelist H. G. Wells, procrastinate to the end. His last words were "Go away. I'm all right."

Some people are still second-guessing themselves, even on their deathbeds. Considered to be one of the greatest painters of all time, Leonardo da Vinci said, "I have offended God and mankind because my work did not reach the quality it should have." Others can't admit they're wrong. While reprimanding his men for taking cover during the Battle of Spotsylvania, Union general John Sedgwick's last words were "They couldn't hit an elephant at this distance."

Some famous last words are taken up and used as rallying cries. When terrorists hijacked United Airlines Flight 93, passenger Todd Beamer was heard saying, "Are you guys ready? Let's roll" just before passengers tried to retake control of the plane before it crashed. The phrase was so inspiring it came to symbolize heroism, self-sacrifice, and initiative in tough situations.

Jesus' last words were brief. There were only three: "It is finished." But what a rallying cry they are! Finished. Done. Satan has lost. Heaven has won! There is hope for us and a future in a place where pain, sickness, and suffering are banned for eternity. For all eternity, nothing will separate us from God ever again.

Jesus' last words are the ones that make every day on this dark earth bearable. Those last words He said are a promise to us that He will come back for us one day when they will become the first words of our eternity. When earth shudders to an end, "In the midst of the angry heavens is one clear space of indescribable glory, whence comes the voice of God like the sound of many waters, saying, 'It is done'" (Ellen G. White, *The Great Controversy,* p. 636). Can you think of any other words you'd rather hear?

September 12

Comeuppance

> But at midnight Paul and Silas were praying
> and singing hymns to God, and the prisoners were listening to them.
> Suddenly there was a great earthquake, so that the foundations
> of the prison were shaken; and immediately all the doors
> were opened and everyone's chains were loosed. **Acts 16:25, 26, NKJV.**

Lights! Camera! Action!

Scene: *Philippian Jail. Camera pans in to a view of Paul and Silas, who have just been severely beaten with rods. Their feet are fastened in stocks so they can't even change position to get more comfortable. Paul and Silas are complaining loudly. They put their heads together to plot their escape.*

Paul: Here's what we'll do: you call the jailer over. Tell him you've got a sliver in your eye or something. When he gets close enough, I'll grab him. I have a knife in my belt that those bullies didn't find earlier. You take it and slit his throat. Got it?

Silas *(nodding):* Yeah, it's a plan. But what about the rest of the prisoners? Should we let them out or leave them here?

Paul: We'll let them out. They're probably thieves and cutthroats. Let them pay back those jerks who beat us.

The story of Paul and Silas in the Philippian jail would have had a very different ending if Hollywood had written it. We're all about revenge. No movie worth its salt would let the bad guy off without getting punished, usually in the most gruesome way imaginable. And audiences cheer: "Yeah! He got what was coming to him!"

God's way is the complete opposite of Hollywood. Paul and Silas didn't kill their jailer. They didn't even plot about it or sit around hollering curses and threats. Instead they prayed and sang hymns, not quietly, but out loud so the whole jail could hear them. They didn't try to escape, and even after God sent an earthquake that knocked down the jail walls, they didn't take advantage of it to escape. Instead they stayed put and witnessed to the jailer and everyone in his house, and they were all saved.

In Hollywood the bad guy usually gets killed in the end. In God's version of the story the bad guy gets saved and goes to heaven. Which ending do you prefer?

September 13

Life Without Limbs

Be cheerful no matter what; pray all the time;
thank God no matter what happens. This is the way God wants
you who belong to Christ Jesus to live. I Thessalonians 5:16-18, Message.

In 1982 Nick Vujicic was born without arms or legs. He could have wallowed in self-pity and anger. In fact, he could still be wallowing and I wouldn't blame him, would you? I've been on crutches a couple times and that was hard enough. I can't imagine not being able to even wipe my own nose, especially during allergy season.

But Nick didn't wallow. Sure, he questioned why he was the kid born with no arms and legs and what kind of purpose his life could ever have when his handicap was so staggering. But even though Nick didn't have limbs, he had something far more important in his life: Nick had God, and God gave his life purpose and the ability to encourage and motivate people.

If you're tempted to think he lives a sheltered life stuck in a wheelchair, you're sorely mistaken. Just check out YouTube for some videos of Nick playing golf, surfing, and skydiving. God gave his life so much purpose that Nick now runs an organization called Life Without Limbs. He travels all over the world giving motivational talks to kids and grown-ups alike.

"I think emotional and mental pain is probably worse than physical pain," says Nick. "I think we don't realize that I have no arms or legs, but we all have disabilities of some sort—some fear, . . . some wishes that didn't come true, things we wish would be better. But we know that God works for all things together for the good of those who love Him and that God is faithful. We will fail God, we will fail our family, and our family might fail us at times, but God never fails us."

So often we look at the negative circumstances in our lives and we can't move past them. We're stuck. What we have to remember is that no matter what we're facing, God allowed that to come into our lives. There are no coincidences, remember? If God allows something in our life, it's because He knows how it will help us in some way or how it will witness to others. Nick Vujicic's limbless life has witnessed to *millions* of people that God can use someone who is willing to be His hands and feet even if they have none of their own. What is the witness of your life saying to people who know you?

From Worthless to Priceless

But God demonstrates His own love toward us,
in that while we were yet sinners, Christ died for us. **Romans 5:8, NASB.**

What is the value of one human being? In dollars and cents, I mean. Well, the U.S. Bureau of Chemistry and Soils decided to spend some of our taxpayer dollars to figure out just how much the human body would be worth if it was broken down into chemicals and minerals and sold. Turns out, depending on the ups and downs of the stock market and based only on the elements we're made from, we're worth a little less than a buck.

That's not very positive, is it? You'll spend more on lunch than you're actually worth. On the other hand, if you sold all of your pieces and parts that can be used in medical treatments or for experimentation and research, you'd make a whole lot more. Your body could be worth anywhere from $10,000 to $100,000, depending on how it's used.

The only trouble with both of these scenarios? You have to be dead to make any of that money, which means that alive, you're worthless. Aren't you glad that God places our value much higher than humankind does? He places our worth so high, in fact, that Jesus left the place we long to go to come to the place we yearn to leave. He didn't leave heaven with a "Hey, Dad, I'm going to pop down to earth to save humanity. I'll be home for dinner." *He left heaven knowing He might never get to go back.* Ellen White tells us that as He hung on the cross, "the Savior could not see through the portals of the tomb. Hope did not present to Him His coming forth from the grave a conqueror, or tell Him of the Father's acceptance of the sacrifice. He feared that sin was so offensive to God that Their separation was to be eternal" (*The Desire of Ages,* p. 753).

Jesus wasn't just willing to live on earth as a man for a while and suffer a cruel death for us. He was willing to give up everything—even His own existence—to save humans. Now tell me how much we're worth. We're priceless!

September 15

Fading In and Out

*So, friends, take a firm stand, feet on the ground and head high.
Keep a tight grip on what you were taught, whether in personal conversation
or by our letter. May Jesus himself and God our Father, who reached out
in love and surprised you with gifts of unending help and confidence,
put a fresh heart in you, invigorate your work,
enliven your speech.* **2 Thessalonians 2:15-17, Message.**

I don't listen to the radio a whole lot, but when I do I flip between two Christian stations. Whichever one is playing better music, or has a more interesting program on, or isn't airing a commercial is the one I'll tune in to. I mostly listen to the radio while I'm in the car, so I never catch a whole program; my trips are too short. In spite of that, though, I do manage to catch a lot of good information and inspiring songs.

Unless it's yucky outside, that is. When the wind is blowing and the rain is pelting my windshield, the radio stations fade in and out. Sometimes they just drop out altogether for minutes, hours, or even days at a time. I don't know about you, but listening to dead air is pretty boring, so I either find another radio station or put in a CD. If the radio station blinks back on for a while, I might miss it and whatever message it was hoping to bring to me because I'm just not paying attention to it anymore. It's too fickle, coming in and out like that, and my attention span isn't long enough to stay focused on it.

This is exactly what happens when we're on-again, off-again Christians. This is the kind of person who can spout Bible verses off the top of their head, who carry a Bible with them everywhere, who tell you they'll pray about your problems, but who also bad-mouth their friends, don't practice what they preach, use foul language, or break rules whenever they feel like it. Do you know this kind of person? (Be honest: are *you* this kind of person?)

Our message has to be consistent if it's going to be effective. If *you* don't even believe what you're saying, how can you expect anyone else to believe it? Christianity isn't something we can take a vacation from; it should be who we are at the center of our being. If it's not, we're living a lie, and soon people will tune us out.

Look critically at your life. Does it live up to your message? Why or why not? If it doesn't, ask God to help you be more consistent.

Good Grief

I heard a voice thunder from the Throne: "Look! Look!
God has moved into the neighborhood, making his home with men
and women! They're his people, he's their God. He'll wipe every tear
from their eyes. Death is gone for good—tears gone, crying gone, pain
gone—all the first order of things gone." The Enthroned continued,
"Look! I'm making everything new. Write it all down—each word
dependable and accurate." **Revelation 21:3-5, Message.**

A 17-year-old boy I know watched his father die from lung cancer within a year of his diagnosis. One of my 13-year-old students lost her mom to cancer. Another girl I know was 10 when her dad died suddenly. Death is no respecter of age. The people who died were not what we would call old. All three of these kids were very young when they lost their parents, even though there were seven years between the youngest and the oldest.

Grief is awful. It's painful. Being physically wrenched from someone you love hurts. You may even say that there's nothing good about it at all. But there really are a couple good things about grief. For one thing, it gives us a measure of comparison. We already know that death is devastating. If you've ever stood by the side of a freshly dug grave and watched someone you love being lowered in, you know how devastating death can be. Compare that feeling with heaven. In heaven, there won't be any more death and dying. It'll be over. Finished. No one will ever die again. Can you imagine how awesomely wonderful that will be?

Grief also gives us the opportunity to rely on God for comfort. People can be comforting during times of loss, but God is the ultimate comfort. Only He knows what it is really like. For three days He lost His Son. He knows the kind of suffering we endure when we lose someone. He also can't wait to come back and wipe away our tears for good.

The other good thing about grief is that it gives us the opportunity to comfort one another. It especially gives Christians the chance to share with people the reason for their faith and hope. We can tell people about the time coming when there won't be any more tears or sorrow, when death will be just a faint memory of something unpleasant that used to happen when we were on this dark earth. In heaven we'll hardly be able to remember the sadness we passed through when we lost someone. Everything will be new. God will be in the neighborhood living with us, making His home with us. I hope He lives right next door. Don't you?

To Tattle or Not to Tattle

If the godly give in to the wicked, it's like polluting a fountain or muddying a spring. **Proverbs 25:26, NLT.**

'm going to tell your mom you're playing with a knife," one kid will threaten another.

"Don't be a tattletale," the kid will taunt back, as if tattling is some horrible thing.

What do you think would have happened to humanity if Eve offered the apple to Adam after she'd taken a bite and he refused to touch it and told her he was going to tattle on her? I don't know, but when I get to heaven, I think I'll ask God.

To tattle or not to tattle, that is the question. It doesn't seem like much of a question to me. What's so wrong with tattling, anyway? Since when did it get such a bad rap? People often see tattling—squealing, ratting, narcing, telling, informing, whistle-blowing—as being a sneaky, conniving activity reserved for people who think they're better than others. Not only is that perception false, but it pressures people into staying silent about activities they ought to be hollering about.

When I was in high school, some boys on my bus were smoking marijuana. It gave me a headache. I knew the bus driver knew what they were doing because he kept glancing in the rearview mirror, but he never said anything. I wanted it to stop, but I wasn't brave enough to knock on the principal's door and say, "Hey, guess what some guys are doing on the bus."

Today if I wanted to leave an anonymous tip about shifty behavior at my high school, I'd go to www.schooltipline.com, leave my tip, and no one would be the wiser. But this happened before the Internet. Fortunately we still had things such as paper and pens, so I sent the vice principal a letter. The very next day those boys were called into his office. I don't know what he said to them, but I know they never smoked pot on my bus again.

Exposing bad, or dangerous, behavior can be risky, but it must be done. Someone once said that the only thing needed for evil to triumph is that good men do nothing. Imagine what would have happened if David had taken one look at Goliath and found a good hiding spot instead of a slingshot. We must stand up to evil knowing that God has our back and is on our side. Even if we are as small as David and face a beast of an adversary like Goliath, with God on our side we cannot fail.

Learning Curve

A wise man will hear and increase learning, and a man of understanding will attain wise counsel. **Proverbs 1:5, NKJV.**

I love to learn. I admit it. Learning is fun. I'll try almost anything new—from learning a new language, to learning a new sport (such as hooping), to trying to master a new art technique with my paints or my spinning wheel. It could be almost anything; I just love learning.

What I *don't* like is learning curves. A learning curve is that stage between loving something new, trying to learn it, and actually acquiring the skills necessary to be able to *do* it. After you've gotten past the learning curve and you can do whatever it is you've been learning, then you still need to keep getting better at it to *master it*—in other words, to be able to do it well.

Learning curves are rough, and more than one person has given up in frustration when trying something new, deciding that it's just not worth it, which is sad. Think about what might have happened if, say, Orville and Wilbur Wright, after one crash too many, had decided that it was too much trouble to try to build an airplane that would fly.

The thing that will get you through a learning curve is practice. You've heard the expression "practice makes perfect"? It certainly does, but the fuel for practice is persistence. You have to want to learn something to keep at it, benefitting from your mistakes, trying again when you fail time after time. Practice builds muscle memory, which will help you get really good at whatever you're trying to learn.

Learning can be a slow process, that's for sure. But the results are worth it. Even if you only learn how to juggle or get a spoon to stick to your nose, you've still learned something. You've engaged your brain. And you'll even have a party trick to trot out at the next family get-together.

But why stop there? Learn something big, new, and exciting. Choose something that you've always wanted to do, something that fills you with a sense of anticipation. The sky's the limit. And when you hit that learning curve, hang in there. It'll be worth it. I promise.

Assault With a Deadly Weapon

For the whole law can be summed up in this one command:
"Love your neighbor as yourself." **Galatians 5:14, NLT.**

Jacqueline Saburido was driving home with some friends when their car was struck by a drunk driver. Two of her friends were killed instantly, and Jacqueline was trapped inside the car. Paramedics who happened to be passing by put out the initial fire, but before they could free Jacqueline it started again, trapping her inside for 45 seconds before the fire truck arrived to put it out. Jacqueline was badly burned over 60 percent of her body. She's had more than 120 operations. Doctors didn't expect her to survive, but she did. Now she campaigns against drunk driving. You can see her story on YouTube.

Let me ask you a question. If someone shot you, would it matter whether they did it because they were drunk, preoccupied, or just horsing around? Probably not. What would matter most is whether or not you lived through it, right? You'd probably also be concerned with how much damage you'd have to live with, like Jacqueline, right? Why it happened probably wouldn't matter as much as how to cope afterward.

But it should. You have a license to handle a deadly weapon every time you get behind the wheel. A car is not a gun, but it's just as deadly. Think about it: a car is much bigger than you. It moves a whole lot faster. It weighs quite a bit more. All it takes is a few seconds when you're not paying attention—texting, talking on the phone, changing the radio station, dialing up a new song in your iPod, swatting a friend in the back seat, nodding off, taking a drink, eating something—to steer that car toward someone and change their life forever. You're driving a loaded weapon; handle it carefully.

Reggie Shephey, the drunk driver who hit Jacqueline, was sentenced to 14 years in jail and fined $20,000, but he says that's nothing compared to the life sentence he'll have to live with knowing how much damage and death he caused. Although Jacqueline says that Reggie destroyed her life, she still was able to forgive him.

If you were driving along, minding your own business, would you want your life to change as dramatically and as horribly as Jacqueline's did? Then why would you risk changing someone else's? Love them and drive safely.

Poor Little Rich Kid

*I will be a Father to you, and you will be my sons and daughters,
says the Lord Almighty.* **2 Corinthians 6:18, NIV.**

My Dad is the richest man in the whole world. You think I'm kidding, but I'm not. He's richer than Donald Trump and Bill Gates put together. If you took all the money in the whole world and put it all together in the same place He'd still have more riches than all of that. And since I'm His kid, He'll give me whatever I need.

Did I mention that I'm adopted? Say, would you like my Dad to adopt you, too? Then we'll *both* have the richest Dad in the whole world. You know, Dad loves us so much there's nothing He wouldn't do for us. And if we want to help our friends, He'll even write us a blank check. We can use as many of His resources as possible to help them. So what do you say? Let's go rob a bank!

Whoa! Why are the richest kids in the world robbing banks? Crazy, isn't it? And yet it happens every day. God's children, the richest people in the universe, go out and rob banks instead of asking God to supply all their physical, emotional, and spiritual needs. Talk about crazy. Whenever we look to things other than God to make us happy, we're robbing banks, and we always end up disappointed.

The excitement of playing that new video game wears off. The thrill of dating the new person gets old when their faults start showing through. The fun of shopping till you drop stops when you get home and it's all over. The pleasure of eating that whole box of chocolates ends when the box is empty. Nothing exciting lasts forever, and then we're back where we started.

When God created us, He created us perfectly, and inside each one of us is a perfect, God-shaped hole that only He can fill. Nothing else will fill that hole inside us—nothing, no one, nada. Only when we finally recognize that we don't need to look outside God to find happiness or fulfillment and instead rely on God alone to supply all our needs will we ever be completely happy and satisfied.

What do you use to fill that God-shaped hole inside your heart? Today, let God fill it and supply everything you need.

September 21

Do UR Feet Stink?

How beautiful on the mountains are the feet of those who
bring good news, who proclaim peace, who bring good tidings,
who proclaim salvation, who say to Zion, "Your God reigns!" **Isaiah 52:7, NIV.**

Feet. Almost everyone has two of them. Either you love them or you hate them, or you don't give them a second thought until someone complains that they stink. They're underappreciated, those feet. They go about their business carrying you from place to place, not asking a whole lot, just calmly plodding or racing through the day getting you around.

Did you know that an average person walks about 10,000 steps every day? Girls walk about three miles farther than guys each day. During your lifetime you'll walk enough steps to take you around the entire planet four times. That's about 115,000 miles.

Of course, you know what all that walking causes: sweaty feet. A pair of feet contains about 250,000 sweat glands, and they can make a half pint of sweat every day. No wonder your feet stink. Dude, get some odor eaters!

Despite the fact that the feet aren't particularly lovely to look at and are often rather smelly, the Bible says they can be beautiful when they bring the good news of salvation to the world. Do you want beautiful feet? Forget the pedicure. Use your feet to carry you to places where you can tell people that this old world is not our real home or our final destination. Use your beautiful feet to bring the good news around the world.

Have you ever heard of a prayer walk? That's when you go walking, either alone or with a partner or group, and pray for people in all the places you're walking through. Or, if you live in the country, you can pray for anyone you want. We believe that God's Word is living and active and that "it will accomplish all I want it to, and it will prosper everywhere I send it" (Isaiah 55:11, NLT). On your prayer walk, recite scriptures as you walk. Think about the words of Bible verses being invisible ribbons that you are laying out that people will walk through. Pray that God's Word will prosper and change everyone who crosses it.

Presto Chango

So letting your sinful nature control your mind leads to death.
But letting the Spirit control your mind leads to life and peace.
For the sinful nature is always hostile to God. It never did obey God's laws,
and it never will. That's why those who are still under the control
of their sinful nature can never please God. **Romans 8:6-8, NLT.**

If you like apples, this is probably your favorite time of year, and I wouldn't blame you; it's my favorite time of year too. Right about now is when we start picking apples. Unless you've had a fresh apple, right off the tree, you've never had a *real* apple. If you haven't, I sympathize; I've never had a fresh mango, and that makes me sad.

So let's go apple picking. Here's a big, fat, juicy-looking Macintosh apple. Not hungry right now, you say? That's OK. You don't have to eat it right now. Why don't you make applesauce with it and then you can pack it in your lunch tomorrow? Go ahead. I'll watch. Just make some sauce. Get saucing. Go ahead. You can do it.

What do you mean you can't make sauce just by holding the apple? Of course, you're right. You have to heat the apple in order to make sauce. Silly me. OK, so if we wait long enough the apple will heat itself and turn into sauce, right? Wrong again? We have to put the apple into a pot over the stove and heat it up? You mean the apple can't change itself into applesauce?

Silly, right? Maybe, but how many times have you tried to change yourself—to be a better Christian, to love God more—and been no more changed than the apple in my hand? We don't expect an apple to change into applesauce without help, but we expect to become poster children for Christianity all on our own. It won't happen. We need God to change us. "It is impossible for us, of ourselves, to escape from the pit of sin in which we are sunken. Our hearts are evil, and we cannot change them. . . . Education, culture, the exercise of the will, human effort, all have their proper sphere, but here they are powerless. They may produce an outward correctness of behavior, but they cannot change the heart; they cannot purify the springs of life. There must be a power working from within, a new life from above, before men can be changed from sin to holiness. That power is Christ. His grace alone can quicken the lifeless faculties of the soul, and attract it to God, to holiness" (Ellen G. White, *Steps to Christ,* p. 18).

September 23

Can't Wait

But godliness with contentment is great gain.
For we brought nothing into the world, and we can take
nothing out of it. But if we have food and clothing, we will be
content with that. **I Timothy 6:6-8, NIV.**

Have you ever caught yourself saying, "I can't wait until _____ [fill in the blank]"? When you were little, you probably couldn't wait until you were in elementary school. Then when you were in elementary school you couldn't wait until junior high, and then high school, and then college. If you're in high school, you probably can't wait to get your license. If you're driving, you probably can't wait until you get a job. If you're working, you probably can't wait for vacation.

There's always something we're wishing for. If it isn't a state of being it can be almost anything else: to live in a different place, to have different friends, to have more money, to have better clothes, to know more, to be better at something, to be smarter. The list is endless because although we all want something, it's not usually the same thing. We all have different wants.

The trouble is that if we live our whole lives in a state of constantly wanting something that we don't have instead of being content with what we do have, we'll reach the end of our lives and realize we were never happy. We'll realize we were always trying to get to a different place and we never fully appreciated the place we were in or the people we were with. And that would be a real shame because I guarantee you that no matter who you are, where you live, or what your circumstances are, there are things you can be grateful for.

Christians always have something to be grateful for, and we don't have any further to look for it than the cross. We have been saved by the King of the universe! Aren't you grateful for that? So maybe it doesn't change the tough situations in your life, but it can. Knowing you've been saved leads to knowing who saved you. And He _will_ change your life, one thought, one action, one step at a time.

The next time you catch yourself saying, "I can't wait until . . . ," stop yourself and instead list 10 things you're grateful for right now. If you find you're saying it often, keep adding to your list and keep it posted somewhere where you can see it. Remind yourself often to thank God for all the blessings He's put into your life _right now_. Ask Him to help you be content.

September 24

Double-Dog Dare

*Then the devil took him up and revealed to him
all the kingdoms of the world in a moment of time. "I will give you
the glory of these kingdoms and authority over them," the devil said,
"because they are mine to give to anyone I please. I will give it
all to you if you will worship me." Luke 4:5-7, NLT.*

Have you ever been on the top of a very high mountain? Man, the view is amazing. If it's a clear day you can see for miles. From the top of Mount Mansfield, the highest peak in Vermont, you can see across Lake Champlain into New York, and by mountain standards Mount Mansfield isn't even all that big.

When Satan tempted Jesus in the wilderness after He'd spent 40 days fasting, he found the highest place he could for the best view. Then he spread before Jesus all the kingdoms of the world. "I'll give them to you," he said. "They're mine and I can give them to whomever I want. All you have to do is worship me." He didn't say, "I double-dog dare you," but he might as well have.

It doesn't seem like much of a temptation to us, really. After 40 days of fasting we'd probably have been more interested in an all-you-can-eat buffet. But saving humanity was the whole reason Jesus came to earth. And here was Satan offering humanity to Him. No pesky cross to worry about; just take them. There was only one little hitch: Jesus had to worship Satan. That would be a little like one of the books I've written offering to make me a millionaire if I'd worship it. Fat chance. Not even if it dared me. Not even if it double-dog dared me. A million dollars, you say? Well . . .

That's the trouble with dares, they usually involve something pretty tempting. For Jesus the temptation was in taking the easy path to getting what He wanted most. For you it might be fame for performing a stunt no one else can do, drinking more alcohol than your friends, or car surfing. For me it might be getting a million dollars so I could retire to a tropical island somewhere. We all have our weak points.

The only safe way to deal with dares of any kind is not to engage with the darer. That was Jesus' policy. He told Satan, "The Scriptures say, 'You must worship the Lord your God and serve only him'" (Luke 4:8, NLT). Just walk away, no matter how many dogs are daring you.

September 25

The Little Boy
and the Snake: A Parable

So put to death the sinful, earthly things lurking within you. Have nothing to
do with sexual immorality, impurity, lust, and evil desires. Don't be greedy,
for a greedy person is an idolater, worshiping the things of this world.
Because of these sins, the anger of God is coming. **Colossians 3:5, 6, NLT.**

Jesus often told stories, or parables, to help people understand important things. Stories capture the imagination, and figuring out what the elements of the story stand for helps people to get the point of the story and remember the lesson. I'm sure you'll figure out what this story is about; different versions of the story are told worldwide.

There once was a little boy. As he walked down a path he came across a rattlesnake. "Please, little boy," the snake said, "I am very old. Will you pick me up and carry me to the top of this mountain so I can see the sunset one more time before I die?" The little boy knew he shouldn't get anywhere near the snake; after all, it was poisonous.

"No, I won't," he said. "Because if I do you'll bite me, and I'll die."

"I promise not to bite you," the snake said. "Please bring me to the top of the mountain."

The little boy felt sorry for the snake. It looked old and pitiful. He decided that it would be OK just this once. He picked up the snake in his arms, and carrying it close to his chest, he brought it to the top of the mountain where they watched the sunset together.

Afterward the boy carried the snake back to his home, fed it, and gave it a comfortable place to sleep. The next morning the old snake asked to be brought back home so it could die. The little boy had been carrying the snake around since the day before and nothing bad had happened, so he figured he would be safe enough. He picked up the snake and carried it back to its home. Just before he put it down the rattlesnake reached over and bit him in the chest.

"Ah!" cried the little boy. "You bit me! Why did you do that? Now I will die."

The snake smiled. "You knew what I was when you picked me up."

We are the little boy, and sin is the snake. No matter how innocent and feeble a sin looks, no matter how safe we feel playing with it, sin is sin, and nothing changes that. If we play with it, we can expect to get bitten. Sin is never safe.

September 26

You Are What You Eat

Then God said, "Look! I have given you every seed-bearing plant throughout the earth and all the fruit trees for your food." **Genesis 1:29, NLT.**

Did you know that our first parents, Adam and his lovely wife, Eve, were vegetarians? They were probably also vegans, since the food God gave them to eat didn't include any animal products, such as milk, cheese, or eggs. Their diet was fruit and every seed-bearing plant—the animals were for petting and cuddling. It wasn't until after the Flood that God told humanity which animals could be eaten, because eating them wasn't part of His original plan.

In 1863 Ellen White had a vision about health reform. God told her what kind of food to eat and how important it was to get proper exercise, enough rest, and to trust in God to keep our bodies healthy and strong. At the time Mrs. White thought that you had to eat meat in order to be strong and healthy, but she did what God instructed and cut out most meat. In 1894 Mrs. White went completely vegetarian.

Now so many Seventh-day Adventists are vegetarians that researchers often study us when they study vegetarianism to see if what a person eats makes a difference in quality of life. It does! Not only do vegetarians tend to live longer than people who eat meat, but they have fewer instances of many diseases, too. And animals like them better. (Just kidding!)

In America more than 7 million people are vegetarians; about 1 million are vegan (they don't eat any animal products, such as milk, cheese, or sometimes even honey). But almost half—42 percent—of those vegetarians are people ages 18-34. They have more than one reason for not eating meat. Some are concerned about the treatment of animals, some are looking to get healthier, others are worried about food safety, and some want to lose weight. All of those reasons are good, but the best one is the one God gave to Ellen White: because our physical health affects our spiritual health. We use our brains to communicate with God. They are part of our bodies, and they are only as clean and clear as the food we nourish them with. Doesn't it make sense to feed them the best fuel possible?

If you aren't a vegetarian already, try a vegetarian challenge. For one day (or one week, or one month), don't eat any meat. If you're already a vegetarian, help out with a vegetarian cooking school or encourage your friends to give vegetarianism a try.

September 27

What's Your Idol?

You shall have no other gods before Me. **Exodus 20:3, NKJV.**

B ob had his television propped up on a table, and he was sick of seeing it up there. He decided it needed a proper cabinet, and since he was a carpenter, he figured he'd make one himself. Every evening after he got home from work he spent time building a beautiful entertainment center to put his television in.

One night his friend Jim stopped by. Jim watched Bob work for a while. "So," Jim said finally, "I see you're building an altar for your idol."

This funny—and true—story brings up a good point: what is an idol? Are you worshipping idols without even realizing it? Are televisions really idols? How about smartphones? iPads? computers? the latest and greatest movie star, sports figure, or singer?

Basically an idol is a false god. A false god is anyone or anything more important to us than the true God, and we know who He is. God directed us not to put any god before Him. That means that anything or anyone can *become* an idol. We don't have household idols—little statues—like people in Bible times (and even some modern religions), but we don't have to. We can make almost anything into an idol. That's the danger.

How? One way is to rely on someone or something to save us from boredom, from stress, from unhappiness, from loneliness, from any negative thing. God alone can save us. This is how it works: you come home after a lousy day. You collapse in front of the television and numb your mind for a few hours. Bingo: you've made an idol.

Is television bad? Not all by itself. It's how we use it that makes the difference. If you watch television in a balanced way to learn, or even for entertainment, it's a tool. If you medicate your brain with it to avoid feeling bad, you've made it into an idol.

Other ways we give someone or something more importance than God could be ditching church for an outing with friends, playing computer games instead of reading the Bible, or listening to our friend's advice even when it goes against what we know God wants. Tear down the idols in your life; track them down and destroy them one by one. God didn't make "You shall have no other gods before Me" the first commandment for nothing. Love God with your whole heart and soul, and ditch your idols.

Praise God

Who compares with you among gods, O God?
Who compares with you in power, in holy majesty, in awesome praises,
wonder-working God? **Exodus 15:11, Message.**

Have you ever been stranded in your spiritual life? Stuck in a rut you just can't seem to get out of? You study your Sabbath school lesson . . . on Friday night, but since you cram it in you can't remember much about it in Sabbath school class the next day. You sit through church but later can't remember what the sermon was about. You *want* things to be different; you just can't seem to dynamite yourself into making any changes.

Or maybe you've got a really vibrant devotional life and you get charged up in church. You're involved in a couple ministries, but lately it's all started to feel like a chore instead of a blessing. Even your prayers feel dry and stale. God seems far away and all you've got left is the busyness of serving Him. You feel stuck, and you don't know how to get out. You really want that closeness with God back.

Praise God! I don't mean praise God that you're stuck. I mean, literally, praise God, even if you don't feel like it. In fact, *especially* if you don't feel like it. It's easy to praise God during the good times when we feel good and God feels close. But we can't act only on our feelings. The Bible says: "Let us continually offer to God a sacrifice of praise" (Hebrews 13:15, NIV). The Merriam-Webster dictionary says that to sacrifice is "to suffer loss of, give up, renounce, injure, or destroy especially for an ideal, belief, or end."

Sacrifice *costs* something. If it was easy it wouldn't be a sacrifice. We have to put aside the way we feel and offer a sacrifice of praise to God because above all He is good and merciful and loving. No matter how we feel at any given moment, God does not change. When we are able to make this kind of spiritual sacrifice it shows that we are maturing as Christians. More important, it makes God happy. The Bible tells us that "with such sacrifices God is pleased" (Hebrews 13:16, NIV).

Dedicate a notebook as a praise journal. Date each entry, and start every sentence with "Praise God for . . ." Write every praise you can think of. Keep writing until you can't think of anything more to praise God for. Repeat daily. See if your spiritual life doesn't improve immediately.

273

Dunked

Now as they went down the road, they came to some water.
And the eunuch said, "See, here is water. What hinders me
from being baptized?" Then Philip said, "If you believe with
all your heart, you may." And he answered and said, "I believe
that Jesus Christ is the Son of God." **Acts 8:36, 37, NKJV.**

Jason was getting to be about the right age for baptism, and people were starting to ask him when he was going to get dunked. He hadn't been baptized earlier because he was afraid of going under the water, but now that he was older that wasn't a big deal anymore. Still, he hesitated. It wasn't even that baptism was such a big step, or that he didn't feel ready. What really bothered Jason, although he wouldn't admit it to anyone else, was that he was shy and no way did he want to dress in a big robe, get soaked, and then stand in front of everyone he knew, dripping wet with his hair plastered to his head. No way. No how. No thanks. There had to be a better way to prove that he loved God and was committed and wanted to be a Seventh-day Adventist. Didn't there?

Sorry, Jason, but there's really not. Jesus was our example in everything so there was always a reason He did, or didn't do, something. One of the first things Jesus did was to be baptized by His cousin, John, who did so much baptizing he got the nickname "John the Baptist." John's whole ministry was based on two things: calling people to repent of their sins, and inviting them to be baptized as confirmation of what they'd done. If they didn't need to get wet to do that, John could have just preached and then asked for a show of hands.

Being baptized unites us with Christ and also with the church. Trying to be a Christian without being baptized is like trying to be a free agent. It doesn't work; Christianity is a team sport. Christians need fellowship and we can only get that by being an active part of our church. When we all contribute our talents and ideas we function as the "body of Christ." There's no better way to learn how to love others than by working with them—the people we like and the ones we don't like so much—toward common goals.

If you haven't been baptized yet, search your heart and discover the real reason. Should you let it stand in your way? Look! Here is water. What hinders you from being baptized?

Very Important Date

Oh, let me warn you, sisters in Jerusalem, by the gazelles, yes, by all the wild deer: Don't excite love, don't stir it up, until the time is ripe—and you're ready. **Song of Solomon 2:7, Message.**

admit it: the white rabbit in *Alice in Wonderland* is one of my favorite literary characters, although the one I know best is the little cutie from Walt Disney's animated version. You know, the one whose snuffly voice is bemoaning the fact that he's late, he's late, for a very important date. I wonder who his date was. I wonder why a rabbit is dating in the first place?

Rabbits don't. Date, that is. Teens do, but do you ever wonder why? Sure, boys and girls are attracted to each other. If they weren't, none of us would be here right now talking about it. But what's the rush? Is there really any point to "going steady" if you're only going to turn around in a month or so and break up and start all over again? There's got to be a better way, don't you think?

When Alejandro was 14, he liked a girl in his class who liked him back. She was too shy to talk to him, though, so she'd send him e-mail. Alejandro couldn't care less about e-mail, but he wasn't much of a talker either. He didn't answer her e-mails, she couldn't talk to him; it was a stalemate. Eventually they broke up. She cried a lot. He didn't seem to care.

Years later, when they were seniors in high school, they became good friends. They often ate lunch together in the cafeteria. They even talked to each other. When she moved away, they wrote each other letters. They're still good friends. I can't help thinking they could have avoided a whole lot of heartache if they'd just started out as friends in the first place.

The whole goal of dating is to find someone to marry . . . eventually. So why start so soon? Sure, some kids meet, date, and get married right out of high school. But very few (if any) of them stay together. They haven't had time to grow up yet and to find out who they are and what they really want out of life. It's a lot harder to explore and find yourself when you're married to someone who is also exploring and trying to find themselves.

Why not give dating a rest for a while? Try concentrating on just being friends with members of the opposite sex. Do you notice a change in yourself or others? Is it good? bad? not noticeable? While you're waiting for the right person to come along, pray that God will help you to recognize them when the time comes.

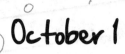

October 1

A Proverb a Day

Let the wise listen to these proverbs and become even wiser. Let those with understanding receive guidance by exploring the meaning in these proverbs and parables, the words of the wise and their riddles. **Proverbs 1:5, 6, NLT.**

A proverb is a short saying that usually has a moral. It's often catchy, and people tend to repeat it so often that sometimes the meaning is almost lost because it's so familiar. For example, have you ever heard someone say, "The early bird catches the worm"? Do you know what it means? It was first recorded in a book called *A Collection of English Proverbs*, by John Ray, in 1670. Of course, back then the actual proverb was "The early bird catcheth the worm." It means that if you're prepared and make an effort, you'll be successful.

Many cultures have proverbs, but they tend to sound strange to us if we didn't grow up hearing them. Here are a few from other countries:

African proverb: I have been bitten by a tsetse fly. (This means that someone who lent you money will pester you until you pay off your debt.)

Asian proverb: The old horse in the stable still yearns to run. (This means that older people still have things they want to accomplish.)

Spanish proverb: Since we cannot get what we like, let us like what we can get. (This means we should be happy with what we have.)

Italian proverb: After the game, the king and pawn go into the same box. (This means that everyone is equal.)

Finnish proverb: Even a small star shines in the darkness. (This means that you don't have to accomplish big things to make a difference.)

You probably know that the Bible has a whole book of proverbs. Many of them (about 3,000) were written by King David's son Solomon. Because he was the wisest man on earth, it was practically his job to write wise sayings. You might also know that there are 31 chapters in the book of Proverbs—one chapter for each day of every month. This month, read the chapter of Proverbs that matches the day of the month. If you start now, you'll read the whole book by the end of the month. Next month, repeat.

What's in Your Closet?

Can all your worries add a single moment to your life? And why worry about your clothing? Look at the lilies of the field and how they grow. They don't work or make their clothing, yet Solomon in all his glory was not dressed as beautifully as they are. **Matthew 6:27-29, NLT.**

"Clothes make the man." At least that's what they say. A lot of people buy into that concept though. It's not only that they like clothes or fashion; it's that they care about what people think of them based on the clothes they wear. One teen said, "I feel like having the clothes makes me more important, or better than everyone. . . . I am literally *obsessed* with my appearance, and I can *never* have enough of anything. It's kind of sad, but the society we live in has pushed this on us."

Teens aren't the only ones trying to influence people through the way they dress, but they are often the ones who worry the most about clothes. Do they have the right kind? Do their clothes match? Do they look cool or dorky? They worry because they're still experimenting to find their own style, and, whenever there's experimentation going on, there's bound to be mistakes. Very few adults can look back on their teen years without cringing over some of their fashion choices. You, too, will probably make mistakes.

It's natural to be concerned with the image we're projecting, particularly as Christians because we're representing more than ourselves; we're representing Jesus. That's why we shouldn't get sucked into the world's anxiety about and obsession with fashion. God does not care if we're stuck in last year's fashions because we can't afford to replace our clothes with what's new this year.

The only garments that we need to be concerned about are the ones that God Himself will give us: kindness, compassion, love, faithfulness, peace, obedience, patience, joy, loyalty. These are the garments that God clothes us in. They never go out of style; they never wear out. We don't need to worry about where to buy them or how to afford them, because we can only get them from God, and He's happy to give them to us whenever we ask.

How much do you worry about clothes, styles, and fashion? Are you happy with your answer, or do you think it's an area of your life that could use some change? How many of God's garments are in your closet?

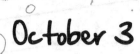

October 3

Fluff And Nonsense

So roll up your sleeves, put your mind in gear,
be totally ready to receive the gift that's coming when Jesus arrives.
Don't lazily slip back into those old grooves of evil, doing just
what you feel like doing. You didn't know any better then; you do now.
As obedient children, let yourselves be pulled into a way of life shaped
by God's life, a life energetic and blazing with holiness. God said,
"I am holy; you be holy." I Peter 1:13-16, Message.

Be holy. That's a tall order for sinful, fallen people such as us. Our nature says, "Nah, be sinful instead. It's easier." And it is. It's a whole lot easier to be pulled along by whatever is happening or whoever is talking than to make an effort to go our own way and choose for ourselves what to participate in or talk about. If this old world was an ocean, we'd be swimming against the current; it's hard work.

We can't do it alone. God has to help us. But we can't float there like lumps, and not expect to put out any effort at all. We'll never get any stronger unless we fight that current. Our brains develop strength, just like our muscles, when we exercise them. It doesn't just happen one day—poof!—and all of a sudden we find we're deep thinkers able to understand all the mysteries of the Bible that yesterday we thought was dry and difficult. We have to do the work.

"Unless the mind is educated to dwell upon religious themes, it will be weak and feeble in this direction. But while dwelling upon worldly enterprises, it will be strong; for in this direction it has been cultivated, and has strengthened with exercise. The reason it is so difficult for men and women to live religious lives is because they do not exercise the mind unto godliness. It is trained to run in an opposite direction. Unless the mind is constantly exercised in obtaining spiritual knowledge and in seeking to understand the mystery of godliness, it is incapable of appreciating eternal things" (Ellen G. White, *Testimonies for the Church,* vol. 2, p. 189).

This kind of spiritual strength has to be built up slowly. Start by reading something you would consider spiritually "deep." *Steps to Christ,* by Ellen White, is a small book that would make a good beginning. Before long you'll be able to grasp higher and higher religious themes, and God will use this new depth of knowledge to help you grow in spiritual maturity. He will help you to become holy as He is holy.

Dead Man Walking

> As for you, you were dead in your transgressions and sins,
> in which you used to live when you followed the ways of this world
> and of the ruler of the kingdom of the air, the spirit who is now
> at work in those who are disobedient. All of us also lived among
> them at one time, gratifying the cravings of our flesh and following
> its desires and thoughts. Like the rest, we were by nature deserving
> of wrath. But because of his great love for us, God, who is rich
> in mercy, made us alive with Christ even when we were dead in
> transgressions—it is by grace you have been saved. **Ephesians 2:1-5, NIV.**

No, "dead man walking" doesn't refer to zombies; it's actually a term used in prisons when someone who has been sentenced to death makes their final walk on the way to their execution. As they walk to their death they are "dead men walking."

A nun who is against the death sentence, Sister Helen Prejean, wrote a book called *Dead Man Walking*, which tells of her experiences being a spiritual advisor to two men who received the death sentence and were later executed. One of the men, Robert Lee Willie, was convicted for horrific crimes and never showed any real remorse. One of his victims who survived was later able to forgive him with God's help and was glad that someone had been able to reach out to him with God's love. She said, "She [Helen Prejean] did something for Robert Willie that I never could have done. She went to him and personally told him about God."

You may think this has nothing to do with you because either you don't work in a prison or in prison ministry or because you're not in prison. But it has to do with you for two reasons: (1) we were all "dead men walking" before we became Christians, and (2) "dead men walking" are all around us. We have a responsibility to these people. They are dead in their sins, and they don't even know it. We need to tell them about God's great love; we need to tell them that they can be alive in Christ. Our life doesn't have to end with death. God has something better planned for us.

The prison of sin doesn't have bars we can see. We don't have to get permission to visit its inmates. The people imprisoned in sin may not even realize how trapped they are because they are so used to their cells. It's up to us to tell them how they can be free. The question is Will you reach out to the "dead men walking"?

279

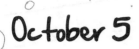

October 5

Blame

But he was pierced for our rebellion,
crushed for our sins. He was beaten so we could be whole.
He was whipped so we could be healed. **Isaiah 53:5, NLT.**

All week I've been driving around with a busted back door and windshield on my car. It's been raining, so when I'm not driving I have to cover the smashed window in the back of my car with a piece of plastic, but since I can't see through it, I take it off to drive. I've been all over town in my busted-up car, and I just know that everyone who has seen it is thinking, *Whoa, what a lousy driver she is. I'd better not get too close. Looks like she was rear-ended. Probably jumped on her brakes trying to avoid a squirrel and made some poor person slam into her. I hope they're OK.*

I'm sure that's what they think. But that's not what happened at all. In fact, I didn't even get into an accident with my car. One of my family members backed my car into a tree. *Pop* went the windshield, and the door caved in so much that I can't open it. I wasn't even in the car at the time. But it's *my* car. I *own* it. I *drive* it. I'm the one people see sitting behind the wheel most of the time. I'm the one they *think* crashed it. And me? I just want to hide until it's all fixed and perfect again and until I can drive around without people judging me for something I didn't even do.

Being judged for something you didn't do is difficult. It's one thing to deserve people's bad opinion, but when it's undeserved, you just want to scream, "You don't understand! It's not my fault!" Yet Jesus died an outlaw's death for something He never did, and not once did He say, "Hold on one second here. I am completely innocent. It's these people who are sinners. I'm just taking their punishment. I didn't do anything wrong." Everyone who saw Him being punished judged Him. Can you imagine what they thought as He stumbled through town all bloodied up, lugging His cross? "Man," they probably said, "what a sinner that guy must be. I'm glad I'm not him."

But Jesus never sinned! Not even once! Instead He was judged for me and for you and for every other person who ever lived. In small ways, day in and day out, people continue to judge Jesus based on the actions of His followers. I have only one car to reflect badly on my driving skills; Jesus has millions of us Christians running around all over the place reflecting badly on Him. Before you head out the door today, take a minute to think about the way you'll represent Jesus to the world. Ask Him to help you represent Him well.

Bombardment

When the devil had finished tempting Jesus,
he left him until the next opportunity came. **Luke 4:13, NLT.**

When I was in grade school, we used to play a game our gym teachers called "bombardment." We'd choose teams, and each team would line up on opposite sides of the gym. There was a line in the center that no one could cross. The teachers gave us a lot of small, squishy balls. The object was to run up to—but not over—the line and throw the ball at someone on the opposite team. Not one at a time, mind you; everyone did this at the same time. There were balls flying everywhere.

The object was to hit someone on the other team, and because you couldn't look everywhere at the same time and balls were flying all over, sooner or later you'd get hit. As soon as you were hit you were out of the game and had to go watch from the sidelines. I loved this game when I was a kid. Turns out I'm still playing it, only I don't like this new version so much.

Here's how it works in real life: Satan has all the balls. He and his evil angels pelt them at me. I try to dodge them. God has drawn a line that Satan can't cross. But there are a lot of balls. They're coming from all directions. Sooner or later, just like in the game of bombardment, I get hit, and I'm out of the game for a while.

The thing about temptations is that Satan doesn't just hit us with one temptation. He hits us again and again and again. At first we dodge them, but over time it gets harder, and he's relentless. We can't even call a time-out.

The Bible only records three temptations at the end of the 40 days when Jesus was in the wilderness after His baptism. Think how many times Satan must have bombarded Jesus during the 40 whole days before that. When he still couldn't hit Jesus with one of his temptations, he "left him until the next opportunity came." Until we're in heaven there will always be another opportunity for Satan to try to hit us and get us out of the game.

If you've been hit with one of Satan's temptations and you're sitting on the sidelines waiting to get back in the game, don't be discouraged. Go to Jesus. No matter what the score is right now, in the end Jesus wins the game, and we're on the winning side.

Can't or Won't?

Work hard so you can present yourself to God
and receive his approval. **2 Timothy 2:15, NLT.**

When I was in high school, I ran track and field. Because I came from a small town and there were only a couple of us girls on the team, we also threw the shot put and the javelin. We were never serious contenders, because we were so puny. The big, beefy girls from other schools would climb off their buses and laugh at us. They always won, too. But when it came to running, we had a shot.

My dad rarely had a chance to come to my races, because he was working. But one time the meet was on our home field. I'd signed up for all the smaller races as well as the long jump and the dreaded shot put and javelin, even though I didn't have a chance. What I hadn't signed up for was the mile. I figured that after I ran all my other races I'd be too tired to do well in the mile, so why set myself up to fail?

My dad had other ideas. He was there to see me race, and he wanted me to run the mile. He made me sign up despite the fact that I protested every second before the race. I was too tired; I didn't want to run. But he wouldn't relent. So I lined up with the other runners knowing I'd come in dead last. After a quarter mile I passed my dad where he was watching me and asked if I could stop. I was dead last. He shook his head. At the half mile? No. Three quarters of the way through I was lagging behind, with no chance to catch up. Hadn't I proved my point? I couldn't win this race. Just before my final lap my dad threw up his hands in surrender. "Fine, quit," he hollered.

At that moment I knew I hadn't given it my all, and now that I *could* quit, I didn't want to. I was also a distance runner with a reputation for pouring it on at the end of the race, so I kicked it into top speed and began passing people. My burst of speed didn't come soon enough to win me the race, but it proved to me—and probably to my dad—that I might have had a chance if I'd given everything I had.

It's easy to make a halfhearted attempt. We do it to our heavenly Father sometimes, too. "See?" we whine. "It's too hard; I can't do it." But if we attempt anything with that kind of attitude, the only thing we *can* do is fail. We can only do our best when we stop believing that we can't and start believing that we can. After all, if with God's help nothing is impossible, what are we whining about?

Dating a Volcano

But mark this: There will be terrible times in the last days.
People will be lovers of themselves, lovers of money, boastful, proud,
abusive, disobedient to their parents, ungrateful, unholy, without love,
unforgiving, slanderous, without self-control, brutal, not lovers of the
good, treacherous, rash, conceited, lovers of pleasure rather
than lovers of God— having a form of godliness but denying its power.
Have nothing to do with such people. **2 Timothy 3:1-5, NIV.**

She had dated him off and on for four months, but she hid a shameful secret that many of today's Christian young people experience. Sixteen-year-old Alma* had gotten the attention of David, who was popular, fairly good-looking, and well liked by peers at school and at church. He was involved in sports, had good grades and nice parents, and participated in various church activities. On the surface he seemed attractive and exciting. What Alma didn't know was that hidden under all his popularity, good grades, and church involvement was a violent temper.

The first time he got angry with her was because she wasn't ready to leave when he arrived to take her to church. Then he hit her when she said that she didn't feel comfortable doing certain physical things with him. David insulted her, called her names in front of her friends, put her down whenever he could, threatened to leave her for her best friend if she didn't give in to him, and became more and more physically violent.

Alma eventually found the courage, through prayer and with the support of a Sabbath school teacher, to tell her parents, and together they reported David to the authorities. It took time for Alma to heal from the emotional scars that David had inflicted on her soul, but now she speaks to and helps other young people by sharing her story of the danger of dating violence.

Dating violence can erupt in many ways, and while it's usually directed at girls, sometimes guys are the ones being abused. The one thing that keeps it going is silence, and shame fuels the silence. If you are being abused, *it is not your fault*. You do not deserve to be treated badly. Dating violence can turn deadly. Ask God to give you the courage to get adults involved and to make the violence stop. You are not weak; you are worth it.

---

* Names have been changed.
Submitted by Julián Anderson-Martín, M.A., L.L.P.C.

October 9

Guess Who

As the Scriptures say, "No one is righteous—not even one. No one is truly wise; no one is seeking God. All have turned away; all have become useless. No one does good, not a single one." **Romans 3:10-12, NLT.**

How would you like to play a little guessing game with me this morning? I'm going to give you some details about the life of a famous person, and you're going to try to guess who it is. Ready?

- He persecuted people.
- He hated one group of people so much that he made it his mission in life to destroy them.
- He went from house to house and dragged men and women out, sending them to prison.
- He approved their outright murder.
- He used the law so that he could legally get away with arresting people and no one would be able to complain about it.
- His speeches were full of threats and hatred of this group.
- He went out of his way to track them down and punish them.

Are you ready to guess? Do you think you know who it is? The answer might surprise you. If you guessed Adolf Hitler, you'd be wrong, although the description certainly fits Hitler. No, the man described above is Saul, better known to us as . . . the apostle Paul.

What? How can that be? How could someone who hated Christians this much end up being someone God used as a great witness through his suffering and preaching and also through his writings in the Bible?

There can be only one answer to that question: grace. Saul/Paul, as is every single one of us, was rotten to the core. There was no more goodness in him than there is in us. His life was changed the very same way our lives can be changed—by the power of the Holy Spirit. Don't ever let Satan convince you that you're too sinful to be saved. Just remember how Paul started out. If Saul can become Paul, we can be just as dramatically transformed.

Mad Dog

Keep watch and pray, so that you will not give in to temptation.
For the spirit is willing, but the body is weak! **Matthew 26:41, NLT.**

He was such a cute puppy, all ears and tail and puppy breath with a big old worried frown that made him seem like a wise old dog instead of a 3-month-old puppy. Turns out there was a reason for that worried frown: Max, my German shepherd, has issues. Lots of them. One of his issues is that he's so attached to me that he can't be more than two feet away from me at any time, which means that I spend most of the day tripping over him. Another one of his issues is that I can't go anywhere without him; he feels it just wouldn't be safe. There's a reason the police like to use German shepherds; they're extremely protective. They are also aggressive.

Before Max was a year old, no matter how often I brought him to doggie day care to play with the other puppies, no matter how much training I gave him, no matter how much I worked with him around other dogs, he tried to kill any dog he saw when we were walking. Once when we were hiking, some pugs came running up the trail off their leashes. I jumped off the trail, pulling Max with me, but one of the pugs ran right up to him, barking and snarling in his face. Max picked up that pug and shook it like a rag doll. It was OK, but I was pretty shaken up.

Max is what they call a Czech shepherd, which means his breeding is based in Czechoslovakia, where German shepherds are bred for their protectiveness and not their social skills. It turns out that his issues were mostly the result of his breeding, and even though he grew up in a good home, had plenty to eat, and was socialized as a puppy, nothing in the world was going to make him a different dog.

The best I could do was protect him from himself. I learned how to be super careful about where I brought him. I never take him anywhere off his leash, and I watch him carefully and warn anyone who approaches that he isn't friendly.

Max is just a dog; he doesn't realize there's anything wrong with him. People, on the other hand, usually know when they've got problems. We know what our weaknesses are, and we can ask God for help to resist them. Although our flesh is weak, when our spirits are willing we will have all heaven on our side. When we keep on our guard, the Holy Spirit will show us the traps Satan has laid for us so we can walk right on past them.

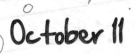

Love Changes Things

*If I could speak all the languages of earth and of angels,
but didn't love others, I would only be a noisy gong or a clanging cymbal.
If I had the gift of prophecy, and if I understood all of God's secret plans and
possessed all knowledge, and if I had such faith that I could move mountains,
but didn't love others, I would be nothing. If I gave everything I have to the
poor and even sacrificed my body, I could boast about it; but if I didn't
love others, I would have gained nothing.* **I Corinthians 13:1-3, NLT.**

It was the Gainesville Tornadoes against the Grapevine Faith Lions in a football game that would change lives, although the Tornadoes didn't know it when they arrived at Grapevine Faith Christian School. The first clue they had was that Faith fans made a spirit line for them to run through complete with a banner that they could crash through at the end that said, "Go Tornadoes!" There were fans in the bleachers on *both* sides of the field, something Gainesville had never seen before.

The boys thought the Faith fans didn't have enough room, so they just spread out . . . until the game started and the fans on their side of the field started cheering them on—*by name.* They even had their own actual cheerleaders. It was a strange experience. Usually the other team's fans were a little afraid of them. You see, Gainesville is a maximum-security correctional facility. The players? Kids with convictions for drugs, assault, and robbery.

It all started with Faith's head coach, Kris Hogan. He sent an e-mail around to parents asking them to cheer for the other side. Some of them were confused and wanted to know why. Hogan told them, "Imagine if you didn't have a home life. Imagine if everybody had pretty much given up on you. Now imagine what it would mean for hundreds of people to suddenly believe in you."

"I see the world in a different way now," said one of the players after the game. "I mean, I don't just see like I'm the victim no more. So much love, 'cause, you know, I came from a broken-home family, so I mean, having all that love, it just rolls my spirits up."

The Faith team sent each Gainesville player home with a bag of food, a Bible, and an encouraging letter from a Faith player. Only God knows how their love will change lives, but the people at Grapevine Faith had love—real love—for the kids from Gainesville, and they showed it.

Land Ho!

From one man he made all the nations,
that they should inhabit the whole earth; and he marked
out their appointed times in history and the boundaries of their lands.
God did this so that they would seek him and perhaps reach out for him
and find him, though he is not far from any one of us. **Acts 17:26, 27, NIV.**

Christopher Columbus almost never made it to America. In 1476, on his first trip into the Atlantic Ocean, he almost died. French privateers attacked his ship off the coast of Portugal. (Privateers were basically hired pirates whose king let them steal from and harass the ships of enemy countries as long as they brought their loot back to him.) They burned his ship, and Columbus had to swim to shore, where he made his way to Lisbon, Portugal.

Eventually he set sail for what he hoped was Asia but turned out to be the Bahamas, though Columbus was convinced that it was Asia. He explored the area, discovering the present day island of Haiti and the Dominican Republic. Eventually he even landed on the mainland in Venezuela. But he believed until his dying day that he had reached Asia.

Even though he is credited with discovering the Americas and is now famous and has a holiday in his honor—Columbus Day, which is celebrated today—Columbus's story doesn't have a happy ending. He treated the natives badly and made them slaves, and eventually his titles and a lot of his riches were taken away from him.

The life of an explorer can be scary. It can be dangerous. But it is always exciting because you never know what you will discover. God created us all to be explorers, not only of the world—and even the universe—but of a friendship with Him.

Although we are each born with a deep need to know God, not everyone sets out on a journey to find Him. Many people are content to sit back and let life go by. They are afraid of what they'll find if they locate God. They're afraid He'll want them to give up things that they cherish. But God isn't about giving up things; He's about giving us more than we could ever hope or ask for. When we explore with Him, we'll discover things that we never even knew existed. Set a course for God today; sail into His world.

October 13

Beast in the Bath

What has been will be again, what has been done will be done again; there is nothing new under the sun. **Ecclesiastes 1:9, NIV.**

Have you ever wondered who the first person was who watched an egg emerge from a chicken's bottom and said, "I wonder what that tastes like"? Or who the first person was who looked at a lobster and thought, *Yum, yum?* Who was it who thought pigs' feet should be eaten? Who thought caviar (fish eggs) might taste good on crackers? I have no idea who those people were, but you can be sure that if I had been standing nearby, I would not have said, "Right on, let's try that!"

Eaten any tomatoes lately? In 1519, when Cortez found them growing in Montezuma's garden, he brought seeds back to Europe with him. People planted them to look at, but they didn't eat them. They thought tomatoes were poisonous. Their Latin botanical name means "wolfpeach," because the French botanist who named them thought tomatoes were the same thing a Greek physician had written about that was used to kill wolves. Obviously somebody along the line decided to brave death and see what they tasted like. The rest, as they say, is history.

Whoever ate that first tomato did us all a huge favor, but if that person had keeled over dead, everyone would have said, "Well, we said it was poisonous." If that individual had dropped dead on the spot, do you think everyone watching would have said, "Me too! Let me try one of those red thingies"? I doubt it, but you never know. I wouldn't think anyone would rush right out to try sniffing bath salts after hearing reports that they turn people into growling, raving lunatics, but the National Institute on Drug Abuse is reporting an alarming number of calls to poison control centers for that very thing. Even the police are concerned. Whatever is in the bath salts gives people superhuman strength, making them very dangerous during their psychotic freak-outs. Videos taken of people flipping out on bath salts will scare any sane person; users look possessed and have even been called zombies.

Every year people try newer and stranger things to see how it makes them feel; what has been done will be done again. This will never change. But just because everyone is participating in the latest nonsense doesn't mean you have to follow them. God created us thinking, reasoning, intelligent individuals. You can choose not to follow the crowd and instead make your own path to fun and excitement, the kind you'll be able to remember the next day.

Leap of Faith

So let us come boldly to the throne of our gracious God.
There we will receive his mercy, and we will find grace to help us
when we need it most. **Hebrews 4:16, NLT.**

On October 14, 2012, I was one of more than 8 million people who watched as Felix Baumgartner was slowly lifted by balloon to the edge of space. He then climbed out onto a tiny little platform and said, "I know the whole world is watching right now, and I wish the world could see what I can see. Sometimes you have to go up really high to understand how small you really are." Then he jumped. Felix was 24 miles above the earth. During his fall he broke three records and gave scientists a lot of data to study that will hopefully help save the lives of pilots and space travelers in a disaster some day.

Dustin Gohmert, head of NASA's crew survival engineering office, said they've been working on self-contained space escape systems but they hadn't made much headway since 1960. Why? Because that's when Joe Kittinger jumped from 19.5 miles up. Until the day Felix jumped, no one had gone higher, so no new research could be done, which just goes to prove that if you always do what you've always done, you'll always get what you always got.

Let's face it: It can be hard to venture past your comfort zone. David didn't go out every day and spar with giants, and look what he did . . . with God's help. Gideon spent more time hiding in wine presses than he did leading troops into battle, and look what he did . . . with God's help. The other apostles would have voted Peter "most likely to deny Jesus," and look what he did . . . with God's help. Are you sensing a pattern here?

With God's help we can move past our safety zones and venture into the land of unexplored faith where God is waiting for us. He wants to meet us there and show us how far we can really go . . . with His help. But if we stay safely anchored in our comfort zone, we'll never get to taste the thrill of following God with abandon, of stepping off of that tiny little platform and giving ourselves over into His hands without being able to control the outcome. If we're going to make a leap of faith, we have to trust God to hold us up. He won't let us down.

If you have a chance, watch the footage of Felix's historical jump. Imagine that it's you standing on that little platform preparing to jump. How would you feel, and what would you say to the whole world as they watched you?

October 15

Spiritual Suicide

Call to Me, and I will answer you, and show you great and mighty things, which you do not know. **Jeremiah 33:3, NKJV.**

Have you ever stopped breathing for any length of time? Maybe clocked yourself to see how long you could hold your breath? Right now the record for holding your breath while being still is 22 minutes and 22 seconds. It's held by a German man, Tom Sietas. Now, I should tell you that Tom's lung capacity is 20 percent larger than normal, which is why he started competing in the first place. A scuba instructor remarked that he could hold his breath for quite a long time. Turns out, he really can. He's set records for holding his breath without moving (static apnea) and swimming a distance while holding his breath (dynamic apnea.)

If you held your breath right now, you wouldn't come close to 22 minutes. Part of the reason is because you haven't trained, and part of it is because to get to that record Tom had to breathe pure oxygen before his attempt. Without breathing pure oxygen before competing, Tom's record is 10 minutes and 12 seconds, so you can see it makes a difference.

Still, 22 minutes and 22 seconds isn't a long time at all if you compare it to the rest of his life. If he lives to be 80, which isn't even really that old, 22 minutes is nothing in comparison. Yet he could live only 22 minutes without breathing, which just goes to show how important breathing is. If you don't breathe, you die.

Prayer is to the spiritual life what breathing is to the physical life. If you were able to stop breathing (you can't; you'd lose consciousness and start breathing again automatically), you'd die. If you stop praying, you will spiritually die. There is no automatic response of your brain to keep you praying if you stop. If we stop praying, we're committing spiritual suicide. But God made us creatures with a free will. If our will is not to talk to Him, He won't make us.

There are a lot of things we don't know but God does. He created us, our world, and everything in it. Each day He holds out His hand to us and offers to walk with us as He did with Adam and Eve, opening our eyes so that we can see both the physical and spiritual world. Will you take His hand today?

Think About It: Oswald Chambers said, "Prayer does not fit us for the greater work. Prayer *is* the greater work." What do you think he meant by that?

Identity Theft

If anyone tries to flag you down, calling out, "Here's the Messiah!" or points, "There he is!" don't fall for it. Fake Messiahs and lying preachers are going to pop up everywhere. Their impressive credentials and dazzling performances will pull the wool over the eyes of even those who ought to know better. But I've given you fair warning. **Matthew 24:23-25, Message.**

Hi there! Good to see you! Excuse me? What did you just say? Did you wake up on the wrong side of the bed or something? I've never heard you talk that way before. Where did you learn to curse like that? And what are you doing? Are you stealing that chocolate bar? What's going on here? You've never acted like this before. Hey, wait a minute . . . something's not right. Are you sure you are who you say you are?

Oh, no! Someone has stolen your identity! Not likely, you say? Think again. In the United States someone's identity is stolen every three seconds. More than 8 million Americans will have their identity stolen this year, and they won't even find out until it's too late and they have to go through the painstaking, tedious process of getting it back again.

Right now there could be someone claiming to be me using my credit card to buy a big-screen TV, or a sports car, or a grand piano. Or they could be using my Social Security number to get their own credit card in my name and then use it to buy something illegal. People will think it's me, but it's not.

Identity theft is nothing new. In fact, it's the first crime that ever happened in the entire universe. The Bible tells us that Lucifer wanted to be God so much that he put himself up as God. Then he started trying to make the other angels believe it. Some of them actually did, and Lucifer and those that did were all kicked out of heaven together. So Lucifer started in on Adam and Eve, who bought his story hook, line, and sinker. And he's still impersonating God today, trying to get us to worship him in all sorts of different ways.

The Bible says that in the end-times he'll become even bolder about impersonating God, and he'll actually appear as the Messiah. But Jesus stole his thunder by telling us what was coming so that we could be prepared. How? The best way to be able to identify something that's fake is to know the real thing. The better you know Jesus, the less likely you'll be fooled by the impostor.

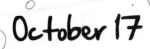

October 17

Under Pressure

A good person produces good things from the treasury of a good heart, and an evil person produces evil things from the treasury of an evil heart. What you say flows from what is in your heart. **Luke 6:45, NLT.**

L et's say you keep your wallet in your back pocket. If you had something to put into it—oh, yay!—how would you take it out and put your loot in? I suppose that if you were really talented, you could use your feet. But you'd have to be seriously double-jointed. You probably couldn't bend far enough to use your mouth. That leaves your mind; can you move things with your brain? Me neither. So I guess that makes your hands the only part of your body with which you can remove your wallet and add any new treasure to it.

In the same way, our hearts contain all our "treasure," and the only way we can add new treasure is through our minds. That means whatever passes through your mind gets stored in your heart and becomes your treasure. If I asked you what sort of treasure you had stored up, what would you say? Do you think you know? Let's find out how well you know what's in your heart. List or consider:

The past five televisions shows or movies you've watched: _____

The past five books you've read or games you've played: _____

The past five Bible verses you've memorized:_____

The past five people you've helped: _____

The past five jokes you've told:_____

Look back over your list. What does your treasure look like? Is it rustier than you thought it would be, or is it bright and shining? The Bible tells us that what we say flows from our hearts—where our treasure is. We hide our treasure (and our trash) all the time. Most of the time we don't even realize that we're hiding it. Not until things start heading south and life is out of control will everyone else see what we hid there. What you really think and how you really feel will come spilling out of your mouth like water over a broken dam. It will be made up of everything you hid down there every day.

Look over your list again. Is there any trash you could replace with treasure? What do you wish you could have written instead? How can you hide treasure in your heart?

Good Job

So I saw that there is nothing better for people than to be happy in their work. That is why we are here! No one will bring us back from death to enjoy life after we die. **Ecclesiastes 3:22, NLT.**

What would you say if I gave you the keys to a candy shop and said, "There you go; take anything you want." You'd probably squeal, "Yippee! Get out of my way!" For about a half hour you'd be thrilled, trying one confection after another. But as you started to slow down, you might even start to feel a little sick of candy. That's when you'd realize something: Too much candy is not a good thing.

It sounds good. It even tastes good—for a while. But sooner than you think, you'd get sick of it. You might even be willing to trade it for something such as fruit or (gasp) even vegetables.

The same thing happens when we do nothing but play all the time. Without work to balance us out, we can't even enjoy fun as much as we could if we worked hard. When God created Adam, He didn't leave him in the garden and say, "There you go. Have fun now." God gave Adam a job to do. "God took the Man and set him down in the Garden of Eden to work the ground and keep it in order" (Genesis 2:15, Message). From the beginning God knew that we would enjoy our free time more if it was balanced with work.

Ellen White wrote: "If they would have pure and virtuous characters, they [children] must have the discipline of well-regulated labor, which will bring into exercise all the muscles. The satisfaction that children will have in being useful, and in denying themselves to help others, will be the most healthful pleasure they ever enjoyed" (*Counsels on Health*, p. 187).

Finding a job that gets you outside moving around and exercising your muscles instead of your thumbs isn't as hard as you think. No matter where you live there's bound to be a need for landscape help, yard work to be done, or even someone to shovel the sidewalk. If nothing else is available, you can "adopt" a stretch of road and green it up: walk it frequently with a trash bag and pick up litter. Be sure to wear gloves or use a trash grabber tool. Do you like animals? Be a dog walker around your neighborhood or at your local shelter. You can also check with state and national parks to see if they have any employment opportunities.

After a few hours in the fresh air burning calories and exercising your muscles and lungs, you'll be amazed at how much more fun it is to play or hang out.

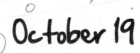

One Gift

The king went to Gibeon, the most prestigious of the local shrines,
to worship. He sacrificed a thousand Whole-Burnt-Offerings on that altar.
That night, there in Gibeon, God appeared to Solomon in a dream:
God said, "What can I give you? Ask." **I Kings 3:4, 5, Message.**

For a young squirt Solomon was already a pretty smart cookie. He was smart enough to know that he could stand to get a whole lot smarter. When God appeared to him in a dream and offered him one gift—whatever he asked for—Solomon didn't hesitate. He asked for wisdom. Why? Not so he could play TV game shows and win all the prize money. Not so he could get into the *Guinness Book of World Records* as the smartest man who ever lived. Not so he could be the president of Mensa, the largest and oldest high-IQ society in the world. He wanted to be wise so that he could rule God's people fairly.

He could have asked for anything at all; God didn't offer him that one gift with restrictions on it. Solomon could have asked to be able to fly. He could have asked to live longer than anyone in history. He could have asked for a million bucks. He could have asked for his song to go to number one on the radio charts. It says a lot about Solomon that he didn't ask for anything for himself, but for God's people. God thought so too. He was so pleased with Solomon's request that He gave Solomon gifts he hadn't even asked for as a bonus.

Put yourself in Solomon's sandals for a minute. What if God offered you one gift, anything you wanted? What would you ask for? I thought about it for a while, and I would ask for trust, complete trust in God. Why? Because I don't need to be fabulously wise as long as I trust God for everything in my life. If I was able to completely trust God for everything, I could have perfect peace too—a bonus gift. I'd never question why anything happened to me, good or bad, because I'd completely trust God to take care of every detail of my life. I would never have to worry about anything in the future because my trust in God would give me confidence that no matter what happened, it would be God's plan for my life.

God has many gifts to give His children. The trouble isn't that He doesn't offer them to us; it's that we don't ask. We're content to go through life as beggars, when He wants us to be wealthy beyond our wildest imaginings. Check your Bible and make a list of gifts God wants to give us. What gift would you ask for? Why?

Fill My Cup

"Please, sir," the woman said, "give me this water! Then I'll never be thirsty again, and I won't have to come here to get water." **John 4:15, NLT.**

et's try a little experiment. Go get a glass. Put it into a large bowl so that you don't have to worry about spills. Now carefully fill it up to the very top with water. Next, find some hard objects (rocks, marbles, beads, etc.) that will fit inside the glass and not be damaged by the water. Ready? OK, let's get started.

Take one of the objects and carefully drop it into the glass. Observe what happens. I'm not a physicist, but I know enough about science to guess that the hard object you dropped into the glass displaced some of the water, which came sloshing out of the glass. Now drop in more objects and observe what happens. Continue to drop in objects until you can't fit in any more.

What happened to the water? I predict that a lot of it ended up in the bowl, because the mass of the objects didn't leave enough room for the water. Go ahead and clean up your mess and set up the experiment again, but this time, instead of hard objects, we're going to drop soft, absorbable objects into the water (such as sponges.) If you have one or two ordinary kitchen sponges, cut them up into small pieces that will fit into the glass. Slowly and carefully drop them in one at a time, letting each one absorb water before you drop in the next piece.

What happened? I predict (if you added the sponges slowly enough) that the sponges absorbed the water in the glass. Very little, if any, of the water should have ended up in the bowl this time. Why? Instead of displacing the water (pushing it out to make room), the sponges absorbed the water (they took it in).

Now imagine that you are the glass. The water is the Holy Spirit. Jesus fills you with His Holy Spirit. What you drop inside your glass determines how much of the Holy Spirit you keep inside. If you drop in things that push the Holy Spirit out (secular television, books, movies, games, even friends), your glass will empty. If you drop in things that absorb the Holy Spirit (Bible study, prayer, lesson study, church, spiritual conversation, and books), your glass will stay full.

The point? If we want Jesus to fill our cups so that we won't ever be thirsty again, we need to be careful that we aren't displacing the Holy Spirit with secular interests. What are you dropping into your glass?

BFF

I no longer call you servants, because a servant does not know
his master's business. Instead, I have called you friends, for everything
that I learned from my Father I have made known to you. **John 15:15, NIV.**

I know something about you that you may not know. I know who your BFF is. *That's crazy*, you think. *You don't even know me, how could you know my BFF?* Or maybe you don't have a BFF, so you think that clearly I have no idea what I'm talking about. That's where you'd be wrong. I know your BFF very well. Question is: How well do you know your BFF?

For instance, do you spend time with Him when you wake up every morning? Do you talk to Him throughout the day? Do you go to Him with problems? Do you thank Him for gifts? Do you proudly talk about Him with your other friends? Do you invite Him along on your activities (or do you ditch Him and go places where He wouldn't want to be seen)? Is He the first one you talk to in the morning and the last one you talk to at night? Do you read His letters, or are they stuck in a pile of laundry somewhere on your bedroom floor?

No matter what kind of experience you've had with friends in the past, you can totally trust your BFF. He wants to be part of everything you do. You are so important to Him that He drops everything the instant you turn to Him for help, guidance, or just a chat. He's there for you 24/7. How many of those hours do you spend with Him? Ellen White says you should "cultivate the habit of talking with the Savior when you are alone, when you are walking, and when you are busy with your daily work. Let your heart be continually uplifted in silent petition for help, for light, for strength, for knowledge. Let every breath be a prayer" (*The Ministry of Healing,* p. 300).

As your BFF, Jesus wants to be the one you go to for help, the one you spend the most time with, the one you lean on for support. He's always with you. He cares about everything in your life. He can help with any problem you face. What more could you possibly ask for in a BFF? And the best part? When He says He's your best friend forever, He really means *forever.*

Chances are you have a human BFF, too, and that's great; God made human beings with a need for companionship. But the greatest need God placed in humans is for Himself. Are you allowing Him to fill that need in your life, or are you trying to fill it with something else?

The Sky Is Falling

Heaven and earth will pass away, but my words will never pass away.
But about that day or hour no one knows, not even the angels in heaven,
nor the Son, but only the Father. **Matthew 24:35, 36, NIV.**

It's been confirmed. The world is going to end very soon. According to Harold Camping, a preacher from California, the world will end on October 21, 2011. Oh, wait, it's 2015. If you're reading this, I guess we're all still here. We can safely throw that prediction in the wastebasket with all the others.

Camping originally predicted that the world would end in May 2011, but when that didn't happen, he revised his date, saying he'd gotten the math wrong. But October 21, 2011, came and went, and nothing happened, except that a lot of people were very disappointed. Some people sold all their possessions and used the money to purchase billboard space to announce the end of the world in an attempt to save as many people as possible. Others gave the money to Harold Camping's ministry. Some traveled from state to state in cars painted with warning messages. Does any of this sound familiar?

It should. In its early days our own denomination went through something similar on October 22, 1844, when the believers lived through the Great Disappointment. People have been saying the world was going to end ever since Adam and Eve ate the fruit. A lot of them think it's going to end soon. They're right, of course. But anyone who sets a date will have it wrong. Regardless of how soon you think the world will end, no one will ever know for sure when it will happen. Jesus says that even *He* doesn't know. Only God the Father knows the exact date and time.

One thing that we do know is that we need to be ready no matter when the earth will end. While God may not be asking us to go out and sell everything we have and take to the roads in a van painted with signs, we need to keep in mind that part of the very name of our church (*Advent*ist) means that we believe God is coming, that He is coming *soon*, and that we must be ready.

Do you know what the mission of your church is? Check it out at www.adventist.org/world-church/name-mission/index.html. Make a list of ways you can cooperate with God and your home church to reach the world with the message of His soon return. Ask the Holy Spirit to give you the power and wisdom to reach out to those who are lost.

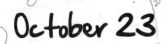

Helpless

*And my God will meet all your needs according
to the riches of his glory in Christ Jesus. To our God and Father
be glory for ever and ever. Amen.* **Philippians 4:19, 20, NIV.**

I just got some bad news, and there's nothing I can do about it. I feel helpless and frustrated because I want to do something, *anything,* to help, but it's out of my hands. When we run smack-dab into a wall such as this, the usual response is to say, "Well, I can't do anything about it. The only thing left is prayer." But this is about as backward as can be. Prayer should never be our last resort; it should be our first line of offense.

God has promised to meet all our needs. We must trust Him to do that. There will be times you're at the end of your rope hanging on with your fingernails, or plastered up against a brick wall you can't climb or even see over. Maybe you're struggling with some kind of addiction. Maybe you've gotten your relationships in a tangle and whatever you say or do just makes things worse. Maybe you're watching someone you love self-destruct. You feel helpless. You can't change anything.

That's OK—*you* don't have to change things. Your job is to trust God to work in and through the situation for His glory. That's what should shine out from every situation: God's glory. It should be evident in your attitude of calm trust as you wait for Him to work. It should be apparent in your confidence in Him, your absolute certainty that He is in control. It will be stamped in your acceptance of whatever happens in your situation.

What we must keep in mind is that there's a difference between our needs (which God supplies) and our wants (which He might not). No one wants to go through pain or suffering, but sometimes that's what's needed to draw us, or someone else, into a closer relationship with God. That's God's top priority.

It's hard for us to see how God can use bad situations toward a good end. We can't see everything the way God can; our finite minds are too small. We just have to trust Him and remember that no one is ever helpless who can hand a situation over to God and praise Him for the outcome without knowing what that will be. As Elisabeth Elliot said: "God is God. Because He is God, He is worthy of my trust and obedience. I will find rest nowhere but in His holy will, a will that is unspeakably beyond my largest notions of what He is up to."

Big Dreams, Small Steps

So the wall was completed on the twenty-fifth of Elul, in fifty-two days.
When all our enemies heard about this, all the surrounding nations
were afraid and lost their self-confidence, because they realized that this work
had been done with the help of our God. **Nehemiah 6:15, 16, NIV.**

Have you ever faced a big project and felt overwhelmed by the sheer amount of what needed to be accomplished? It doesn't really matter what it is you're trying to do, whether it's reading the Bible through in one year, quitting smoking or drinking, or passing a difficult class. All big projects have some things in common. Their size makes us want to give up before we even get started. Yet, like Rome, they can't be finished in a day. In order to tackle any large project successfully, you have to break it down into smaller parts and conquer them one at a time.

Nehemiah had a great job working for the Persian government, and life was fine and dandy, until one day he was talking to some of his fellow Jews and learned that the walls and gates of Jerusalem were broken down, leaving the city vulnerable to attack. How could the people defend themselves when their city had no walls? As you can imagine, building walls around an entire city is a big construction project.

Nehemiah didn't let that discourage him though. He got permission to leave his job so he could take over building the walls. He rallied the people, and they finished in 52 days, which proved even to their enemies that God was working with them.

It wasn't all smooth sailing. Not everyone wanted those walls to be rebuilt. Nehemiah and his helpers had to deal with death threats, curses, false accusations, and assassination attempts. You're not likely to face such serious obstacles, but discouragement is just as likely to force you to quit. Here are some tips to help you when you face a big, daunting project:

1. Ask God for help. No matter what you're trying to do, if God is on your side, as He was on Nehemiah's, you know you can push through to the end.

2. Take it in small steps. Don't expect to finish the whole project in one day. Biting off more than you can chew will only discourage you and make you want to quit.

3. Keep at it. Even when you feel like quitting, regularly put in some time on your project. Over time it will get done.

4. Have a sense of humor; it will help you see the bright side when you feel like quitting.

October 25

I'll Trade Ya

Then he turned to Jesus and said, "Lord, I believe in You! Please, remember me when you set up your kingdom." Jesus turned His head toward him and said, "I promise you today, when I return with the glory of my Father, I will take you home with me to paradise." **Luke 23:42, 43, Clear Word.**

This afternoon in lunchrooms all across the United States (and for all I know, the whole world) kids will be bartering. It'll be like a scene at the New York Stock Exchange. The confident: "Got a Ring Ding! Who'll trade me for a muffin?" The desperate: "Mom sent me a stupid apple. Please, will somebody trade me for a cookie?" The hopeful: "Carrot sticks, who wants 'em? They're yours for half a sandwich." The concept of bartering is pretty simple: I have something you want; you have something I want; let's trade. Both parties win because they both get what they want.

Although it doesn't really matter if you're trading something of greater or lesser value—as long as you get what you want in the end—no one wants to get the short end of the stick during a trade. For instance, if you have a car and you barter it for a pair of sneakers, you're going to feel like you got cheated. The items being bartered must be of the same value, more or less. If you traded your used car for a new boat that was worth about the same amount, you'd walk away from the transaction feeling a whole lot better than if you walked away with a pair of sneakers, even if they were new.

You could also barter something for a service. People often try to barter with God in this way: "Please, God, if You give me the new iPad, I'll pray every night before I go to bed." However, just as was the case for the thief on the cross, the only thing we have to offer God is our great need of Him. The thief was dying; he couldn't even offer God service for the rest of his life. He had nothing—*less* than nothing really! But God didn't look at him and say, "You've got nothing I can use. Sorry." His need was what God wanted.

God wants my need and your need, too. That's what we "barter" for God's grace. We give Him our need, and He gives us His grace. It's a great deal for us because we don't have anything of value, and yet God will trade us the one thing that has eternal value. God's grace, our entry fee to heaven, is priceless.

Passing the Baton

The disciples, seeing the Master with their own eyes,
were exuberant. Jesus repeated his greeting: "Peace to you.
Just as the Father sent me, I send you." **John 20:20, 21, Message.**

When I was in middle school, we had field day every year. This was the best day of the whole school year. Not only did we not have to do any schoolwork, but they let us play games all day long. There were running games and jumping games and throwing games. My first year in that school I could hardly believe my good fortune.

And then I got to the jumping contest. You had to run as fast as you could, and when you reached a line in the ground you jumped as far as you could. (In track and field they call this the long jump.) I jumped so far that the teacher who was keeping track made me do it again because he thought I had gone past the starting line. Twelve feet and one inch I jumped. I was in the fifth grade. Everyone was amazed.

Then it was time for the foot races. There was one girl, Julie, who had always won the blue ribbons in the foot races. That year I gave her some competition. We traded off coming in either first or second for every race. Later, when the school decided to send a team to the regional track-and-field events at the local high school, they chose three boys and me for the relay team. The boys were not happy because I was a girl, but I was faster than any of the other boys, and they wanted to win.

In a relay race the most important part of the race is passing the baton. The person who is carrying it is running as fast as they can, and they can't slow down, or they'll lose time. The person who is taking it can't fumble and drop it, or they'll waste precious time picking it up so that they can continue the race. Once you grab that baton you have to run as fast as you can and pass it to the next person running. I was more nervous about dropping that baton than I was about running around the track.

After Jesus rose from the dead, He passed the baton—the job of spreading the good news—to His disciples, and it has been passed down from one generation of Christians to another ever since. When you became a Christian, it was passed to you. This is your race; run it well, remembering that Jesus will give you everything you need to run your best race.

And the relay race? We won. I still have the blue ribbon.

October 27

O Great Whachmacallit

If anyone is ashamed of me and my message, the Son of Man will be ashamed of that person when he returns in his glory and in the glory of the Father and the holy angels. **Luke 9:26, NLT.**

I have three sisters, which was a little confusing at times for our grandmother. When she wanted to call one of us, she often went through the whole roll call before getting to the one she wanted. It was, "Céleste, Faith, Aimee, no, um, Joy, could you come here, please?" Most of the time we already knew whom she wanted, so the other three sisters would just ignore the call. Sometimes we even answered to the wrong name if she yelled for the wrong one of us. We knew what she meant. It wasn't a big deal.

Depending on the situation, names can be vitally important. You wouldn't, for instance, pray, "Dear Satan, save me," when you really mean, "Dear Jesus, save me." In this case, the name is vitally important. The Bible tells us that there is no other name under heaven by which we can be saved (see Acts 4:12). Only Jesus can save us.

But lately I've noticed a trend. Christians who don't want to offend non-Christians have taken to calling God by names He never called Himself. They'll say we need to pray to "Spirit," or the "Presence," or our "Higher Power." While most people know what they mean, those names are open to interpretation; they can mean anything, really. There is the Holy Spirit, and then there are evil spirits—which one are they praying to? Anything can be a "Presence," and "Higher Power" does not specifically mean God, but any power you believe to be higher than yourself that can help you.

If we use such vague words as these when we really mean God or Jesus or the Holy Spirit, we show a cowardly streak that won't please God. Jesus told people flat out that if we are ashamed of Him, He'll be ashamed of us when He returns with God the Father. Never be ashamed of the only name under heaven that can save us. Never water down the message of the gospel by using weak words to talk about God. Be proud of being a son or daughter of God, and let God worry about who gets offended hearing His name.

Try This: There are many names for God in the Bible. Each one describes a different aspect of His character. Look them up and write down your favorites. Use them when you are praying or praising God.

Who's in Charge Here?

Don't let anyone look down on you because you are young, but set an example for the believers in speech, in conduct, in love, in faith and in purity. **I Timothy 4:12, NIV.**

I was talking to a young man the other day about taking a turn on the platform at our church. "Absolutely not," he replied so strongly that I had to ask why. "Because," he informed me, "I was forced to get up in front of people at my school whenever there was a special program. Now that I've graduated, I don't have to do that anymore." This young man was, however, a deacon at church. He was serving in a way that felt comfortable to him, and I couldn't argue with that.

There are times God will call us out of our comfort zones. Moses, for example, wasn't keen on public speaking either. When he found out God wanted to send him with a message for Pharaoh, he looked around, tapped his chest, and asked, "Me?" Surely God had someone else in mind. He put up such a stink about it that God finally said Aaron could go with him and speak for him, so in the end it took two men to do that job, which is some pretty creative job sharing.

God usually calls us to serve Him in positions that fit our strengths, though. Are you good with numbers? You could help the treasurer. Are you good with people? You could be a greeter. Like to sing? You could lead out in the song service. There's a job for everybody in the body, young or old, so thinking that you are excused from serving in the church because you are young just won't cut it.

This is *your* church. You will inherit it someday. It will be your responsibility to keep it growing. Wouldn't it be great to get some experience running it before you have to take over? Great, because now is a perfect time to learn. As members we each have a duty to contribute in some way to the church. We can't sit back and let others do all the work and receive all the blessings.

The church has different positions for a reason; not everyone is alike. All personality types can contribute in some way. Think about the positions in your church and decide which ones you'd like to help with. Then talk to your pastor about serving in your church. Go ahead, make their day!

October 29

Heart Surgery

I will give you a new heart and put a new spirit in you;
I will remove from you your heart of stone and give you a heart of flesh.
And I will put my Spirit in you and move you to follow my decrees
and be careful to keep my laws. **Ezekiel 36:26, 27, NIV.**

Dr. Dwight Harken was a young U.S. army surgeon during World War II, and he got mighty sick of seeing so many soldiers coming back from the front lines full of shrapnel, especially when it was lodged in their hearts. Leaving it was dangerous, but taking it out was fatal. Stuck between a rock and a hard place, Dr. Harken did what most determined people do: He began experimenting to find a solution to his problem.

Eventually he did find a way to cut into the wall of a still-beating heart and remove the shrapnel, and the first heart surgery was performed. After this success doctors started trying to fix other heart problems that required surgery. However, they were under severe time restrictions, because the brain could go only so long without the oxygen carried by the heart, which was under reconstruction. Discoveries in lowering body temperature to lengthen the amount of time someone could undergo surgery led to even more complicated heart surgeries.

In 1967 Dr. Christiaan Barnard performed the very first heart transplant by taking the heart from a woman who had died in a car accident and putting it inside a man, who lived for 18 days until the drugs he was taking to help his body accept the heart weakened him and he died. And that was the problem with transplanting hearts: the body saw it as a foreign object and rejected it. It wasn't until Dr. Norman Shumway discovered cyclosporine, which helped keep the body from rejecting its new heart, that heart transplant patients begin to thrive.

God has been performing heart transplants far longer than doctors have, and our bodies react the same way to the new hearts God gives us. When He replaces our hearts of stone with hearts that can feel, our sinful minds try to reject them. Only by constantly filling our lives with the Holy Spirit—the same way heart transplant patients must continue taking cyclosporine—can we keep our minds from rejecting God's new hearts. With the Holy Spirit our new hearts will allow us to live useful, productive lives for God. While there are many more patients needing new hearts every year than there are hearts available, everyone who wants a new heart from God can have one. Have you asked Him for your heart transplant yet? Do it today!

October 30

Calm in the Storm

Jesus was sleeping at the back of the boat with his head on a cushion. The disciples woke him up, shouting, "Teacher, don't you care that we're going to drown?" When Jesus woke up, he rebuked the wind and said to the waves, "Silence! Be still!" Suddenly the wind stopped, and there was a great calm. Then he asked them, "Why are you afraid? Do you still have no faith?" The disciples were absolutely terrified. "Who is this man?" they asked each other. "Even the wind and waves obey him!" **Mark 4:38-41, NLT.**

On October 30, 1938, actor Orson Welles narrated an episode of a radio drama that caused mass hysteria. It was presented as a series of news bulletins that described an alien invasion by Martians that was taking place in Grover's Mill, New Jersey. People listening to the broadcast were seriously freaked out. They thought it was a real news broadcast and panicked, fleeing their homes.

As I type this, mass hysteria is building once again, but this time the threat is very real. A superstorm called Hurricane Sandy is making landfall on the East Coast. By the time you read this, Sandy will be ancient history. You'll either remember it as the storm of the century, or the storm that turned out to be a dud. But right now people are scared. They've stocked up on food and water, bought batteries, and battened down all the hatches. Now that there's nothing left to do but wait, they're flooding Facebook with their terror. And the storm hasn't even hit the coast yet.

Sandy could be bad news for lots of people. I know; I lived through Hurricane Irene last year, and it wasn't pretty. But feeding on the fears of others is not how Jesus wants us to live. Fear is Satan's territory. We serve the Creator of the wind and the waves; what can we possibly be afraid of?

After all the storm drama on their boat, the disciples were quaking in their sandals, but Jesus just looked at them and asked, "Why are you afraid? Do you still have no faith?" If we have faith in Jesus to take care of us, there won't be a storm strong enough to shake our confidence. When times get tough and things get hairy, when everyone around us is running around in a panic, we'll be able to point to Jesus and say, "My God is greater than anything you can throw at me. 'Even the wind and waves obey him!'"

Trick or Treat?

Don't participate in the things these people do. For once you were full of darkness, but now you have light from the Lord. So live as people of light! For this light within you produces only what is good and right and true. Carefully determine what pleases the Lord. Take no part in the worthless deeds of evil and darkness; instead, expose them. It is shameful even to talk about the things that ungodly people do in secret. **Ephesians 5:7-12, NLT.**

If you ask 10 Christians whether or not we should celebrate Halloween, you'll probably get 10 different answers. Some people feel there's no harm in dressing up in costumes and going to silly parties at which you bob for apples and try to eat doughnuts off a string. Others believe that participation means we approve of Halloween and all that it stands for. Halloween, by the way, has pagan roots in Samhain, a festival of sacrifice to appease Celtic gods in which celebrants wore costumes to hide from roaming ghosts.

Some Christians use Halloween as a ministry opportunity. They have parties for neighborhood children and provide safe, clean fun and games giving peace of mind to anxious parents who fear poisoned Halloween candy from strangers. Others hand out Christian literature to trick-or-treaters along with candy. Some Christian kids trick-or-treat to raise money for good causes.

The Bible doesn't talk about how we should treat Halloween, whether to participate or ignore it. Instead it instructs us to live as people who have light. No matter what you think of Halloween personally, you have to admit that God can use a holiday with dark beginnings to give us a wonderful opportunity. One night every year our mission field comes right to our door!

In the United States Halloween is the second-biggest commercial holiday; Americans spend about $6 billion on it. I think someone not far from my house spent most of that creating an entire zombie apocalypse on their lawn. The rest is probably spent on candy. Why not take some of that money and buy tracts or copies of *Guide*, *Primary Treasure*, or *Our Little Friend*? Pass them out when the little tricksters come to your door. Be sure your church information is stamped on them somewhere so that the people you give them to will know how to find your church later.

Happy Wovember!

But since you are like lukewarm water, neither hot nor cold,
I will spit you out of my mouth! **Revelation 3:16, NLT.**

Maybe you've figured out by now that I live on a farm. I grew up on a farm too. Not a dairy farm, though my grandmother had one of those. Or a pig farm, though my uncle had one. Or a chicken farm; another uncle had one of those. I grew up on a small homestead farm. We had goats, hens, pigs, rabbits, and my horse.

On my farm I have animals I can use in my fiber arts—fiber art is art made using materials from animals and plants that are generally called "fiber." Yarn is fiber art; so are sweaters, woven tapestries, scarves, and lots of other creations. Fiber art takes many forms, but the one thing they all have in common is that they are made of animal or plant fiber.

Because I make a lot of things with the wool from my sheep, rabbits, alpaca, and llama, I am interested in information about wool. When I found out that a group of people nicknamed November "Wovember," I had to check it out. It turns out that Wovember is all about getting people to wear 100 percent wool and appreciate that the material their sweater or socks or scarf came from was produced by 100 percent real sheep. If your sweater is made with 50 percent wool and 50 percent acrylic, that means it's only half wool. The other half is "fake" wool. People who care about keeping it real want it to be *all* real.

God wants us to keep it real too. He wants us to be 100 percent Christians. In fact, in Revelation He says He'll spit half-and-half Christians right out of His mouth. That's pretty strong language, especially coming from God, but He wants to be sure that we know how important it is that we are committed to Him 100 percent of the time. This Wovember, take some time to get your life real with God by making Him part of all of it, not just half of it.

Try This: Draw a pie shape. Write down areas of your life in each slice of pie: school, home, work, church, personal time, clubs or activities, etc., and put a dot somewhere on each slice to show how much God is involved in that area. Put the dot close to the center if God is involved and toward the edge if He's not. Now connect the dots. Is your line lopsided? Can you see which areas need work? Ask God to help you invite Him into those areas of your life.

November 2

Is it Well?

*And so she departed, and went to the man of God
at Mount Carmel. So it was, when the man of God saw her afar off,
that he said to his servant Gehazi, "Look, the Shunammite woman!
Please run now to meet her, and say to her, 'Is it well with you?
Is it well with your husband? Is it well with the child?'"
And she answered, "It is well."* **2 Kings 4:25, 26, NKJV.**

How much do you really love God? What if you lost everything the way Job did? Would you still love Him? Whoa, that's the real test, isn't it? I mean, it's easy to love someone who helps you out, takes care of you, gives you good gifts, and blesses you. It's a lot harder to love Someone who allows bad things to happen to you. Isn't our first question always, "How could God love me if He allowed _____ [fill in the blank]?" And then we get angry and our next question is "Why should I love God if He's going to treat me like that?"

Actually, you could say that we find out just how much we love God when something bad hits us hard. That's when we have to decide whether we love *God* or only what He *does for us.* That's the decision Horatio Spafford had to make. First, his only son died of scarlet fever. Then all his property was wiped out in a fire. Deciding that his family needed a holiday, Horatio booked passage on a ship, but just before it sailed he was delayed by business, so he told his wife and four girls to go on ahead and he'd meet them. Nine days later he learned that the ship his family had been on had sunk, and only his wife had survived.

He sailed on the next ship out of New York to join his wife, and as the ship passed over the place where his daughters had drowned, he stood at the railing and looked out at the water. I can only imagine what he was thinking. When he returned to his cabin, he wrote a hymn: "It Is Well With My Soul." Say what?

The words of his hymn echoed the words of the Shunammite woman whose only son had just died. What did these two know so that they could say all was well when they were faced with the worst kind of tragedy? They both knew one important truth: No matter what happens in life, God can be trusted. He can be trusted to support us, love us, and save us, and for that we owe Him our absolute gratitude and loyalty.

When sorrows like sea billows roll, remember that whatever our lot, God has taught us to say, "It is well, it is well with my soul." Is it well with *your* soul?

What's in Your Way?

Oh yes, you shaped me first inside, then out;
you formed me in my mother's womb. I thank you,
High God—you're breathtaking! Body and soul,
I am marvelously made! I worship in adoration—what a creation!
You know me inside and out, you know every bone in my body;
You know exactly how I was made, bit by bit,
how I was sculpted from nothing into something.
Like an open book, you watched me grow from conception to birth;
all the stages of my life were spread out before you,
the days of my life all prepared before
I'd even lived one day. **Psalm 139:13-16, Message.**

Patrick Henry Hughes is pretty awesome. In his entire school career he got almost all A's—only three B's. He was a member of the Cardinal Marching Band at his college and graduated magna cum laude from University of Louisville as a Spanish language major. He speaks fluent Spanish.

He's a virtuoso pianist (he started playing the piano when he was only 9 months old), vocalist, and trumpet player. He's won or finished very high in numerous musical contests. He's been featured on television shows and in magazines. He's recorded two CDs and written a book, *I Am Potential.* He's a motivational speaker and travels the world with his dad encouraging people to overcome obstacles and reach their full potential.

Oh, and did I mention that Patrick was born blind and unable to straighten his arms and legs? He's confined to a wheelchair and has had to have steel rods surgically attached to his spine to correct scoliosis, a curvature of the spine. Patrick says that it's not important that God created him without sight and unable to walk; God gave him incredible musical gifts. That's what he focuses on. Patrick doesn't even see his disabilities; he can see only his abilities.

How about you? Are you reaching your full potential? Think about everything Patrick has to overcome just to get out of bed in the morning, and then compare it to your life. Do you have anything you can really complain about, or do your problems seem a little smaller by comparison? No matter whether they are overwhelming mountains shadowing your life or tiny little speed bumps, God can help you over them. He created you; He knows everything about you. Only God knows how to help you reach your fullest potential. Only you can trust Him to help you reach it.

November 4

Operation Christmas Child

One day some parents brought their children to Jesus
so he could lay his hands on them and pray for them.
But the disciples scolded the parents for bothering him. But Jesus said,
"Let the children come to me. Don't stop them! For the Kingdom of Heaven
belongs to those who are like these children." And he placed his hands on
their heads and blessed them before he left. **Matthew 19:13-15, NLT.**

Do you know what time of year it is?

It's *that* time of year: the time of year that people around the country are starting to fill shoeboxes for needy children in an all-out missionary effort called Operation Christmas Child. Run by Samaritan's Purse, a Christian relief and evangelism organization, Operation Christmas Child's mission is "to demonstrate God's love in a tangible way to needy children around the world, and together with the local church worldwide, to share the good news of Jesus Christ."

Remember when you were little and looking forward to Christmas and all those *presents*? Well, imagine receiving a shoebox full of presents if you were a little boy or girl who lives in extreme poverty in the garbage dumps of the Philippines, the orphanages in Macedonia, or one of the many other places shoeboxes are sent. Wouldn't you be excited? But these children don't simply receive presents. They also receive the good news that Jesus loves them.

Dejan, a young Macedonian man, received an Operation Christmas Child box along with an invitation to attend church when he was living in an orphanage. Now 26, he says that he feels called to reach out to other children who are underprivileged and abused. He's active in youth ministry and helps to feed the children of Gypsy families living at the city dump in Skopje. Their soup kitchen feeds 80 to 120 kids daily.

"When Jesus told the disciples not to forbid the children to come to Him, He was speaking to His followers in all ages—to officers of the church, ministers, helpers, and all Christians. Jesus is drawing the children, and He bids us, 'Suffer them to come;' as if He would say, They will come, if you do not hinder them" (Ellen G. White, *The Ministry of Healing*, pp. 42, 43).

Pack a shoebox and help a child meet Jesus. Go to www.operationchristmaschild.org to find out how to get involved.

Cast Your Ballot

The first thing I want you to do is pray. Pray every way you know how, for everyone you know. Pray especially for rulers and their governments to rule well so we can be quietly about our business of living simply, in humble contemplation. This is the way our Savior God wants us to live. **I Timothy 2:1-3, Message.**

This morning I woke up and discovered that America had elected President Obama for another term in office. When you read this, it will soon be time to hold another presidential election. If you aren't old enough to vote, maybe you don't care. But you should. Every American, voting age or not, should care about who governs the country. Why? That's the privilege and responsibility of everyone living in the greatest free country on earth.

God has His hand on the United States. Ellen White tells of seeing in vision the Battle of Manassas, Virginia, during the Civil War. The Southern army had the better position, but the North marched into battle confident they would win. The men were reckless and boasting, as though they'd already won, but by the time they reached the battlefield, many were fainting and in need of food. They fought desperately, and both sides suffered large losses. The dead and dying were all around.

The Northern soldiers rushed on, recklessly pushing the Southern army back. However, God knew that in their exhausted condition they were heading for great destruction that would bring rejoicing in the South, so He sent an angel to turn the tide of the battle. The angel waved his hand backward and caused great confusion in the Northern ranks. The Northern soldiers thought their troops were retreating, although in reality they weren't, and they turned and joined the retreat.

Because the destruction suffered by the Southern army was so great, they didn't have the heart to boast. They were confused about the outcome of the battle, because they had been so sure they'd win. They'd had the advantage and should have been able to defeat the North easily. But God was punishing them for the sin of slavery. He was also punishing the North for allowing slavery to go on so long.

God cares deeply about our nation, and we should too. When you're praying, remember our president and all those in charge of this great country. The better they do their jobs, the longer we can go on bringing the gospel to all the people who need to hear it.

Practice Makes Perfect

I am warning you ahead of time, dear friends.
Be on guard so that you will not be carried away by the errors
of these wicked people and lose your own secure footing.
Rather, you must grow in the grace and knowledge
of our Lord and Savior Jesus Christ. **2 Peter 3:17, 18, NLT.**

D o you ever get sick of having fire drills? evacuation drills? lockdown drills? The alarm goes off, you dutifully parade out of school or to the designated safe place, and you wait around for someone to "check" the school over and tell you it's "safe," even though you know it's only a drill. You probably think drills are a waste of time . . . until the emergency happens for real.

A teacher I know told me that she'd been stuck for three hours in a lockdown with her class—only it wasn't a drill. Men with guns had been spotted in the school parking lot. This was not a drill, but because they'd had so many drills, the teacher and her class knew exactly what to do. They waited quietly until school officials ended the lockdown after discovering that the men were only hunters who were where they shouldn't have been.

The things we practice become easy for us. It's the same no matter what we practice. If we practice playing an instrument, we can play better. If we practice a sport, we perform better. If we practice complaining, we become complainers. Whatever we repeat, we get good at doing. Doesn't it make sense then that we should be careful what we practice?

This goes for your mind, too. If you allow your mind to fill with negative thoughts and you don't do anything to redirect them, you are practicing negative thoughts, and soon they will become negative feelings and actions. Allow only positive, uplifting thoughts into your mind.

Our characters are made up of the things we practice. When we practice good traits, we have good characters, so you know what happens when we practice bad traits. We can make our characters strong by making positive choices—practicing positive character traits—every day. The best thing you can do to cultivate positive character traits is to study your Bible and pray every day. In God's Word you'll find many great traits you can practice: patience, love, kindness, sympathy, endurance, and forgiveness are just a few.

Make a list of positive character traits you'd like to have. Ask God to put circumstances, people, or opportunities into your life so that you can practice those character traits.

I Tink I Hab a Code

Then Jesus said, "Come to me, all of you who are weary
and carry heavy burdens, and I will give you rest. Take my yoke upon you.
Let me teach you, because I am humble and gentle at heart,
and you will find rest for your souls. For my yoke is easy to bear,
and the burden I give you is light." **Matthew 11:28-30, NLT.**

It's about this time of the year that people all around you will start dropping like flies, struck down by the common cold. Twenty-two million school days will be lost to sickness, and I'll bet you wish they could all be yours. While you may have to share sick days with the rest of America, hopefully you won't share your cold with them, too, because if you do a good job of taking care of yourself, you could skip the cold and flu season altogether. Wouldn't you rather spend your school-free days doing something fun instead of moping around on the couch trying to breathe?

Because one of the most common ways the cold is spread is by touching something infected with a virus and then touching your eyes, nose, or mouth, you can avoid a lot of germs by not touching your face and by washing your hands well and often. Most people don't wash their hands long enough to be effective. The Centers for Disease Control and Prevention recommends washing your hands with soap in running water for 20 seconds. You can count out the seconds or sing through "Happy Birthday" twice.

When God created Adam and Eve there was no sickness in the world. They didn't need to get flu shots or take antibiotics or worry about spreading germs when they sneezed (but you do, so remember to sneeze into your elbow or a tissue). But even before there was a special need for humanity to rest, God gave us Sabbath.

Every seven days we're called to step aside from our hectic world for 24 hours to rest and worship God. He knew that we would get busy and overworked, stressed out, and tired. It would be all too easy for us to stop taking care of ourselves. It's particularly important during this contagious time of year to spend time resting with Jesus, handing over our burdens, and letting Him teach us. It's a sure cure not only for the cold but for whatever ails us.

Think About It: How do you spend Sabbath? What would the perfect Sabbath be for you? Take one step to come closer to your perfect Sabbath this week.

November 8

Bucket List

Delight yourself in the Lord; and He will give you the desires of your heart. **Psalm 37:4, NASB.**

Have you made a bucket list yet? Although the list got its name from the expression "kicking the bucket" (and yes, it is a list of things you want to do before you die), it's not just for old folks who are closer to bucket-kicking time than teens. Anyone can have a list of things they want to accomplish or experience during their lifetime. In fact, the sooner you start, the more things you have a chance to do during your life.

To make your own bucket list, all you need are ideas. Think about it for a minute. If you could do anything at all—swim with dolphins, volunteer at a homeless shelter, sing "The Star-Spangled Banner" at a ball game, read the entire Bible, learn how to paint—what kind of things would you want to do? No cheating now—these have to be things that you really want to do. They can be far-fetched, such as skydiving, or just require a lot of commitment, such as learning Greek and Hebrew so you can read the Bible in its original languages.

See if you can come up with 100 items to get started. Of course, just because you have a list now doesn't mean you have to do everything in order, unless you want to. Feel free to bounce around and check off items as you accomplish them. You can keep the list in a notebook or in a document on your computer. It doesn't matter as long as you can keep track and keep working on your list.

It's important to have things to look forward to and goals to work toward. Not only do they keep us from getting stuck in negative thinking or dwelling on past mistakes, but they prevent Satan from finding ways to tempt us to do dangerous or questionable things out of sheer boredom. Before we get the first item scratched off on our bucket lists, Satan will try to convince us that God doesn't want us to have any fun and that following Him is boring and unexciting. This just proves that Satan is a liar, because God Himself says that if we delight ourselves in Him, He'll give us the desires of our hearts. I want the desires of my heart, don't you?

Don't leave your bucket list in your head. Take the time to write it down. The act of writing will strengthen your commitment to trying some of the things on your list. Now choose one and go have fun!

Safe Place

The Lord is my rock and my fortress and my deliverer;
the God of my strength, in whom I will trust; my shield
and the horn of my salvation, my stronghold and my refuge;
my Savior, you save me from violence. **2 Samuel 22:2, 3, NKJV.**

It was a silly accident. I was trying to put some mugs into the cupboard, and one slipped out of my hands. I tried to catch it between my arm and the shelf before it crashed onto the floor. (Don't try this at home.) I caught it, but the mug broke and sliced my arm. I ended up in the emergency room trying to hold my arm together until a doctor could stitch it up.

Before they can do that, though, they ask you a lot of questions. I had to tell the nurse all about what had happened and how I'd cut myself. As soon as I finished, she gave me a look full of significance and asked, "And do you think your home is safe?"

I'd just finished telling her that I'd cut myself on a mug in my kitchen. How safe was that? But the way she was looking at me made me feel as though she was talking in code. I said, "Yes?"

"Good," she said, and looked relieved. When the blank look on my face didn't go away, she sighed and patiently explained, "We ask that in case there's any abuse in the home."

I felt like the last kid in math class to finally understand how to solve the problem. She was making sure I knew I was safe in case I was making up a story and had really been hurt by someone at home. I was able to tell her that no, my house was messy, but it was safe. Still, it was nice that she had asked. It was nice to know that even though I wasn't being abused, there was help out there if I needed it.

Every single human being is valuable, and no one should ever be abused physically, emotionally, mentally, or even virtually. If it happens to you or someone you know, don't stand for it. Abuse can survive only in silence, so raise your voice against it. Shout out—roar if you have to. You are worth it. God paid the ultimate price for you; that's how valuable you are to Him.

When we're scared, it's hard to know where to go. Go first to God. He has promised to be our shield against the darkness of violence. He is the high tower we can run to when we need a place of safety. He'll fight for you and lead you to people who can help: parents, pastors, counselors, teachers, or even the police. He will save you from violence.

November 10

Everyone's a Critic

Do not judge, and you will not be judged. Do not condemn,
and you will not be condemned. Forgive, and you will be forgiven.
Give, and it will be given to you. A good measure, pressed down,
shaken together and running over, will be poured into your lap. For with
the measure you use, it will be measured to you. **Luke 6:37, 38, NIV.**

Anamarie was visiting a new church. She had fun with the other teens in her class. She enjoyed the lesson study because the leader was awesome and taught in many creative ways rather than preaching at the students. She liked the music and the pastor's sermon. Her family was thinking about moving to the area, and she was excited that they would become part of this dynamic church group. Until . . . her parents were talking to the pastor, and a woman from the church pulled Anamarie aside and told her that she shouldn't be wearing pants or makeup, because they were sinful.

On the way back to their hotel room, Anamarie's parents asked her how she'd liked the church. She tried hard to remember the excitement she'd felt because she could see how enthusiastic her parents were about the church, but all she could remember were the woman's frowning criticisms about her appearance. She dreaded the thought of going back to that church.

Have you ever been in Anamarie's shoes? Teens seem to get more than their share of criticism from well-meaning church members. There's a reason for this. Partly it's because teens are still trying to find their own sense of style. In their explorations it's easy to offend people whose ideas about what is and what is not appropriate are set in stone. Partly it's because adults sometimes feel it's their duty to correct teens. Whatever the cause, criticism can lead to bad feelings on both sides. But the good news is that you're responsible for only one side: yours!

As important as it is not to judge, criticize, or condemn others, it's also important that we forgive people when they do those things . . . to us. It may be one of the hardest things you ever have to do, but it's important to do it. If you don't, it could drive you from church altogether, and then Satan wins. Score one for the devil. I don't know about you, but I'd rather not give Satan any easy wins.

Think About It: Put yourself in Anamarie's situation. How would you have reacted? How can you prepare yourself for criticism so you can react in a Christlike way?

Ditch the Diet

"Please test your servants for ten days: Give us nothing but vegetables to eat and water to drink. Then compare our appearance with that of the young men who eat the royal food, and treat your servants in accordance with what you see." So he agreed to this and tested them for ten days. At the end of the ten days they looked healthier and better nourished than any of the young men who ate the royal food. **Daniel 1:12-15, NIV.**

There is a big difference between your diet and dieting. Your diet is everything that you put into your mouth on a regular basis. If you always have toast and peanut butter for breakfast, then bread and peanut butter would be a part of your diet. If you only have chocolate pecan pie a couple of times each year, it wouldn't be part of your diet, but something you eat occasionally. *Dieting* is what you do when you start tracking and controlling your diet. If you measure out your food and keep track of your calories for the day, and eat or don't eat certain foods, then you are dieting.

Sometimes it seems as if everyone in America is on some kind of diet. The list of the different kinds of diets you can be on is never-ending. Every year someone thinks up some new kind of diet that everyone has to try until they get sick of it. While many diets work if you do them correctly, not all diets are safe, and very few people are able to stick to a diet for the rest of their lives. As soon as they stop dieting and go back to their regular way of eating, they gain their weight back. (And those pounds usually bring friends along with them, so people end up weighing more than they did before they started dieting.)

And that's the problem: Dieting is hard. No one wants to be on a diet for the rest of their lives. That's good news and bad news. No one *should* be on a diet for the rest of their lives. But everyone should have a healthy diet that they can live with forever. Any nutrition expert in the United States will agree with Seventh-day Adventists that the best diet includes lots of fresh vegetables, fruits, grains, nuts, and seeds. Loma Linda University has put together a vegetarian food pyramid to help you choose which foods are healthy enough to be part of your daily diet. Check it out at www.vegetariannutrition.org/food-pyramid.pdf.

What's your diet like? How much does it look like the diet Daniel and his friends ate to become the healthiest and best nourished? What changes could you make today to give your diet a makeover?

November 12

Friends Don't

Treat others the same way you want them to treat you. **Luke 6:31, NASB.**

D o you have any friends? Sure you do—probably lots of them. If you looked up and saw a couple of your friends chatting and laughing just as they were about to walk off the side of a cliff, would you warn them? shout? scream? wave your arms? I'm sure you would. That's what friends do. And if one of your friends were swimming and you saw a shark sneaking up on them, would you warn them? alert a lifeguard? make some noise? something? Sure you would. That's what friends do, right?

We love our friends. If we see them on a crash-and-burn course, we try to stop them. Even if they think they know what they're doing, we try to save them from their own stupidity. Why? Because we care about them, and we want the best for them. That's why it's important to choose good friends. If they mess up, help them out and give them a hand to get back on track. If you watch their backs, hopefully they'll watch yours.

You've probably heard of peer pressure, otherwise known as "my friends made me do it." It's usually used in a negative way. By taunting and bullying and sometimes even just by example, teens influence others to follow their behavior. In bad cases this can cause someone to start drinking, smoking, having sex, or doing drugs, but peer pressure works both ways. Not only can we influence people to do bad things, we can also influence them to do good things. That's called positive peer pressure.

By your good example you can influence your friends to steer clear of drugs, eat healthier, consider praying about problems, talk out conflicts with their parents, get better grades, attend church, or stop swearing. There's no end to your good influence. Just remember to use your powers for good and not evil. We are each responsible for the influence we have on others, whether it's bad or good. When in doubt, ask yourself this question: Am I treating this person the way I would like to be treated?

Take It to the Streets: Consider your friends. When it comes to influence, who's got the most power? Is it the friends with the positive influence or the ones with the negative influence? What does that tell you about your group of friends? If you are being negatively affected by the influence of your friends, think about making some new ones. It could save you a world of regret.

November 13

Speechless

*But he said to me, "My grace is sufficient for you,
for my power is made perfect in weakness.
"Therefore I will boast all the more gladly about my weaknesses,
so that Christ's power may rest on me.* **2 Corinthians 12:9, NIV.**

It's not often that I'm speechless. It tends to happen when I get nervous. And I tend to get nervous in uncomfortable situations, when I'm just not sure what to say at all. What do you say to someone whose friend or relative has just passed away? What do you say to someone sitting by a hospital bed waiting for someone they love to die? What do you say to the person who's dying? What do you say to someone whose parents have just announced that they are getting divorced? What do you say to someone whose father was just arrested? What do you say to someone whose sister was just gunned down accidentally in a drive-by shooting? What do you say to someone who just got dumped? What do you say to the friend who just found out they have AIDS?

You and I may not know exactly what to say to these hurting people, but God knows what they need. Sometimes they do need our words of reassurance or comfort. If you can't think of anything reassuring to say, you can always read a psalm for someone. Many psalms are prayers crying out to God for mercy, help, and comfort. They often contain promises of God's assistance and can be claimed for someone who is hurting. For example: "_____ [friend's name] waits quietly before God, for their victory comes from him. He alone is _____ [friend's name's] rock and their salvation, their fortress where they will never be shaken" (see Psalm 62:1, 2, NLT). You can even highlight verses you have prayed for someone in their own Bible so they can reread them later.

People don't always need words. Sometimes a hurting person really just needs someone to listen. Sometimes they need someone to hold their hand and just *be* there. Because we are used to a constant flow of information and data, silence can be awkward and uncomfortable, but we need to remember that silence is not bad, and it doesn't always need to be filled with words.

Because we are Christians, friends often treat us like experts on difficult subjects when they're in trouble. Or they may look to us for answers when they have problems. If you don't know how to help someone, first offer to pray for them. Prayer is always a good response to any need. Then direct them to a youth leader, pastor, or other trustworthy adult who can get them further help.

November 14

Survival Skills

Be good to me, God—and now! I've run to you for dear life. I'm hiding out under your wings until the hurricane blows over. I call out to High God, the God who holds me together. He sends orders from heaven and saves me, he humiliates those who kick me around. God delivers generous love, he makes good on his word. **Psalm 57:1-3, Message.**

Where I live we get big snow. This is great if you like winter sports, which I do. Snow makes for great skiing, snowshoeing, sledding, and, when you scrape it off the ice, skating. After one big storm I decided to go snowshoeing along a trail I hike in the summer. The only problem was that the temperature warmed up and the snow started to melt, which made it as wet and heavy as cement. It was a huge effort to slog through it, and I got tired quickly.

I was only halfway along my usual route and about a mile from my car when I realized it was all I could do to pick my legs up one after another to take the next step. I started wondering what I would do if I got so tired I couldn't walk any farther. What would happen if I didn't make it back out of the woods? I wouldn't be the first person stuck in the woods overnight during the winter, but I would be one of the least prepared. I hadn't told anyone exactly where I was going, I had no phone with me, and it was going to be dark soon. I was completely unprepared to face a survival situation in the winter at night.

Eventually I was able to make it out of the woods, and the experience made me really start thinking about being prepared. I hadn't been really prepared when I'd left home that day, because I'd planned to come right back. I didn't have anything I needed to survive for more than a couple hours in the cold out there in the woods.

You may not face miles of snow-covered trail, but every day you need survival skills. As you head out to school today someone could offer you drugs on the bus or sex behind the bleachers, or you could be bullied in the locker room. Do you have survival skills to get you out of those dangerous situations? If you don't, now is the time to start planning, not when you're in the middle of the situation.

When he was in a jam, David prayed to God for protection. But David was also a skilled warrior; he used his God-given brains and brawn to prepare himself for the enemy's attacks. God may or may not help those who help themselves, but He always helps those who call on Him.

Body Art

Do not cut your bodies for the dead, and do not mark your skin with tattoos. I am the Lord. **Leviticus 19:28, NLT.**

These days it would be hard to throw a cell phone and not hit someone with a tattoo. Despite the fact that tattoos are expensive and painful to remove, more and more people are having their bodies painted with artwork. Christians are no exception. Some feel that it's OK to get them as long as the symbols or words they have tattooed onto their bodies reflect their Christian beliefs, because they are then a witness to the unbelieving world.

It's tempting to think this makes tattoos OK; they are such a large part of our culture, and their coolness factor goes up every year. It's only natural to want in on the fun of something that seems as harmless as decorating skin. But tattoos come with a lot of questionable baggage. Although tattoos can't be viewed strictly as the badge of rebellion they were originally intended to be (as so many different kinds of people now wear tattoos), Christians have a moral responsibility not to cause people to stumble. If getting a tattoo would cause Christians or non-Christians to question the sincerity of our beliefs or to stumble in their own beliefs, we should avoid them. Our message about Jesus is too important to trip someone up over a tattoo.

According to the Mayo Clinic, moral concerns aren't the only thing to consider when it comes to tattoos; simply *getting* a tattoo is risky business. The dyes used in tattoos can cause allergic reactions, especially the red, green, yellow, and blue dyes. Itchy rashes at the tattoo site can appear even years after you get a tattoo. Skin infections are also possible. Then there are granulomas, bumps that form around the tattoo ink, and keloids, which are raised areas of scar tissue.

But the most dangerous health risk is blood-borne diseases like tetanus, hepatitis B, and hepatitis C, which you can get from equipment contaminated with infected blood. These are nasty characters that will put you in a seriously bad mood for a really long time. Not to mention that some employers won't hire people with tattoos, and some of those who will hire have policies forcing employees to cover their tattoos during work hours.

If you still have questions about whether or not you should consider getting a tattoo, read over today's text and ask yourself if God could make the answer any clearer.

Eat for Strength

Happy is the land whose king is a noble leader
and whose leaders feast at the proper time to gain strength
for their work, not to get drunk. **Ecclesiastes 10:17, NLT.**

I have a confession. I have driven my own car since I was a teenager, but I don't have any idea how to fix it. I can't change a tire. I can't put jumper cables on it when the battery dies. I can't even change the oil. But there is one thing I know about my car: I know that I have to put gas in the tank if I expect it to go anywhere. I can't put milk in the tank. I can't put orange juice in the tank. I can't put water in the tank. It's got to be gasoline.

I know this because the folks who built my car wrote a whole book about how to take care of it. It's called an owner's manual, and it tells me exactly what to do (and not to do) to my car if I want to keep it running well. Now, I don't have to do what they say. I can put honey in the gas tank if I want to. It's my car; I can do what I want. No one can stop me. That's my choice. But whatever happens to my car if I don't follow the instructions in the owner's manual are the consequences. If I do whatever I want to my car, I have to accept that it may stop doing what it was created to do.

It's the same with our bodies. God, who created us, gave us an instruction manual that tells us exactly what we can safely put into our "engines" to keep them running well. We can choose to follow those instructions and enjoy good health. Or we can ignore them and leave ourselves open for illness and disease. We're already starting with a strike against us: we live on a fallen planet. Even if we eat the healthiest diet in the world, we can still get sick simply because of all the pollution, chemicals, and additives in our environment and food supply. Doesn't it make sense to give ourselves the best chance at good health that we possibly can?

Ignore this week's nutritional villain or hero that magazines are screaming about, and instead take a look at the kinds of foods God created for us to eat in the first place. Fruits, vegetables, nuts, grains, seeds . . . these are all whole foods full of vitamins and nutrition. We're eating for strength; we need to give our bodies the best fuel possible.

Take a look at your own diet. Is there anything you're eating now that isn't the best for you? What would it take to get rid of it? Add, or at least try, one new food each week this month and next.

Spaceship in the Backyard

By faith, Noah built a ship in the middle of dry land.
He was warned about something he couldn't see,
and acted on what he was told. The result? His family was saved.
His act of faith drew a sharp line between the evil of the
unbelieving world and the rightness of the believing world.
As a result, Noah became intimate with God. **Hebrews 11:7, Message.**

Have you seen Rashid lately? He's gone completely off the deep end. You will never believe what he's doing. Get this: He's building a spaceship. You heard me right. Guess where he's building it— in his backyard. It's huge; it's like 10 stories high, and it's about three times longer than a football field. I'm telling you, it's a good thing he's got a big backyard.

"His parents don't seem to care. I saw his mom yesterday, and she said he's waiting on some parts he got by mail order, and in the meantime he's been going to that big warehouse store—you know the one where you can buy things in bulk—and stocking up on supplies. She said anyone who wanted to go with him could have a place on the spaceship. Supposedly everyone on the whole earth can fit.

"Why is he building it? That's a good question; that's what I asked her. She said that God told him a giant asteroid is going to hit the planet, and everyone will die unless they get on the spaceship and get clear of the earth's atmosphere before it hits. No joke. That's what she said. She had a straight face, too; I think she believes him."

Does this conversation sound fantastical to you? It's exactly the kind of conversation people were having when Noah was building the ark. They had never seen rain before, yet Noah said it would rain so hard that the earth would be flooded. He built a boat, a *huge* boat, on dry land. He said God talked to him and told him what was going to happen. If Noah lived next door to you right now, wouldn't you think he was crazy?

Walking by faith looks like that; it looks crazy from the outside. Walking by faith equals believing in things you can't see (such as a flood) or can't understand (such as rain). It's believing in them because God tells you they are real and not because you can explain them yourself. Faith always requires action on our part. Even though Noah had never heard of rain when God told him to build the ark, Noah started building. If you pray for rain and God tells you He's going to send it, get your umbrella out, because it's coming.

Priceless

See, I have engraved you on the palms of my hands;
your walls are ever before me. **Isaiah 49:16, NIV.**

The Kohinoor Diamond is priceless. No one knows exactly how much it's worth, because it's never been sold. It's been stolen a lot, bartered, and gifted, but never sold. Maybe we'll never know how much it's worth, because right now it's part of the British Crown Jewels—in fact, it's in Queen Elizabeth's crown, which is on display at the Tower of London—but the whole collection is worth $10 to $12 billion, and the Kohinoor is one of the most expensive diamonds in the collection.

Doesn't it sparkle when the light hits it? Prince Albert, who had it cut by Mr. Cantor (who worked on it for 38 days), was disappointed because after the diamond was cut, it didn't sparkle as much as it had before. Still, it's a pretty thing, and as we said, priceless. Would you like to have it?

Oops, I dropped it in a can of oil. Now it's all covered in nasty, sticky oil. Do you still want it? Are you sure? It's really gross. You'll have to wash it. Oops, dropped it in the gutter. Who knows what else is on it now? Lots of nasty germs, I'm sure. Do you still want it? Oops, dropped it again, into the sewage system of New York City. Major bad smells down there, but I can see it. Do you still want it? Really? You still want it? Even though it's all disgusting? You must really value it. I suppose, after all, no matter how dirty it is, it's still worth so much that it's priceless.

How many times in your life have you felt as sticky, gross, and disgusting as the Kohinoor Diamond down there in the sewer? People might look at you and think you're not very valuable—not looking (and smelling) like that. But God reached down from heaven and plucked you right up out of the sewer. He washed you off, and there you sit in His hand, sparkling the way you were meant to. Even after all you've been through, you never lost your value to Him. He always loved you, always cared about you, always wanted you, even when you gave up on yourself.

Right now, this very minute, what do you estimate your value is to God? Based on current, past, and future market value, I can tell you: You're priceless.

Betcha

*But people who long to be rich fall into temptation
and are trapped by many foolish and harmful desires that plunge
them into ruin and destruction. For the love of money is the root of all
kinds of evil. And some people, craving money, have wandered from the true
faith and pierced themselves with many sorrows.* **1 Timothy 6:9, 10, NLT.**

As I write this entry, everyone in America who has purchased a Powerball ticket is holding their breath right now. Why? Well, the estimated jackpot is $425 *million*. Of course, the winner won't get that much money. The amount of money they'll actually get to see is $278.3 million, but still, that's probably more money than you get for an allowance, right? It's nothing to sneeze at.

What these people may not realize is that the chance they will win the lottery is about 1 in 176 million. That means that if you were standing in a crowd of 176 million people during a thunderstorm, the chances that you would be struck by lightning are about the same as winning the lottery. To put it another way, did you know that in the United States each year approximately two people are crushed to death by vending machines? Odds are 1 in 160 million that one of those people will be you, which means that you have a better chance of being pulverized by a vending machine than you have of winning the lottery.

That doesn't stop people from buying lottery tickets and hoping to hit the jackpot. And most of them won't have a real problem with gambling. But thousands will, and they won't find out until it's too late. Addiction is sneaky that way. Once you're hooked, it'll be with you the rest of your life. It'll be something you have to avoid, try to ignore, and fight the pull from as it tries to drag you back.

Gambling may not even seem like a problem to most people, yet many gamblers' lives are destroyed by huge debt, and their every waking moment is spent thinking about the excitement of that next game. But even that is not the biggest problem with gambling. The Bible tells us that looking for fast money lures us away from God. When we're focused on gambling and hitting the next big jackpot, not only aren't we relying on God to provide for us, we're off chasing the pot of gold at the end of the rainbow instead of following God.

Have you ever thought about gambling? Do you think it's harmless? Is getting rich quick worth losing your faith over?

Snakebite

Their grapes are poison grapes,
their grape-clusters bitter. Their wine is rattlesnake venom,
mixed with lethal cobra poison. **Deuteronomy 32:32, 33, Message.**

When Rory called home, she was crying hysterically and didn't know where she was. Her mother said, "She kept saying, 'Mom, can you come get me?' but she had no idea where she was—and we live hours away. I've never been that scared—she could barely speak." Rory's parents told her to give her phone to someone who could tell them where she was. They called campus security at her school. When the officials found her, her face was covered with blood from breaking her nose when she fell, something Rory didn't remember doing because she was so drunk. Turns out she'd been drinking a concoction of very strong alcohol with friends.

Rory was an athlete and honor student who had never been in trouble, which just goes to show that even smart kids can get duped into drinking alcohol. The trouble is that when teens drink, they tend to binge-drink, and binge drinking is extremely dangerous. Dr. Mary Claire O'Brien, an emergency medicine doctor, says they're seeing kids come in to the emergency room with sky-high alcohol levels, four or five times the legal limit for driving. "That's the level at which 50 percent of people die," she says.

Energy drinks are partly to blame; teens are mixing them with alcohol. Alcohol makes you sleepy, which eventually makes you pass out and stop drinking, but caffeine keeps you awake to drink much more than you might have otherwise. "By the time many of these kids get to the hospital, they have to be put temporarily on respirators because of depressed breathing," Dr. O'Brien says.

Worse, a study of high school students found that hard liquor is replacing beer in drinking games, meaning that teens who play are consuming huge amounts of alcohol. But the teen brain is extremely sensitive to alcohol, and drinking kills off brain cells quickly. Researchers found that just one high dose of alcohol destroyed a significant amount of brain stem cells.

We're born with only so many brain cells. When they die, they're gone forever. The poison of alcohol will kill them just as surely as rattlesnake venom mixed with cobra poison would. Be kind to your brain cells; don't kill them off with alcohol. You'll need each and every one of them to get through life. God can accomplish much more through you if you're not brain-dead.

Checkup

Examine yourselves to see if your faith is genuine.
Test yourselves. Surely you know that Jesus Christ is among you; if not,
you have failed the test of genuine faith. **2 Corinthians 13:5, NLT.**

You've probably had a physical—or checkup—more than once in your life. Chances are you have one every year or every couple of years. Physicals are important for keeping track of our health. By knowing what is normal, doctors can tell us when something abnormal is going on in our bodies. Maybe you feel great, but you're tired all the time. During your physical your doctor discovers that you're anemic, and that's what's causing you to be tired.

In the same way that we need to have physical checkups, we should have a spiritual checkup to be sure that our faith is actually growing. Take a few minutes to take your spiritual temperature to see if you are growing toward God or away from Him.

Give yourself a spiritual checkup by answering the following questions:

1. When was the last time I talked to God? (Should be yesterday at the latest, but five minutes ago would be even better.)

2. What are God and I working on in my life right now? (Hint: your answer shouldn't be "nothing that I can think of.")

3. How is God making a difference in my life right now?

4. Do I have an active and growing prayer list that God and I go over every day?

5. When was the last time I read the Bible? (Hopefully this morning!)

6. How am I taking my faith to the streets? What outreach or church activities am I involved in, and why? (This is a motivation check; are you participating because your friends are, or are you participating because you want to do God's work? Being happy to do spiritual activities with your friends isn't wrong, but it shouldn't be the main reason you participate.)

7. Can I feel God's power in my life more or less every day?

Remember, if you aren't actively growing toward God, you're moving away from Him. The move may be so slow you don't notice unless you're really paying attention. However, if you constantly work on having a closer relationship with God, then you won't be able to drift away. Instead you'll grow closer to Him and more like Him each day. If your answers disappointed you, how can you improve them (get more spiritually healthy) before your next checkup?

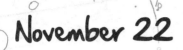

November 22

Mercy

Here's a word you can take to heart and depend on:
Jesus Christ came into the world to save sinners.
I'm proof—Public Sinner Number One—of someone who could
never have made it apart from sheer mercy. And now he shows me
off—evidence of his endless patience—to those who are right
on the edge of trusting him forever. I Timothy 1:15, 16, Message.

If you could go see one band or performing artist—just one—who would you choose?

For me that's an easy question. I'd pick Jars of Clay, my favorite band *evah*. For years I hoped they would come to a state near me—not my actual state, you understand, because it's small, and the only bands that play here are usually just stopping by on their way to Montreal. I would be happy if they would just come to one of the states somewhere near me.

This summer they were supposed to play in a neighboring state, but they got rained out. That's as close as they had ever come. So you can understand how shocked I was to find out that not only was Jars of Clay coming to play a concert near me, in my own state, but they were coming to my very own town! I bought my tickets so fast that there were skid marks on my credit card.

Now, can you imagine that I'm standing in line, ticket clutched in my sweaty little palm, and I see you? You're not dressed like you're going to a concert. In fact, you're in rough shape. You're dressed in rags, and you smell just awful. And your hair? Nightmare. You look at me with big puppy dog eyes and say, "I really, really want to go see the concert. Can I have your ticket?"

My ticket? Are you crazy? Nobody is getting my ticket. I planned for it. I paid for it. I got all dressed up. I'm waiting in line. I have every right to see Jars of Clay perform. But you look so sad—wait, are you crying?—that finally I sigh and say, "OK, here; take my ticket and go see Jars of Clay," and I hand over my precious ticket.

And that, my friends, would be mercy: getting something you don't deserve at someone else's expense. God showed us the greatest mercy by letting us into heaven on Jesus' ticket. We stood there in filthy clothes having a bad hair day, and before we could even ask, Jesus kindly gave us His ticket and His place. We got to go inside where *He* should have been to hear the angels sing, while He stayed outside where *we* should have been.

Still Small Voice

> The Lord said, "Go out and stand on the mountain
> in the presence of the Lord, for the Lord is about to pass by."
> Then a great and powerful wind tore the mountains apart and shattered
> the rocks before the Lord, but the Lord was not in the wind. After the wind
> there was an earthquake, but the Lord was not in the earthquake.
> After the earthquake came a fire, but the Lord was not in the fire. And after
> the fire came a gentle whisper. When Elijah heard it, he pulled his cloak
> over his face and went out and stood at the mouth of the cave. Then a voice
> said to him, "What are you doing here, Elijah?" **I Kings 19:11-13, NIV.**

Air traffic controllers are folks who keep all the airplanes flying over our heads from crashing into each other and help them land safely, one at a time, in various airports all across the United States. They have an extremely important job that's very stressful and challenging. Around the world it's considered one of the most difficult jobs there is. If you held the fate of hundreds of people in your hands and relied on communication equipment that could blink out at any time, wouldn't you be a little stressed out? Yeah, me too.

If you'd like to get a taste of what air traffic control is all about, you can listen in on radio conversations between air traffic controllers and pilots at your favorite airport. Just check out www.liveatc.net. Imagine you're a pilot flying a plane full of people, and suddenly you decide you're sick of listening to the air traffic controller. You'd rather listen to your favorite tunes. So you switch them off and plug in your iPod instead. How would you feel if the plane you were piloting crashed and burned because you chose to stop listening to the person who was keeping you safe?

Yet that's what people do every time they take drugs or drink alcohol. I worked with a man once who speaks to hundreds of kids every year to warn them about the effects of drugs and alcohol. He's passionate about his work because he knows what it's like; he used to use drugs and alcohol himself. "Do you know what the worst thing is?" he asked me once. "When you're under the influence of drugs and alcohol, it dulls your mind. You can't hear God's still small voice anymore."

Make sure you can hear God's still small voice when He asks you, "What are you doing here, _____ [fill in your name]?" Then follow His directions to get safely back home.

November 24

Exposed

Don't fool yourself. Don't think that you can be wise merely by being up-to-date with the times. Be God's fool—that's the path to true wisdom. What the world calls smart, God calls stupid. It's written in Scripture, He exposes the chicanery of the chic. The Master sees through the smoke screens of the know-it-alls. I Corinthians 3:18-20, Message.

I f I told you that cigarettes were "sensuous and luxurious," would you believe me? That's what a sign advertising cigarettes outside my neighborhood Quik Stop tried to tell me. I didn't believe it because I know better. I know that cigarettes will make you cough like an old clunker in the morning, stain your fingers and teeth brown, and make your breath, clothes, car, and everything exposed to the smoke smell like an ashtray. It's also very likely they'll give you lung cancer. I've watched people die from lung cancer, and it's not pretty. But if I was trying to sell them to you, I'd never tell you that.

Fortunately the government requires that cigarette manufacturers put a label on every pack stating something like: "SURGEON GENERAL'S WARN-ING: Smoking Causes Lung Cancer, Heart Disease, Emphysema, and May Complicate Pregnancy." Despite the warning, people still buy and smoke cigarettes. Although the United States was the first country to make tobacco companies put a health warning on cigarettes, we sure aren't the only ones. Other countries are even blunter about their warnings than we are. Italy's cigarette packages have a variety of messages. One flat out says: "Smoking kills."

Although tobacco companies know that smoking cigarettes causes cancer, they still work very hard to sell them. They want to make money, and it doesn't matter whom they harm in order to do it. They'll say anything to sell cigarettes. If they can get you to believe that smoking will somehow make your life better, they can make you take that first puff, and then, because they put addictive chemicals into their tobacco, they'll have you hooked.

Lying for profit is nothing new; it was Satan's first gig. The same lines that worked on Eve still work on us today: "If you do this, you'll be like God." Any sin has this at its root. Sin is always an effort for us to make ourselves like God. It's important to be able to see through the smoke screen to the truth. Ask God to blow the smoke away from Satan's lies and expose the truth so you can walk in it.

Human Beings

If someone claims, "I know him well!" but doesn't keep his commandments, he's obviously a liar. His life doesn't match his words. But the one who keeps God's word is the person in whom we see God's mature love. This is the only way to be sure we're in God. Anyone who claims to be intimate with God ought to live the same kind of life Jesus lived. **I John 2:4-6, Message.**

Once upon a time there was a goat who wanted to be a dog. Now, I don't know how much you know about goats, but if you've ever seen one, you'll know that there is no way anyone would mistake it for a dog. First of all, most goats have horns, and dogs never do. Dogs bark; goats bleat. Dogs have paws; goats have hooves. Dogs eat meat; goats eat grass.

But this goat wanted to be a dog. So he trimmed off his horns, taught himself how to bark, and tried to hide his hooves whenever he could. Then he went inside the house and curled up by the fire. When the man who lived there came home, the goat ran to the door and barked. He licked the man's face and acted as though he was happy to see him. When the man went to bed, the goat curled up on the floor by his bed. He was tired; it's hard work being a dog when you're a goat.

The goat stuck with it. He learned how to play fetch. He learned how to guard the man's house. He even managed to plug his nose and eat dog food, even though it was disgusting. But he never felt comfortable being a dog; it just wasn't in him. Finally one day he gave up and went outside to eat grass. When the man came home that night, his "dog" was gone, but he had a really great goat outside.

There's a popular saying that goes something like "I'm a human being, not a human doing." We are human beings; that's what we are. The things that we do don't make us human beings; they just make us human beings who *do* something: human *doings.* When one of those things is being a Christian, we become people who do what Christians do. But we don't become Christians by doing what Christians do any more than the goat can become a dog by doing what dogs do.

Fortunately, we have something the goat doesn't have. We have a Creator God who can make Christians from human beings. You can try to be a Christian all you want, but you won't actually be one until you turn yourself over to God. Ask Him today to change *you.*

November 26

The Acknowledgments

Enter into His gates with thanksgiving, and into His courts with praise. Be thankful to Him, and bless His name. **Psalm 100:4, NKJV.**

When you're reading a book, do you ever stop and read over the acknowledgments? This is the place where the author takes time to give a shout-out to all the people who supported him or her through the writing of the book. For particularly grateful authors this list can be quite long, and most people probably won't take the time to read through a bunch of names of people they don't know receiving thanks for things they don't care about. "Thanks to my good pal Sammy for bringing me a pizza when I was trying to write chapter four. And a big thank-you to my writing group for all the great comments . . ." Unless your name is listed in there somewhere, what do you really care about how grateful they are, anyway?

Authors are fortunate in that they have the opportunity to thank the people who have helped them finish a big project, but just because you're not an author doesn't mean you can't take time to appreciate the people in your life who have helped you, supported you, or guided you since last Thanksgiving at this time. In fact, this is a perfect time to take a moment and let the people in your life know how much you love and appreciate them. Why not start a new Thanksgiving holiday tradition of acknowledgments? Why should authors have all the fun?

If you consider your life since last year as a book you've just written, who are the people you would thank, and what would you thank them for? Make a list of their names and the reason you are grateful to them. Don't worry if it sounds cheesy; have you ever once thought someone sounded cheesy when they were thanking you for something? Me neither. If you like, when your list is complete, share it with your loved ones during Thanksgiving dinner.

Take It to the Streets: This activity can be done alone. You don't have to read it aloud at the Thanksgiving table, but imagine the looks on the faces of the people you are grateful to if you did. If you want company, invite others to share their own acknowledgments. Who knows, maybe you'll even find yourself in their list and realize that you helped them without even knowing it. Consider making the acknowledgments a Thanksgiving tradition. And while you're thanking folks, don't forget God. Our deepest gratitude should be toward Him and all He's done for us in the past year. Be thankful to Him and bless His name!

November 27

Thanks Living

Jesus asked, "Didn't I heal ten men? Where are the other nine? Has no one returned to give glory to God except this foreigner?" And Jesus said to the man, "Stand up and go. Your faith has healed you." **Luke 17:17-19, NLT.**

Today many people all over America will be counting their blessings as they help themselves to seconds (or thirds) of mashed potatoes and to-furkey. But how many of those people will take that same attitude of gratitude with them for the next 364 days? Probably not many.

Science is just beginning to understand what Christians have known all along: Gratitude is good for you. The trouble is that we have so much to be grateful for that we take it for granted. Usually it isn't until we lose something that we begin to understand how important it was to us: our health, our job, our family or friends, our ability to do something we love.

An article in the *Wall Street Journal* quoted Robert Emmons, who is considered a pioneer in the area of gratitude research, as saying: "As simple as it sounds, gratitude is actually a demanding, complex emotion that requires 'self-reflection, the ability to admit that one is dependent upon the help of others, and the humility to realize one's own limitations.'"

The article goes on to say: "Being grateful also forces people to overcome what psychologists call the 'negativity bias'—the innate tendency to dwell on problems, annoyances, and injustices rather than upbeat events. Focusing on blessings can help ward off depression and build resilience in times of stress, grief, or disasters, according to studies of people impacted by the September 11 terror attacks and Hurricane Katrina."

Of the 10 lepers that Jesus healed, only one came back to thank Him. Only one was grateful and focused on his blessings. The others disappeared from the Bible account, scattered back to their homes and families. Only one realized he'd been given a gift, sought out the Giver, and said thank You. God showers us with gifts every day. Have you said thank You?

Dietrich Bonhoeffer, German pastor and martyr, said: "In ordinary life we hardly realize that we receive a great deal more than we give, and that it is only with gratitude that life becomes rich." Today, write down a list of what God has done for you. Take the time to share it with someone else; exchange lists if you can. Do your own experiment. Keep a journal of things you are grateful for and see if it makes a difference in your mood and how you see life.

Thankful

So to keep me from becoming proud, I was given a thorn in my flesh, a messenger from Satan to torment me and keep me from becoming proud. Three different times I begged the Lord to take it away. Each time he said, "My grace is all you need. My power works best in weakness." So now I am glad to boast about my weaknesses, so that the power of Christ can work through me. **2 Corinthians 12:7-9, NLT.**

When I was in tenth grade, one of my best friends was a dude we called Snaz, which was what he told us to call him, and he was scary enough that most people generally did what he said. Snaz and I were the only two students in a Seventh-day Adventist academy who weren't actually Seventh-day Adventists at the time. That gave us a common bond. We were the rebels; we could get away with stuff the churchy kids couldn't. Snaz had even been in a gang.

That's kind of funny to think back on now, because both Snaz and I are as close to God as we can get, and we wouldn't have it any other way. I still keep up with him because he's on Facebook, and I see what he's up to. In 2003 he was deployed in Iraq, where he was injured in an explosion. The force of the blast knocked him out, and when he came to he had a cut on his arm and a slight limp. He thought he'd been one of the lucky ones, one of the ones who had walked away without any life-changing consequences.

But he started to notice things that weren't quite right. His vision was off, and his limp began getting worse. Tests later showed that he had suffered a traumatic brain injury, and several parts of his brain had been affected. Today he struggles with many physical difficulties, but the part that will surprise you is that he is *thankful*.

"I have learned humility," Snaz says. "I was once a very proud man who thought it was great to be able to run younger men and women into the ground and barely break a sweat. Now, many times, I need help just getting my shoes on. To walk any great distance is a massive chore, yet I am thankful. Not because it is difficult, but because it has made me a much more humble and compassionate man to those who are hurting."

It's not easy to see disabilities the way God sees them. He gifts them to us so that we can rely on Him all the more. And when we do, His great power shines through our weakness with more brilliance than it otherwise could.

Just the Opposite

What I don't understand about myself is that I decide one way, but then I act another, doing things I absolutely despise. So if I can't be trusted to figure out what is best for myself and then do it, it becomes obvious that God's command is necessary. **Romans 7:15, 16, Message.**

Have you ever wanted to do something, but no matter how hard you try, you just can't seem to be able to make yourself do it? Or you want to stop doing something, and no matter how hard you try, you can't stop? You are not alone. If you are human, you struggle with that problem. You may even know that what you are doing is wrong and that it is bad for you, but you just can't seem to stop.

I know—I've been there, done that. So has Kara, a first-year college student. She says, "In high school I was completely anti-partying and anti-drugs, I thought they were the worst thing in the world. And now that I do it, I feel like a hypocrite. I told my friends over and over that they need to be careful, and here I am doing the same thing. I don't know what to do about that! My prayer is that God gives me a clear view of the plans that he has for me. I pray that I can be light that can look back on my past and say, 'Yeah, I did those things, but now I am free, and God has changed my life.'"

While Kara might be struggling right now, she's on the right track. She recognizes that only God can change her life. Admitting that we can't help ourselves is the beginning of giving God our problems. We can see what we're doing wrong when we compare our behavior with God's law, but that only convicts us; it proves that we're guilty as charged. Grace is our "get out of jail free" card; only when we accept Jesus' sacrifice on our behalf can we be saved. And only with Christ's power in our lives changing us one step at a time, one day at a time, are we *able* to change.

Those things, as Paul says, that we despise and don't want to do, we'll stop doing them. Not because we finally work up enough willpower to do it, but because God will change us from the inside out. Not only will we despise those things, but we won't want to do them anymore, either. When Satan tempts us, it will be like trying to get us to eat dirt; we won't have any interest. That's what the power of God working in our lives does: it changes us from the inside out and makes us people who can overcome anything.

Tarnished Reputation

And when Saul had come to Jerusalem, he tried to join the disciples;
but they were all afraid of him, and did not believe that he was a disciple.
But Barnabas took him and brought him to the apostles.
And he declared to them how he had seen the Lord on the road,
and that He had spoken to him, and how he had preached boldly
at Damascus in the name of Jesus. **Acts 9:26, 27, NKJV.**

Paul had a big problem. He'd done such a good job of persecuting Christians that he had quite a reputation. He was so famous, in fact, that even without nightly news, radio, or Internet, Christians everywhere were scared to death of him. It was no wonder that no one believed him when he showed up in Jerusalem claiming to have had a change of heart. Even the disciples were afraid of him.

Fortunately for Paul, he knew a guy named Barnabas who could vouch for him. Barnabas had to take Paul to the disciples himself and stand up for Paul. He had seen Paul in action in Damascus and knew that he wasn't a fraud. For Barnabas it was probably a bit like showing up at a pool party with a shark and trying to convince all the swimmers that it had become a vegetarian and really wasn't going to eat any of them for lunch. Because the disciples knew and trusted Barnabas, they finally accepted Paul, but I bet they watched their backs for a while.

New Christians often have bad reputations that they have to live down. People who knew them in their sin-filled lives don't believe that their change is genuine or that it will last. Christians in the churches they hope to join want to see proof before they'll believe those sinners are safe to have around. They need someone like Barnabas to stick up for them, encourage them, introduce them to friends, and teach them how to behave in the church.

Being like Barnabas isn't easy. He stuck his neck out. If Paul had been pretending to be a Christian in order to spy on the disciples so he could arrest them, Barnabas would have been blamed as a traitor for betraying them. Barnabas had to be a strong character. He had to trust Paul and God and his own judgment. And he could have been wrong. If we stick up for sinners who are trying to live down their reputations, we can be wrong too. But Barnabas didn't let that risk stop him, and neither should we.

Do you know a new Christian trying to live down a reputation from their former life? Take them under your wing and be a Barnabas to them.

Your Wildest Dreams

God can do anything, you know—far more
than you could ever imagine or guess or request
in your wildest dreams! He does it not by pushing us around
but by working within us, his Spirit deeply and gently within us.
Glory to God in the church! Glory to God in the Messiah,
in Jesus! Glory down all the generations! Glory through all millennia!
Oh, yes! **Ephesians 3:20, 21, Message.**

Right about now the upscale department store Neiman Marcus is probably releasing their Christmas catalog of posh gifts that most people can only dream about, which is probably why the most expensive ones are called fantasy gifts. These such things as a dancing fountain installation for $1 million, a yurt called Dream Folly decked out with antiques and luxuries that is a steal for $75,000, a Ferrari that can go faster than 200 miles per hour for $395,000 (that's almost $2,000 per mph!), and a $250,000 Hacker-Craft speedboat. There are cheaper items, of course, but "cheap" is a relative term, and nothing in this catalog is what I think of as cheap.

I did not grow up in a rich family; we didn't have a lot of worldly wealth. I learned how to make do and reuse things—it's a great skill to have. I still use it because I don't have a lot of worldly wealth now. But I trust God to provide for my needs, and He always does.

Still, I always shoot low. I always ask for just enough. I'm always skimpy with my prayers. I even used to doubt that God wanted me to have nice things. I doubted God was *generous*. Can you imagine that? The God who gave us an entire planet, stars, sun, moon, solar system, oceans, animals, and ultimately His own Son is the very *essence* of generosity.

God *wants* to give us good things. Jesus tells us that God wants to give us good things even more than the humans who love us want to give us good things. He's waiting for us to ask. God has all the resources of heaven and earth. We could ask all day, every day, for the rest of our lives, and everyone we know could ask too, and He'd never run out of resources. Be bold! Ask God for whatever you need; if you see someone else in need, ask for them, too.

Try This: In a notebook, write down on the left side your requests, and on the right side, write down how God responds. See if He doesn't give you more than you imagine or guess or request in *your* wildest dreams.

December 2

The Cross in Christmas

"You are a king, then!" said Pilate. Jesus answered,
"You say that I am a king. In fact, the reason I was born
and came into the world is to testify to the truth.
Everyone on the side of truth listens to me." **John 18:37, NIV.**

It happens every year about this time. People start wishing each other a "Merry Xmas." Eventually, someone, usually a Christian, will protest, saying that non-Christians are trying to take Christ out of Christmas. This is a tricky subject, because in many ways people *are* taking Christ out of Christmas. Religious-themed Christmas carols can't be sung in public schools anymore. Some towns won't allow a Nativity scene to be set up. There is a movement in some places to replace "Merry Christmas" with the more religiously neutral "Happy Holidays."

But when Christians take offense, they don't make any friends for Christ by making snarky comments to people who may or may not even believe yet. One year someone I know threatened to unfriend anyone who posted "Xmas" as part of their status on Facebook. And a friend of mine soundly thrashed someone who posted a message containing the abbreviation "Xmas." What kind of impression of Christ's followers does that give? Not a good one. Imagine if you offhandedly referenced "Xmas" and someone slammed you for it. What would you think of Christians? Probably that they are all snobbish and bad-tempered. There isn't anything remotely resembling the Christmas—or Christian—spirit in that, is there?

I'm not a big fan of the abbreviation, but I'd never given it much thought until the firestorms began cropping up each Christmas. There would be the unthinking, in-the-Christmas-spirit people, and the outspoken Christians waiting in the wings to pounce on anyone who so much as whispered the abbreviation "Xmas." When my friend was chastised for using "Xmas," it made me give some thought to the abbreviation.

What is an "X" but a cross? Isn't it perfectly acceptable to put a cross in Christmas? After all, Jesus was born specifically to die on the cross. His birth led to His death on a cross. If you think about it, including a cross in Christmas not only honors Christ's birth but points directly to His saving death . . . on the cross.

No doubt you've seen the Christmas versus Xmas debates raging. What do you think? Be prepared to defend your answer to others, because 'tis the season.

Two Hands

The world of the generous gets larger and larger;
the world of the stingy gets smaller and smaller.
The one who blesses others is abundantly blessed; those who
help others are helped. **Proverbs 11:24, 25, Message.**

One of the things everyone looks forward to at Christmas is getting presents. And why shouldn't we look forward to it? When we're very small, one of the first things we remember about Christmas is all the new toys we get. We see the pile of pretty packages stacked up under the tree and try to imagine what wonderful goodies are inside. Everyone is excited to watch us open our presents. Getting presents is fun!

Then we grow up, and suddenly people expect us to give *them* presents. When I was in high school, I used to spend Christmas Eve running around the mall trying to buy Christmas presents for everyone on my list. I made an effort to find something I thought they would like, but obviously I didn't put much thought into it beforehand.

Just why are we giving presents, anyway? Is it something that's required? For example, if Aunt Sally gives me a present, then I have to give her a present, too. Or are we giving gifts to show the special people in our lives that we love them? It makes a difference because giving gifts at Christmas can become a chore if our hearts aren't in the right place. If you are spending money you worked hard for at a part-time job when you could have been having fun instead, you can even start to resent having to blow it on gifts for other people.

This is one case in which attitude really matters. While the Christmas holiday isn't focused on gifts (hopefully it's focused on Jesus!), we have to admit that in our culture it's a large part of our celebration. The evangelist Billy Graham said, "God has given us two hands—one to receive with, and the other to give with. We are not cisterns made for hoarding; we are channels made for sharing." Make sure your heart is in the right place this Christmas season so your gifts will flow in one hand and out the other.

Giving gifts is about more than money. The object is to give from your heart, cheerfully and happily, not grudgingly. If money is tight, make gifts for your loved ones, or give service coupons for things like washing someone's car or packing their lunch for a week. There are many ways you can get creative with gifts. Surf the Internet for more ideas.

December 4

Text Me

Therefore you shall lay up these words of mine in your heart and in your soul, and bind them as a sign on your hand, and they shall be as frontlets between your eyes. **Deuteronomy 11:18, NKJV.**

Pop quiz: How many Bible texts can you recite from memory?
A. Five to 10
B. 10 to 20
C. 20 to 30
D. 50 or more
E. Texts? Forget single texts—I can recite whole books of the Bible.

If you think E is a misprint, guess again. Ben Stevens, a theologian from Berlin, Germany, said he'd never been very good at memorizing Bible texts until he asked for some advice from his friend Paul Larson. Paul not only memorizes scriptures by the chapter, but he performs a one-man act in which he does nothing but recite entire epistles. (You can find him on YouTube. Search "Paul Larson Romans.") Ben says that Paul is on track to have memorized the entire New Testament by 2015. Ben wanted to know his secret; frankly, so did I. Do you?

There are many ways to memorize portions of Scripture, involving writing out texts or entire sections and carrying them with you, reviewing them again and again. Books have been written to teach methods for this type of learning. But here's how Paul does it. He chooses a book to learn and then listens to an audio recording of it. He breaks it down into manageable sections and listens to it every day for three months.

The first month the material is all new to him. By the second month he starts to remember parts of it. By the third month all he has to do is tweak what he's learned. Paul uses his iPod to listen to whatever portion he's working on while he runs errands and does housework.

Using Paul's method, Ben has memorized the first eight chapters of John. He says, "It is the inspired Word of God, and in committing it to heart, we are in fact internalizing the God-revealed answers to the mysteries into which every society in all human history has desired to look. Could there be a greater privilege or more worthwhile investment for a Christian?"

Treasures

*"Don't hoard treasure down here where it gets eaten
by moths and corroded by rust or—worse!—stolen by burglars.
Stockpile treasure in heaven, where it's safe from moth and rust and burglars.
It's obvious, isn't it? The place where your treasure is, is the place you will
most want to be, and end up being."* **Matthew 6:19-21, Message.**

Put it down; put it down, or I'll shoot you in the face!" At first Abdullah Shakeri, aide to the Dubai royal family, thought the men were joking. Shakeri was carrying two suitcases full of money. Inside was £2 million (about $3 million) for the royal family to spend on holiday. (I know who I want to go on vacation with next year!) He had put one suitcase into the trunk, or boot, as the Brits call it, when the armed men came up from behind him.

When they repeated their threat and told Shakeri to run or he'd be shot, he realized they were serious and ran into a nearby shop. The thieves grabbed the cases and fled. Police found the money later, along with two of the thieves. I'm sure the royal family was very happy to get its petty cash back.

Everybody, it seems, wants money. Some people want it so much that they work all the time and squirrel it away like Ebenezer Scrooge, Charles Dickens' character in *A Christmas Carol*. Some people, such as the gang who stole the Dubai royal family's vacation money, want it so much they take it from other people . . . at gunpoint if necessary. Others invest their money in things: land, stocks, bonds, businesses. Sometimes these things pay off, and other times they fail, and the money is all lost.

Money is not a bad thing. God knows that we need money to live. The trouble comes when we want money so much that we have an unhealthy attitude about it. God doesn't want us to store up treasures—money and possessions—here because that's not what we're here for. We're here to tell everyone the good news. We can trust God to take care of our needs.

Sacrificial giving is giving even when it "hurts." This kind of giving is personal. It means that while you are supplying someone else's needs you yourself may have to go without. This principle doesn't just relate to money; it could relate to time or talents. This week, find at least one way to give sacrificially.

December 6

Pray Tell

*Live creatively, friends. If someone falls into sin,
forgivingly restore him, saving your critical comments for yourself.
You might be needing forgiveness before the day's out. Stoop down
and reach out to those who are oppressed. Share their burdens,
and so complete Christ's law. If you think you are too good
for that, you are badly deceived.* **Galatians 6:1-3, Message.**

You have friends, of course, but do you have a group of friends who really care about you as a Christian? Do they care about your struggles and your needs? Do you have friends whom you can call when you need prayer for something you're going through? Do you have friends who will support you even when you fall down, instead of blabbing your problems around school or making fun of you? Do you have friends who will hold you accountable, who will encourage you to do what's right even when you don't feel like it and you want to give up? Do you have friends who will jump in and help when there's a need somewhere?

We all need those kinds of friends. They are the type of people Paul was encouraging us to be for each other when he wrote to the Galatians. Life is hard on us; our friends shouldn't be. Especially not our Christian friends. People in the military form exceptionally close bonds with each other because they are fighting a common enemy, and so are we. But finding these sorts of friends doesn't just happen. We have to search for them and collect them like priceless objects.

You might have to get creative about finding them. Maybe you have some friends online who would be willing to start a prayer and support group to encourage each other. Or you could have friends at school. Don't wait for them to make the first move. They could be waiting for you to suggest forming a group. You never know until you ask.

Building a small group for encouragement and support may be a good way of joining two worlds if you don't attend a church school. You can bring your school friends and your church friends together. You want a small enough group that everyone can stay in touch easily through texting, e-mail, phone, or in person.

Some ideas: Start a prayer chain. Choose someone new each day that everyone in the group shows support to by sending an encouraging message or by praying especially for them. Pick out a service project that you can all work on together. Forgive each other, love each other, and work together to spread the gospel. That's real Christian unity.

Great Day in the Morning

For they are spirits of demons, performing signs,
which go out to the kings of the earth and
of the whole world, to gather them to the battle of
that great day of God Almighty. **Revelation 16:14, NKJV.**

President Franklin D. Roosevelt proclaimed December 7, 1941, a date that would "live in infamy," meaning a state of extreme dishonor. If you haven't been dozing off in history class, you probably know why—on this day all those years ago, the Japanese bombed Pearl Harbor, causing the United States to declare war on them the very next day. Considering that the reason they bombed Pearl Harbor was to prevent the United States from interfering with attacks they had scheduled, it sounds like somebody made a boo-boo when they came up with that plan.

If you just compared casualties, you might come to a different conclusion. The United States lost 2,402 American lives that day, and 1,282 were wounded. The Japanese had only 65 lives lost or wounded. That's just lives, which can't be replaced or rebuilt. The United States also lost all kinds of equipment, ships, and planes, but the Japanese losses were light. If you looked only at that battle, you might have been tempted to surrender right then.

Compared to Japan, the United States was a big, hulking giant, but a lot of their military power had just been crippled or destroyed. Did that lose the war for us? No. Many people sifting through the ashes of Pearl Harbor, mourning loved ones, might have been tempted to think resistance was futile after such a barbaric surprise attack. But no matter how bleak it might have looked from ground zero, history doesn't record that Japan won the war. They didn't lose through any one huge battle, but over time they experienced many losses that finally forced them to admit defeat.

Does that sound like any story you're familiar with? Been through any Pearl Harbors lately? We're involved in a war, and every day is one that will live in infamy. From here it sometimes doesn't seem like it will ever end, or that we can ever win. Watch the news or read a newspaper and tell me it doesn't seem like the enemy is doing some serious winning. Except that he's not. It only looks that way down here in the ashes.

There's a great big battle coming. We've got the inside scoop. We already know how it will end. So does the enemy, and he's getting desperate. As well he should: the day of God is coming, and it's gonna be a great day.

December 8

Perfect Peace

People with their minds set on you, you keep completely whole, steady on their feet, because they keep at it and don't quit. Depend on God and keep at it because in the Lord God you have a sure thing. **Isaiah 26:3, 4, Message.**

Have you ever gone through something difficult and felt worried, anxious, or upset? Me, too. In fact, that's how I go though most difficult experiences. That is, until lately. Recently God's been showing me how to stick with Him like glue. He is teaching me to bring my mind back to Him constantly throughout the day. I'm learning how to trust Him with everything in my life, not just the hard things. Even the easy things that I think I can handle myself turn out better when I'm getting help from God to do them instead of doing them alone.

Right now I'm going through a very difficult experience. My favorite pet—a little blue rabbit named Fergal—ripped the ligaments in his jaw. Apparently he got his bottom teeth stuck around the cage wire and pulled too hard to get them out. Now his jaw doesn't work. The vet says that if he can learn how to eat on his own again he'll live. Otherwise he'll have to be put down, because eventually he'll starve to death.

I prayed for him all the way to the vet's office. I prayed for him in the waiting room and in the examination room. Because I have placed myself in God's care, everything under *my* care is in God's care, too, and the Bible tells us that God cares about the fate of every living creature, even little sparrows. "Are not two sparrows sold for a copper coin? And not one of them falls to the ground apart from your Father's will" (Matthew 10:29, NKJV).

The verse that keeps coming into my mind is: "You will keep in perfect peace all who trust in you, all whose thoughts are fixed on you!" (Isaiah 26:3, NLT). Thoughts, though, are slippery things. It's almost Christmas right now, and I find myself wondering how I'll cope if I have to have Fergal put down just before Christmas. *Stop! Fix your thoughts on Me.* Which rabbit will come to live upstairs if I have to put Fergal down? *Stop! Fix your thoughts on Me.* How I will ever be able to stop crying if . . . *Stop! Fix your thoughts on Me.*

Again and again I have to stop, regroup, and place my trust and my confidence in God. I have to trust that God loves me, will not let me face anything He knows I won't be able to handle, and has my best interests in mind. And that is more than good enough for me. Is it good enough for you?

Bad Hair Days

We can rejoice, too, when we run into problems and trials,
for we know that they help us develop endurance.
And endurance develops strength of character, and character
strengthens our confident hope of salvation. **Romans 5:3, 4, NLT.**

Have you ever had the kind of day when you wake up in the morning and you're already grumpy? It's all downhill from there. We all have those kinds of days. I'm having one right now. Nothing has gone right since my feet hit the floor, and I just want to crawl right back into bed and skip the whole day. But that would be a silly waste of time, wouldn't it?

Bad days come to us all. No one likes them, but everyone has them. When you're in the middle of one, it seems like it will never end. Problems and trials—the stuff that makes up your average bad day—are supposed to help us develop endurance, but what they more often turn into is failure and discouragement. If we don't develop endurance, we can't move on to strength of character, which strengthens our confident hope of salvation. So bad days leave us feeling helpless, hopeless, discouraged, and alone.

What's the answer? That's easy. We have to start looking at bad days the right way, as hurdles to jump over, not huddle under. Bad days will always have us beat until we do one simple thing: surrender. Not to the bad day, but to God's plan for us through the trials and problems that seem so overwhelming. You can't do that by gritting your teeth and hanging on by your fingernails. It starts slowly, way before you even open your eyes on the bad day.

Marathon runners are famous for their endurance, but they do not jump out of bed one day with the ability to run 26 long miles. They develop their endurance slowly, one short run at a time, which leads to longer runs, and finally to a marathon. In the same way, we develop Christian endurance through trials; one small trial at a time. If we don't, we'll never have the strength to make it through the marathon of a bad day full of trials, problems, and tests.

Someone who has run a marathon knows that no matter how they feel at mile 1, or mile 10, or mile 17, or mile 23, the marathon will end at mile 26.2. They can hang on to their hope that it will end because they've done it before in training. They have seen the finish line. Run your small races—irritations, upsets, and disasters—faithfully, and God will give you the endurance you need to run through a whole bad day and cross the finish line with confidence.

December 10

Too Much Information

Let the words of my mouth and the meditation of my heart be acceptable in Your sight, O Lord, my strength and my Redeemer. **Psalm 19:14, NKJV.**

Have you ever spilled your guts to someone and then later felt sick about it, wondering if you said too much? If so, you, my friend, have over-shared. While oversharing with people has always been an occasional problem, social networking has taken it to a new and dangerous level. Things you say; pictures you post; and events, groups, and people you like are all easy for your friends to share with their friends at the click of a mouse. Suddenly your likes, dislikes, tastes, and preferences have been seen by hundreds, some-times thousands, of people you never intended to see them.

Ashley Johnson's public Facebook gripe about cheap customers who tied up one of her tables for three hours got her fired from the restaurant at which she was a server. Rachel Ross, 15, posted an invitation to a party at her house while her parents were away at a wedding. Dozens of *adult* gatecrashers who saw the invite online crashed the party and trashed the house.

Lane Sutton, a 15-year-old social media coach, has these suggestions to help teens avoid oversharing:

1. Share with real friends, the kind you can see face to face and trust.

2. Turn off location-based apps and settings that will tell others exactly where in the world you are at any given moment. Some apps display this infor-mation for everyone to see.

3. Turn off instant sharing from apps that track your activity.

4. Update your privacy settings every three months in case policies have changed.

When it comes to sharing, some things are universal. We are accountable for the words we speak, whether they are spoken out loud or in pixels. As Christians we are accountable not only to the people we speak to and about, but to God, who is represented by the things that we say. When it comes to sharing, God is the only one we can safely overshare with. For anyone else, think hard before you speak or type. Once they leave your head, those words will always belong to you. Be sure they're ones you don't mind keeping, and bear in mind this biblical advice about oversharing: "Too much talk leads to sin. Be sensible and keep your mouth shut" (Proverbs 10:19, NLT).

Crash Landing

And then he told them, "Go into all the world and preach the Good News to everyone. Anyone who believes and is baptized will be saved. But anyone who refuses to believe will be condemned." **Mark 16:15, 16, NLT.**

It's a beautiful day. You're flying to visit your grandma on the other side of the United States. The plane is crammed full of passengers; every seat is taken. Just before the flight attendant starts distributing peanuts and hand wipes, the pilot comes on the intercom. "Ladies and gentlemen, I'm sorry to inform you that both wings have fallen off the plane, and we're going to crash. We're so high up that the impact will incinerate every bit of the plane when we land."

Instantly panic breaks out. People are screaming, yelling, crying, and hyperventilating. They all know they are about to die, and there's nothing anyone can do about it—until you stand up, raise your hands, and say, "Please, everyone, keep calm. I happen to know that there are exactly the right number of parachutes on the plane so that everyone who wants one can safely evacuate. Simply line up in an orderly fashion, and I'll begin handing them out right now."

How many people do you think would line up for a parachute? I'm guessing it would be every one of them, and chances are pretty good that there would be a lot of people cutting line to get them, too. Now, this story is an allegory about witnessing, so each part of it represents something else. In this case, you represent yourself. The other passengers on the plane represent the entire population of the world. The parachutes represent salvation. The pilot represents the Holy Spirit. The flight attendant is just in the story to hand out peanuts and hand wipes.

Now, when you think about witnessing, if you're like 99.9 percent of people you probably get sweaty palms and heart palpitations because you think that in order to witness *you have to convince people to become Christians.* That's not actually true. We really have a pretty easy job. We just have to deliver the good news: We get to stand up and tell everyone that there's a parachute available for everyone who wants one. Pretty easy, right? The Holy Spirit (portrayed by the pilot in our story) is the one responsible for convincing people they *need* a parachute. If He had announced the plane was crashing but no one believed Him, they wouldn't have paid any attention to you when you offered to hand out parachutes, right? When it comes to witnessing, all we have to do is extend the invitation. The Holy Spirit will convict people when the time is right.

December 12

Climbing the Walls

*So I decided there is nothing better than to enjoy
food and drink and to find satisfaction in work. Then I realized that
these pleasures are from the hand of God.* **Ecclesiastes 2:24, NLT.**

I am scared of heights. There, I said it. I can't look over the side of a cliff without feeling woozy. I can't climb a ladder without getting dizzy. And those glass elevators that go up the sides of buildings? They are very scary. So what business do I have thinking about trying out rock climbing? That's a very good question, and I'm glad you asked.

First, let me ask you a question: When was the last time you did something fun that wasn't exactly in your comfort zone? Have you challenged yourself lately? Have you tried something you've been wanting to do but never actually did because it made you nervous? I'm not talking about something you *shouldn't* do. I'm talking about something healthy and fun that you'd like to try but just thinking about it makes your stomach drop a little.

It's easy to get into a rut and just do the same things we've always done simply because we've always done them. And if you're happy about that, there's no real reason to change. But if there's something you've been wanting to do, you shouldn't let fear stop you either. Fear can be healthy; it can keep us from being careless and getting hurt, it can keep us from rushing into something recklessly, and it can prevent us from doing something foolish. But if we aren't careful, it can also prevent us from having good, wholesome fun.

I've always liked trying new things, but I don't like how uncomfortable it sometimes makes me feel. Let's face it, beginners at anything usually make silly mistakes. I hate looking stupid, such as the time I tried downhill skiing and had to be rescued by the ski patrol. But riding down the mountain on the back of a snowmobile was a lot safer than trying to ski a hard trail I wasn't ready for. Trying something new often means being willing to look silly while we're learning. Making those beginner mistakes may feel like the end of the world at the time while you're feeling embarrassed, but they usually aren't. I can laugh now about my rescue even though it wasn't very funny at the time.

So why am I going to try rock climbing even though I'm scared of heights? Because I know that healthy pleasures are from God. And if you think it's exciting down here, just imagine what God's got in store for us in heaven. Space skydiving, anyone?

Snapshots of God

Take a long, hard look. See how great he is—infinite, greater than anything you could ever imagine or figure out! **Job 36:26, Message.**

Even though there are no physical photo albums in which we can see pictures of God, Jesus, or the Holy Spirit, people still have images of God in their minds. Sometimes they see God as being stern, handing out punishments to the Israelites when they made one bad choice after another and openly rebelled against Him. They often see Jesus as being kinder than God, telling people to turn the other cheek instead of taking an eye for an eye. The Holy Spirit can seem like a vague haze, who may or may not be very real to us.

This is our own human way of putting God in neat little boxes that we can understand, but the truth is that God is beyond our understanding. God is "greater than anything you could ever imagine or figure out!" Aren't you glad we don't have to figure out God in order to love, obey, trust, follow, and believe Him?

Still, because we are visual people and God is invisible, we want to fill our albums with snapshots of God. That's fine; God wants us to know Him as our Father, our friend, and our God. As we have personal experiences with God, as we read the Bible and learn more about Him, as we pray for ourselves and the people in our lives, each time we have an interaction with God, we're taking a picture to add to our album.

Have you ever seen a trick photograph? They're usually real pictures that someone has doctored in Photoshop to make them appear to be something they are not. Some of them are very good: a cat with the jaws of a shark, a zebra with the head of a fish, a goldfish with legs like a dog. I'm sure you've seen some too. Trick photography is great when it's just pictures you're looking at, but when someone shows us a doctored-up picture of God, it's not so amusing. It can look very real. The only way you can tell it's a fake is if you know what God *really* looks like. Don't be fooled by fake photos, and be careful that you don't put them into your scrapbook about God, even if you realize they're fakes. They aren't worth hanging on to. You never know when someone will look through your photo album, see the fake photos, and get confused.

Take a look through your mental picture album at the pictures you've collected of God. Which ones are your favorites? Are there any doctored pictures you need to throw away?

December 14

Dried Up

On the last and greatest day of the festival,
Jesus stood and said in a loud voice, "Let anyone who is thirsty
come to me and drink. Whoever believes in me, as Scripture has said,
rivers of living water will flow from within them." John 7:37, 38, NIV.

Unless a person lives on an island surrounded by the ocean or has seen satellite images of the earth from space, it may be difficult to comprehend that the majority of our planet is covered with a massive amount of water. In fact, about 70 percent of the earth's surface is covered by water. About 96.5 percent of the water on earth is in the oceans. With all that water it's hard to imagine how we can get so thirsty.

But you can't drink ocean water. If you were to fall overboard in the middle of the ocean, you would eventually get so thirsty that water would be all you could think about. Even though you would literally be floating in water, you'd be the kind of thirsty that pastes your lips together and makes your tongue stick to the roof of your mouth. You might as well be in the middle of the Sahara; you'd have the same amount of water to drink.

While you probably don't have to worry about drifting around in the ocean for days, it's not the only time you have to be concerned about dehydration—not drinking enough water. Your body is about two-thirds water. You can easily become dehydrated if you lose more water than you replace. If it's hot and you sweat a lot, if you drink caffeinated beverages, if you are sick, or if you exercise a lot, your body will lose fluids. If you don't replace them, you'll become dehydrated, and your body won't operate as well as it should.

Being thirsty is one way to tell that you need to drink water, but by that time you could already be dehydrated. The best prevention is to drink lots of fluids. Not all fluids are equal; drinking anything with caffeine in it will make your body lose fluids. When you drink matters too; if you're going to be playing sports or exercising, you should drink water before and during your activity. Every 20 minutes you should stop for a water break, and keep drinking after your activity ends.

Our constant dependence on water is probably one of the reasons Jesus used water as an illustration of Himself; He knew that water was something we would always need and would always be looking for, just as we always have a need for Him and should keep looking for Him. Being well hydrated will help us perform at our best, and being filled with spiritual water will keep us functioning at our spiritual peak. We need both kinds of water to survive.

Junk-Food Junkie

For I have told you often before, and I say it again
with tears in my eyes, that there are many whose conduct shows
they are really enemies of the cross of Christ. They are headed for
destruction. Their god is their appetite, they brag about shameful things,
and they think only about this life here on earth. **Philippians 3:18, 19, NLT.**

True or false: It's possible to be addicted to food.

True. Especially junk food.

Scientists studying lab rats at the Scripps Research Institute in Florida discovered that rats got addicted to bad food in the same way that people get hooked on cocaine and heroin. Why? According to the study, they found that our brains react the same way to junk food as they do to drugs.

The scientists divided a bunch of rats into three groups. They gave the first group a healthy diet. They gave the second group a healthy diet and a limited amount of junk food. They gave the third group all kinds of fattening foods, such as cheesecake, fatty meat products, cheap cakes, and chocolate snacks.

The third group, as you can imagine, got awfully fat, and they started bingeing on the food. Chemical substances in the food made them feel good, but after a while it took more and more of the food to make them feel as good, so they ended up eating a lot more. The researchers noticed the very same effect in rats who were given cocaine and heroin. They needed more and more of the addictive substance in order to feel good. When the scientists tried to take the rats off their high-calorie, junk-food diets, the rats stopped eating altogether for two weeks.

Junk food is just that: it's junk. The good news is that God made lots of natural foods we can't get addicted to. You can eat all the carrots, apples, potatoes, spinach, and beans you want to. They are all healthy and completely safe (unless you have a food allergy to one of them). They will nourish your body and make you strong. Ask God to bless your food, and *bon appétit!*

Think About It: On average, how much junk food do you eat? Consider your diet honestly. Are you a junk-food junkie? Do you need help overcoming a food addiction? If so, talk to your parents and ask for their help in finding treatment. Recognizing you have a problem is the first step in overcoming it.

December 16

Babes in the Hood

Marriage should be honored by all, and the marriage bed kept pure, for God will judge the adulterer and all the sexually immoral. **Hebrews 13:4, NIV.**

Are you counting down the days until Christmas? The story of Jesus' birth is so familiar to us that sometimes we don't really stop to consider all the details. For example, when was the last time you thought about the fact that Jesus was born to an unmarried teenage mother? Teen pregnancy is an extremely difficult situation in today's world, but back in Mary's day she could have been stoned to death if Joseph had given the word. Before the angel talked to him, Joseph thought the same thing as the rest of the town when they discovered Mary's pregnancy: that she'd had sex with some other man.

Mary, of course, had done no such thing. Jesus was created by God's Holy Spirit passing over Mary. But this had never happened before in the history of the world, so you can imagine that anyone who counted the months between the date Jesus was born and the date Joseph and Mary actually got married would think something was fishy. Jesus grew up with people who knew His story and looked down their noses at Him. That kind of gossip gets around quick.

Of course, Joseph stuck with Mary and eventually married her. He raised Jesus as his own child, and there were other children in the family as well. All in all it's a pretty happy ending for what could have been a tragic story. Each year in the United States about 750,000 teen girls are finding themselves in a similar situation with a different beginning and a much sadder ending, whether in abortion, adoption, or the struggle to raise a child before the teen mom is even an adult herself, with or without the help of the baby's father.

No matter how a teen pregnancy turns out, a study found that only one in two teen moms manages to finish high school and get a diploma, as compared to nine out of 10 teen girls who don't get pregnant. While friends may not completely forsake a pregnant teen, life changes with a baby on board. Activities become limited, and many are just plain out of the question. Instead of taking their own time growing up, teen moms discover the world becomes all about baby. When you bring someone into the world, you are responsible for that person . . . for the next 18 years.

Take It to the Streets: Talk to your youth group leader or pastor about the possibility of volunteering some time at a teen pregnancy center if there is one in your area.

Picture This

That night there were shepherds staying in the fields nearby,
guarding their flocks of sheep. Suddenly, an angel of the Lord appeared
among them, and the radiance of the Lord's glory surrounded them.
They were terrified, but the angel reassured them. "Don't be afraid!"
he said. "I bring you good news that will bring great joy to all people.
The Savior—yes, the Messiah, the Lord—has been born today in Bethlehem,
the city of David! And you will recognize him by this sign: You will find
a baby wrapped snugly in strips of cloth, lying in a manger." Suddenly,
the angel was joined by a vast host of others—the armies of heaven—
praising God and saying, "Glory to God in highest heaven, and peace
on earth to those with whom God is pleased." **Luke 2:8-14, NLT.**

I love the Christmas story, don't you? Whenever I read it, I feel as if I'm right there in the middle, first with Mary and Joseph, so relieved when Baby Jesus is born safely, then sitting in a cold field with the shepherds, keeping a sharp eye out for predators and getting an eyeful of glory instead. Can you picture the looks on their faces when the whole sky filled with singing angels? Their faces must have shone with lingering light as they made their way to worship the Child.

The Christmas story, like the Christmas season, is about Jesus from beginning to end. It doesn't matter what the world wants to celebrate at this time of year. From Santas to shopping malls, all the worldly trappings of the season can't begin to approach the majesty of the event Christians celebrate. When we begin to understand that God Himself, in the person of His Son, was born to a poor couple, wrapped in rags, and placed into a feed trough for animals, we'll drown out the world singing with the angels, "Glory to God in highest heaven, and peace on earth to those with whom God is pleased." The Messiah has come for us!

Why not start your own Christmas tradition this year by reading the Christmas story in the book of Luke first thing when you wake up Christmas morning? Don't worry. Your presents won't go anywhere. Maybe your whole family would like to sit with you on the couch and listen while you read aloud. If not, cuddle down into your own warm bed and read out loud quietly to yourself . . . it adds a nice sense of occasion. You may end up liking this tradition so much that you bring it with you when you start your own family. Can you think of any better way to begin Jesus' birthday celebration?

December 18

Great Responsibility

And the Lord replied, "A faithful, sensible servant is one to whom
the master can give the responsibility of managing his other household
servants and feeding them. If the master returns and finds that the servant
has done a good job, there will be a reward. I tell you the truth, the master
will put that servant in charge of all he owns." **Luke 12:42-44, NLT.**

Roland placed an order online for an item he was really excited to buy. It was pretty expensive, but Roland figured that was OK because he had the money, and he had a job. He was supposed to be saving up for college and a car, but he had plenty of time to do that . . . eventually. Two weeks later his job dried up, and suddenly Roland had no money coming in, an expensive game system, and no car to take him to job interviews.

Some people think that the Bible says money is the root of all evil. It actually says the *love* of money is the root of evil. That's because if we expect money to take care of us, we're putting it in the place of God; we're making it an idol. God knows we need money. The trouble starts when we stop relying on Him to provide for us and we use up all our money on things we don't need.

We can't expect a free ride. In 2 Thessalonians 3:10 Paul gave the believers this rule: "The one who is unwilling to work shall not eat" (NIV). Even if we can get away with being lazy, we shouldn't. It's not Christian. Work was always part of God's plan for humanity. Even in the Garden of Eden, Adam and Eve had work to do. Working keeps us healthy and active and keeps our brains engaged. Of course, work didn't wear Adam and Eve out; they found it refreshing. We can find work rewarding, too, as long as we balance it with rest and fun.

God lends us the money we need to get along down here, and in turn we manage His money—and His resources, too—using it however He directs us. It's a great responsibility and takes planning, thought, and prayer. We can't handle our finances carelessly and expect good financial health.

Think About It: Do you have a budget? Do you know how much you make every month and what your expenses are? Do you have a savings account? If you answered no to any of these questions, talk to your parents or a guidance counselor about finding some tools to help you manage your money so it doesn't end up managing you.

Cheater Pants

Whoever walks in integrity walks securely, but whoever takes crooked paths will be found out. **Proverbs 10:9, NIV.**

They say cheaters never prosper, and they don't. But it can be really maddening when they seem to get away with it for a while. When you've studied for days, ignoring your friends and turning down invitations to fun activities, and someone in class cheats and ends up with a better grade, it's possible to think all your hard work wasn't worth it after all. Maybe you would have been better off cheating too. No one has to find out, right?

Wrong. There are all kinds of shortcuts in life. You can make a living out of getting away with stuff. You can park in places you aren't supposed to just because you know no one can stop you. You can bend and break rules if you think the consequences aren't bad enough to stop you. Maybe you'll pay for it, maybe you won't. You can even take advantage of people who are weaker or slower than you are. If a clerk gives you back too much change at the Quik Stop, you don't have to return it. You could slip it in your pocket, and they wouldn't even find out until they cashed out their drawer at the end of their shift and realized that they didn't have the correct amount.

There are crooked paths going from every place to every other place. You don't have to take the long, straight path that requires actual work and might take longer and cost you more. But don't ever be tempted to think that cheaters make out better in any way. Part of the training God gives us when we travel the straight path is the opportunity to face harder situations that cost us more.

For one thing, it builds our muscles for the really hard stuff ahead. Any coach will tell you that an athlete who skips practices won't be of much use on game day. For another, no one respects a cheater. Any athlete who has ever used drugs in order to win and has been kicked out of their sport when they are discovered can vouch for the fact that it wasn't worth it. What good is being on top for a few moments when you could stay there for the long haul? Integrity—being honest and dependable—will last much longer than the temporary thrill of cheating.

Have you ever been tempted to take a crooked path because the straight one seemed tougher? What made you stick to the honest way? If you didn't, what could you do next time to help you stay the course?

December 20

Seek Him

*Now after Jesus was born in Bethlehem of Judea in the days
of Herod the king, behold, wise men from the East came to Jerusalem,
saying, "Where is He who has been born King of the Jews? For we have seen
His star in the East and have come to worship Him." Matthew 2:1, 2, NKJV.*

Let's drop in on Baby Jesus, shall we? There He is, wrapped in swaddling clothes, lying in a manger. Joseph is sleeping; he's exhausted from the long walk from Nazareth and the racing around all day to find a place where Mary could have her baby. It's been quite a night. The shepherds have just left, praising God, and Mary is about to fall asleep herself.

But she's wakened from her drowsy stupor by three strangely dressed men leading camels. They have flowing robes and are carrying ornate caskets filled with gold, frankincense, and myrrh. Mary sits up and shakes Joseph awake. "Psst, honey, would you get a load of these characters? What do you think they want?"

These are the three Wise Men—Gaspar, Melchior, and Balthasar—otherwise known as the Magi, who have seen a new star in the east and followed it to find the baby King, the one Herod is so worried about. Right? Well, not exactly. While the Bible does talk about Wise Men visiting Jesus from the east, it never says there were only three of them—only that there were three gifts. It also doesn't tell us their names. And it doesn't say anything about them visiting Jesus at the time of His birth. In fact, the Bible says they found Him when He was a young child.

The most important information the Bible gives us about the Wise Men is that they sought Jesus. They didn't look up into the heavens one night, notice a new star, realize what it meant, and sit around waiting for Jesus to grow up and come find them. They saddled up their camels (or strapped on their sandals) and headed out to find Him. And that, my friend, is what made them wise.

Christmas is right around the corner, and celebrating Jesus' birth gives us all one more opportunity to "seek the Lord while He may be found" (Isaiah 55:6, NKJV). Today wise men still seek Jesus. They don't wait for the pastor to bring Him to their door. They don't wait for their parents to sit them down for a lecture. They actively seek Him in Bible study, in the Sabbath school lesson, in the sermon, in acts of generosity and kindness to others, in prayer. And when they find Him, they worship Him.

December 21

Presents

*They entered the house and saw the child with his mother,
Mary, and they bowed down and worshiped him.
Then they opened their treasure chests and gave him gifts of
gold, frankincense, and myrrh.* **Matthew 2:11, NLT.**

Speaking of the Wise Men, did you notice that they didn't come to visit Baby Jesus with empty hands? Of course not! It was a birthday party, after all. When you go to a birthday party, you bring presents. Now, there is plenty of debate about how our own tradition of giving Christmas presents started and whether or not Christians should exchange gifts for Christmas, but the one fact no one can argue with is that when the Wise Men presented themselves to Jesus after their long journey they did three things: they bowed down, they worshipped Him, and they gave Him gifts.

In a few short days we'll be celebrating Jesus' birthday. I can't think of a better way to honor Him than to follow in the footsteps of the Wise Men (hey, they aren't called the Wise Men for nothing). While most of the world concentrates on the secular parts of the holiday season, we, as Christians, have the privilege of worshipping our King and Creator.

We can bow before Him. Bowing, which is lowering the torso and head, is a gesture of respect. Kneeling is pretty much the same thing. This demonstrates our total dependence and respect for God. It's a physical sign of the state of our heart, bowed before Him.

We can worship Jesus. Worship isn't just something that happens at church. Worship has many outlets: praying, singing, praising God, serving Him, meditating on or reading Scripture, thanking God, obeying God. Worship is not one particular thing but the attitude of our grateful hearts and our desire to show our love to God.

We can give Him gifts. There are only three more shopping days left until Christmas—what are you going to get Jesus for His birthday? If you've left your shopping until late, I have good news for you: what Jesus wants money can't buy. It's simply your heart. That's all. But feel free to offer Him your service and other nonmonetary gifts as well. Get creative!

Try This: Write out your gift to Jesus on a slip of paper, put it in an envelope, seal it, and tuck it into the branches of your Christmas tree or a stocking set aside for Jesus. Invite your family to participate. On Christmas morning, take turns reading the presents you're giving Jesus.

357

December 22

God's Special Gift to a Soldier

Whatever is good and perfect comes down to us from God our Father, who created all the lights in the heavens. He never changes or casts a shifting shadow. **James 1:17, NLT.**

Heather, a soldier serving her first deployment in Iraq, found herself far from home during Christmas. Her unit had been living in tents since March, and they were being moved into trailers. On Christmas Eve the unit assembled to begin taking down the tents they'd been living in. Around the tents were piles of sandbags, but it had been raining steadily since Thanksgiving, turning the sandbags into wet mud balls that were hard to empty. No one was in a good mood.

One solider found a small Christmas tree and held it up, asking, "Anybody want this?"

Heather was thrilled; one of her favorite memories from Christmases past was putting up the tree and decorating it with strings of beads and handmade ornaments. Before she could say anything, the soldier threw the tree on the ground and began stomping on it, yelling, "I hate Christmas!" again and again. Soon other soldiers joined him, and Heather could hear the pretty ornaments popping under their boots. Crushed, she began to cry, glad for the first time for the rain that hid her tears.

Later she reported to the mail warehouse to pick up and deliver her unit's mail, a job she'd volunteered for so she wouldn't have to wait for it to be delivered. She was still stung by the incident with the tree, so the thought of mail didn't raise her spirits. She felt grumpy and selfish because she'd already received all the packages her family and friends had sent.

As she helped sort through the pile of 200 packages, the sergeant helping her called out that she had a package. Heather asked him if he was sure; she wasn't expecting anything. "It's for you," he said, "and here's another." Heather said that's when she knew that even in her selfishness God was thinking of her.

She eagerly took the boxes but didn't know the people who had sent them. She carried them back to her room to open them there. When she opened the second box and took out the tissue paper, she found a three-foot-tall, fully decorated Christmas tree complete with strings of gold beads. She was stunned. "It was as if God Himself had sent it," she says. "I felt as though I was being given a warm, loving hug. I cannot put into words how joyful I was at that moment. I had never felt as loved as I did then."

358

December 23

Love Notes

The Lord says, "I will rescue those who love me. I will protect those who trust in my name. When they call on me, I will answer; I will be with them in trouble. I will rescue and honor them." **Psalm 91:14, 15, NLT.**

Along the route I walk, a young homeless man sometimes camps out among the trees. He's like an elusive forest animal; I've never actually seen him. But I've seen his camp from the sidewalk. Other walkers have seen him, and one was worried enough that she called the police to find out if he was dangerous. Turns out the bridge he usually lives under was having some repairs done so he'd moved temporarily. The police assured the woman that he was harmless, and she spread the word to the people she met along that route.

He doesn't usually stay very long. Even if you can't see his camping area, you know he's there because of the love notes. He writes messages to someone named Dana and posts them on the roadside. The latest one says, "Merry Xmas, Dana. The Elm." I'm not sure if "the Elm" is the tree he's camped under or his nickname. This summer one sign said: "I miss you and love you, Dana. The Elm." I sure hope Dana sees them. It would be a shame to miss out on these expressions of love posted for all the world to see.

I wonder how many of God's love notes we miss. The dollar you just happen to find when you forgot lunch money. The job that opens up just when you need it. Something you've wanted but couldn't afford given to you out of the blue. These are not coincidences; they are love notes from God.

The Elm's love notes are right there out in the open, and sometimes God's are just as obvious, but not always. Sometimes you really have to look to spot them. We take His blessings for granted, but we shouldn't. Nothing good happens to us because Satan wants it to, so we should realize that every good thing comes from God.

Of course, if we want a love note from God we don't need to look any further than our own Bibles. But when God steps out of its pages and turns up in person in our lives in some tangible way, it would be a shame if we didn't recognize Him. Look for God's love notes in your life today.

December 24

The Gift

> But now that you've found you don't have to listen to sin
> tell you what to do, and have discovered the delight of listening to God
> telling you, what a surprise! A whole, healed, put-together life right now,
> with more and more of life on the way! Work hard for sin your whole life
> and your pension is death. But God's gift is *real life*, eternal life,
> delivered by Jesus, our Master. **Romans 6:22, 23, Message.**

Tomorrow is the big day. For weeks now you've been planning and buying and wrapping and anticipating the moment the people on your Christmas list will open the present that you chose especially for them. There was probably at least one super-special gift; something you know will surprise the socks off someone on your list, something you can't wait to see them open. Can you imagine at that happy moment when they opened your gift, if they oohed and ahhed over it, and then whipped out their wallet to pay you back?

Wouldn't you be insulted? "It's a gift," you'd say indignantly. "I don't want to be paid back. I want you to enjoy it. I chose it just for you."

But isn't that what we do each time we try to "earn" salvation? It's a free gift, God's gift to us. A present. Wrapped in love. Trying to earn it is like trying to pay God back for His gift. It can't be done.

God doesn't want to be paid back, which is a good thing, because we can't pay Him back. His gift is perfect, and we aren't. Even the good things we do aren't anywhere close to perfect. In fact, the Bible says that "all our righteousness [is] like filthy rags" (Isaiah 64:6). "Everything that we of ourselves can do is defiled by sin. . . . When we submit ourselves to Christ, the heart is united with His heart, the will is merged in His will, the mind becomes one with His mind, the thoughts are brought into captivity to Him; we live His life. This is what it means to be clothed with the garment of His righteousness. Then as the Lord looks upon us He sees, not the fig-leaf garment, not the nakedness and deformity of sin, but His own robe of righteousness, which is perfect obedience to the law of Jehovah" (Ellen G. White, *Christ's Object Lessons*, pp. 311, 312).

Tomorrow as you open your gifts, won't you take a minute to thank God for His perfect gift? Ask His Holy Spirit to come into your life and help you to grow more like Him in every way. That is the real gift—the real spirit—of Christmas.

Secret Admirer

This is how much God loved the world:
He gave his Son, his one and only Son. And this is why:
so that no one need be destroyed; by believing in him,
anyone can have a whole and lasting life. God didn't go to all the
trouble of sending his Son merely to point an accusing finger,
telling the world how bad it was. He came to help,
to put the world right again. **John 3:16, 17, Message.**

Have you ever had a secret admirer? Maybe you found a note in your locker or got an e-mail or a text from someone you didn't know confessing how much they liked you, or maybe it was just an anonymous flower on your desk that tipped you off. Someone liked you; someone you didn't know. Kind of exciting, isn't it? Knowing that we've attracted the attention of someone unknown is kind of thrilling, isn't it?

As exciting as it can be to have a secret admirer, can you imagine how much better it would be if the special someone who loved you declared their undying devotion by filling an entire cathedral with a professional orchestra and choir performing a love song especially for you? And then that special someone engaged a whole crowd of messengers to spread the news around so that everyone knew just how much you were loved? And after all that they gave you a priceless gift, the kind of gift that was so unique, so one-of-a-kind, that it could never be replicated. How would you feel then?

Admit it: you're kind of blown away now, aren't you? This is no secret, blushing, hiding, maybe kind of love. This is the sort of passionate love only declared by people who are totally committed and don't mind everyone knowing it. They want to shout it from the rooftops and invite everyone to the wedding.

Does that kind of love sound familiar? It should. It's the kind of love God has for us. Aren't you glad there's nothing secret about God's love for us? I am!

Think About It: In the description above, where was the cathedral? Who played in the orchestra and sang in the choir? Who were the messengers? What was the priceless gift? Who declared their love? Who was so extravagantly loved? Hint: It all happened on Christmas about 2,000 years ago.

December 26

Sin Differently

My beloved friends, let us continue to love each other since love comes from God. Everyone who loves is born of God and experiences a relationship with God. The person who refuses to love doesn't know the first thing about God, because God is love—so you can't know him if you don't love. This is how God showed his love for us: God sent his only Son into the world so we might live through him. **I John 4:7-9, Message.**

All sin is sin. It doesn't matter if it's small, big, accidental, or on purpose. Sin is still sin, and that is how God sees it. He also sees our motives and intentions, which is something we, as human beings, can't see in each other. If you and I were standing on a cliff having an argument, and I slipped and pushed you over the edge by accident, God would know that even though technically I was responsible for your death, it wasn't something I meant to do; it was an accident. Police, hearing passersby talk about the fight we were having, might get a different impression entirely. As humans we can only judge someone by what we see with our eyes or hear about them by what they or others tell us. We can't tell how a person really feels in their heart.

That doesn't stop us from passing judgment on them, though. In fact, most of us are very quick to pass judgment on other people even if we don't know them well or don't have all the facts in the matter we're judging. We humans also put sin into compartments. There are biggies, such as murder, theft, and adultery, and little stuff—cheating, swearing, or lying. It would be easier for us to forgive someone who swore at us because we bumped into them than someone who stole our life's savings.

But all sin, big and small, hurts God. Yet He still sent love into the world before we repented, *while we were still sinning.* He didn't wait for us to realize we were sinning and how much it hurt Him to forgive us; He forgave first. When we realize this, we can love first, too. We can forgive first, too. We can overlook the sin and love the sinner, not because we like what they are doing, but because we know God, and God is love, and that's how He loves us. He gave us His own love as an example.

When we understand that love, we can safely leave the heavy stuff, such as judging people, to God. He's the only one who is qualified to handle it.

Twilight of Evil

When God, your God, cuts off the nations
whose land you are invading, shoves them out of your way
so that you displace them and settle in their land, be careful that
you don't get curious about them after they've been destroyed before you.
Don't get fascinated with their gods, thinking, "I wonder what it was like for
them, worshiping their gods. I'd like to try that myself." Don't do this to God,
your God. They commit every imaginable abomination with their gods.
God hates it all with a passion. **Deuteronomy 12:29-31, Message.**

Zombies, vampires, wizards, witches, and werewolves. If the current craze for the supernatural is still at a frenzy when you read this—and I know Satan will work quite hard to be sure it is—then you'll hardly be able to exist without hearing about a new book, movie, or fad featuring some of the scariest critters Satan has been able to conjure up.

You know, of course, as a Christian, that such things don't really exist. You even know that Satan is behind any supernatural evil, whether society realizes it or not. What you may not know is that even though you don't believe in the reality of zombies, vampires, werewolves, and other creatures, it is very dangerous to take an interest in their stories. In his book *The Screwtape Letters* C. S. Lewis said: "There are two equal and opposite errors into which our race can fall about the devils. One is to disbelieve in their existence. The other is to believe, and to feel an excessive and unhealthy interest in them."

As I write this, a vampire mega-saga has just ended, and new reports are starting to scare people more than the thought of imaginary vampires: teens, inspired by the movies and the books they came from, are starting to act like vampires, biting each other and even "feeding" on each other's blood. These kids probably didn't think they'd end up wanting to bite someone when they got interested in vampires, but that's how Satan hooks us; before we know it, we're affected.

Health experts warn that biting can have serious consequences. Up to 15 percent of human bites can become infected, and blood-borne diseases such as HIV, hepatitis, and syphilis can be passed on. A far greater consequence is the harm that is done to our salvation and our relationship with God when we listen to and play with demons. Scripture tells us demons are real; it also tells us to submit ourselves to God so that we can resist them, and then they will flee from us (see James 4:7). Stay close to God and send the devils packing.

December 28

Texting

For everything that was written in the past was written to teach us, so that through the endurance taught in the Scriptures and the encouragement they provide we might have hope. **Romans 15:4, NIV.**

Breaking news! A recent survey discovered that 66 percent of people have a fear of being without their Bible. In fact, in an effort to keep God's Word close almost half of the people interviewed said they have at least two or more Bibles. Since the discovery a name has been given to the fear: nomophobia.

How do you feel about the study? Are you part of the 66 percent of people who fear being without their Bible? Oh, wait—slight correction. The study wasn't about Bibles, it was about cell phones. Now it probably makes more sense because, really, who is afraid of being without a Bible? We *should* be as attached to it as we are to our cell phones, but sadly, we're not.

Imagine what would happen if we had our Bibles on us at all times—in our pockets, in our backpacks, in our purses. If we left it somewhere accidentally, we'd be frantic, looking all over the place for it until we found it. While everyone around us was exercising their thumbs sending texts, we'd be getting texts from God, texts that could change our life. We could use our Bible in an emergency to call 9-1-1 to God; we'd always get through, and help would be instantaneous.

Why don't we do this? Why don't Christians carry their Bibles everywhere with them? I had a friend in high school whose father was a pastor. It was a public high school, but she carried her Bible with her right along with her books. I remember being both impressed and scared for her, as if she was carrying around a "make fun of me" sign. As far as I know, no one ever did make fun of her.

It would make an interesting experiment, wouldn't it? Maybe in a couple years there *would* be a name for fear of being without your Bible. Wouldn't that be something?

Why not start a trend with your friends of carrying your Bible everywhere you carry your cell phone? I challenge you, and anyone you can talk into participating, to bring your Bible with you to anyplace you'd have your cell phone for one whole month. At the end of the month, reflect: Did having your Bible with you 24/7 change anything? Did you read it more often? Did anyone comment on it? Do you want to continue?

Redeemed

At one time you all had your backs turned to God, thinking rebellious thoughts of him, giving him trouble every chance you got. But now, by giving himself completely at the Cross, actually *dying* for you, Christ brought you over to God's side and put your lives together, whole and holy in his presence. You don't walk away from a gift like that! You stay grounded and steady in that bond of trust, constantly tuned in to the Message, careful not to be distracted or diverted. **Colossians 1:21-23, Message.**

If you traveled to the town of Cateura in Paraguay, you'd find a slum built on top of a landfill; in other words, a dump. The town/dump receives 1,500 tons of new garbage every day. Most of the families living in the town/dump work in it, recycling the trash and selling it. That includes the children. They are so poor that they have to work in the landfill instead of going to school to get an education that might help them escape their poverty.

In this very unlikely place, you'd find something else that you'd never expect to find: beautiful music. In fact, you'd find an entire orchestra, but it wouldn't be filled with ordinary violins, cellos, and other classical instruments. One of the landfill workers, Favio Chávez, is also a musician. Working with these kids in the landfill, Favio decided he wanted to give them something positive in their lives. He started to teach them music, sharing his own instruments. When he ran out of instruments, he decided to try making some from the garbage the town was built on. He created the Landfill Harmonic Orchestra, giving kids instruments, music, and something beautiful in a land of garbage.

We know we should be responsible in how we handle our garbage. We have recycling bins, and we know what items to place in each bin so that they get recycled correctly. But often we're not so careful about people. We throw them away on the garbage heap of life when they are broken. Sometimes we even find ourselves sitting on the top of the landfill, thrown away by people we thought loved us.

While we may look at someone society has thrown away and see nothing but garbage, God sees the potential in each and every one. He can craft us into instruments who will not only sing His praises but will inspire the people around us with His creativity and compassion toward those who are rejected. That's called redemption. What music will God make of your life today?

December 30

Laughing Matter

*A happy heart makes the face cheerful,
but heartache crushes the spirit.* **Proverbs 15:13, NIV.**

Have you ever laughed so hard tears that ran down your face and you got the hiccups? Sometimes things are just that funny. Whether you're giggling, chortling, chuckling, or guffawing, God created us with the ability to be cheerful, to laugh, and to enjoy fun times. In fact, being happy will help us to be healthier people. Happiness is good for us.

But not everyone who laughs is actually happy. Laughter and jokes are sometimes a cover for sadness or depression. There's a story about a man who went to the doctor because he was so sad that he didn't see how he could possibly go on living. The doctor put an arm around the man's shoulder and said, "I have just the thing for you. You must go see Grimaldi the Clown. He's the funniest man alive. I saw him a couple nights ago, and I'm still laughing."

"But Doctor," protested the man, "*I* am Grimaldi the Clown!"

Joking can also be a way to beat someone to the punch by making fun of the very thing for which you're afraid someone else will pick on you. If you laugh about it first, it takes the sting out of the intended cruelty, and also lets everyone know you're OK with it—even if you aren't. But humor should never be used to tear down anyone—you included. Using humor in this way against someone else would be bullying, and using it against yourself would involve lying by pretending that it doesn't bother you. You can't make fun of yourself and enjoy it.

We know that God has a sense of humor because He gave us one when He made us, and the Bible says that we are made in His image. I like to think that we can see some of His humor expressed in some of the funny creatures He made for earth, such as the platypus or the giraffe.

No matter what our lives are like here, whether we hide our sadness behind a grin like Grimaldi the Clown, or work through it to cheer ourselves up, we know that we will all laugh in heaven. Jesus told His disciples that although there will be tears here, in heaven we'll laugh (see Luke 6:21).

Do you know anyone who uses humor to hurt others? The best thing you can do is not participate. Laughing at their cruelty will only encourage them. Instead, try to distract them by changing the subject, or tell them up front you don't consider that type of humor to be funny.

Go With God

> Now all glory to God, who is able to keep you from falling away and will bring you with great joy into his glorious presence without a single fault. All glory to him who alone is God, our Savior through Jesus Christ our Lord. All glory, majesty, power, and authority are his before all time, and in the present, and beyond all time! Amen. **Jude 1:24, 25, NLT.**

Today is New Year's Eve. It's the time of the year when we stand poised to step into a fresh new year full of opportunity and promise. But before we do, it's nice to take a minute to look back and see how far we've come since last New Year's Eve.

Think about the struggles you've faced, the obstacles you've overcome, and the trials you've endured. What have you learned this year that you can bring with you into the next year? What lessons has God taught you that you never want to forget? Jot them down on the inside flaps of your Bible or in your journal. Consider them milestones, markers of where you've been as you traveled through the year.

They say that people who do not learn from their past are doomed to repeat it. Don't spend this next year walking over the same ground you already covered. Break new ground instead. Let God take you even further than you were able to go last year. Don't get stuck in a spiritual rut; go on a grand adventure with God, exploring new territory and finding new ways to serve Him.

Traditionally, lots of people make New Year's resolutions today . . . and break them by next week. Instead of writing down a list of things you can't possibly hope to accomplish this coming year, why not take a few minutes to give some serious thought to what your spiritual goals are for the coming year? Consider new habits you can begin, and add to promising habits you've started. If you began reading your Bible regularly this year, why not add scripture memorization? If you've started having daily devotions, try adding a prayer journal. Ask God to show you ways you can grow in Him this year. Ask Him to direct your journey.

Pray that every new step you take this year will bring you closer to God, as surely as it will bring you one step closer to great joy in His glorious presence. Stay in God, walk with God, and live through God this year and every one that follows.

Notes:

"I have set
before you life
and death,
blessings and curses.
Now choose life."
Deuteronomy 30:19, NIV